Studies in Classics

Edited by
Dirk Obbink & Andrew Dyck
Oxford University/The University of California, Los Angeles

A Routledge Series

STUDIES IN CLASSICS

DIRK OBBINK AND ANDREW DYCK, *General Editors*

SEX AND THE SECOND-BEST CITY

SEX AND SOCIETY IN THE *LAWS* OF PLATO

Kenneth Royce Moore

Routledge
New York & London

Published in 2005 by
Routledge
Taylor & Francis Group
270 Madison Avenue
New York, NY 10016

Published in Great Britain by
Routledge
Taylor & Francis Group
2 Park Square
Milton Park, Abingdon
Oxon, OX14 4RN

Printed in the United States of America on acid-free paper.
10 9 8 7 6 5 4 3 2 1

International Standard Book Number-10: 0-415-97273-6 (Hardcover)
International Standard Book Number-13: 978-0-415-97273-4 (Hardcover)
Library of Congress Card Number 2005013414

Library of Congress Cataloging-in-Publication Data

Moore, Kenneth Royce, 1972–
Sex and the second-best city : sex and society in the Laws of Plato /
Kenneth Royce Moore.
        p. cm. -- (Studies in classics)
Includes bibliographical references and index.
ISBN: 0-415-97273-6 (alk. paper)
1. Plato. Laws.   2. Sex--Greece--History to 1500.   3. Sex role--Greece--History to
1500.   4. Homosexuality--Greece--History to 1500.   5. Greece--Social conditions--
To 146 B.C.   I. Title.   II. Series: Studies in classics (Routledge (Firm)) (Unnumbered)

HQ13.M56 2005
306.76'6'0938--dc22   2005013414

Taylor & Francis Group
is the Academic Division of T&F Informa plc.

Visit the Taylor & Francis Web site at
http://www.taylorandfrancis.com

and the Routledge Web site at
http://www.routledge-ny.com

Contents

Abbreviations

PLG	Bergk, Theodor ed. *Poetae Lyrici Graeci,* 4th edition. Teubner: Leipzig, 1878–82.
DK	Diels, Hermann ed. *Die Fragmente der Vorsokratiker,* 10th edition, ed. by W. Kranz. Weidmann: Berlin, 1951–2.
Diels-Schubart	Diels, Hermann and Wilhelm Schubart eds. *Anonymer Kommentar zu Platons Theaetet (Papyrus 9782), nebst drei Bruchstücken philosophischen Inhalts (Pap. N.8; P. 9766, 9569) unter Mitwirkung von J. L. Heiberg bearbeitet von H. Diels und W. Schubart.* Weidmann: Berlin, 1904.
GH	Dover, Sir Kenneth J. *Greek Homosexuality.* Duckworth: London, 1978.
GPM	———*Greek Popular Morality in the Time of Plato and Aristotle.* Oxford, 1974.
FGrH	Jacoby, F. ed. *Die Fragmente der griechischen Historiker.* Brill: Leiden, 1926–1958.
PCG	Kassel, R and C. Austin eds. *Poetae comici Graecae.* de Gruyter: Berlin, 1968.
IG	Kern, Otto. *Inscriptiones Graecae.* Walter de Gruyter & Co.: Berlin, 1913.
LSJ	Liddell, Henry George and Robert Scott revised and ed. by Sir Henry Stuart Jones. *A Greek-English Lexicon,* 9th edition. The Clarendon Press, Oxford, 1994.
Frag. ep.	Kinkel G. ed. *Epicorum Graecorum Fragmenta.* Vandenhoek & Ruprecht: Gottingen, 1988.
FHG	Müller, C. ed. *Fragmenta Historicorum Graecorum.* Firmin Didot: Paris, 1841–72.
TGF	Nauck A. ed. *Tragicorum Graecorum Fragmenta.* 2nd edition. Hildersheim: Olms, 1962.
RP	Ritter, H. and L. Preller. *Historia Philosophiae Graecae,* Eighth ed. Edward Wellmann: Gotha, 1898.

Currency Conversion

(late 5th–early 4th centuries)[1]

'Money implies poverty'.
—Iain M. Banks[2]

1 Athenian talent (36,000g silver)	=	60 *minai* = 6,000 *drachmas*
1 *mina* (600g silver)	=	100 *drachmas*
1 *drachma* (6g silver)	=	6 *obols* (1g each)
1 Kretan Stater (12g silver)	=	2 Athenian *drachmas*

Series Editors' Foreword

Studies in Classics aims to bring high-quality work by emerging scholars to the attention of a wider audience. Emphasizing the study of classical literature and history, these volumes contribute to the theoretical understanding of human culture and society over time. This series offers an array of approaches to the study of Greek and Latin (including medieval and Neolatin), authors and their reception, canons, transmission of texts, ideas, religion, history of scholarship, narrative, and the nature of evidence.

While the focus is on Mediterranean cultures of the Greco-Roman era, perspectives from other areas, cultural backgrounds, and eras included as important means to the reconstruction of fragmentary evidence and the exploration of models. The series reflects upon the role classical studies has played in humanistic endeavors from antiquity to the present, and explores select ways in which the discipline can bring both traditional scholarly tools and the experience of modernity to bear on questions and texts of enduring importance.

Dirk Obbink, Oxford University
Andrew Dyck, The University of California, Los Angeles

Acknowledgments

I should like to express my sincere gratitude to all those who have helped me, along the way, towards the completion of this book. It is to them that I dedicate it with alacrity. First and foremost, I must thank my loving parents and grandparents who have supported me and my academic research unconditionally in emotional and monetary terms all throughout. I extend special thanks to Nathan Wood and Charlotte Bjuren who have always been on my side and provided me with inspiration and insight when I most needed it. All of my teachers should be praised here but I shall only mention a few for want of space and time. I must thank the English and Classics faculties of Birmingham-Southern College (especially Susan K. Hagen, Jane Archer, Michael McInturff, Samuel Pezzillo, Fred Ashe, Roger Casey and John Tatter) for giving me my start upon what has been a most interesting academic career. I thank the Classics and Philosophy faculties of the Florida State University (especially Leon Golden, Bill and Nancy deGrummond, Jeffrey Tatum, Russell Dancy, Maria Morales, James Sickenger and Justin Glen) for having faith in my abilities and pointing me in the right direction. And I should especially like to offer my sincere gratitude to the School of Classics at the University of St. Andrews (especially Stephen Halliwell, Jill Harries, Jonathon Hesk, Harry Hine and Sir Kenneth Dover) for inspiration and insight as well as tremendous support in general. I should like to express my special thanks and compliments to Greg Woolf and Tom Harrison of St. Andrews for being superb supervisors and friends whose efforts I can never hope to repay fully by word or deed. Without Greg and Tom this book would not have been possible. I am particularly grateful to Karen Stears, of the University of Edinburgh, for helpful advice and insight. Let me also mention my good friends Andy Hughes, John Hardy, Bojan and Dragan Masic (and their mum), Dave Waters, Dave Edwards, John-Mark Glover, Michael Dempster, Alan Stewart, Alan Reid, Brian Stuart, Zev Paul, Amir Tehrani, Emanuella Giangregorio, Cherie Briant, Kennen Blanning, David Darwin, Shari Tharp, Tom Wagner, Betty Grant, Kathy Twilley, Dalton Turner, Thomas Kiedrowski, Joel Beaman, India Van Brunt, Agnes Baxter, Austin Moore, Charles Cushing, Allie Thomas, Ray Jackson, Rob and Eric Caves (and their mum), Steven Bailey,

Shawn Castleman, Tom Cox, Kennen Blanning, Ralph Young, Trevor Henderson, Ian, Gordon and Kenny Anderson, Kenny MacDonald, the good people at Project Archelogos in Edinburgh, especially Dory Scaltsas, and the Fence Collective. I dedicate this work of mine to all of the above and many others unnamed. But, perhaps most of all, I dedicate it to the living memory of Plato, son of Ariston and Periktione, without whose love of wisdom—indeed without whose life—the world would surely have been bereft of considerable light.

Preface

For nothynge is more easye to be founde, then be barking Scyllaes, rauenyng Celenes, and Lestrygones deuowerers of people, and suche lyke greate and vncredyble monsters; but to fynde cytyzyns ruled by good and holsome lawes, that ys an excedynge rare and harde thynge.

—St. Thomas More[1]

Like all literary utopias since his era, Plato's *Laws* proposes a radical re-invention of society in keeping with the tenets of a philosophical agenda. As with later utopias, an integral feature of this proposed social change entails a significant revision of popular sexual morality. It would be inaccurate to assert that, in the following chapters, I have dealt with every aspect of that which we would today refer to as sexuality that may be found in the *Laws*. A significant number of salient points have been considered but there remains ample space for further study. These subjects here chosen for analysis are sufficient to fill the pages of this book. It has been a great pleasure to discover a wealth of information which will provide interesting topics of inquiry for considerable time to come.

The approach that I am employing here combines elements of modern Cultural Studies, Marxist-Feminist Theory and 'Queer' Theory along with the long-established methodologies of the Classics. In this way, this text brings to bear a potent arsenal of diverse scholarship on Plato's final *opus*. Some might rightly inquire why one should take such measures and consider the *Laws* in the light of modern theories of sexuality. What could so ancient a text have to tell us about sex and society in the world of today? Not only has Plato, in the *Laws*, undertaken to theorise about no less than the construction of a hypothetical culture from the ground up (surely a very relevant issue for the modern world), he has also provided us with considerable insight into the subject of sexuality and the manner by which many aspects of it may be controlled and directed through socialisation and the calculated influences of authority. Contemporary criticism, especially that which deals with the use of language with regard to sex, serves to illuminate this inquiry in ways that many traditional approaches alone could not. Plato was actively contributing to an ancient discourse on human sexuality. Our modern conceptions partake of the same intellectual continuum and our on-going examination of it stands to benefit from a more holistic approach. Re-examining ancient ideas in this way will contribute to our growing body of knowledge.

Sex is a complex issue that has yet to be resolved. This examination of the *Laws* of Plato seeks to achieve a deeper understanding of sexuality as a natural phenomenon, as force for social change and itself as subject to change. A significant portion of Magnesia's social programming is based on the control of human sexuality through a calculated scheme. The 'artificiality' or 'constructedness' of sexuality in the *Laws* as the product of directed socialisation towards clear ideological and philosophical ends should be emphasised. This bears particular significance to the (post)modern, post-Freudian world. The broader understanding that I am here attempting will not only add to our overall knowledge of the past but it may also shed some light on our present and future.

The chapters of this book have been divided along thematic lines in order to provide a fairly comprehensive coverage of issues of sex and society in the *Laws*. The first chapter details the modern critical methodologies that will be utilised throughout the text as well as providing some relevant background on ancient views on sexuality as we understand them today. Chapter II deals with the *Laws* as an historical artefact and providing relevant background information on the text and its place amongst the Platonic *corpus*.

The breakdown of the remaining chapters is as follows. Chapter III examines the educational programme for Magnesia, the city to be founded, as outlined by Plato's narrator, the Athenian Stranger. It is here that he expresses the revolutionary proposition that women should be educated equally (or almost as equally) as men. Chapter IV considers the Platonic concept of *andreia* (courage and/or manliness) which figures prominently in the philosophical framework of sexual ideals to be impressed upon Magnesia's hypothetical citizenry. Chapter V looks into the official 'myth of the family' and the values associated with it along gendered lines. It considers the Magnesian family's utilitarian function in this hypothetical society. Chapter VI examines the role of women in Magnesia and how that role is to be shaped both by the Platonic ideal of *andreia* and the physical constraints of the female sex—both perceived and otherwise. Chapter VII deals with the complex issue of same-sex relations in the *Laws*. Chapter VIII contains my general conclusions.

The overall aims of this work are several. First, it is important that the *Laws* should be brought again into the light of scrutiny. As mentioned above, it has been perhaps the least examined representative of Plato's entire *corpus* in modern times. Yet, it has much to offer to almost anyone who would undertake to peruse it. The *Laws* is one of the world's first examples of a written constitution (albeit hypothetical) and, as such, deserves considerable prominence for that fact alone. It explores many significant prospects of societal administration and social regulation that bear relevance to the modern world. Plato has demonstrated a number of methods by which a society may be directed and controlled, along specific lines, with the aid of philosophy, psychology and rhetoric. Some might say that the twentieth century (not to mention the eighteenth and nineteenth centuries with their revolutionary advents of constitution-building) has been largely characterised by just such an approach to the government of peoples. Surely the twenty-first century will continue to proceed along a similar path.

Whatever we may think about his methods, Plato appears to have had the noblest of ideas in mind in composing his *Laws*. Its end was conceived to be no less than the maximum degree of happiness and virtue for the hypothetical citizenry. The 'second-best' approach (second-best because the ideal is perhaps beyond mortal achievement) is designed to correct human failings with philosophically enlightened legal prescriptions. The administration of these by 'a rigid theocracy' is perhaps a dangerous example in the wrong hands.[2] The manner in which Plato's works have been employed, or might yet be employed, as always remains the domain of the current generation at any given time. Totalitarian and democratic regimes in the past have utilised his ideas, in their own ways, according to their own particular ideologies. Plato's theoretical excursions may be fairly said to have provided a means by which to change the world. His tools are not weapons of war or implements of terror. Rather, he has demonstrated that our thoughts and our words are the most powerful resources that humanity has at its disposal and that their careful employment can change the minds of others.[3] To change people's thinking is to change the world. These and other similar ideas will continue to induce lively debates long into the future. But for now let us turn to the *Laws*, as the Athenian Stranger suggests, 'beguiling the time with discourse, and so complete our journey at leisure'.[4]

Chapter I
Modern Theory, Ancient 'Sexuality'

The past is a foreign country. They do things differently there.
—L. P. Hartley[1]

We mythologists know very well that myths and legends contain borrowings, moral lessons, nature cycles, and a hundred other distorting influences, and we labour to cut them away and get to what might be a kernel of truth.
—Isaac Asimov[2]

Well, man, you're doomed to repeat it otherwise. There's continuity and there's foolishness.
—Keith Richards[3]

Let no one say that we have reached every conclusion about human sexuality. The topic remains in the crucible of modern cultural theory and is hotly debated in all media. No cultural artefact that addresses this issue should be disregarded; although, all such artefacts should be weighted according to their merits. In November of 2001, a BBC2 television documentary on modern taboos pointed out that, roughly since the 1970s, male fashion advertisements and icons of pop-culture have become increasingly homoerotic. Perhaps surprisingly, these adverts are not geared exclusively toward homosexuals. Their primary demographic target consists of those men who would probably identify themselves as unequivocally heterosexual. This trend of increasing homoerotic representation shows no sign of subsiding in the near future. It is perhaps possible to speculate that certain shadowy members of the gay-male community have perpetrated some cunningly engineered conspiracy—but such a thing seems altogether unlikely. There must be some other reason why homoerotic imagery that idealises the male form in such a manner that could readily be construed as sexual is considered to appeal so positively (enough to sell clothes, jewellery, cigarettes etc.) to presumably heterosexual men. The BBC television programme, perhaps wisely, offered no explanation for this queer phenomenon.

No complete explanation is likely to emerge for some time yet to come and we must not take the (albeit) influential medium of television as the best possible academic source on the matter. It certainly is not. However, the clear presence of homoeroticism curiously aimed at heterosexuals that is being highlighted, does perhaps hint at the fact that the sort of paradigms that Western culture is currently utilising for the delineation of sexual categories are somewhat less adequate to the cause than might have been generally supposed. While such issues are examined today within many institutions of higher learning and other similarly sheltered venues, they remain unsettling conversation for the vast majority of other people (including even some of the scholars who specialise in the subject). The reasons for this are numerous and complex. Ultimately, we must admit to some ignorance, at this stage in our development, as to precisely how something as essential as human sexuality actually functions. This is why academics must continue to examine the matter as thoroughly as possible. It can only be to our benefit to plumb its depths, questioning our assumptions and past theories as we go, in seeking a greater understanding. The fact that most people tend to feel so strongly about this subject, despite our impoverished comprehension of it, highlights the necessity for more careful study.

The ancient Greeks make an interesting port of call from which to embark on this ongoing examination. We know with a reasonable degree of certainty that their attitudes toward sex were different from our own. From there the matter of discerning particularities becomes much more difficult. Comparing modern sexuality with the ancient Greek equivalent presumes some clear understanding of the former by which to contrast the latter. It also assumes some understanding of ancient Greek analogues and some general agreement on what the evidence that we have extant actually means. Acquisition of the one, sadly, seems to be almost as daunting a task as the other. But the fact that the problem is difficult should not dissuade one from trying. It is probable that the illumination of ancient Greek sexual mores will also shed considerable light on modern sexuality. The ancient Greeks, free as they were from the Judeo-Christian ideological legacy as well as having existed prior to and apart from the Renaissance-continuum, may have much to tell us about this difficult subject. They lack the 'distorting influences' of modern culture and society and their more 'recent' antecedents. The Greeks too had cultural and historical influences affecting their view of sexuality. The examination of such things is the essential to the aims of this text.

Is either of these psychosexual states, ancient or modern, somehow more 'natural' than the other? This is probably not the case. Both represent situations of various types in which the given culture influences and conditions human psychology. The modification of human behaviour through cultural influences could be called 'natural' inasmuch as culture may be seen as an evolutionary development. Can one separate the natural (genetic) influences on sexuality from the external (cultural) influences with impunity? Whatever the totality of their relationship, the latter certainly affect the former.

I am labouring under the premise that Classical scholarship should utilise such methodological techniques as represented by Cultural Studies in the broader sense. It is the purpose of this chapter, at least in part, to clarify this point in greater detail and to expand upon it. It would be erroneous to assert that the modern academic forces engaged in the Classics are exclusively occupied, ostrich-like, with sifting through the past without regard for the present or the future. This is not the case in the least. The Classics in particular may be regarded as a means of 'backing into the future'. That is, with scholarly recourse to the ancient past, we may project something of the path of events yet to come. Our contemporary re-reading and reinterpretation of ancient texts serves to form our present intellectual *zeitgeist* as well as laying the foundations for future ways of thinking. As Cartledge says, 'the ancients themselves not only invented the Western canon but constantly interrogated and reinvented it, and much of what we regard as modern literary theory traces its genealogies to ancient literary criticism and rhetorical theory'.[4]

Clearly derived from the methods of the Classics, modern Cultural Studies is a distinct and separate area of academics. Under the influence of Derrida, Foucault and others, English Lit., History and Sociology have adapted its methodologies. The study of the Classical world is ripe for approaches derived from Cultural Studies. Both it and the Classics are closely related and, by no means, mutually exclusive. The latter hold within their domain vast resources of cultural data that can yield an untold wealth of information about our world today as well as help to shape the thoughts that bring about its future. We can never guess when some new innovation in the Classics may bear valuable fruit. The relatively recent advents of Cultural Studies and Sexuality-based theories serve to bolster traditional methods and augment their potency for scholarly discourse. 'It turns out', as Cartledge says, 'that, with the rise of gender and cultural studies approaches, its sophisticated sexiness and self-consciousness have more to say to us than to earlier readers'.[5] Our own self-reflection, through the application of modern critical methodologies to the Classics, may be considered to be one of the most important cultural achievements that we have inherited from the ancient Greeks.[6]

It was not unknown to the ancients that a culture produces art.[7] We may broadly posit that the subjects indicated by the term *art* should comprise many phenomena such as literature, history, philosophy, painting, architecture etc. but it is not exclusive of other disciplines or media. Since art is always the product of individuals within a particular cultural context, the prospect that the art produced by a given culture bears certain of the ideas and ideals of that culture should not be cause for much surprise. Modern scholarship can deduce many things about the past from studying its artefacts. By extension, numerous insights may be uncovered about our own culture either through examining our artistic and other productions or when viewing them in contrast to another culture—past or present. Yet the discoveries made by us today that yield insight into the distant past, along with our implicit connection with that past as part of a continuum, are often obscured by our own subjectivity (or the indirect influences of the subjectivity of one or more of our forebears).

There is no such thing as a disinterested reading. The subject of this study, the *Laws* (itself an interested artefact of the 4th century B.C.E.), was intentionally selected and it has been screened through my chosen 'lens' of sexuality and critical theory. Such choices reflect an interested reading of Plato, his thoughts and times. Even with the limitations imposed by these subjective selections, this particular re-reading of the *Laws* in respect to sexuality connects with a broad spectrum of thought both ancient and modern. As indicated earlier, the subject of human sexuality in this era is both topical and controversial.[8] It is an aim of this examination that it should aspire to a broad political and social relevance. In this way, it will contribute to an on-going and enlightened discussion of a subject of such importance as sexuality in relation to culture and, to some extent, sexuality as the product of culture.

The modern English term 'sexuality' is problematic when used in relation to the ancient Greeks. Whenever it is invoked, the reader should understand that it refers to the equivalent paradigm (about which there is much contention) that was a feature of ancient culture and that remains somewhat elusive to our present understanding. There are a number of ways to deal with this problem. One may take a traditionally historicist approach and say that coming to grips with the implicit *otherness* of the ancient Greeks requires a periodisation of ancient cultural and social institutions based on the extant sources and archaeological evidence. Alternatively, one may choose to accept that their *otherness* is implicitly beyond our comprehension. Thus 'by ignoring the marked similarities between classical and modern cultures (and equally within the cultures of the Greek and Roman worlds)', as Golden and Toohey say, some '*reconstruct* or even invent an ancient world that is so foreign, so completely different in its characteristics as to be near impenetrable'.[9] Other scholars such as Foucault, Dover, Halperin and Konstan, adopting elements from New Historicism, attempt to formulate a theory of *otherness* based on their interpretation of the sources in accord with their own historical theories. This approach has sometimes been regarded as biased. In part as a reaction to these, Davidson has attempted to liberate the ancient sources from modern prejudices in order to produce a different model of ancient sexuality. His approach is also arguably subject to a comparable imposition of modern prejudices even while seeking to exclude them. All of these methods represent interested reconstructions (as does this book) but they also strive to broaden our understanding of a very complex subject. Each has its merits and demerits. All contribute to the sum of our knowledge.

Drawing clear boundaries to delineate all the facets of 'sexuality', ancient or modern, is a task that largely falls to the psychologist, the cultural theorist and the philosopher (although, perhaps poets do it best). It is an ambitious endeavour. Before undertaking this examination of sexuality and society in the *Laws* of Plato, it is first necessary to define the use of terms and to outline some of the critical methodologies to be utilised as well as presenting an albeit limited overview of the state of the art of modern theory. This applies both to Classical scholarship and other methodologies. Is ancient sexuality so different from its modern equivalent, in theory and in practise, as to present too much of an impediment to contemporary minds? Surely one must not proceed under such an assumption. To discuss this complex subject adequately, however, is almost impossible without the use of precise, technical language.

Let us turn now to Sexuality-based Theory and the sexual politics of language. The terms 'sex' and 'gender' are often employed to mean more or less the same thing; i.e., the label for the category to which belong the classes 'male' and 'female'.[10] This should present a simple formula for distinguishing the nominal differences between the bearers of XX and XY chromosomes. However, as with the problem of delineating ancient sexuality, form this point the issue becomes much more complex. Along with the incipient chromosomal makeup of a given individual, in this or any culture, there are likewise myriad social and psychological conventions on what constitutes 'being a man' or 'being a woman'. When one makes reference, for example, to a member of the male or female sex of, e.g. a Latin American nation of the early twenty-first century, a certain stereotype or archetype may emerge. This will probably differ from the same archetype for women and men in, e.g., Germany or France (or most anywhere else—although one should expect some similarities across cultures). These cultural differences, however minute or grandiose, constitute another category called 'sex-' or 'gender-roles'. In addition to these, above and beyond societal influences (yet affected by them) is the individual's own 'sexual identity' or 'gender identity' that fits into the greater category of their state of 'sexuality'. This concept has a profound impact on an individual's overall self-identity and is influenced by and influences that sense of holistic identity.

A difficulty with accepting such terms as 'sex' and 'gender' *carte blanche* is that they frequently accrue, sometimes in vague and uncertain ways, bits and pieces of meaning from all over and outwith the super-category of sexuality and beyond thus generating much confusion. Frequently, allowing for regional variances, these terms can gain political weight and become the centres of heated debates even on matters of state policy. At the moment, North American academics seem to prefer to avoid the term 'gender' in favour of 'sex', in designating XX and XY individuals, and 'sexuality' as the label for the broader category of things entailed by sexual difference. British scholarship currently appears to prefer the term 'gender' for these same things. It is perhaps fair to hazard that there is something innately problematic about the implicit assumptions made by either of these choices of terminology.

The original preference was to employ 'gender' as a catch-all phrase for matters related to sexuality in late-twentieth century academia. It could be considered, as Scott indicates, 'one facet of what might be called the quest of feminist scholarship for academic legitimacy in the 1980s'.[11] It had come a long way up to that point in terms of obtaining greater academic legitimacy. Previously, from the Victorian era to the 1960s, some type of 'women's studies' had existed. Although popular morality often limited this discourse to areas such as the particulars of child care, housekeeping and whether or not women should have the vote.[12] Student and teacher activism in the 1960s and '70s brought this subject more decidedly into the light of day. Gender theory has undergone more transformations since the 1980s and the term 'gender' has attained, as we have seen, varied levels of significance.

'Gender' may be used to designate modes of behaviour entailed by social relations between and amongst the biological sexes. Some might ask such questions as: 'Does he/she behave appropriately for a boy/girl? A man/woman?' There is an implied suggestion in such questions that we somehow know what it means to behave like or to be either. But these matters are always part of an ongoing cultural debate. Society can set specific gender or sex roles that may be rigidly enforced at times and in such a way as to limit participation by a given XX- or XY-enhanced individual in a particular context—public or private. Gender may also be employed in the sense of rejecting biological explanations (or biologically based arguments) such as those that would support selective female subjugation on the grounds that women have the capacity to give birth and men, while barren, tend to be physically stronger. 'Gender', as Hall indicates, then 'becomes a way of denoting "cultural constructions"—the entirely social creation of ideas about appropriate roles for women and men'.[13] Thus construed, it may be regarded as a social category imposed on the (biologically) sexed individual.[14]

Part of the problem in the first place—a reason for carefully considering these terms—has to do with the manner in which the sexes have been traditionally regarded. This is especially true in the case of women; however, men too are integral to the situation. 'In a sense', as Butler states, 'what women signify has been taken for granted for too long'. Unquestioned values encourage certain 'blind' assumptions in terms of how people construct sex roles in particular. As a consequence, women became '"fixed," normalised, immobilised, paralysed in positions of subordination'.[15] This is the product of language and the way people think with regard to language. The definitions of words thus come to shape the world that those words describe.

Several ideological camps have developed different approaches in order to elucidate the matter of dealing with the signifier 'gender' as a social construct. Theorists who examine patriarchy have elected to view the construction of gender in terms of a perceived male 'need' to dominate the female. Post-Hegelian approaches define male domination as the resultant psychological effect of a desire on the part of men to transcend their state of alienation from the reproductive act beyond their procreative contribution through sexual intercourse.[16] The significance placed on the continuity of generation in this theoretical model tends to emphasise the primacy of paternity. It also denotes the real work (labour) and social reality undertaken by women in childbirth whilst relegating it to a subordinate status. The argument follows that sex roles have been largely devised by the (male) rulers of a given society in order to impress women into very cheap or slave-like labour. This type of labour, controlled by men and performed by women, however extends beyond biological sex, societal, gender or sex roles into the broader realm that could be referred to alternatively as gender or sexuality.

Sex is not only a matter of discourse, as with women's' status in society, it also possesses a quality of materiality.[17] Many Marxist-feminists have claimed as their goal the liberation of the subverted labour of sexuality with a view toward freedom from male enforced dominance. Women's liberation, according to O'Brien, resides in 'an adequate understanding of the process of reproduction' and an appreciation of the contradiction between the nature of women's reproductive labour and male-generated ideological mystification'.[18] Others, like McKinnon, look to subject/object relationships involved in the construction of sex roles within societal views of sexuality. They tend to adopt an especially economic stance. According to McKinnon, 'sexuality is to feminism what work is to Marxism: that which is one's own, yet most taken away'.[19] She elaborates her point on subject/object relations as follows:

> Sexual objectification is the primary process of the subjugation of women. It unites act with word, construction with expression, perception with enforcement, myth with reality. Man fucks woman; subject verb object.[20]

Sexuality, a construction of society, is here identified as a function of dominance/submission or subject/object relationships—generally designed to the greater benefit of the XYs. McKinnon and O'Brien are, at least in part, reacting against an orthodoxy that maintained sexuality to be an inherent fact of nature around which social conventions 'naturally' formed. The notion that society, in no small part, constructs sex roles challenges this 'essentialist' or 'fundamentalist' view.

There is a clear indication amongst the Marxist-feminists as to who is responsible for constructing the traditional sex roles. Capitalistic patriarchy is seen to bear the blame. The Marxist-feminists reject the essentialism of the argument that the necessities of reproduction 'naturally' determine the sexual division of labour under capitalism.[21] Marxist-feminists have augmented their efforts by way of the works of the French post-structuralist philosophers such as Foucault and Derrida. The former's insistence that sexuality is constructed in historical contexts and his conviction that the current sexual revolution requires serious analysis resulted in many feminist critics making 'sexual politics' the focus of their attentions.[22] This approach combines the examination of socio-economic contexts with the 'psychic structuring of gender [or sexual] identity'.[23] Psychology entered the spotlight.

Anglo-American academics have worked largely in the area of psychologically oriented object-relationships. Chodorow and Gilligan (who based her work on Chodorow) are two North American scholars who have greatly contributed to this research. They, as with my own work, are concerned with moral development and behaviourism and how these relate to the societal construction of sexuality.[24] The continental (largely French) school, in contrast, is based on structuralist and post-structuralist readings of Freud in terms of linguistic theory. A key figure for continental feminists is Jacques Lacan.[25] Both of these schools of thought are concerned, as Scott says, with 'the processes by which the subject's identity is created; both focus on early stages of child development for clues to the formation of gender [or sexual] identity'.[26] Object-relations theorists stress the significance of actual experiences whereas the post-structuralists emphasise language and communications in the development of sexual identity and sex roles. Both methods are useful and both posses innate drawbacks.

Disagreement between these and other scholarly approaches is a healthy sign and suggests that progress is being made, and will continue to be made, in this complex area. None of their theories necessarily helps one pin down any universal sexual language that can be employed in the discussion of ancient sexuality in relation to Plato's *Laws* or anywhere else. I include them to give the reader a sense of the academic tradition in which this examination participates and to provide some theoretical foregrounding in relevant areas. Part of the problem perhaps lies in seeking such universalities (across vast gulfs of space and time) in the first place. The ongoing discourse on sexuality does, however, illustrate the importance of terminology and stresses the necessity of attempting to attain some degree of clarification.

It may be noted that the term 'sex' has at least the double meaning of that which designates XX and XY individuals as well as, in common jargon, being the customary signifier for the physical act of sexual intercourse. The term 'gender' can mean both a biological status and a broader reference to the cultural/natural phenomenon that one might also call sexuality. Gender, unlike sex, does not generally connote the act of intercourse itself—rather, it deals with physio-psychological issues relevant to it. Implicit in either term is the (modern) notion that one's biologically sexed condition somehow must be a determinate factor in one's psychosexual identity within specifically defined parameters.

Some confusion may arise when referring to one's gender to mean either one's biological XX/XY status or one's socially enforced role or one's sexuality—however culturally constructed or natural. Gender could be any one of these depending on context. Both terms are equally blurry in their ideological import. Sex, in common usage, has all the same signifying potential—that is, covering essentially the same areas of definition—as does gender. One could easily construe sex to denote a biological status exclusively rather than a psychological/social/cultural condition. Some will doubtless prefer to utilise gender in the scientific sense, as a clinical term, to denote a physical condition and/or a psychological condition. Both terms are equally blurry in their ideological import. Sex, in common usage, has all the same signifying potential—that is, covering essentially the same areas of definition—as does gender.

I have chosen to utilise terms such as 'sex', 'sex role', 'sexual identity' and 'sexuality' rather than 'gender', 'gender role' and 'gender identity' throughout this text. This does not mean to suggest that 'sex' is somehow correct and 'gender' is somehow not. These choices appear to allow for marginally more clarity in discussing these subjects but this is, as always, open to debate. The reader should understand my use of the term 'sex', unless otherwise indicated, to signify the popular binary opposition of a biological condition composed of the two categories of male and female. It is always the case that any use of this word will also bear implicit connotations of its connections to the greater category of that which we call sexuality. This term encompasses a number of psychological conditions as well as physical ones. Sex, while indicating XX or XY status, is implicitly connected with sexuality. Even so, I must remain effectively constrained by my choice of words. As the post-structuralists amongst others have argued, the use of language is as significant as the use of bodies with regard to the politics of sex.[27]

Feminist critical theories, such as those mentioned above, inform my examination of Plato's *Laws*. Another similar methodological approaches also figures prominently into it. 'Queer reading', or 'queer theory', as it has been called, arose as a form of criticism largely out of Marxist-feminist, cultural-materialist and Marxist-humanist traditions. I take exception to the term 'queer theory' since it implies another kind of theory that is 'normal'. I would prefer to employ a more general phrase such as 'criticism of sexual identity'. 'Queer', in any context, contains implicitly negative connotations. 'When the term has been used as a paralyzing slur', as Butler indicates, 'as a mundane interpellation of pathologized sexuality, it has produced the user of the term as the vehicle and emblem of normalisation'.[28] This book strives to be no such vehicle of prejudice. Even so, perhaps to highlight the inequity of the dichotomy between the 'queer' and the 'normal', the former will be employed in discussing it here (sometimes with inverted commas). Contrary to popular belief, queer theory is not the sole domain of those who consider themselves homosexual. Echoing Athenian democratic sentiments, anyone who wishes may feel free to undertake such examinations utilising this theoretical approach.[29]

Central to this sort of reading are analyses that expose the inner workings of norms and trends within given cultures. Science plays a significant role in such cultural inquiries, as does art.[30] Works by writers such as Oscar Wilde, Percy and Mary Shelley, Virginia Woolf, Tennessee Williams, Ezra Pound and Truman Capote are fertile ground for undertaking a 'queer reading'. These works of literature, whenever historically generated, contain expressions of sexuality, of same-sex relations and of human nature as regards sex in general. Other notable examples include all the ancient Greek writers that are mentioned below, the Hebrew *Talmud*, Islam's *Koran,* the gospels of the Judeo-Christian Old and New Testament, the works of Shakespeare and Milton to name a few. One begins by taking any such work as may be replete with (or even sometimes largely bereft of) material relating to sexuality and examining it as a product of a given culture and time in context. It is necessary to bear in mind that any such cultural artefacts will never reveal all there is to know about human nature at any given time nor about sexuality.

We can take a lesson from more recent history as an example with which to draw some interesting contrasts. A given society with particular views on sexuality that differed markedly from our own was that of Tudors. In Bray's book, *Homosexuality in Renaissance England,* he follows Foucault's logic in saying that early-modern Britain did not possess the contemporary notion of 'homosexual'.[31] There were such terms as buggery and sodomy but these were largely considered particular acts unto themselves and not necessarily a class or mode of behaviour particular to an individual's identity (except perhaps in a broader sense of one who is especially lecherous).[32] Such terms were part of a category that represented, as Bray says, 'a more general notion: debauchery; and debauchery was a temptation to which all, in principle at least, were subject'. Committing sodomy did not make one necessarily effeminate and transvestism amounted to 'a vice in its own right'.[33] It was not until the 19th century, with cultural, historical and technological forces at play, that the individual who engaged in same-sex activity was perceived as a specific kind unto itself. The fact that the term 'homosexual' was an invention of Victorian pseudo-psychology, and did not exist as a singular concept prior to that, is essential to my re-reading of ancient sources. It should also not be ignored with regard to our current paradigms.

Modern concepts of sexuality—and particularly the notion of 'homosexuality'—have arisen out of a lengthy historical process that incorporated features of Judaeo-Christianity and the epistemology inspired by it. The particular concept of the homosexual may be traced at least to 1892 with the efforts of one Charles Gilbert Chaddock who is credited with having introduced the term by the *Oxford English Dictionary* (although the word itself did not actually appear in the dictionary until the 1976 edition).[34] Prior to this advent, there was a notion of sexual 'inversion' associated with those who pursued same-sex relations. Inversion was the dominant term used to designate this state of 'deviancy' throughout most of the nineteenth century.

This idiomatic expression, as Halperin indicates, 'referred to a broad range of deviant gender behaviour, of which homosexual desire was only a logical but indistinct group, while "homosexuality" focused on the narrower issue of sexual object choice'.[35]

The legacy of this distinction has been profound and far-reaching. With the advent of the concept of homosexuality (and heterosexuality), a new taxonomy emerged in which a number of previous distinctions were obliterated in favour of a new and rather monolithic ideology. The differences between 'active' or 'passive' sexual partners, 'normal' and 'abnormal' sexual roles, 'masculine' and 'feminine' modes, pederasty and lesbianism that had traditionally operated in earlier discourses were all subsumed under a single category with relatively little effort to distinguish one from the other.[36] They were all deemed part of the same perceived dysfunction. This new taxonomy failed to evolve a clear technical language with which to examine human sexuality. Old prejudices reasserted themselves on the subject and made it, at the very least, a problematic issue for academia in later times.

It is possible to posit, with relative security, that there was no such thing as ancient Greek homosexuality. As indicated, our modern notion of homosexuality is a direct result of more recent historical processes. This highlights the necessity to avoid the term when talking of the ancient Greeks—'same-sex' (e.g. intercourse, attraction, etc.) will have to suffice for this. The Victorians and their immediate heirs did not merely repress all things sexual (not the least of which was the "unspeakable vice of the Greeks"); they regulated and policed sexuality through the changing of cultural conventions. Through this process of altering the dominant cultural paradigms the homosexual, as Foucault says, 'became a personage, a past, a case history, and a childhood, in addition to being a type of life, a life form, a morphology, with an indiscreet anatomy and possibly a mysterious physiology . . . the sodomite had been a temporary aberration; the homosexual was now a species'.[37] The 'homosexual', thus clinically categorised, was isolated from normal individuals and socially ostracised as the quintessence of the *other*. On account of the active policing of this category by forces seeking what they perceived as 'normalisation', individuals such as Oscar Wilde and others of his fellow outcasts frequently had cause to mourn. Our current conceptions of homosexuality are clearly derived from those of our Victorian forbears and this trend of thought follows like a thread stretching from the distant past to the present. Evidence of this has inevitably been left behind in texts as well as in works of art.

One of the functions of so-called 'queer theory' is to expose and discuss issues of sexuality, including and beyond the role of women, in order to take account of the often hidden or neglected issues of same-sex relationships and their implicit 'sexual politics' both within and without the 'homosexual' sphere. Subject/object relations, performative models and linguistic usages figure prominently in this theoretical approach. Works of art, taken as a production of culture, reveal volumes about those who have laboured to produce them and those for whose consumption they were intended. This is particularly true of the subjects of 'queer theory'. 'We', as Sinfield asserts, 'don't mind texts having political projects, of course; we believe that every representation, with its appeal for recognition—It is like *this,* isn't it—is political'.[38] The absence of a same-sex theme in a work of art may be just as important as its presence. If states of sexual orientation are regarded as cultural constructs, then terms like 'homosexuality' and 'heterosexuality' may be cast as linguistic devices that demonstrate some of the sexual-political views of people of a given era and place.

Can sexuality be deliberately 'constructed'? Who would argue that Western attitudes toward sex have not undergone significant change in the last fifty years alone? One way in which the volatility of sexual values may be observed is through a significant shift in attitudes toward the (perceived) 'natural' roles of women and men that have taken place from the end of the nineteenth century to the beginning of the twenty-first. Presumably women and men have not changed considerably in terms of their physiological qualities in that span of time.[39] Any significant changes will have been largely in psychology and, in terms of both cause and consequence, culture. Scrutiny of this situation has led some modern theorists to suspect that how we view ourselves as sexual entities is in no small part the result of social conditioning psychologically induced from an early age by the values and attitudes that a given society proffers for imitation and regards as acceptable/unacceptable.[40] In this way, a considerable number of people's views on sexuality may be 'constructed' by a governing agency or a ruling class so inclined to undertake the regulation of sexual matters with propaganda and 'spin'. As I will later demonstrate, Plato's narrator in the *Laws* envisions just such methods of social control that are designed to be persuasive and to favour certain sexual ideas and ideals over others.

In a society that allows its citizens to question its values freely, individuals may assume a more active role in shaping the contemporary discourse on sexuality. Alternatively, a given society may prescribe its models of behaviour whilst precluding the free participation of others in that same capacity. One way of constructing sexuality is for a society to define the accepted roles for men and women, according to specific criteria of norms, and then actively (and sometimes forcefully) encourage them to adhere to these models as if they were 'natural' law. The employment of specifically engineered language is as integral to this process of influence as are the performative models presented for imitation.

The observation that personal views of sexuality are in no small part a result of cultural and psychological factors imposed on the individual from outside him/ herself not only applies to modern times. It should, if the theory is sound, hold true at all points in the development of human civilisation. The process by which societal norms of sexuality are implemented perhaps underwent a parallel development concurrent with and integral to that of civilisation itself. It is ongoing. Therefore, the process by which sex roles have developed (or been constructed) within, e.g. the ancient Athenian city-state, Sparta and Krete make up significant elements of our common heritage. These and others have influenced modern thinking on sexuality through their contribution to the connected continuum of human ideological advancement.

Amongst the ancient Athenians, Plato in particular has left no small mark on the subject of sexuality and his narrator in the *Laws,* undertaking no less than the creation of a new society, has outlined some specific sexual mores to be upheld by his hypothetical citizenry. A primary method that he employs consists of redefining the virtue of 'manliness' in particular terms and then enforcing the imitation of specific performative models for both men and women. This value system is to be inculcated by means of various civic institutions and official state doctrines concerning its 'naturalness' and 'correctness'. It provides a neat paradigm for a process of social control.

Nature probably plays more than a propagandistic role in constructing sexuality. It functions alongside socialising influences. It is possible to assert that many of the psychological aspects of perceived sex roles are socially defined according to relatively arbitrary values imposed by groups in power at a given time. The only 'natural' sexual attributes, therefore, would appear to be those peculiar to each sex as regards its differences relative to reproduction. It is also possible to theorise that, due to the two primary sexes' various physiological differences, there are also some behavioural attributes that are sexually specific. These fundamental attributes would appear to be, according to Darwinian evolution, somehow helpful toward the cause of human survival.

Sexual values and society are locked together in a close relationship. Advanced social units (e.g. city-states) regarded their own survival as the basis for most of their sexual regulations. This perhaps resulted in a particularly 'manly' concept of honour that is often associated with warfare.[41] At some stage in our history, states and religions began to engineer moralities deliberately, on whatever metaphysical and authoritative groundings, that greatly influenced their societies' views on sex. As Vance indicates, 'the history of the construction of sexuality in modern, state-level society shows that sexuality is an actively contested political and symbolic terrain in which groups struggle to implement sexual programs and alter sexual arrangements and ideologies'.[42] This appears to have held true as much for Classical Greece as for modern cultures.

Amongst the natural influences affecting sexuality one might enumerate such things as the weather, geological phenomena, proximity to food/resources, genetics etc. Under the category of 'nurture' (culture) one might include politics, law, fashion, religion (cultic activity, mysticism etc.) along with the moralities favoured by these. Both natural and cultural influences have an impact on the sexual values of a given society. The points of convergence between them, as indicated earlier, may be so numerous as to collapse their apparent differences altogether into a state of indeterminacy of meaning. Even if a culture has intentionally constructed its sex roles out of a perceived necessity for survival and self-perpetuation, one is not prevented from observing the particular social (artificial) response to natural phenomena. For example, a given culture may base its conception of manliness on a natural tendency for most men to be physically stronger than most women. Therefore, athletic prowess and martial skill would be important facets of sexual identity. In such a society, to have been born a male might automatically oblige one to partake of athletic and warlike activities in order to live up to the established ideals of masculinity. Or, a given society might do completely otherwise in all respects. It depends on the chosen set of values present in a culture in concert with the influence of natural factors.

There have been, and continue to be many attempts to (re)construct the modes of behaviour of ancient Greek men and women based on surviving source material. Philosophers, historians, orators, dramatists and others have all added to a cultural discourse on sexuality in the ancient world.[43] Such evidences as we have, however, only indicate what a relatively small number of people believed and wrote. Their representations are often idealised or culturally biased in some way. Additionally, the reading of ancient sexuality through the views of modern thinking on the subject adds a further dimension of distortion to our interpretations. Translating the term 'sex', not only across languages but cultures and time as well, presents a significant problem. This is especially true in the case of sex's modern meaning of 'sexual intercourse', or even 'sexuality'.

The ancient Greek phrase τὰ ἀφροδίσια, a general term used to express a number of sexual nuances including sexual intercourse, literally means 'the things of Aphrodite'. There is really no direct translation for τὰ ἀφροδίσια into English except perhaps the archaic use of 'venereal' that maintains in its etymology the divine name of Venus but now denotes a less than divine state. There is no truly equivalent term in ancient Greek for the English word 'sex' in its common or scientific sense. The modern impact of this term makes it largely useless as a viable translation for τὰ ἀφροδίσια. The ancient Greeks spoke of what we think of as sex in relation to gods such as Erōs and Aphrodite who probably functioned, at least in part, as mental abstractions for human decisions and deeds.[44] These deities are integral to interpreting the cultural *ethos* and psychological world-views contemporary with those times. We have to make recourse to a similar abstraction in attempting to discern their views. Pangle, in his discussion of this problematic concept, helpfully suggests for τὰ ἀφροδίσια the paradigm 'erotic things'.[45] Again, this is less than a perfect equivalent for the English term 'sex' (even simply in the sense of fornication) but the Greek term may be construed as bearing comparable significance. The situation becomes more complex when we compare and contrast the sex roles and sexual identities of today with those considered to have existed amongst the ancient Greeks.

What did they think about masculinity and femininity? Or, perhaps a better question would be: what were the dominant notions that they held on the subject, as we have them, amongst the extant texts? Absolute knowledge of these things is probably unobtainable. No comprehensive understanding of human sexuality has ever obtained a consensus about all the particulars of this vast and difficult subject and we should not expect the ancient Greeks to have done so either.[46] The study of sexuality is an ongoing cultural discourse that remains open to many considerations and shows no evident signs of concluding in the foreseeable future. There is no reason to assume that the ancient Greeks should have any ready answers for us about how they viewed sex categorically outlined in a handbook. What we have is an imperfect picture of ancient sexual practices and values based on the words of certain authors. These, at least, indicate that private and social relationships between women and men were strikingly different in many ways from those of modern, Western civilisation.

Female participation at most levels of society outside the home seems to have been rather limited. We do hear of some foreign women in Classical Athens who were well educated but it remains impossible to deduce the average level of education of citizen-women across the spectrum in ancient communities.[47] A rather rigid sexual dichotomy appears to have existed and this appears to have been especially true amongst the upper classes. Ancient Athenian citizen-men lived at home with their wives and families but practised their careers primarily in the public sphere of the *polis*. By contrast, citizen-women appear to have been generally restricted to the private sphere of the *oikos* (funerals, weddings and religious festivals being the major exceptions to this rule). This division of the sexes extended also into education and sex role stereotyping and, as with societies today, started from an early age.

It is possible that by the fourth century some women were, from time to time, educated on an equal footing with males but there were no legal conventions that mandated this across the board.[48] An example testifying to the existence of educated women in Classical Greece is the gravestone of Phanostrate, presumably one of the first female physicians in Athens.[49] The laudatory nature of her epitaph implies that not only was Phanostrate highly educated but that she was highly respected as well. It may be that she was something of an exception in this capacity or, perhaps, that she was representative of some of the changes happening in the fourth century. Classical Athenian girls seem to have been, on the whole, significantly less educated than boys (if it is fair to say that they were educated at all) although some were evidently taught to read and write. That they had some level of learning is implied but not definitively known.[50]

There appears to have been a popular (male) attitude to the effect that Athenian citizen-women, if not all women, were 'secretive' and 'cunning'. This may have developed because they displayed such qualities resulting from their enforced segregation in the private sphere. It may also have been largely a matter of (mis)representation in the media of the time. Xenophon, through his narrator Ischomachos, wrote that 'it is seemly for a woman to remain at home and not to be out of doors; but for a man to remain inside is a disgrace'.[51] Those women who fell outside the usual boundaries of citizen-wives seem to have been either foreigners or prostitutes. It is difficult to separate the real, about which relatively little is known, from idealised representations. The ruling male-elite amongst the ancient Athenians seem to have considered this situation in which respectable and feminine women keep to the private sphere and men rule the public to be the natural state of affairs. Women would have been socialised into this set of beliefs from the earliest possible age. The relationship that existed between the sexes is a necessary foreground to addressing deeper issues.

How does one discuss ancient sexuality? As with the status of women in Athens and elsewhere, we seek to reconstruct an image, based on the extant sources, and then develop paradigms accordingly. Again, more than a little significance resides in the manner of language that one employs. It should be stressed that no such terms as 'homosexual' or 'heterosexual' existed in the ancient Greek world. As indicated above, it is more correct to utilise 'same-sex' or 'mixed-sex' to denote the sexual relations that transpired between individuals. The ancients did distinguish between different types of sexual practise. The terms employed, as with their modern equivalents, were politically charged and held broad social significance. Again, there are profound differences between their paradigms and our own.

These differences highlight the necessity to clarify more of the incompatibilities inherent in reading one culture through the views of another. At this point in history, in the industrialised West, we have developed sub-categories unavailable to the ancients that compose the greater category of sexuality and denote several perceived types of sexual identity.[52] Three major sub-categories have arisen to account for the dominant forms of sexual expression. 'Homosexuality' is used to refer to a state in which one chiefly has sexual relations, emotions, thoughts and/or attractions to members of the same sex. 'Heterosexuality' refers to a state in which an individual of one biological sex chiefly experiences such attractions, emotions, thoughts and/or deeds with members of the other sex—sometimes (inaccurately) called the 'opposite' sex. 'Bisexuality' tends to mean a state wherein these erotic sentiments are aimed toward members of both the male and female sex (both together and/or separately) with whom one might engage in sexual intercourse. There are other categories such as 'transgendered' and 'eunuchdom' that skirt the edges of the modern definition and, there are others still beyond these.[53] The tripartite system outlined above is the one that is mainly recognised but some prefer to envisage a bipartite system that excludes 'bisexuality' and refuses to acknowledge any other states than 'homosexuality' and 'heterosexuality' however defined. Others believe that these designations are all erroneous fictions and that people should be identified as sexual beings with a range of options, inclinations and preferences whether fully availed or not.

Whilst modern pop-culture may jokingly refer to ancient sexuality in terms of the stereotypes of today, any serious approach to the issue must consider matter in appropriate detail. Cantarella's summary account of ancient Greek sexuality stresses its difference:

> The Greeks were certainly bisexual, in the sense that when they were boys they were loved by a man, while in the first years of their own adulthood they preferred to make love to adolescent boys. Later in life they chose women, and even when they were married they were allowed to have their *paidikia* . . . but even in ancient Greece, inevitably, there were men whose impulses were directed decisively if not exclusively towards a single sex (whether the female or the male).[54]

Again, a term like bisexual, as with homosexual or heterosexual, cannot truly apply to the ancient Greeks in the same manner as it is employed in modern English. Otherwise, Cantarella's formulation generally describes the situation as we understand it. Many attempts have been made to reconstruct the sexual values of the ancients in terms that we can comprehend. The dominant trend in modern scholarship since the sixties has been to assert that the primary sexual mindset of Plato's era consisted of a fairly rigid polarity in terms of sex roles and sexual practice. The boundaries of this paradigm are described as a masculine/active state and a feminine/passive state.

The model developed by Foucault and Dover depicts intercourse not so much as mutual activity between two equal individuals; rather, it portrays it as something that is decidedly done to one by another.[55] The sex act, so conceived, polarises and divides its participants into two distinct and opposite classifications. This view is ultimately phallocentric and places greater significance on the active agents (penetrators) whilst marginalizing the passive recipients of penetration. As Halperin describes, 'the insertive partner is construed as a sexual agent, whose phallic penetration of another person's body expresses sexual "activity," whereas the receptive partner is construed as a sexual patient, whose submission to phallic penetration expresses sexual "passivity."'[56] The relationship between active and passive partners, perceived here largely in terms of dominance and submission, is characterised as that between a social superior and a social inferior. This sort of relationship is considered to occur more often than not between people of differing ages and social standings, thus highlighting the disparity in status.[57]

There is a stage in their development when some citizen youths could undertake the 'passive' role with relative impunity. Later, when they reached adulthood, there appears to have been more of a stigma associated with anally receiving another man's penis. This stigmatisation does not appear to be fully commensurate with modern homophobia. The *symposion* and the *gymnasion* were primarily institutions of the upper classes that bore particular associations with same-sex intercourse. Both of these venues provided occasion for male-male sexual desire to be physically realised within an acceptable cultural context. By at the early 6th century B.C.E., at least, some of the ancient Greeks seem to have regarded it as perfectly natural that an attractive male should arouse the same degree of sexual excitement in another male as one might expect would a beautiful woman.[58] Interestingly, it appears that a same-sex lover was considered capable of the same obsessive longing, devotion and self-sacrifice that later romantic literature would associate with the passions between members of the opposite sexes.[59] Even so, in relationships between adults and youths, overt sexual excitement on the part of a 'junior' partner appears to have been less than ideal.[60] Sustained same-sex relationships, such as that between Pausanius and Agathon in Plato's *Symposium* (177d, 193b–c), were probably rather unusual. A number of ancient Greek sources, along with others, appear to have regarded the concept of same-sex marriages as a source of humour and contempt.[61]

It seems to have been difficult for an Athenian man or youth to engage in erotic affairs with citizen-women since they were usually kept indoors and almost always under some kind of supervision before and after marriage.[62] Owing to this segregation, it was perhaps easier for freeborn males to partake of erotic forays with members of the same sex (along with, potentially, non-citizen women and youths) without running the risk of 'deflowering' an unwed virgin or committing adultery with a citizen-woman—either of which could incur severe penalties if caught.[63] There were additional incentives for engaging in temporary (but accepted) same-sex liaisons with youths who had not reached their civic majority. Such relationships in ancient Athens entailed an educational aspect as well as potential for social advancement.[64] Humphreys offers a formulaic description of this phenomenon:

> . . . a boy was first *erōmenos,* the object of romantic passion, introduced into adult society by an older lover who took his father's place as a model of adult behaviour; later he became a lover and educator of younger boys in his turn . . . he would not drop out of the life of the gymnasium and *andron* until some time after marriage, when his own sons were beginning to grow up . . . this was regarded as the normal sequence of sex roles–mockery of homosexuals [sic] in comedy is directed only at those who deviate from this norm.[65]

Eventually a freeborn male citizen was expected to marry and beget heirs. Exclusive, long-term relationships between members of the same-sex would have been impractical to this end. We do not know how often an adult male might have continued to be an *erōmenos* or *erastēs* with other men in the *symposion,* the *gymnasion* or elsewhere; although, one may infer that some men would have had male lovers 'on the side', as it were, for the remainder of their lives.

Dover and Foucault's (re)construction of the sex roles of ancient Athenian men and women seems to overemphasise the deviant quality of engaging exclusively in same-sex intercourse. Their theory posits that there existed two extremes into which most men would have fallen: the manly penetrators (often associated with *hoplites*) and the unmanly *kinaidoi*. It supposes that, amongst the citizen-soldier class, displays of bravery and masculine prowess were the standards of behaviour. These idealisations are thought to have upheld a specific model for imitation, however imperfectly, in reality. Dover argues that the self-definition of the community as a 'vigorous elite' was an important theme in terms of cultural identity.[66] In the words of Xenophon, 'the pursuit of honour (*philotimīa*) is not a natural component of the irrational animals nor of all human beings; those who have a natural desire for praise and honour are at the greatest distance from cattle—they are considered to be men, no longer merely human beings'.[67] Aiskhines asks Demosthenes whether the Athenians would prefer to have at their defence 'ten thousand *hoplites* like Philon, with bodies as well-made as his and souls as disciplined, or thirty thousand *kinaidoi* exactly like you?'[68]

Certainly not every *erōmenos* was regarded as a *kinaidos*. Both of these terms, consequently, refer to the states of desiring and being desired. The term *kinaidos* appears to have (at least sometimes) indicated a sexual pathic given to repetitively gratifying the excessive desire for pleasure.[69] There is, however, no way of determining how often desires led to acts of sexual congress. Dover and Foucault maintain that the *kinaidos* was an adult male-citizen who preferred being passively penetrated rather than engaging in active penetration. A key tenet of the penetrator/penetrated model is that the *kinaidos* was generally considered to be effeminate and 'womanish'.[70] Dover asserts that the status of *kinaidos* was associated with sexual promiscuity, 'womanliness' and passively subjecting one's self to another man's sexual penetration—incompatible and contrary to the manly role of the *hoplite*. The *kinaidoi*, as Foucault says, seem to have consisted of those who were 'automatically assumed, according to the protocols that polarised penetrators and penetrateds, to desire to be penetrated by other men, which assimilates them to the feminine role'.[71] In a society where displays of bravery (*andreia*, which also means 'manliness') were paramount, one who did not behave appropriately, or who did the opposite of what was expected, as Winkler says (following Foucault's lead), might be subject 'to symbolic demotion from the ranks of the brave and manly to be identified with the opposite class of women'.[72]

Societal forces reinforced the symbolic paradigms. Grosz, in keeping with continental academics, argues that 'sexual difference was imagined in the past and was largely unconstrained by what was known about this or that bit of anatomy, this or that psychological process . . . it derived instead from particular rhetorical, cultural and political exigencies of the moment'.[73] This may be an over-generalisation and is somewhat reductive. It particularly stresses the significance of language and culture in relation to sexuality. But practising the art of rhetoric or entering into the political arena entail more than words alone. There were models of masculinity that public speakers upheld in terms of physical manner and deportment. This had broader, propagandistic effects on the populace as a whole. 'Rhetorical theory and practice', as Gunderson says, 'and their interrelationship thus offer an overt example of the process of subject production'.[74] What better way to advertise an accepted sexual norm than through the expected modes of behaviour of those persons most in the public eye?

Performative modelling is one level of ancient sexual construction and personal psychology is another. Halperin maintains that ancient sexual relations functioned in terms of individual perceptions of power and status. These, he argues, were played out through acts that reinforced dominance and submission.[75] Negative qualities are ascribed to the submissive partner. The penetrator/penetrated model suggests that an adult male citizen subjecting himself to the role of being a sexual 'patient' must have been publicly perceived with abhorrence. As evidence for this, Winkler cites Aiskhines' rhetorical encouragement to those who desire boy-lovers to seek out their quarries amongst foreigners and *metics* so that citizen-boys may avoid social demotion.[76] Dover and Foucault argue that men who had the desire to be penetrated by other men recanted the 'proper' masculine role, which was thought to be naturally superior, in favour of an inferior, 'feminine' role.[77] Aiskhines seems to confirm this attitude when he writes that Timarkhos was 'a man who is male in body but has committed a woman's transgressions' and, echoing Plato's narrator in the *Laws*, 'outraged himself contrary to nature'.[78] I shall presently return to the case of Timarkhos.

This theory of accepted ancient Greek social norms also extends to 'boy love'. The object of desire in question would have been socially inferior and thus more readily subjected to the role of sexual 'patient' by an older male who would have been higher on the social scale. It must be stressed that ancient 'boy love' is not the same thing as the modern concept of paedophilia. The differences between ancient and modern culture preclude so easy a comparison. There are also problems with including 'boy love' in the same category as same-sex intercourse between willing adults. At least, there is a difference between a willing and an unwilling participant and it is difficult to determine (even for us today) exactly what age constitutes an 'age of consent'.[79] The active/passive dichotomy and the implicitly *masculine* role of the lover and the *feminine* role of the beloved may be applied to 'boy love' as well as to same-sex relations with older males. But did it signify a zero-sum relationship? The sheer amount of poetry and other literature devoted to the pursuit of youths seems to suggest something beyond this.[80]

The penetrator/penetrated model is not the end of the discussion. It represents a major step in our understanding of ancient sexuality. One may object that it is not an accurate representation. Davidson argues that the problem lies in the interpretation of ancient sources through the distorting effects of modern values. Other influences may have also affected Dover and Foucault's zero-sum model. Something like it may have held true more so for ancient Rome, 'where', according to Davidson, 'there does indeed seem to be evidence (still less than in modern cultures) of a metaphorical use of sex as domination and triumph'.[81] The relatively recent social force of homophobia could also have influenced Dover and Foucault's theory, perhaps inclining it to stress the 'deviancy' or 'inferiority' of the penetrated's role.

Even so, it would be unfair to dismiss them outright. Their work represents the culmination of considerable thought and research on the subject. Davidson's theories too have their limitations. A new formulation that incorporates both academic camps seems to be the correct way to proceed. There is clearly something pertinent to the observation that the ancient Greeks (especially the Athenians) applied significance to sexual relations in terms of who was, as it were, 'on top'. Certain values were attached to the act of sexually penetrating another individual, who, in turn had (not insignificantly) been penetrated by that person. But what does this mean? A careful re-examination of relevant sources is essential.

As I have said previously, ancient evidence is far from clear in indicating the precise quality of ancient sexuality. If the sort of implications that Dover has proposed existed, then there should be textual material to sustain this view. Yet the ancient authors, as ever, are reluctant to lend so much unambiguous support. For example, Bain, after an exhaustive search to locate uses of the Greek verb *pugizō* (πυγίζω—to bugger), found only one Classical example. It occurs in an inscription on an early fifth-century cup from Gela in Sicily that reads 'Who wrote this will bugger him who is reading it'. The context is lost and it might be referring to any number of potential situations about which we know nothing. Nonetheless, Bain writes that this represents 'clear evidence that such practices [i.e. aggressive uses of the verb] existed also in the Greek world'.[82] It is arguably the case that one instance of an aggressive use of *pugizō* did exist. We have no evidence of any others. It could just as easily be the case that the missing context of this one instance of the verb could indicate a playful, possibly even erotic, rather than aggressive usage. But this is presently unknowable and it is dangerous to speculate on such uncertain ground.

The zero-sum model is further problematised when one considers another important term already mentioned above. *Kinaidos* (κίναιδος) is, as Davidson says, 'a very rare word in classical Greek and its usage seems quite respectable', at least, 'respectable' compared to Dover's interpretation of it.[83] It is only to be found in Plato, Aiskhines and in one dubious comic fragment that would appear to make its employment as an explicit reference to anal penetration rather doubtful.[84] Plato's use of *kinaidos* in the *Gorgias* refers to an individual whose existence is devoted to the pursuit of pleasure and who lacks self-mastery (consistent with a similar theme in the *Laws*).[85] A man who voluntarily surrendered his 'masculine' identity for the 'feminine' due to a lack of self-mastery in the face of pleasure could be regarded in a negative manner.[86] Aiskhines never uses *kinaidos* to refer *directly* to Timarkhos whom

Dover and others assume to be a sexual 'patient' and therefore subject to aggressive ridicule. Instead, he makes reference to the *kinaidia* of Timarkhos' patron Demosthenes and 'here and elsewhere the word is associated with effeminate dress like that of an adulterer, *moichos*'.[87] The law quoted in Aiskhines, as Dover indicates, 'said nothing of "unnatural practices", "gross indecency", and the like, and thus it appears not to have imposed any penalty on those who submitted to homosexual [sic] acts for love or fun'.[88]

It may have been irrelevant whether the *kinaidos* was penetrator or penetrated. What appears to matter most is his (perceived or reported) hedonistic pursuit of pleasure. It is this that is associated with effeminacy—a 'womanish' insatiability especially for sexual pleasure. The condition of being a sexual pathic was later described in the Aristotelian *Problemata* as a state of 'insatiability', or *aplestia,* rather than having anything necessarily to do with being penetrated by a man's penis *per se.*[89] Effeminacy and 'softness' then, in the case of the *kinaidos* have less to do with the perceived cultural stigma about being penetrated. It particularly indicates an inclination toward luxury and the pursuit of too much pleasure.[90]

Eurupröktos (εὐρυπρωκτός), literally 'wide-arsed', may be 'seen as an attack on whorishness (excessive penetration, or even what we would have to call "anal eagerness"), rather than on the submission to another's penetrative actions in itself'.[91] Again, the implication appears to be that of partaking of sexual pleasure to excess. It does not seem to indicate that those who receive anal penetration are necessarily inferior. Neither does it specifically point to their 'passive' submission to a dominant penetrator. 'Wide-arsed', however, is clearly an example of invective and may at least be said to stress the consequences of excessive penetration on the penetrated's anatomy. It seems correct to view it as a form of comic ridicule directed at the penetrated. It is, however, more difficult to determine the degree of negativity that this term might or might not have denoted. Is one who is identified as *eurupröktos* not seen to have been actively partaking of sexual pleasure?

Katapugōn (καταπύγων) is another word that potentially presents some problems to the zero-sum model. It was employed to mean something like 'lecherous'. When Lysistrata uses this term, for example, despairing of the female sex as 'completely *katapugōn*', she would seem to be making a statement about women's perceived lack of sexual self-control.[92] Dover has asserted that this usage in Aristophanes indicates contempt felt by the active penetrator for the passive penetrated and that *katapugōn* here implies a complete sexual pathic.[93] It is possible that an ancient Athenian audience might have recalled, at that point in the play, a stereotype of the sexual pathic, but there appears to be no firm basis to assume, therefore, that lechery necessarily indicates a pathic state. Just as some early twentieth century cinematic melodramas might recall certain popular notions of women being given to excessive flights of fancy or emotion, there is no reason to generalise that people actually behaved like that, on the whole, or that those popular notions were somehow correct or accurate for describing a cultural norm.

Dover has translated the verb *laikazō* (λαικάζω), employed in comic sources, in the aggressive sense of the modern English invective 'fuck'. Despite the fact that Jocelyn has demonstrated that this word refers exclusively to fellatio, Dover insists that this makes no difference and has continued to render it as 'get fucked', etc.[94] Some uses of *laikazō* may be said to denote disgust (whether the act of fellatio involved men or women). But these, as Parker indicates, reflect certain ancient Greek notions on contamination and pollution (*miasma*) more so than anything else.[95] There seems to be little or no indication of *laikazō* being employed to indicate aggression, dominance or submission. Dover's intractability on the matter is worthy of note as is his lack of evidence for refuting Jocelyn and Parker.

There is at least one potential example of aggressive penetration of one man by another that offers some evidence for the zero-sum theory to have functioned in a specific context.[96] The notion that penetration could occur as an act of domination is found in at least one source. We are told that there was a law in ancient Athens whereby a man who caught a seducer (a socially defined, inappropriate sexual partner) in the act of sexual intercourse with his wife, mother, daughter or concubine (a clearly delineated illegal deed) was permitted either to slay the offender outright or, if he chose, he could maltreat the seducer in some humiliating manner.[97] Types of maltreatment could and sometimes did include shoving 'radishes' up his anus and forcefully extracting the offender's pubic hair.[98] The insertive aspect of this procedure, if it was ever practiced in reality, does denote an aggressive form of penetration—although not necessarily with an actual penis. But it refers to a situation in which dominance and submission of a particular sort are implicitly occurring in a specific context beyond normative sexuality.[99] The context is one of intentional humiliation with an express purpose of aggression. The same concept cannot be generalised to include all incidents of sexual penetration. Some types may clearly be acts of dominance (e.g. in the instance of rape) but, in the case of a loving relationship, there is no reason to presume that sexual penetration should amount to much more than one aspect of a mutually enjoyable experience.

Finding evidence for a zero-sum relationship in same-sex congress by recourse to ancient conceptions of rape is also problematic but it is possible to observe some interesting contrasts. Xenophon has drawn a comparison between same-sex intercourse and the sort of *hybris* associated with the rapist. Does it support for the zero-sum model? He appears to vilify the (male) practitioners of same-sex, saying:

> But you compel sexual relations before they are required, trying everything and using men as women; thus you educate (παιδεύεις) your friends, committing *hybris* against them through the night.[100]

Omitowoju interprets this according to Dover's model indicating that it means that the 'issue must be passivity and penetrability, which normatively characterise the female in sexual relationships and which insult a man's or a youth's sexual honour'.[101]

The passage does appear to be favouring sexual intercourse between a man and a woman over any other type. But Omitowoju may have erred in drawing such conclusions from Xenophon. Who is being condemned? Is it just those men who 'use men as women'? Might it not be those who are 'trying everything *and* using men as women' [emphasis mine], and those who also 'compel sexual relations before they are required'? In what way do such individuals commit *hybris* against their friends? Is it not because, presumably, in 'trying everything' they might not only engage in penetrative sexual intercourse with their friends, but with their friends' wives and children as well? Or does the *hybris* reside in the assertiveness of the act as Omitowoju suggests?[102] The fault here seems to be that of an uncontrolled sexual appetite. Xenophon's statements are subject to debate, but it appears rash to draw conclusions about a whole sexual mindset based on a few lines that ultimately reflect only one individual's particular views—and those with less clarity than we would prefer.

The Athenian Stranger in the *Laws* also seems to contradict the zero-sum formulation in characterising the 'active' male partner, along with the 'passive', as both being weak (in a sense more 'feminine') in respect to their self-control over the desire for pleasures. He is not alone in reckoning that same-sex intercourse is exceedingly pleasurable and that the compulsive pursuit of it could amount to a loss of self-mastery. Xenophon's Sokrates considered the transformation from self-mastery to the slavery of excessive Desire to be a swift one, although habituation is considered to encourage and entrench such a state. 'Miserable wretch', he says, 'are you considering what will happen to you if you kiss a beautiful youth: instantly to be a slave instead of a free person . . . '.[103]

It is possible that one who proved to be a slave to pleasure could be construed as dangerous to the stability of the *polis*. Aiskhines alleged that Timarkhos originally held sufficient property to place him in the highest economic range, the liturgical class, but his 'madness' for erotic pleasure and all forms of sexual indulgence caused him to consume his paternal estate.[104] In the selection of a general to defend the city or of a custodian to manage a farm, Xenophon indicates that someone who is an honourable master of his own pleasures should be preferred over the shameful slave to them—nowhere does he imply that same-sex intercourse is unnatural or disgusting or necessarily wrong.[105] It is the excessive pursuit of these pleasures that is deemed harmful.

Plato's Athenian Stranger and Xenophon's Sokrates are not the only ones to criticise the 'penetrator' in male, same-sex relations for failing to master himself. Plato's emphasis on the lover's failure is perhaps somewhat more vehement than most other sources but it is by no means unique. Timarkhos' friend Misgolas was allegedly the subject of ridicule in several comedies due to his excessive fondness for *cithara*-boys. Aiskhines refers to his comic reputation and condemns another of his friends, who has been known in the past to have been a 'penetrator', Hegesander, in the same terms as Timarkhos. He asks: 'tell me fellow citizens, in the name of Zeus and all the other gods, since this man has defiled himself with Hegesander does he not seem to you to have prostituted himself with a prostitute?'[106] Theopompus condemns the Macedonian Companions as effeminate prostitutes and male-whore-keepers. Similarly, the men who take advantage of Agathokles' 'whorishness' are criticised for their complete lack of self-control and Menon is harshly rebuked for having an *erōmenos* older than himself.[107] 'The negative portrayals', as Davidson writes, 'of Timarchus as enslaved to desire, of Hegesander or the Macedonian Companions as "prostitutes", are not ameliorated one iota by allusions to their "positive" role as "penetrators"'.[108]

Self-mastery when faced with temptation appears to be a more important feature of ancient Greek sexuality than the matter of who penetrated whom. One may posit that there were those who desired to be penetrated to an excessive degree and these were seen as particularly effeminate through their lack of self-control. But there were others whose desire for penetrating made them equally 'effeminate' in the eyes of their peers for the same basic reasons. That there were 'penetrators' and 'penetrateds' is beyond doubt. The sort of emphasis that Dover, Foucault and others propose to be applied to them, especially in terms of dominance/submission and zero-sum, seems unnecessary and perhaps slanted. The roles of penetrator and penetrated were important in other ways. Men frequently penetrate women when engaging in mixed-sex coupling. It is not unreasonable to consider, in the case of same-sex couplings, that the question of who penetrates whom may contain explicit assumptions about the sexual character of such persons in relation to traditional male-female idioms. At least, one may see it that way if one wishes to do so.

What we are left with is a conceptualisation of human sexuality that, while in some ways evidently quite similar to our own, is strikingly alien in many others. There are at least some points that can be made with relative certainty. Marriage did not necessarily imply monogamy for either party (whatever the ideal). Sexual intercourse could and did transpire between members of the same sex and amongst mixed sexes. It might sometimes be potentially reproductive in certain instances or it might not. In the cases of men with women and men with men, somebody was usually, at some point or another, penetrating somebody else who was in turn being penetrated. A clear sense of negativity was associated with those who did these things to excess inasmuch as certain other people knew about it and chose to draw attention to the fact. It may be that the negativity that some have identified with the penetrated is the normal quality of reproach specific to those who were seen to be partaking too much of this type of sexual pleasure—just as there was a kind of reproach, as indicated above, for those who partook of penetrating others to a perceived degree of excess.

Again, our sources may not have been representative of the general attitude of the time. The opposing theories of ancient sexuality demonstrate that it was at least as complex as its modern equivalent and underline the importance of continuing to seek clarification.

In conclusion, it can be deduced that sophisticated, socially defined sex roles existed amongst the XXs and XYs of ancient Greece. It cannot, however, be deduced to what degree these ideal roles were actually enforced or even popularly accepted. This chapter has sought to stress that no consensus on this existed amongst the ancients. Modern theory can help illuminate many of these issues. But we must take care to separate modern prejudices from the application of theory as much as feasible. This is not an easy task and it is not always possible to know when one is being prejudicial. Dover and Foucault's theories perhaps reflect some bias (notably that of the male penetrator) whilst excluding arguments and evidence that undermine these. Davidson is also biased in his opposition to them. The matter is too complex to be resolved by unilateral views.

A vast discourse exists today across many academic fields on the subject of sexuality and its relation to society and the individual. A comparable cultural discourse also took place in the ancient world. All of the statements that have been made in this chapter, grounded as they are in modern theory and ancient context, probably represent only the 'tip of the iceberg' of ancient sexuality. One considers the evidence available and attempts to reconstruct an imperfect image from it. Then, as now, there were certain sexual conventions in effect but their conceptual evolution was (and is) in a state of perpetual flux and re-definition. The following chapters of this text address such concepts of ancient sexuality that are present in Plato's *Laws* and contrast these with related cultural data in light of modern scholarship.

Chapter II
The *Laws* in Context

Mankind will not be rid of its evils until either the class of those who philosophise in truth and rectitude attain political power or when those who are the most powerful in cities, under some divine dispensation, really get to philosophising.

—Plato[1]

They've used genetics, physics, philosophy, literature, er, sport, all to enhance the basic human condition and elevate it to the highest level . . . They'd be a worrying prospect, a potential über-race bent on domination, if they weren't all pacifists.

—Dr. Who?[2]

This chapter considers Plato's text as an artefact in context along with the holistic project of Magnesia as its subject. The *Laws* (**NOMOI**) was probably composed during the last twenty years of its author's life (his death is given as c. 348 B.C.E.) and, as such, it is generally regarded as his final philosophical treatise.[3] It is thought to have been written in the 350s and early 340s, although, as Saunders indicates, 'some passages may conceivably be earlier'.[4] This was a time in which the formal codification of laws and the production of printed text were in vogue. As Nightingale says, 'the Athenians had grown more "document-minded" and were beginning to place more trust in written texts'.[5] Plato, in a sense, was on the 'cutting edge' of this literary phenomenon.[6] However, despite the greater cultural emphasis on the written word, the transmission of his text presents us with several uncertainties from the start.

A 'rough' version of the manuscript of the *Laws* may have come into the possession of Philippos of Opus, a member of the Academy, who probably edited and arranged it in some way. The extent of his involvement is a complex matter and fraught with historical uncertainty. Philippos, according to Morrow, 'is apparently the same as the philosopher referred to in the *Suidas* (s.v. φιλόσοφος) who divided the *Laws* into twelve books (adding the thirteenth, i.e. the *Epinomis,* said to be his own composition) and is probably identical with Philippus from Medma mentioned by

Stephanus of Byzantium [6th c.e.]'.[7] The sources from late antiquity, however, had a less than accurate picture of Plato's era.

The *Laws*' alleged editor is likely the same Φίλιππος ὁ Μενδαῖος whom Proclus (5th c.e.) described as a mathematician and student of Plato's.[8] The *Index Herculanensis* identifies him as both Plato's pupil and secretary (ἀναγραφεύς) toward the end of the Athenian philosopher's life.[9] None of the extant sources suggest that Plato had two students by the name of Philippos. Alexander of Aphrodisias referred to him as Φίλιππος ὁ ἑταῖρος Πλάτωνος.[10] Diogenes Laertius (3rd c.e.) is unfortunately our earliest source on the transmission of the text of the *Laws*. He wrote that Philippos of Opus 'revised' or 'copied the *Laws* whilst they were still in wax'.[11] This has sometimes been taken to mean that Philippos acquired Plato's wax-tablet manuscript after he died to have it copied and that he perhaps edited the text in its final form.

The author of the *Prolegomena*, probably embellishing on what he read in Proclus, wrote that Plato left the *Laws* not only uncorrected but also 'confused', saying that 'if the work now seems properly organised, that is not due to Plato, but to a certain Philippos of Opus, who later became the successor (διάδοχος) to Plato's school'.[12] In many respects, he appears to have got it wrong. His reports, as Taran says, 'about the unfinished state of the *Laws* is in all likelihood only an inference of his based on a conflation of Proclus' first argument against the Platonic authorship of the *Epinomis*'.[13] Philippos was never in fact placed in charge of the Academy. Speusippos, Xenokrates and then Polemon succeeded Plato in that order. As for the reputed degree of disarray, Aristotle never referred to the *Laws* except as if they were the *ipsissima verba* of Plato. The *Suidas* consequently, mentioning only the division into twelve books, does not directly state whether there was any rewriting involved.[14]

The extent to which Philippos edited the *Laws*, if at all, remains a subject open to speculation. There is nothing in Proclus about the alleged state of disorder in which Plato left his final work. The division of the text into chapters occurred after Philippos' lifetime and significantly later than the fourth century B.C.E.[15] The phrase 'in wax' appears to refer to wax-tablets. It could be taken metaphorically to mean that the *Laws* lacked editing. It is possible to suggest that Philippos was left in charge of 'tidying up' the drafts and then taking them to the copy house. According to Diogenes Laertius, 'some say that Philippos transcribed (μετέγραφεν) Plato's *Laws* which were ἐν κηρῷ'.[16] The term μετέγραφειν could mean 'to transcribe/copy' as well as 'to rewrite/correct'.[17] It appears unlikely that Diogenes meant the latter.[18] It may not be possible to know whether the text as it stands is Plato's work *in toto* or what parts of it may have been solely authored or at least modified by Philippos or later hands. However, 'in wax' probably should be taken to refer to Plato's drafts, composed on relatively inexpensive wax-covered tablets, on which the text would have been written and edited prior to being sent for copying onto expensive papyrus. Philippos' role appears to have been to copy Plato's final draft (perhaps replete with numerous corrections in his own, no doubt, 'characteristic' handwriting) into a more legible form for the copyists to transcribe. If he was in fact Plato's personal secretary and confidant, such a degree of involvement seems perfectly reasonable and altogether necessary.

The question of authenticity of authorship is not the principal concern of this book. I presume *a priori* that the *Laws* is Plato's and that it was his final work. As such, it reveals a new phase in terms of both his literary style and philosophical approach. It differs significantly when compared to the *Apology, Republic* or any of Plato's earlier works. The *Laws* falls into the category of the so-called 'late dialogues'. In these the style is plainer and, as Saunders says, 'analysis and exposition far outweigh dramatic interest'.[19] The sense of difference is heightened by the fact that the character of Sokrates is altogether absent from the *Laws*. He was a mainstay of Plato's dialogues who appeared, albeit in a diminished capacity, even in the *Sophist, Statesman* and *Timaeus* (although he is absent from the dubious *Epinomis*).[20] In his place as the principal speaker of the *Laws* we have the somewhat didactic persona of the Athenian Stranger (ΑΘΗΝΑΙΟΣ ΞΕΝΟΣ) who bears no little resemblance to Plato's Sokrates.[21] This elderly gentleman meets up with two other characters (Megillus the Spartan and Kleinias the Kretan—also identified as elderly) on the road from Knossos. They are on a pilgrimage to an unspecified 'chapel of Zeus' when the three of them fall to discussing good and bad laws.[22] The other two interlocutors request that the Athenian Stranger, who has displayed a superior understanding of wise legislation, outline the laws that would make a good constitution for a hypothetical colony.

This discourse, being on the very nature of law and government, had and still has considerably wider political ramifications. It was written in an era when 'colonies were springing up all over the place', as Robinson and Groves say, and 'discussion about what a "perfect" society would be like was quite a practical concern and not just an academic exercise'.[23] Another potential inspiration for such a discussion was in part hostility felt by the author against the Athenian democracy and its imperialistic ambitions. Perhaps, as Brisson says, the *Laws* was 'proposing a reactionary adaptation of the Athenian legislation of Plato's time'.[24] This enmity on his part may have been exacerbated by the judicial murder of Plato's famous mentor Sokrates at the hands of the Athenian law courts in 399. Toynbee, going farther than Brisson, has declared that the *Laws* reads 'almost like a deliberate rejoinder, point for point, to the eulogy of Athens in Perikles' Funeral Speech'.[25] This conclusion is exceedingly reductive and no longer taken seriously in modern academia; however, it approaches a basic truth. Plato's Sokrates scathingly criticises Perikles' scheme of paying jurors in the *Gorgias*. There he indicates, as Ostwald paraphrases, that the 'commons are like animals that Perikles corrupted instead of tamed'.[26] The *Laws* does in fact address many of the fundamental issues of the role of government and citizens. Whether it is specifically a 'reaction' to the faults of democratic Athens-*cum*-Perikles is another matter that will probably never be fully resolved.

Plato's criticisms of Athenian democracy are well known and can be seen in the *Republic* and elsewhere.[27] Since these are delivered in the medium of the dramatic dialogue (and not in outspoken comedic performances or public speeches), Ober describes Plato as fitting 'the role of the rejectionist external critic'.[28] This means that he was more detached in his criticism than, e.g., Aristophanes, who may be characterised as an internal 'immanent' critic of democracy. Amongst its other negative qualities, Plato perhaps felt, as Ostwald says, that the Athenian democracy represented 'a force imposing a tendency to conform to an establishment mentality dictated by the ignorant mob and stifling rather than nurturing the intelligence of the educated citizen'.[29] It is, as always, dangerous to speculate too much about an author's motivations. One should hesitate to attribute the inspiration of Plato's final work to any specific cause or event. He was always interested in the philosophical underpinnings of law and morality. His complaints against democracy make up a significant part of the *Laws*' context, as they must, but remain only one facet of the 'big picture'.

How does Magnesia compare with *Kallipolis?* The *Laws* represents no less than the theoretical founding of a new and experimental type of city-state. The plan is more than a little reminiscent of that outlined in the *Republic*—although the differences are profound. The interlocutors generally agree that any *polis* governed by laws (as opposed to righteous philosopher kings/queens under the guidance of transcendentally ineffable 'Goodness') can never be an ideal state. It will always be second-best (δεύτερος).[30] Where law governs, injustices invariably transpire. The ideal state should be ruled by just men and women who share their property communally (as in the *Kallipolis*) without recourse to mundane laws. The proper application and execution of the Athenian Stranger's plan of constitution is meant to engender an increasing desire to seek the realisation of the ideal. Through growing understanding, the laws of Magnesia may be improved along with the subjects they govern. Magnesia may become more like *Kallipolis* over time.

There is no reason to assume that the *Laws* might somehow serve as a constitution or legal code, added as an afterthought, for the *Kallipolis* of the *Republic*. Magnesia and *Kallipolis* are by no means the same place. Some of the differences between these two 'republics' are rather striking but it would be dangerous to jump to the hasty conclusion that the former was written as a sort of working constitution for the latter. Brisson believes that the *Laws* is an attempt to modify the unrealistic expectations of the *Republic* and, as such, it 'must be read as an original project for the organisation of the City, which takes into account the developments found in the *Timaeus, Critias* and *Philebus*'.[31] It is true that the *Laws* and the *Republic* both deal, at least in part, with the founding of new societies that could be considered rather, if not wholly, utopian.

The *Kallipolis* of the *Republic* represents the *ideal* and unrealistic form that a state might take whereas Magnesia signifies a condition that is more realistic yet somewhat less than the ideal. 'The state that Plato describes in the Laws is therefore not a Utopia', as Morrow says, 'it has a definite location in Greek space and time'.[32] The *Republic* (probably written in the 380's and/or 370's) is imaginary and represents a quest for the definition of Justice more than a practical guide to ideal government. The *Laws,* also describing an imaginary city, is not centrally concerned with finding a morally absolute definition—although it presumes the existence of just such a thing.

There are other significant points of connectivity between these two mythical *poleis. Kallipolis* is to be a society governed by philosopher-kings (and queens), with absolute authority.[33] They are trained to *know* the moral ideals for their society as well as being exposed to the Form of the Good that imparts to them such knowledge.[34] These are sometimes called the 'Perfect Guardians' and comprise a very small and elite class. The 'Auxiliary Guardians' are less thoroughly trained in philosophical matters and serve their masters and the state in the capacities of administration, maintaining civil obedience and order and undertaking the defence of the state in times of conflict.[35] These 'Auxiliary Guardians' possess only a partial comprehension of the reasons behind the rules they enforce and lack the greater apprehension of their metaphysical foundations—as opposed to such superior understanding found in the 'Perfect Guardians'.[36] The third class of *Kallipolitans* contains everybody else: farmers, artisans, merchants, clerks etc. They must willingly and wholeheartedly submit to the rule of their philosophical/metaphysical betters and, with few exceptions, are not generally educated in the ways of the 'Perfect' or 'Auxiliary Guardians'. The *Republic's* narrator expresses his doubts about the proposed enterprise saying that a city like the *Kallipolis* 'can be found nowhere on earth . . . perhaps there is a pattern for it laid up in heaven'.[37]

By contrast, the *Laws* does not seek to establish a perfect *polis* on earth but sets about the task of detailing a next-to-perfect code of laws by which an imperfect, human society may be governed. We should not, as Field says, 'draw any conclusions about a possible change in Plato's views . . . we are expressly told that the provisions of the *Republic* still represent the ideal, but are not regarded as practicable in these circumstances'.[38] The importance of written law is brought to the forefront and, while there is some discussion of rulers with superior moral knowledge, the *nukterinos* council does not function in precisely the same capacity as philosopher kings/queens. Law is supreme, albeit less than perfect, and serves as the instrument for the moral and social regulation of society. Sufficient commentary on its theory and execution is provided as guidance for the future. The Athenian Stranger says that we should 'order our private households and our public societies alike by obeying the immortal element within us, giving the name of law to the ordering of understanding'.[39] The laws of Magnesia, grounded in eternal truths, govern the entire life of the community and they embody and express the philosophical vision of the Good.

Magnesia will have a command economy. There are to be four property classes of citizens in addition to a fifth class—the slaves—who do all of the 'banausic' labour whilst their masters go about the pursuit of *aretē*.[40] These classes are based on income and the stewardship of property. There is the possibility of advancement and non-lateral mixing. Members of the highest of the four property classes are to be matched together for marriage with members of lower classes, and so on, in order that there be balance within the state.[41] This 'enlightened' policy of eugenics is something of a change from that found in the *Republic* where the different 'metals' of the three classes were expressly compelled to avoid intermingling. The 'best' could only breed with the 'best' etc., according to a calculated scheme, in temporary relationships designed to produce offspring.[42]

Balance is to be maintained in Magnesia through permanent marriages with an economic basis in land-division.[43] Each of the prescribed 5040 land units is divided into two parts and no citizen may have more land than any other. Any population surplus exceeding that which can be reasonably contained within the 5040 family units will be shipped off to a colony.[44] Here too is another difference in terms of Magnesia's semi-private landholdings based on the family unit as opposed to the communal property of the *Republic*.[45] One may refer to them as 'semi-private' since these lots can never be purchased or sold. Land division is one of many areas of life directly regulated by the Magnesian state.

The *Laws*, as Saunders says, 'gives a powerful impression of the range of activities under the control of *nomos* (custom, law, habitual practice etc.) in one sense or another'.[46] As in the *Republic*, there are to be Guardians of the Laws whose job it is to police the Magnesian state in every conceivable way and enforce the law in both public and private spheres. Men and women will have to regard them as figures of state authority as they have the power to fine and detain lawbreakers in accord with the city's statutes. There will also be female Marriage Guardians (αἱ τῶν γάμων κύριαι), Market Wardens (ἀγορανόμοι), City Wardens (ἀστυνόμοι), Rural Wardens (ἀγρονόμοι) and various other bureaucrats to regulate and oversee the numerous slaves, the city's educators, other non-citizens and orphans.[47]

Perhaps Plato had a model for his Guardians (both in the *Republic* and the *Laws*) in the form of an Athenian institution that reputedly existed before Perikles. In the council of the Areopagos, as it was prior to Ephialtes (early 5th century B.C.E.), there may have been comparable guardians. Aristotle says that Solon 'assigned the council of the Areopagos to the duty of guarding the laws (ἐπὶ τὸ νομοφυλακεῖν), acting as before as the supervisor (ἐπίσκοπος) of the constitution'. He goes on to indicate that Ephialtes reduced its authority over guarding the constitution and as-signed some of them to the council of the five hundred and others to the *demos* and the popular courts.[48] It is possible that this alleged institution of the pre-Periklean Areopagos was the inspiration, or at least *an* inspiration, for the Athenian Stranger's Guardians of the Laws.[49] Cicero, heavily influenced by Plato, commends 'the Greeks' for establishing officers called νομοφύλακες, who guarded the text of the laws, ob-serving the actions of citizens and calling them to obedience.[50] It is not possible to say whether such guardians actually existed in ancient Athens and, if so, that they were an inspiration for Plato.[51] His *nomophylakes* appear to have more in common with the Spartan *ephors*.[52] As Morrow says, they add a *Lakonian* 'monarchical element in the city'.[53] Their superiors in Magnesia also recollect other Spartan elements rather than Athenian.[54]

Above all the various guardians, and drawn from the eldest of the Guardians of the Laws, is the *nukterinos* council or so-called 'Nocturnal Council'.[55] Its geron-tocratic character is one of many points of similarity to the Spartan *gerousia*, the members of which were also required to be over the age of sixty[56] The Athenian Stranger says that his *nukterinos* council will function in a 'watchdog' capacity, ideally just making recommendations, and will serve to keep the ship of state 'on course'.[57] Its powers, as with the *gerousia*, are considerably broader than this innocent-sounding statement suggests. Its membership includes the eldest Guardians of the Laws and the ministers of education past and present. These influence such areas as education, music, choruses and all civic events that involve the inculcation of morality and ac-cepted ideology. The *nukterinos* council also has also been afforded the unique author-ity, only on rare and special occasions, to alter Magnesia's laws.

Brisson proposes the term 'Vigilance Committee' instead of the more tradi-tional rendering of 'Nocturnal Council'. As he indicates, this body 'sees to it that the laws of the City are based on the order manifest in the universe, [and] becomes the most essential element in the project of the *Laws*'.[58] The term *nukterinos* 'connotes the idea of wakefulness' and, indeed, the 'Vigilance Committee' is meant to meet each day from before dawn until the sun has risen.[59] Morrow suggests that the inspiration for this 'Vigilance Committee' must be the Academy itself since, as he says, 'its stud-ies bear an unmistakable resemblance to those cultivated in Plato's Academy, and the purpose they are intended to serve is identical . . . viz. to apply philosophy to the sav-ing of the city-state'.[60] Like the Academy, the members of the 'Vigilance Committee' will have been inducted into the innermost mysteries of philosophy. Also, not unlike certain of the Academy's membership, they too hold real legislative and administra-tive powers over the state.[61]

Where is Sokrates? There is an observable shift in Plato's literary style from the myth-ical and dramatic qualities found in the early and middle dialogues to the more didactic and expositional character of the later dialogues and, in particular, the *Laws*. The total absence of Sokrates, who has been a constant throughout all of the other extant dialogues of Plato, stands out. As mentioned earlier, he plays a diminished role in the *Sophist, Statesman* and *Timaeus;* however, he is present and active. The Athenian Stranger in the *Laws* performs the part usually delegated to Plato's Sokrates and does this with a style of character altogether familiar and reminiscent of the fictional luminary. There is relatively little discussion, however, amongst the interlocutors and the Athenian Stranger spends most of his time delivering a lecture on his second-best state.

Since Plato died before editing significant portions of the *Laws*, it is impossible to know for certain whether he had meant to change the name of his principal character. Perhaps he intended for the finished piece to have Sokrates as its narrator and he never got around to changing the name of the Athenian Stranger in the drafts. This seems improbable. It is more likely that he intended the work to be published with his primary speaker named 'the Athenian Stranger' and that he presumed his audience would immediately recognise Sokratic elements in him anyway. Sokrates would certainly have been a stranger to Krete. Why resort to such a conceit? Might there have been political reasons? Perhaps the Athenian Stranger should not be identified with the historical Sokrates at all. The choice of 'Athenian Stranger' might constitute a bit of literary license on Plato's part. Such a choice may reflect political factors in the post-399 Athenian world. We may never comprehend his motives for doing this—however interesting they may be to ponder. It is erroneous to presume, as some have done, that the absence of a designated Sokrates somehow indicates that the *Laws* is fraudulent.

What could have prompted Plato, late in his career, to lay aside his earlier style in preference for a more straightforward manner of address? It does represent a ready medium in which to get across ideas whilst limiting dissenting influences. Perhaps there was a more 'human' reason. Given the approximate dates for the *Laws*, it is certainly true that Plato was getting on in years. He would have been in his late seventies or early eighties when the majority of the text was written. He must have known that his death was not far away. Could it have been the case, as Taylor suggests, that Plato did not 'want to look farther and farther into "the beyond," but to come down to earth and realise some of the truth he has seen'?[62] This has some merit but one cannot know with certainty.

It is the case that the vast majority of the text deals with many subjects that could be considered mundane. The *Laws* is mostly legal code and legal theory. Even so, in a significant portion of book X (885–907) the Athenian Stranger posits some inspired metaphysics on the nature and immortality of the soul, general cosmology and the gods. Likewise, in book I (644d sq.), he delivers what is perhaps the only moral fable in the whole of the *Laws*, on the somewhat depressing subject of how mortal beings are mere 'puppets of the gods'. Potentially these two sections bolster Taylor's claim that Plato's change in style reflects his desire to leave behind some of the truths that he has gained in the clearest possible terms for future generations. However, it seems that he is still looking into the 'beyond' when one considers the philosophical backdrop of Magnesia.

The change in style prompts other questions. For example, what does it mean to say that Plato's literary manner was more or less *mythic* at any given time? The subject and treatment of myth in the works of Plato is complex. One might ask, in a manner rather like that of Sokrates, what is meant by the term 'myth' and how, therefore, should one discuss it? Graves gives a list of that which he considers to be not 'true myths', amongst which are 'philosophical allegory', 'political propaganda', 'moral legend' and 'realistic fiction'.[63] This is a conservative reckoning and would appear, on the one hand, to exclude any would-be 'myths' about whose literary inception, as works of fiction, something is known. On the other hand, it accepts and includes a number of myths whose origins are historically obscure.[64] A more recent re-evaluation is more inclusive in scope. Burkert's definition of myth considers it to be a 'traditional tale' with a secondary, partial reference to something of 'collective importance'.[65] This theory appears to excludes Platonic mythmaking. However, one is inclined to wonder precisely when a fable or tale becomes traditional. Establishing what is meant by 'collective importance' also seems an equivocal task.

It is possible to posit a broader interpretation of 'myth' as a concept to include sufficiently 'mythological' material of various sorts. Such instances of Platonic mythologizing occur at points where he has chosen to adapt certain traditionally cultural tales, modifying them appropriately according to his philosophical agenda. There are also some 'myths' that Plato appears to have originated (whether unique creations or peculiar adaptations) specifically for his own ends. These that he originated or modified may not have been traditional when he wrote them down. The fact that many Platonic myths (such as that of Atlantis) have since become traditional after Plato's lifetime further problematises the issue of defining what we mean by a 'traditional tale'.

Plato too has played a role in the definition of myth. He has drawn the distinction between a story that may or may not contain relevant philosophical or 'truth' value and ones with an essential quality that determines their philosophical worth.[66] 'Plato', as Buxton indicates, 'takes important steps towards systematising two distinctions between *muthos* and *logos*: that between *muthos* as unverifiable discourse and *logos* as verifiable discourse, and that between *muthos* as story and *logos* as rational argument'.[67] However, Plato's method for classifying myths according to their value does not appear to be consistent. For example, the types of tales that are to be banned from the *Kallipolis* are referred to as *logoi*. But these also include the sort of *muthoi* that are told to children under the broader designation as *logoi*.[68] Given the nature of the dialogue form (discussed below), Plato is under no obligation to be systematic across diverse dialogues.

The *technē* of mythologizing, for Plato the writer and philosopher, amounts to a sort of tool with which he may shape an argument and deploy it for specific reasons. In the *Laws,* as we shall see in later chapters, this technique is deployed specifically to affect Magnesian sexuality. Many myths that belong to the traditional canon of the ancient Greeks find their way into the Platonic *corpus* and, as such, serve a variety of philosophical ends. These often come from the works of Homer or Hesiod and Plato's narrators frequently have some critical comment to make about them or through them.[69] Such poets, however divinely inspired, are deemed to lack the appropriate understanding to deploy their myths correctly. 'The philosopher', as Murray says, 'is aware of the approximate status of his myths, whereas the poet is not'.[70] Plato's Sokrates criticises the use of myths that miss the mark in terms of truth-value—e.g. that portray the gods and divine heroes as ugly or immoral.[71] The perceived danger of such myths is that they present potentially harmful models for ordinary people who lack the proper philosophical training to make the necessary distinctions. The imitation of these must be curbed. 'In short', as Morgan states, 'only myths conducive to virtue will be allowed, as when Odysseus commands his heart to endure in difficult circumstances'.[72]

There are myths that Plato appears to have originated himself for the express purpose of forwarding his philosophical agenda. Some of these include, for example, the Fable of the Cave, the Line, the Metals, the ancestor of Gyges of Lydia (the tale of the ring of invisibility), the metaphysical Myth of Er in the *Republic,* the Two Horses of the *Phaedrus,* the Myth of the Uranian Age and the Puppets of the Gods in the *Laws.* Some of these (e.g. the Myth of the Metals) may be considered 'noble lies' or exhortatory fables designed to persuade. It is clear in all of these instances of tale telling, as Hesk says, that 'certain situations make lying a moral necessity' for Plato's narrators.[73] They are designed not only to persuade, but also to affect correction.

A broader type of Platonic myth making may also be seen in undertaking such a work as the *Republic* itself or, for that matter, the *Laws.* The whole business of creating (albeit theoretically) an artificial, utopian society is itself a sort of mythologizing on a grand scale. The creation of the *Republic* was so vast and complex a project that it marks one of the major stylistic changes in Plato's writing.[74] It might be fair to regard the character of the *Republic* and *Laws* as on a par with that of Homer's *Iliad* or *Odyssey.* They are all epic-length fictions that, in describing mythical events and persons, entail a comparable level of sophistication. Whereas Homer's myths belong to ages past, Plato's transpire in a speculative future. Both are vehicles of moral and metaphysical guidance.

It would appear, as Murray says, that 'Plato's concern is not so much to free the mind from myth, but rather to appropriate myth from the hands of the poets and construct new myths that will serve the interests of philosophy'.[75] The emphasis lies with *logos*-value (truth-value in terms of philosophical worth and instructive potential) as opposed to *muthos*-value (one could say story- or entertainment-value or persuasive value devoid of acceptable instructive potential). While these Platonic myths might not be completely truthful, they need not be. The ends are deemed to justify the means. Platonic myths are ostensibly intended to fulfil their function of imparting a higher, philosophical truth to those who experience them.[76] When employed on a hypothetical populace (whether Magnesia of *Kallipolis*), they entail specific agendas and have been calculated to achieve these with effective persuasion.

Platonic myths fall into several recognisable categories.[77] As Morgan says, 'we can distinguish three classes: traditional myths such as those told by the poets, educational myths that are intended to exercise social control, and philosophical myths, which are tied to logical analysis'.[78] Even these distinctions may be too rigid. How, for example, should we label an instance of myth told by the poets but altered or amended by Plato's narrator? Are not all Platonic myths somehow 'tied to logical analysis' anyway? All of his uses of myth appear to serve a distinct philosophical purpose—however much they may traverse the boundaries of various imposed categories.

The Myth of the Metals in the *Republic* provides a good example. It is a lie that serves the purpose of exercising social control. Myths of this type, as Hesk says, 'are not to be criticised if the "untruth" of the story conveys a deeper moral truth'.[79] Beneath the Myth of the Metals there is a meaningful philosophical argument, based on logical analysis, on the manner in which humanity ought to be governed according to a specific philosophical agenda. The myth may be little more than a clever encouragement designed to persuade people to follow the rules on the merits of a fable, yet it has 'truth-value' inasmuch as the ends that are anticipated are identified as virtuous and therefore justify the somewhat duplicitous means of their accomplishment.

'Fables' of one particular sort have a prominent place in the *Laws* as in the second-best *polis*. They will be employed propagandistically as a means of social control to effect persuasion. The use of these fables, akin to the so-called 'noble lies' of the *Republic,* corresponds both to known (or at least reputed) Athenian and Spartan practices.[80] It becomes the chief business of the Magnesian government to mould the characters of its subjects and the *Laws'* interlocutors deem the employment of 'fables' to this end justifiable. It is nowhere suggested that Plato has overturned the basic tenet, elsewhere espoused and extolled, that only the one who knows what Justice is can be just. The Athenian Stranger's policies, however totalitarian they may seem to a modern audience, are said repeatedly throughout the *Laws* to aim for the hypothetical Magnesians' maximum attainment of *aretē*. Behind the moral fables, which are informative, is the threat of violence for those who disobey the law. As Bobonich says

'Law still has a penalty or sanction attached to it and Plato is willing to use force and the threat of force on those who are not rationally persuaded to obey'.[81] Subtler methods are preferable for the second-best city, however, and mild, effective persuasion is preferable to coercion. The Athenian Stranger, as Brisson indicates, 'insists on relying on persuasion rather than repression because to use the latter is to admit defeat, which is implied by a lack of respect for the law'.[82]

Plato's narrator uses the term *paramyth* to describe the preambles to the various laws that will be read aloud to the Magnesians. *Paramyth* (παραμυθία) may be loosely defined as 'encouragement' or 'persuasion', and its use here combines philosophical, rhetorical and mythical qualities.[83] The legal preambles possess a kind of 'mythological resonance' and thus fall into the broader category of Platonic mythologizing.[84] They are reminiscent of the philosophical exhortations in the *Republic*. The Athenian Stranger indicates that the lawgiver should not threaten the populace with rules or merely prescribe his philosophically sound decrees, but that he should give encouragement (παραμυθία) and appropriate degrees of persuasion.[85] The legislator will deliver a convincing fiction that is grounded in a (Platonic) truth. It differs from a work of pure fiction inasmuch as the discourse of the Magnesian legislator, unlike that of a poet, must be non-contradictory and based upon reason's rule.[86]

Paramyth is seen to have a positive effect inasmuch as it is undertaken for the good of the subjects in question and society as a whole. Many of these subjects (non-citizens in particular) will be unable to engage in the more complex philosophical discussions that underpin the laws and they will be the ones primarily affected by the oral recitation of the preambles. The citizens of Magnesia will study the text of the laws in school, along with their preambles, and will be expected to have gained some comprehension of the 'inner mysteries' of philosophy and civic ideology by adulthood.[87] I will presently return to the subject of *paramyth* as a special type of rhetoric.

A related use of myth in Plato's works concerns the theme of philosophical 'play'. 'Play', according to Morgan, 'can be a childish game, an educational tool, or a metaphor for philosophical activity'.[88] The educational programmes of the *Republic* and the *Laws* depend on types of structured play (παιδιά) in order to ensure psychic harmony and intellectual development along specific lines. The games that Plato's narrators propose that children should play are designed to promote the attainment of an idealised state of the *psychē*. This is one level of 'play' as mythologizing inasmuch as it becomes a vehicle, like myth, for delivering a philosophical message.

At another level, not unlike 'noble lies' or *paramyth*, 'play' becomes a sort of secondary metaphor concealing complex theoretical underpinnings. Role-playing can be an effective method of philosophical argumentation.[89] This sort of 'play' may embody critical seriousness and sort out an issue by utilising role-playing as a type of logical analysis. As Morgan says, 'in this respect it is analogous to philosophical myth'.[90] A prominent example occurs in the complicated discussion on whether or not same-sex relations should be permitted in Magnesia.[91] The discussion appears to be largely hypothetical and it is worked out through logical analysis. It is a sort of monolithic role-playing game. It is not perhaps role-playing in the modern sense of Dungeons & Dragons, or corporate strategising; rather, the participants engage in a philosophical game of 'what ifs?' led by Plato's narrator in which an important issue is explored. The theme of 'play' as a kind of philosophical exercise, especially in contrast to the 'seriousness' that such 'play' might imply, may be seen throughout the Platonic *corpus*.[92] In fact, 'play' as a means of approaching a problem or administering philosophical *pharmaka* has much in common with other instances of mythologizing in Plato.[93] Not unlike the creative works of the *Republic* or the *Laws,* in Platonic 'play' at large an imaginary 'something' is called into existence and then used to advance a philosophical agenda.

More needs to be said about the dialogue form. Plato's method of presenting his philosophical discourses in dramatic dialogues connects significantly with his use of myth. He, as Dover indicates, 'sets out these "Socratic dialogues" in purely dramatic form, sometimes in near-dramatic form enclosed within the narrative framework'.[94] Plato borrows from a number of literary and dramatic traditions in formulating his genre of philosophical writing.[95] As with many of the myths that he employs, he did not originate the dramatic dialogue. Precedent for it may be found in Homeric dialogues, the Melian dialogue of Thucydides, the *Dissoi Logoi* of the sophists and Athenian stage drama. There is every reason to believe that these were all important influences.

Thucydides' dialogue expresses what Immerwahr calls 'philosophical truths' along with historical theories.[96] The *Dissoi Logoi* does so even more self-consciously.[97] Both package their messages in the accessible medium of the dialogue form. The feature of accessibility is an important part of it. Drama has a wider appeal than dry dialectic. It also has certain advantages in terms of a more formal approach to philosophy. The dramatic dialogue allows Plato's narrators to deal with a problem from many angles. They are able, as Guthrie indicates, 'to set out opposing theories, to show that neither is wholly right and to conclude only that the matter needs more thought'.[98] This represents a major stepping-stone to more sophisticated levels of philosophical analysis.

The Platonic dialogues demand certain imaginary concessions on the part of the reader (or auditor) to the effect that a fictional event, related to drama, epic and myth, is transpiring. It is within this imposed context of such a fictional event (the dialogue) that Plato's narrators and characters undertake to philosophise. The Platonic tradition of employing myths and parables to provide reasoning by analogy may be therefore extended to the mythic framework of the dialogue itself. It is a kind of fictional episode out of which one is invited to derive some philosophical experience.

One may interact with a Platonic dialogue through one's own independent thoughts as well as by imitation (*mimēsis*) of the methods and virtues presented. It is left to the audience to take away what they will, although their choices are often encouraged along specific lines.

Some causal factor for Plato's choice of literary style may be derived out of Sokrates' preference for dialogic discourse in his pursuit of wisdom. Sokrates had employed oral discussion as his characteristic mode of philosophical activity. As a Platonic character, he has variously expressed the limitations of the written word inasmuch as it cannot answer questions or engage in interactive discussions with a living audience. This sort of interaction was his philosophical *modus operandi*.[99] Unlike Sokrates, Plato devised a more formal means of getting across his messages. His approach is striking. Even the earlier dialogues, which are largely 'conversations with Sokrates', indicate Plato's 'involvement with philosophy in a more technical sense'.[100] Other philosophers such as Solon, Pythagoras and Empedokles of Akragas had utilised the artistic medium of poetry in order to convey their ideas.[101] Plato's dramatic dialogue form would appear to represent a quantum leap beyond the methods of these others in terms of effectively transmitting a philosophical agenda or message across even vast gulfs of space and time.

Plato's narrative style in composing his dialogues, as indicated by stylometrical research of the last century, appears to have altered twice in terms of a markedly observable shift. The first significant one is concurrent with the *Republic*. This came, in part, from the literary requirements imposed by the scope of the project and its scale compared to previous dialogues. We can note a similar situation in the *Laws*. The other change occurred sometime between the *Theaetetus* and the *Sophist* when, as Kahn indicates, Plato 'began systematically to avoid hiatus and hence adopt more unnatural word order and sentence structure'.[102] These too may be especially observed in his final work.

There are at least three different types of dramatic dialogue (other than the temporal 'early', 'middle', and 'late' distinctions) in Plato's *corpus*.[103] They are *aporetic* (e.g. *Euthyphro, Laches, Charmides, Lysis*) when they present insoluble problems for consideration and conclude in perplexity. The *protreptic* ones explore inconclusive arguments whilst exhorting the interlocutors (and so the audience/reader) to continue in their philosophical inquiries (e.g. the *Meno* and the *Ion*). Dialectic, from the Greek meaning 'conversation', (such as in the *Republic* and the *Laws*) is the third and most developed type. It is possible that the dramatic style of presentation in the *Laws* deserves to be designated as 'division' rather than dialectic.[104] This is due to the fact that there is virtually no dissent or criticism expressed by the Athenian Stranger's interlocutors. Rather, Plato's narrator 'divides up' all of the various subjects that he wishes to discuss and presents them as a monologue of ideas. Technically, the philosophical style of the *Laws* qualifies as a revised version of dialectic.

Sokratic dialogues typically contain *elenchos*—that is, a procedure of interrogation that leads to refutation.[105] Not all of Plato's dialectical discourses seek to refute an argument without positing something new in its place. Dialectic is the most well known Platonic method by which, through argument and mutual criticism, philosophical truth is to be ascertained.[106] All of these styles (*aporetic, protreptic,* and dialectic with or without *elenchos* and division) depend on the dramatic dialogue form and could not function in the same way without it. This is due to the rhetorical and conversational elements intrinsic in Plato's chosen medium.

In his various dialogues, the dramatised *persona* of Plato as a character is either completely absent or plays no active role.[107] Yet, in another sense, Plato is wholly present. He is the 'puppet master' or 'stage director' who sets the scene for the dialogues and it is he alone who chooses the words of the players. This innovative adaptation of the dramatic dialogue, the sole means of revealing Plato's philosophical thoughts apart from his letters, places him in a mixed category. Is he the first serious academic philosopher? Is he not also a literary theorist who has pioneered a new, hybrid genre? Plato's use of the dramatic dialogue as a medium in which to convey philosophical ideas began a trend that was to have profound implications on the history of Western philosophy.[108]

As mentioned above, the dialogue form has the advantage of involving and engaging the reader/auditor in a very direct way precisely because of its dramatic qualities. The vividness of the scenes (i.e. two or more persons in a setting having a discussion) draws the observer into the dialogue in much the same way that one is vicariously drawn into a play being performed or (today) a film being watched. 'Philosophy presented this way', as Rutherford says, 'is more accessible, more enticing, than formally presented system-building or *ex cathedra* exposition'.[109] Plato's method contrasts sharply with the 'oracular' style of Herakleitos, the divinely inspired utterances of Empedokles or the mind-teasers of Zeno of Elea—while incorporating certain elements from all of them. There are still 'oracular pronouncements' of a sort in Plato. These come as philosophical 'truth' and the higher virtues imparted by metaphysical entities such as the Forms. There are a number of poetic influences in Plato as well as a fair share of mind-teasers.[110]

The dramatic dialogue form reveals other literary borrowings that contribute to its total effect. Plato has incorporated other works and genres into his dialogues in numerous ways. Examples include the transplantation of texts in whole or in part (as in the funeral speech in the *Menexenus* which echoes other examples of this genre and the many quotes from Homer and other poets throughout the Platonic *corpus*) along with incorporation by allusion (as in the many allusions to Euripides' *Antiope* in the *Gorgias*). Also, as Nightingale says, 'Plato can target a genre by incorporating the discourse, *topoi,* or themes that are peculiar to it and readily identified as such: when Callias' slave slams the door in Socrates' face at the opening of the *Protagoras,* for example, we are confronted by a *topos* from the genre of comedy'.[111] Numerous poets are quoted in the dialogues as authorities on ethical matters.[112] When cited, Plato's characters metapoetically recite the piece in question as part of their dialogue.

This technique of incorporating literary borrowings appears to play an important and functional role in Plato's philosophising. It may be the case, as Nightingale writes, that the audience or reader 'is meant to hear both a version of the original utterance as the embodiment of the speaker's point of view (or 'semantic position') *and* the second speaker's evaluation of that utterance from a different point of view'.[113] A probable goal of such 'novelistic hybridisation', as Nightingale and others call Plato's intertextual borrowings, is the illumination of one discourse by means of another. As usual, his incorporation of works of poetry, speeches and comedic techniques are employed in order to advance his philosophical agenda.

This brings us back to the theme of *paramyth* and legal preamble. In the *Laws*, the dramatic dialogue form adapts certain techniques from the field of rhetoric.[114] This appears in the preambles to Magnesia's code of laws that are to be read before the assembled public as a means of information and persuasion.[115] The Athenian Stranger indicates that he got the idea for these legal preambles from the musical and rhetorical practice of delivering a proem before the main musical piece or oratorical speech.[116] He says that, as with both music and rhetoric, the preamble serves as 'a kind of artistic preparation useful for the further development of the subject'.[117]

Why should the subject require 'preparation' in order to be more receptive to the dictates of the laws? Written law, as the Athenian stranger says, is a 'tyrannical prescription' (τυρραvικὸv ἐπίταγμα—722e); it 'orders and threatens like a tyrant or despot who writes his decrees on the wall and is done with it' (859a4–6). The lawgiver can 'soften' the impact of these with recourse to persuasive preambles—the language of which is more exhortatory than prescriptive.[118] 'The basic structural differences between the *polis* in Magnesia and the *polis* of the *Republic*', as Yunis indicates, 'reveal the reason for the turn to rhetoric in the *Laws*'.[119] The citizens of Magnesia are not to be philosopher kings/queens with the full power of state.[120] Magnesia is to be a limited democracy. The majority of people will be directed and exhorted to follow the laws without question. The rhetorical qualities of the legal preambles are designed to aid the Magnesian government in keeping the majority of its populace in line.

Each preamble represents a piece of calculated rhetoric. Failure to take the 'advice' offered in the preamble and thence breaking the law will incur severe penalties of a punitive as well as psychological nature. A Magnesian lawgiver will address himself/herself to the hypothetical populace, reciting the preambles and stating the laws and injunctions and these will be publicly inscribed for all to see.[121] As we have seen, the legal preambles are not merely there to persuade. They are also there to instruct and function as one of many forces in the mass education and inculcation of the citizens.[122] The fact that the *Laws* itself is required reading for the hypothetical

Magnesians underscores the persuasive effects of the written text, in concert with living speech, as a kind of 'drug' (*pharmakon*) acting on their *psychai*[123]

Plato's narrator describes the legal preambles with an analogy to a doctor of slaves—who prescribes his treatments without explanation—and the doctor of a free man who provides an adequate (albeit incomplete) explanation of why the medicine or treatment is good for the patient.[124] This analogy breaks down somewhat, e.g. the lawgiver does not engage in one to one dialogue with the citizens, but addresses them *en masse*. As Nightingale says, 'the good lawgiver creates his preludes and his legal prescriptions long before he comes across any "patients."'[125] Through his deeper comprehension of the science of medicine, the 'free doctor' is at once instructing and persuading the patient. The Magnesian lawgiver, with his/her deeper understanding of the science of politics, delivers the preambles as persuasive pieces of instructive advice to a populace that, on the whole, lacks the lawgiver's specialised *technē*.

The preambles are clearly meant to render the audience favourably disposed toward the speaker and to instruct, in albeit a superficial way thus facilitating general comprehension, about the virtue of the particular law being introduced. The lawgiver who will read the preamble is being cast in the role of a teacher. They are compared with 'a loving and intelligent father or mother'.[126] The lawgiver may be seen as a parental figure (a sort of 'good shepherd') that, through the benefits of greater wisdom, seeks to help others. The 'evangelical' connotations of this have not been overlooked. Yunis considers Plato's legal preambles to have stepped into a fourth state of rhetoric outside the traditional modes of the deliberative, the judicial and the epideictic. He suggests that it might possibly represent the first systematised example of 'preaching' as a rhetorical form.[127] They do, in fact, exhort the Magnesian subjects to obey the laws through the backing of religious authority.[128] Not unlike the later Christian art of preaching, Plato's employment of calculated, instructive discourse is designed to communicate divine matters. The need for mass-appeal directs their verbal 'packaging'. This, along with Plato's adaptation of the dialogue form, constitutes another interesting innovation.[129]

Let us consider ancient ideas about law and custom. The concept of a legal preamble is conceptually related to the later notion of preaching. But they are not the same thing. Something similar may be said of Plato's understanding of the concept of law as opposed to our current paradigm. The title of Plato's text, the *Laws* (NOMOI), itself presents a problem of translation for readers in the modern age. The word *nomos* held multiple connotations and a fluid range of meanings for the ancient Greeks.[130] It appears to have originally had something to do with 'assigned pastures' and 'appropriate dwelling places' but later came to mean something more like 'common usage' or 'custom' as well as 'law' and 'ordinance'.[131] *Nomos* may also be used to denote a 'tune' or 'melody' and this twist of meaning becomes a favourite source of puns in Plato's *Nomoi*.[132]

Themis is an older legal term that expresses a law, as Jones indicates, having been 'given by someone, prince or priest, specially endowed with insight to express the divine will'.[133] It was Zeus' discretion that Agamemnon had been granted the authority to issue his *themistes* to his subjects. These were more like strong advice than actual decrees.[134] Similarly, Zeus gave authority to Minos, in his capacity as judge of those who enter the underworld, in the issuing of *themistes* in answer to the appeals of the dead.[135] Here we find a connection with the *Laws*. The Athenian Stranger also considers his *nomoi* to have been 'divinely' inspired. Apprehension of 'true' *nomos* is akin to philosophical illumination.[136] Such connotations as are invoked by *themis*, this approach has a persuasive quality not unlike the 'noble lie' or legal preamble but it also reflects the deeper, mystical connection between law and divine (Platonic) Reason.

Other terms also contribute to this discussion. *Thesmos* eventually came to be accepted for *a* law as opposed to *the* law amongst the ancient Athenians.[137] A clear distinction seems to be lacking. We have in the same sentence of a speech of Andokides reference to the *thesmoi* of Drako and the *nomoi* of Solon.[138] This is perhaps because the laws of Drako each began with the word *thesmos*. Echoing Ostwald's definition, MacDowell suggests that *nomos* may be distinguished as 'a term for a norm of action recognised by a society, what is agreed to be the right thing to do', as opposed to *thesmos* which is a judgement or decree.[139] However, this distinction is arguable and, as Jones says, 'there was probably no period when the two words [*nomos* and *thesmos*] were not roughly interchangeable'.[140]

'In the latter part of the fifth century', as Dover indicates, 'the realisation that a law, custom or usage must have had an origin at a point in time aroused great interest among intellectuals and expressed itself in argument about *physis* ('nature') and *nomos* ('usage', 'custom', 'practice', 'convention', 'law')'.[141] For example, Demokritos considered it a natural phenomenon that all creatures should beget offspring and rear them but that it was a matter of *nomos* that human parents should expect some returns on their effort from their offspring.[142] Demosthenes indicates that Nature herself will move citizens in the manner that is best but the good citizen should lead the city by argument and explanation.[143] *Nomos* was often contrasted, especially in 5th century Greek discourse, with *physis*; 'the latter represents underlying reality, and the former denotes the patterns by which men try to shape this'.[144] Then as now, there was a perceived connection between *nomos* and *physis*

Efforts were made to clarify the specific functions of *nomos*. In his speech, *On the Mysteries*, Andokides wrote that 'henceforth the *archōns* shall not make use of unwritten law (ἀγράφῳ δὲ νόμῳ); but the decree (ψήφισμα) of the Assembly is to have greater authority than either the rule of the executive council or that of the demesmen'.[145] This reform set the seal on the revised law code adopted by the restored Athenian democracy in 403/2 B.C.E. and, as Ostwald says, 'marks the conclusion of a curious development in Athenian political terminology'.[146] From this time the principal meaning of *nomos,* in both legal and non-legal spheres becomes something like 'statute' or 'law'. It signified an enactment (normally a written or inscribed one) that had either been included in the law code at the time of its ratification or had been added to it through the elaborate legislative process known as νομοθεσία.[147]

In the earlier part of the 5th century, the terms *nomos* and *psephisma* were often used interchangeably. Either word could be employed by ancient Athenian writers (along with the more archaic *thesmos*) in order to denote various shades of the concept of 'law'. Attempts were made at the end of the 5th century to clarify the semantic fields of *nomos* and *psephisma* as well as to codify the laws and iron out their inconsistencies.[148] Thereafter, as MacDowell indicates, it 'was normally assumed that a law (*nomos*) was something more fundamental and more permanent than a decree (*psephisma*)'.[149] As Humphreys says, '*nomos* had to be something which did not easily change . . . the laws of Solon could be called *nomoi* because they had been established for a long time'.[150] A law made a rule concerning some specific activity whereas a decree specified action to be taken in a particular instance. The term *nomos* continued to carry its other non-legal attributes both inside and outside the courts of law.[151]

The notion that *nomos* can mean both something like 'law' and something like 'custom' to the ancient Greeks begets a daunting challenge. How does one approach Plato's use of this term throughout his final *opus* where this problematic term appears as the title itself? In the works of Plato there are variegated uses of this expression with similar but distinct shades of significance. Some examples include a) a conventional linguistic usage (*Krat.* 384d7, 388d12, *Tim.* 60e2), b) a customary practice (*Symp.* 182a7, *Laws* 795a1), c.) a conventional belief (*Gorg.* 482e6, *Laws* 889e6, 890d4, 6, 904a9), d) a norm of individual conduct (*Rep.* 587c2, 604a10, b6, 9, 607a7, *Polit.* 291e2, *Laws* 674b7, 835e5, 836e4), e) a religious practice (*Phaedo* 58b5, *Phaedr.* 256d7) and f) a condition of law and order (*Rep.* 587a10, *Laws* 780d5, 904c9). There is, in Plato and elsewhere, the distinct sense that 'law' is implicitly connected with 'custom'. There was also, in Plato's era, the connotation that their 'constitution' was derived out of some ancestral practice that provided the law with a legitimate foundation—having been derived from established customs.

Nomos in the *Laws* must be something more profound than 'custom' alone. Laws that had been largely unwritten in actual practice will be incorporated into the Magnesian constitution. 'This paradoxical idea is made explicit at 793a–d', as Nightingale says, 'where the Athenian [Stranger] indicates that "unwritten laws" (ἄγραφα νόμιμα) are "ancestral customs" that hold the lawcode together from the very beginning and form the very foundation for the constitution; though they "will make the lawcode longer" (μακροτέρους ποιῇ τοὺς νόμους, 793d5), he adds, the unwritten laws must not be left out'.[152] This represents a more formalised legal system and an advanced step in political science. The inclusion of 'unwritten laws', along with preludes for all the laws (all publicly inscribed similar to the custom at Gortyn), reveal a significant shift from Athenian practice.[153]

The rapid changes in government at Athens in the later part of the 5th century brought this issue of the 'ancestral constitution', or 'ancestral law' (πάτριος νομός), to the forefront for many.[154] There was an intellectual opposition to the restored democracy in Athens at the end of the 5th century. Amongst this group, as Finley says, 'the appeal to the ancestral constitution retained vitality'.[155] It was generally agreed that Solon founded the Athenian *politeia*. It is therefore not surprising that Plutarch wrote his biography whereas Kleisthenes only gets notable mention. Isokrates and his followers, ostensibly eschewing oligarchy, favoured a 'mixed constitution' that hearkened back to some non-specific, idealised past.[156]

Plato took a different approach to the issue. He was about eighteen when Kleitophon moved the amendment that opened the debate on the subject of the 'ancestral constitution'.[157] As a member of one of Athens' more prominent political families, Plato had close personal connections with some of the chief players and a keen eye for the relevant events. When the time came, he set aside the 'historical' discussion, without altogether dismissing it, while introducing a new method based on reason. His philosophy of government never rested solely on 'ancestral' arguments.[158] Certainly Plato reveals conservative tendencies and his views may have also been informed by recourse to an idealised vision of the past. In the *Statesman* we have a possible answer to the debate. Perhaps building on the works of Gorgias and the sophists,[159] Plato's narrator espouses a novel concept: having established that there is a science (*epistēmē*) of politics, he posits that the proof of a correct constitution is that it be based upon science and that it be scientifically administered. The question of whether or not it is historically well grounded becomes largely irrelevant. In his dialogues Plato's narrators typically support a particular formulation of aristocratic rule over any other type. The difference between his aristocracy and that of the real world lies in the role of philosophy in law. 'Correct' rulership is, rather strikingly, a science practised by those who have been properly educated to do it.[160]

In the *Statesman,* the Eleatic Stranger demonstrates that formal legislation in a democratic assembly is actually unnecessary and potentially a very dangerous thing.[161] His analogy describes hypothetical legislators passing and modifying laws on medicine and navigation—subjects about which they know little or nothing—and how such a process will never successfully navigate ships or cure sick people.[162] The best constitution therefore is that which is based on science informed by the superior insights of philosophy. 'That is always Plato's answer:' as Finley says, 'of all existing constitutions, even the best are mere imitations of the true constitution; the debate over ancestral constitution is a waste of time or worse; constitutions cannot be judged by reference to this or that past hero or constitution'.[163]

The laws of Magnesia are philosophically inspired in their creation. Above and beyond all else, it is Philosophy (with its attendant sciences) that is to be the ultimate standard on which the rule of *nomos* is based. The laws' changeability is extremely limited with little or no legislation allowed and only the philosophically illuminated *nukterinos* council permitted to alter them. As Nightingale says, 'the lawcode is conceived as a distinct genre of writing which is not only elevated above all other modes of discourse but is accorded an almost scriptural status'.[164] *Nomos* here means something like rationally, scientifically and philosophically derived laws with permanent binding force. If a historical law is found to be philosophically sound, then it will be utilised.[165] Plato's narrator is no stranger to borrowing from useful sources. He has repeatedly availed himself of the wealth of information present in existing legal codes. The Magnesian *nomoi* have regard for ancient custom and 'unwritten laws', but these are subordinate to the scrutiny of science and the rule of Reason (*logos*).

It is impossible to gauge the influence of all the factors that might have affected Plato's thinking. Even so, there are a number of interesting points of connection that may enrich our understanding of the *Laws*. This is particularly the case in relation to such perhaps seemingly improbable groups as the Kretans, Spartans and Pythagoreans. These along with others form a backdrop to the second-best *polis* and the examination of it would be incomplete without considering them.

The designation of the hypothetical colony and its placement are not insignificant. The name 'Magnesia' does not itself appear until Book VIII, at 848d and thereafter is brought up again at 860e, 919d, 946b and 969a. The site for Magnesia is described as being on a plain in Krete about eighty *stadia* (about 9 or 10 miles) from the coast, along the river Lethaeus (Hieropotamos), with plenty of trees and with limited access to a good harbour.[166] The Athenian Stranger enjoins his hypothetical colonists to honour any local divinities worshipped by the earlier inhabitants of this same site. This may indicate, as Morrow says, 'that Plato remembers—or imagines—an ancient Kretan city named Magnesia'.[167] No evidence of such a city has been found in the region that Plato's narrator has delineated but much archaeological work remains to be done on Krete.[168]

Why might Plato want his Magnesian colony to be situated in this place? Potential answers may be derived from both within and without the text of the *Laws*. At the beginning of Book I, the Athenian Stranger mentions that the Kretans follow Homer in ascribing the origin of their laws to Minos, the son of Zeus. The latter would reportedly hold court with his son every nine years to give him legal advice on the government of the kingdom.[169] He later indicates that 'the laws of Krete are held in exceedingly high repute amongst all the Hellenes'.[170] This appears to be a mostly true statement.[171] According to Herodotos, the Spartans of his era maintained that their *Lykourgan* legislation was derived, in part, from that of Krete.[172] Aristotle discusses one historical account that makes not only Lykourgos but also Zaleukos and Charondas dependent on one Thaletas who was a legislator of Gortyn.[173] He rejects this tradition for chronological reasons but agrees with the tribute to Krete that such a tradition implies, saying that 'the true statesman wishes to make his citizens good and obedient to the laws; we have a good example of this in the Kretan and Lakedaimonian legislators'.[174]

The Athenian reformer Solon (c. 640–c. 560 B.C.E.) was reputed by some to have been helped in lawmaking by the Kretan Epimenides.[175] This perhaps reflects more of what was believed rather than what was necessarily true. The respect that it reveals for Kretan legal traditions appears justified by the inscriptions that have come to light in the past century. The *Code of Gortyn* indicates that the Kretans were not only superb legislators but had developed their skills over a long period of time.[176] An inscription from Dreros, probably not later than 600 B.C.E., was discovered in the 1940s that represents, as Morrow says, 'an early source of the *polis* type of constitution which became a common feature of the Greek states in the classical period'.[177] Saunders has likewise pointed out that a number of the statutes in the *Laws* of Plato have much in common with Kretan legal traditions and, in this way, 'it is not only geographically that Magnesia is close to Gortyn'.[178]

Plato's interest in Krete is not a late development exclusive to the *Laws*. In the *Protagoras*, Sokrates claims to believe that the love of knowledge was more ancient and more truly cultivated in Krete and Sparta than in any other part of Greece (342a–343b). This particular passage is not without its elements of humour but may reflect genuine esteem for the Kretan and Spartan traditions. Plutarch later tells us that, under Plato's influence, Dion of Syracuse sought to establish a constitution 'of the Spartan or Kretan type, a mixture of democracy and royalty, with an aristocracy overseeing the administration of important affairs'.[179] There is more of a Spartan influence to be seen in the *Republic*, but both of these cultures had an effect on Plato's utopia-building.[180]

The notion of a ruling, aristocratic elite is certainly a prominent theme in the *Laws*. Perhaps more importantly, both Krete and Sparta had experienced the effects of deliberate attempts at societal control through the advent of legal codes.[181] Sparta, in particular, had undergone a number of constitutional reforms with results that were readily observable to the Greeks.[182] This was possibly a major reason why it was worthy of study. Plato's Sokrates praises Krete and Sparta on various occasions and, in the *Republic*, he cites 'the Kretan and Spartan constitution' as an example of the best of the imperfect forms of government.[183] One of the main faults of these constitutions was their warlike inclination.[184] More importantly, they only aim at a part of virtue—courage—not the whole of virtue.[185] As with the *Republic*, the *polis* in the *Laws* also seeks to attain the greatest possible happiness (εὐδαιμονία) for all citizens; but, this is inextricably linked with their attainment of virtue (ἀρετή).[186] 'In particular', as Bobonich says, 'the [Magnesian] lawgiver must aim at fostering all the virtues—courage, justice, moderation and wisdom—in the citizens as a whole'.[187]

Despite their defects, Plato's interests in Kretan and Spartan constitutions had a noticeable effect on other members of his Academy. The second book of Aristotle's *Politics* contains a lengthy account of Krete with a careful comparison of Kretan and Spartan institutions and discussion of their historical relationship.[188] Jaeger has indicated that the materials used by Aristotle in this section of the *Politics* were assembled during the period of his residence in the Academy, as he says, 'when Plato was working on the *Laws* and Kretan and Spartan institutions were a favourite subject of discussion'.[189] It may have been the case that Plato and the Academy were attempting to retro-engineer an ideal government based on existing models of past experiments in governmental reform.

As indicated earlier, the Spartan *politeia* underwent a series of revisions and constitutional reforms (one might say 'calculated social planning') followed by some marked success as a consequence.[190] It is impossible to say with certainty what prompted Spartan constitutional reforms. In the 7th century, there had been, as Whitby says, some 'internal wranglings over the constitution' as well as, perhaps more profoundly, the Messenian revolts which seem to have necessitated some deliberate cultural re-ordering.[191] A primary result of these reforms appears to have been the achievement of a more tightly controlled society in which the lives of most citizens and non-citizens were subjected to a kind of intense scrutiny and martial regulation. This process involved, amongst other things, the inculcation of accepted virtues along with a considerable deal of propagandistic exposure to the state's official ideologies.

A number of the Athenian Stranger's policies in the *Laws* appear to reflect Spartan ways of thinking both real and imagined. I examine many of these and other instances of similarity throughout this book where applicable.[192] Although Sparta and Magnesia have different ends envisioned for their respective ways of life, the Spartan influence appears to be quite strong. According to Finley, in the *Laws* Plato seems to have 'combined much Athenian private law with a social and political structure that more closely approached Sparta, in so far as it resembled any existing Greek system'.[193] His version is a unique synthesis of these and other elements.

A group of philosophers who, nearly a century before Plato's time, reputedly took both a theoretical and a practical interest in politics, in a manner similar to Plato, were the Pythagoreans. Iamblichos (4th C.E.) reported that Pythagoras himself paid special attention to Kretan and Spartan legislation.[194] Pythagoras was reputed to have had political dealings in Sicily, Lampaskos and Kroton (to name a few such places), and he may have held a particular interest in the constitutional formulations of Krete and Sparta.[195] The indications that we have suggest a highly political

aspect to early Pythagoreanism. That Pythagoras influenced Plato is generally acknowledged.[196] Volumes could be (and indeed have been) written on the potential
links between Plato and the Pythagoreans. It is not the purpose of my study to explore
that murky realm.

So, why place Magnesia on Krete? Plato's interest in Krete and Sparta seems
beyond dispute. This appears especially true with regard to the codified structure of
their laws and their methods of social control. The Athenian Stranger borrows a great
deal from perceived Kretan and Spartan traditions in framing the constitution for his
Magnesia. Perhaps there would be equal reason to deposit Magnesia in Sparta rather
than Krete. It is possible that he chose Krete because the region was relatively isolated
and less of a military target than Sparta at the time of the *Laws'* composition. The
pursuit of *aretē* demands uninterrupted leisure.

The *Laws* contains all manner of legislation dealing with virtually every aspect of a society. It includes, but is certainly not limited to, such subjects as trade, taxes, welfare,
education, marriage, the rearing of children, penal codes, governmental organisation
and, as particularly concerns this text, moral and sexual conduct. The statutes are
presented in a didactic format with intermittent interpretations. The initial chapters
of the text, as well as some of the closing chapters, contain the largest portion of the
theoretical discussions on subjects relating to government, law and philosophy. Plato's
interests in philosophy included the theoretical side of politics to no small degree.
This is especially true of the *Laws* which is particularly concerned with the proper
government of an idealised *polis*. Plato's Magnesia is a work of fiction. Its theoretical
contemplations find their corollaries in the real world of politics and society only by
way of metaphor and analogy.

Even so, the political impact of the *Laws* on real societies and *poleis* may have
been profound. Plato's aristocratic Academy is thought to have entertained many
political connections. Perhaps the *Laws* may have served as a kind of handbook of
guidelines for its members. These academics appear to have been renowned for their
expertise in political, legal and constitutional studies and, as such, many were retained
as advisors to a number of communities in the ancient world.[197] Their interests and
activities, along with Plato's, point to a kind of indirect practical agenda behind their
theoretical works.

It is important to bear in mind, however, that the political activity of the Academy remains a controversial and disputed subject. I do not seek to resolve this issue
here. Elements of uncertainty make their political activities only a potential context
against which to view the *Laws,* but the implications of this, if true, are well worth
consideration. Much of the Academy's alleged political activity hinges on the validity
of Plato's letters—especially the fifth (in which he introduces his student Euphraios
to King Perdiccas of Macedon), the sixth (in which he recommends two of his pupils

to King Hermeias of Atarneos) and the famous seventh letter to the Dionian party that ruled Syracuse.

There is no indication that the authorship of these letters was regarded with scepticism in the Classical era and this fact alone lends them no small amount of credibility. It was in the fifteenth century C.E. that Ficinius condemned letter XIII as false, followed two centuries later by Cudworth.[198] Attacks on the validity of the Platonic letters reached its climax in the nineteenth century as did attacks on the validity of the *Laws*.[199] The same critics of the letters also cast doubt on the authenticity of the *Parmenides, Sophist, Kratylus* and *Philebus* for similar stylistic reasons. In later decades, these have found more favourable light in the eyes of the critics. Their previous errors may have been due in part, as Morrow says, to a failure to appreciate 'the changes which Plato's style had undergone between the *Republic* and the *Laws*'.[200] The hypersensitivity of some nineteenth century philologists has since given way to more modern critical methods that tend to embrace most if not all of the Platonic letters.[201] Morrow, who accepts all of them with the possible exception of the first, says that the others agree 'in thought, style, and diction' with the acknowledged works of the author.[202] He indicates that this is especially true of the seventh letter. It is doubtless that the subject of authenticity will continue to haunt Platonic scholarship well into the future. It is reasonable to proceed with the assumption that the letters (especially the key political ones such as the seventh) are probably valid.

The contextual effect of the Academy's political entanglements on the *Laws* must remain theoretical. This does not, however, mean that these alleged involvements were not significant. The *Laws,* by its very nature, is a highly political text. The context in which it was conceived and created appears to have been no less political. Many later authorities have thought so. The Academy, according to Vatai, 'made a name for itself in the fourth century by the lawgivers it sent to assorted Hellenic cities'.[203] Plutarch, who identified himself as a Platonist, gives a favourable account of Academics in positions of power. He regarded these as justly opposing the dangerous influences of the Epicureans who, as he says, 'if they write in such matters at all, write on government to deter us from taking part in it'.[204]

Plutarch mentions the Academic Aristonymos who reformed the constitution of Arcadia, Phormio who modified the heavily oligarchic rule of the Eleans, Menedemos who was sent to the Pyrrhaeans, Eudoxos who legislated for his fellow Knidians and Aristotle who advised both the Stagirites and, more importantly, the Macedonians on legal matters.[205] It can be safely assumed that these philosophers benefited from Plato's teaching as well as the financial and other support of their aristocratic families (excepting perhaps Eudoxos and Aristotle who were more, so to speak, *bourgeois*). Eudoxos (4th C.E.) was already established as a famous mathematician and philosopher and, as such, did not depend solely on the auspices of the Academy. Aristotle, while not of the same social class as Plato, had little trouble in finding a place amongst Athenian elites and, later, the courts of aristocrats and autocrats.

Perhaps the Academy's most noteworthy of alleged political successes involved Hermeias the tyrant of Atarneos. Hermeias had risen from the merchant class to dominate his home *polis*.[206] He appears to have cultivated a close relationship with two of Plato's students, Erastos and Korsikos. As scholarly representatives of the famous Academy, they could have been valuable advisors as well as providing some useful 'spin' for the tyrant.[207] Plato had requested that Hermeias look after his students, who were somewhat lacking in worldly experience, and extend to them his protection.[208] Securing from Hermeias his *aegis* over Erastos and Korsikos, themselves two leading citizens of Skepsis, also seems to have secured the protection of Skepsis itself. If so, this induced a condition in which the two philosophers could undertake whatever reforms (or experiments) in Skepsis, and later Assos, that they wished with considerable ease.

Hermeias evidently benefited from his pursuit of philosophy and its application to government as he reportedly took up geometry and dialectics and may have pursued his studies even after the novelty wore off.[209] Arius Didymus, the Augustan-era stoic philosopher, offers an account of the effect that the Academy's agents produced on Hermeias:

> Into the surrounding country he made expeditions; and he made friends of Korsikos and Erastos and Aristotle and Xenokrates; hence all these men lived with Hermeias . . . he listened to them . . . he gave them gifts . . . he actually changed the tyranny into a milder rule; therefore he also came to rule over the neighbouring country as far as Assos, and then, being exceedingly pleased with these same philosophers, he allotted them the city of Assos. He accepted Aristotle most of all of them, and was very intimate with him.[210]

The degree of validity represented by this fragment is open to debate. Even so, both it and Plato's sixth letter seem to corroborate such momentous political involvements on the part of Academics.

Some of the more ambitious members of Plato's mostly aristocratic Academy, we are told, tried to establish themselves in the roles of tyrants. Some evidently succeeded. Klearchos, who studied under Plato and Isokrates, was regarded by the latter as the kindest, most humane and most liberal student in the school.[211] This future tyrant was sponsored for Athenian citizenship by Timotheos in 375, and in 362 Klearchos named his son after the famous Athenian general.[212] However, after gaining his tyranny, Klearchos earned the disfavour of the Academy, as well as that of the philosopher Chion, through his harsh policies and his abusive treatment of local aristocrats.

Other Academics allegedly sought their own crowns. Timolaos of Kyzikos followed in the pattern of Klearchos and revealed a different personality once he had assumed power. We are told that he went from being a benevolent distributor of free grain and money to suddenly overthrowing Kyzikos constitution.[213] Euaeon of Lampaskos was another Academic who reportedly attempted a similar rise to power. His tactics involved loaning money to his native city and, as Athenaios says, 'taking as security the *acropolis* which he retained with the design of becoming tyrant, until the people of Lampaskos combined to resist him; and after repaying his money they threw him out'.[214]

The Academic Chaeron of Pellene may have been more extreme than Klearchos or Timolaos. As tyrant, he allegedly banished all of the male nobility, redistributed their land to their slaves and forced all of the aristocratic women to marry the newly freed and propertied slaves. This seems rather unlikely and may represent Athenaios' attempts at slandering the Academy with embellished half-truths. He seems to be sneering as he writes that 'these were the beneficial results he derived from the noble *Republic* and from the lawless *Laws!*'[215] Timolaos of Kyzikos, Euaeon of Lampaskos and Chaeron of Pellene were all three used by Sophokles of Sunion's legalist, Demochares, as exhibits to justify the ban on philosophers at Athens in 307/6. Chroust, after giving a list of Plato's disciples and associates, concludes that 'one could justly refer to the Platonic Academy as the "seedbed" of political tyrants'.[216] But should one conclude such a thing? Political enemies of the Academy might have desired to spread just such a view. We should bear in mind that Athenaios' assertions in particular are clearly aimed at defaming the Academy. However, as Burkert indicates, 'Plato's Academy was a cult organisation' and there is no inconsistency between this and its political activities.[217] It can be said with certainty that the Academy was well connected to the political landscape of ancient Greece from its inception.

Much more could be said about their other potential political dealings but will be omitted here for want of space and time. One could mention Plato's own involvement in the political affairs of Sicily and his frequent dealings with the Pythagorean philosophers there who sought influence over the courts of Dionysius I and II.[218] There are also the more famous, if perhaps less dramatic, undertakings of Aristotle in the Macedonian court, tutoring prince Alexander.[219] Likewise, one could mention the continued political influence of the Academy after Plato's death when it came under more direct control of his aristocratic family. It seems to have had political interests above and beyond the purely theoretical and, as such, it may have exerted influences over real world politics. One cannot begin to calculate the potential effects of this Academic involvement but it may be more profound than we have yet to realise. The *Laws* should probably be read in light of the evident political interests of the Academy. But we must acknowledge the limitations of our sources. It is a shadowy context, at best, against which to consider the *Laws* but politics and philosophy persist in making strange bedfellows.

In conclusion, the *Laws* is in many ways dramatically different from its Platonic predecessors. It provides a working constitution by which a colony may be founded and a *polis* managed. It reveals an interesting and dramatic study into the very heart of that which makes a society function—that is, the essence of law, government and morality. It may be regarded as a theoretical approach to social engineering in which many important ideas are examined and addressed. The Athenian Stranger utilises a political methodology, involving complex psychological theory that will be deployed to achieve maximum social control. This is particularly observable, as the following chapters will consider, in the realm of sexuality.

The laws and institutions of Magnesia strive to inculcate a particular ideology in its subjects that is intended to encourage their (mandatory) pursuit of Platonic *aretē*. It is a second-best solution to that offered by the *Republic*—a more 'realistic' utopian vision (if this is not a contradiction in terms). It is fortunate that no one will be made to live in his *polis* if they do not wish to do so and he has included no plans for it to undertake expansion.[220] The Magnesians are to remain isolated in their 'brave new world' and only defend themselves if attacked. They are, so to speak, 'pacifistic supermen'.

The *Laws* has a great deal to say about human psychology, society and sexuality in particular. The attainment of a total psychological control over the sexual appetites figures prominently into the Athenian Stranger's formulation of *aretē*. The implicit value of this virtue is to be accepted unconditionally by his hypothetical subjects. Magnesia will be a city-state whose government concerns itself directly in the private lives of its citizens and pays special attention to their psychosexual development. The express purpose of such careful regulation is the production of the maximum degree of happiness and excellence in the populace as a whole. The end of the project is at least benign if not benevolent.

Bear in mind that Magnesia is purely hypothetical. The *Laws* is a philosophical discourse that is couched within the imaginary landscape of dramatic fiction. There is no indication that Plato ever planned to put his theories into practice as outlined in the text. His narrators tell a story that describes how one might construct a near-utopian *polis* and govern it through law and philosophy. It also represents a professional plan of constitution complete with an outline of governmental bodies and complex programmes for social control. It is a mythic tale designed to instruct. As we have seen, it could also have been employed as a guide to political theory and practice. The reported activities of Plato and his students suggest this possibility. We should keenly regard the historical and other contexts as relevant, perhaps recalling Wordsworth's encomium with a more critical eye, 'while the lunar beam of Plato's genius, from its lofty sphere, fell round him in the grove of Academe, softening their inbred dignity austere—'.[221]

Chapter III
Educating Magnesia
Developmental Psychology and Sex Role Stereotyping

So long as the young generation is, and continues to be, well brought up, our ship of state will have a fair voyage; otherwise the consequences are better left unspoken . . .

—The Athenian Stranger[1]

Know you not, therefore, that the beginning of every task is the most important part—especially for any creature that is young and tender? For then is it best moulded and takes well the form that one wishes to impress upon it.

—(Plato's) Sokrates[2]

No examination of sexuality in Plato's Magnesia, as outlined in the *Laws,* could approach the subject adequately without taking into account the important part that education plays in the formation of its citizens' sex roles. Plato's innovations in pedagogy are extremely advanced by modern standards and this holds especially true when they are viewed in contrast with developmental psychology. One of the principal aims of the Athenian Stranger's educational programme is to encourage a type of psychological development along specific sexual lines. He has identified the ideal sex roles that his hypothetical subjects should adopt and designed a state-sponsored system of education in order to inculcate these from the earliest possible age.

Plato's influence on modern educational theory and practice has been undeniably profound. Few if any of his ancient contemporaries (including especially Isokrates, 436–338 B.C.E. and Xenophon, c. 428–c. 354 B.C.E.), had undertaken to develop a more comprehensive and practicable pedagogical methodology. No other single individual's effects on pedagogy has been as far-reaching as his. Whether Beck's claim that 'virtually all idealistic theories of education may be traced back to him' is completely accurate, it nonetheless conveys a sense of Plato's significance to the development of our modern education.[3] Not only has he theorised a working pedagogy for pre-primary, primary and secondary education; with the foundation of the Academy Plato may be said to have invented the University as well.[4]

The philosophical aims of Plato's pedagogical system overshadow its practical applications. Those who praise his innovations have sometimes ignored the metaphysical aspects that underpin his philosophy. Whether in the *Protagoras* or the *Timaeus,* the *Republic* or the *Laws,* the *telos* of a Platonic education is to induce a state of Reason's rule over the *psychēs* of those educated. The achievement of a healthy condition of civic and other virtues must be regarded as secondary to this. Since the Classical era, both liberal and conservative regimes have adapted elements of Plato's pedagogical philosophy to their own ends with varying effects that extend beyond the scope or frame of this book. Plato may claim the dubious distinction of having introduced educational censorship through the expurgation of 'dangerous' subject matter from the school *curriculum,* but he has also had the revolutionary temerity to suggest that females ought to have the opportunity to be educated more or less equally with males. Theirs is a separate but mostly 'equal' education with some limitations (e.g. Magnesian girls have the option to refrain from the study of horsemanship and the arts of war if they so choose) but the core *curriculum* of arts and sciences, as in the *Kallipolis,* is extended to both sexes—as is the option to continue their education beyond the secondary level. Why does the Athenian Stranger in the *Laws* deviate so profoundly from the known standards of Greek culture?[5] The answer appears to be more utilitarian than egalitarian.

Plato's theories on education are impressive and did not appear *ex nihilo* from a cultural vacuum. Many of his notions necessarily derive from his own educational experiences particular to his position within the Athenian liturgical class.[6] His contact with the educational traditions in democratic and aristocratic contexts was fundamental in shaping his views. Sparta too, as we shall see, plays a major role in his thinking. As with the other subjects here examined, it is worthwhile to consider some of the cultural backdrop against which Plato has formulated his theories. This chapter looks at the educational system of Magnesia, in its broader context, in keeping with the overall theme of this book with regard to sex and society.

The Athenian education, in its several incarnations, particularly informs this examination of hypothetical Magnesia. The Spartan system also appears to have had a major influence. 'It is generally agreed', as Nightingale says, 'that the constitution outlined in the *Laws* is characterized by a blend of Spartan and Athenian elements, with Athens making the largest contribution to the mixture'.[7] It is not the case that Plato has merely copied the Athenian education and then added Spartan and other elements. His narrator has taken these ideas and advanced them to a much more sophisticated level altogether.

This system of education with which Plato would have been most familiar was itself largely the product of the wealth of empire. His experiences were peculiar to his class. In democratic Athens, education was not free and its quality depended heavily on the finances of the student's family. Despite this, perhaps for the first time in history more than a few had the opportunity and the means to be educated. This marks a significant historical advancement. In earlier times, education was much less accessible or, when available, widely un-availed due to socio-economic circumstances.[8] The 'programme' developed for upper class Greeks in the Archaic age set the standard for its democratic successor. Some time during or before the era of Homer and Hesiod (c. 9th–8th B.C.E.), youths of high social standing had tutors/slaves to instruct them in letters (mainly poetry), numbers and the arts of martial combat. These subjects may be reductively designated as music and gymnastics—whilst the former was mainly put to use (unprofessionally) at private *symposia,* the latter was meant to improve one's warlike skills.

The 6th–5th century equivalent to this has been called the 'Old Education'. The term derives from a passage of pseudo-Xenophon's *Athenian Constitution* generally referred to as the *Old Oligarch.*[9] 'The Old Education, combining physical exercise and cultural interests, is now rejected by the common people', complains the Old Oligarch, 'they disapprove of it because they know that they cannot cope with it'.[10] This passage appears to provide good evidence for retrospective attitudes (whether literal or literary) about fifth-century Athenian democracy and empire. But is it, as has sometimes been assumed, a fifth-century text that represents a reality of the time? Hornblower has recently cited a number of linguistic and other issues that suggest a later date—probably mid- to late-fourth century.[11] If this is so, then the *Old Oligarch,* as he says, 'becomes a valuable document about fourth-century attitudes to imperialism' but should be regarded as a type of later 'nostalgia' and therefore not an accurate picture of fifth-century life.[12] This is not to suggest that something like the Old Education did not exist.

A comparable pedagogical experience seems to have been exclusive to Athenian aristocratic elites prior to the democratic reforms of the late 6th to early/middle 5th centuries. The tradition probably continued amongst the upper classes for some time thereafter. The study of letters and numbers made up less of the *curriculum* (although these will have been a part of it) than that of 'music' and athletics/gymnastics. It seems to have been designed with the express purpose of preparing upper class, male youths for the aristocratic way of life.[13] This is reminiscent of the practices favoured by Plato's Sokrates for the *Kallipolis* which was a traditional *curriculum* involving 'gymnastics for the body and, for the soul, music'.[14] Training in 'music' superficially covered all aspects represented by the Muses. Basic arithmetic and geometry were included in this as was history, poetry and *mythos.* Significant emphasis was placed on that which we think of today as music or, that is, poetry sung to a musical accompaniment.[15] As

Griffith indicates, recitations of Homer in particular, an integral aspect to this education, 'served as an ideological reinforcement of aristocratic values and processes, a reinforcement endorsed at both public and private levels'.[16]

Aristophanes provides a nostalgic look at the *kitharistes*' school in which aristocratic youths were taught music in the *Clouds*.[17] This tradition is perceived as extending back into and beyond the 5th century to an idealised 'Athens of old'. The transition to the Democratic or New Education appears to have been sparked, to the greater extent, by social and economic causal factors. The growth of trade in the 6th and 5th centuries contributed in no small part.[18] The burgeoning responsibility of the citizen elite caused by the flowering democracy/empire in the 5th century may have increased the demand for widespread literacy. Being able to read and write, as Thomas says, 'was generally seen as a positive force for democracy and its rule by written law'.[19] These and other factors eventually brought about some significant revisions to the *curriculum* of the Old Education as democracy spread the privilege of learning to a broader demographic than had previously been possible. The 'democratisation' of education resulted in a similar 'aristocratisation' through the assimilation of upper-class ideals by some of the newly educated, and newly wealthy, populace. The time of Perikles (d.429 B.C.E.) probably saw the Athenian democratic education at its height. A new system had emerged to cope with increasing demands for higher learning and a number of private schools were founded.[20] More is known of individual schools from the 5th century onwards than in earlier eras.[21]

Education became more diversified and available to classes of society that had previously been excluded from it. Not everyone, however, was literate or even well-educated. Unlike the modern world, being functionally illiterate did not severely limit one's participation in the *polis*. Dramatic performances and public debates were readily accessible to the majority who were probably limited in their ability to read.[22] The growth of education in the democratic era, as Harris writes, 'is clearly connected with, or part of, a growth in the non-aristocratic citizen's belief in his own worth and his own rights and duties'.[23] Education and literacy could aid in social advancement. It would have helped some citizens deal with the finer complexities of government and, by extension, serve to protect their democratic rights from tyranny. A similar attitude to this, as we shall see, is likewise present in the *Laws*.

It is thought that the children of wealthy Athenians began their education earlier and finished later than those of the lower classes.[24] The system was not rigidly formal or especially organised. There was little or no state supervision. The reason for this, as Ober has proposed, is perhaps because a more formalised system would have been regarded as antithetical to the popular democratic ideal of civil liberty.[25] It was largely left to the individual (male) citizen, rather than to the state, to provide an education for himself or his offspring. A *paidagōgos* (possibly a slave who was incapable of manual labour) could be retained to see to the daily rearing of a child aged seven or thereabouts.[26] The *paidagōgos* would take him to school and supervise aspects of his moral development.[27] Such paid tutors or slaves (*grammatistai, kitharistai* and *paidotribai*) instructed their pupils in letters, music and gymnastics.[28] Assuming his resources permitted, a father might continue his son's tutelage for several more years, at a sort of 'secondary' level, from the age of twelve theoretically up to twenty-one.[29] When a student had passed from being a child (παῖς) to s 'young man' (μειράκιον) he might be released from his *paidagōgos* and schoolmasters to commence with his induction into public life.[30] It is thought that the term for 'young man' (μειράκιον) could imply anything from age fifteen to twenty-one depending on the individual in question.[31] On reaching their civic majorities, many citizen-youths would have entered into an apprenticeship for a trade or joined the military.[32]

Athenian youths in the later half of the fourth century, at least, had to undergo a period of military training known as the *ephēbeia* (ἐφηβεία).[33] There is some evidence of the existence of this from about 371/0 B.C.E.,[34] but, according to Marrou, 'it did not receive its full form until much later, immediately after the defeat of Chaeronea (338), after a law for which Epikrates seems to have been responsible and which was passed between 337 and 335'.[35] But did this law establish the *ephēbeia* or merely modify a pre-existing institution? Reinmuth agrees with the 371/0 date for its existence but whether this represents the earliest instantiation of the practice remains uncertain.[36] He also indicates that 'one might with some justification propose the period after the Persian War' as the time of the *ephēbeia's* inception.[37]

Aiskhines the orator spoke of a similar system in which he partook as a youth saying that he served for two years after his childhood as a '*peripolos* of this land'.[38] He uses the word *sunephēboi,* describing his participation in this institution, in reference to himself and his age-mates. Perhaps, in this respect, Aiskhines was something of a pioneer.[39] This term may or may not be the same as the later *ephēbeia.*[40] *Sunephēboi* may refer to a voluntary body of youthful 'territorial guards', at a time when Athens could not afford to pay foreign soldiers, that later grew into a proper institution. 'The ephebeia was a programme of military training', according to De Marcellus, 'but authors of the early to mid-fourth century state, both directly and implicitly, that such training does not exist'.[41] Isokrates, from whom we might expect some insight into this matter, makes no mention of it. He says that his students acquired virtue, 'having just emerged from boyhood', whilst most other youths waste time at drinking parties and in soft living.[42] Plato's narrator in the *Laws* seems unaware of any such existing institution in Athens. In Megillus' discussion of the Kretan *agelai* and the Spartan *agōgē*, which would seem to be the opportune moment to bring it up, there is no reference to any Athenian *ephēbeia.*[43] This would seem to support a later date for its official inception, but the issue remains controversial.

At some point, then, in the fourth century (at least post 371/0 and very possibly post 338/7), when a male youth attained the age of μειράκιον, he would lead a life apart for a period of time before gaining full admission into society. He might not be allowed the status of citizen until he had served his *ephēbeia*. Each year the demes drew up a list of eligible youths, about to reach their civic majority (or 'manhood', ἔφηβος—generally fifteen to twenty-one), and then submitted it to the *Boulē* for approval. Aristotle tells us that an *ephēbe* 'cannot go to law either as a defendant or as a plaintiff, unless it is a matter of upholding an inheritance, arranging the affairs of an heiress, or a priesthood related to the clan'.[44] The period of *ephēbeia* ended when one of several eventualities occurred. It could conclude with entry into the hoplite phalanx, the Athenian navy and/or marriage.[45] Until the *ephēbeia* was over, the young man's relationship to the *polis* was equivocal. As a pedagogical institution, it certainly played a significant role: it appears to have been one of the few truly organised aspects of ancient Greek education outside Sparta.[46] The *ephēbeia* also incurred other, more unsavoury comparisons with Spartan practices.[47]

Here is a connection with Plato. The policy of mandatory military service in the *Laws,* except for the potential inclusion of women, readily corresponds to the Athenian *ephēbeia*.[48] The fact that a text of Plato's, composed in the 350's and early 340's, contains an outline for something like the *ephēbeia* is historically interesting.[49] Although, as we have seen, there is evidence for *ephēbic*-type training in Athens as early as 371/0 (and possibly even earlier), it does not seem to exist as an official institution until Epikrates' law dated between 337 and 335. The fact that Plato's writing and the *ephēbeia* coincide suggests that these ideas were 'in the air' at this time. Even if Epikrates' law only modified the existing institution of the *ephēbeia*, Plato's propositions in the *Laws,* based on Kretan and Spartan customs, might have been an influential factor. It is a tantalising suggestion but, for the present, must be relegated to the speculative realm.

The activities undertaken by youths during their *ephēbeia* amounted to a type of military education that probably also served as a process of socialisation. It is not dissimilar to the practice of mandatory military service in some nation-states of the modern era. Troops known as *peripoloi* existed in Athens during the Peloponnesian Wars but, as indicated above, it is unclear whether or not the *ephēbes* were amongst them at that time.[50] In the fourth century, the *ephēbic peripoloi* would have undertaken their service in the forts surrounding Athens including the Panakton, Dekeleia and Rhamnous.[51] Their role at these forts appears to have been mainly for the purposes of training or, potentially, as backup support in the event of an attack. Young men in their *ephēbeia* tended to enter actual combat only under exceptional circumstances.[52] After about two to three years of his *ephēbeia,* an Athenian youth stepped into his mature, civic role both as heir and citizen.

Female youths did not undertake an *ephēbeia* and their education was less comprehensive than that of males. There is a whole tradition of oral composition by women about which we know next to nothing.[53] This suggests that a kind of learning experience existed specifically amongst women from a very early date. The poet Sappho (7th century B.C.E.) stands out as one of our best exemplars to indicate that at least some women were well educated even during the archaic age.[54] But being educated on an equal footing with males in any century hardly seems to have been the norm.[55] Many women might have learned rudimentary reading and possibly writing. Some may have studied poetry. Subjects such as rhetoric and mathematics appear to have been taught almost exclusively to males.[56] Nevertheless, an example testifying that there were some highly educated women in the mid-fourth century B.C.E. may be seen in the gravestone of Phanostrate who was a female physician in Athens at that time.[57] It is difficult to draw a clear image of women's level and manner of education as it still remains largely based on an argument from silence. 'What is interesting about this controversy', as Pomeroy says, 'is that, numerous though they probably were over the years, the women, absent or present, were not noticed by our ancient authorities'.[58]

Most Classical Athenian girls, if they undertook any studies at all, had severely limited 'educations' compared to that of their brothers, fathers and husbands. It may have been necessary for upper-class women to learn reading and writing to some degree.[59] But they were generally *not* instructed in the use of weapons.[60] There is much contention about that which they did learn. Plato has provided some anecdotal evidence that muddies the picture rather than clarifying it. His narrator remarks at *Laws* 658d that 'educated women', as with most common people, regard tragedy as the best form of entertainment. This may not speak well of their education given some of Plato's writings about tragedy.[61]

Whether or not women were permitted to attend dramatic performances is the subject of an ongoing debate in modern scholarship. A dialogue in Aristophanes' *Peace* seems to suggest that they did attend, but it could be interpreted either way. In a scene from this play, Trygaios and his slave throw barley (*krithai*) into the audience making a bawdy pun to the effect that the women did not receive any but 'come night, their husbands will give it to them' (*krithē*=penis).[62] As Goldhill suggests, the passage may mean 'not that the women were absent but that they were sitting too far back to catch the barleyseeds' but, as he also indicates, 'this sexual humour clearly does not depend on the presence of women in the theatre'.[63] The passage does not confirm their presence or refute it.

There are two other tantalising pieces from Plato which imply that some women might have watched dramatic performances, but both of these occur in hypothetical contexts and cannot therefore be taken as definitive.[64] The passage from the *Gorgias* criticises popular rhetoric aimed at women, men, adults, children and slaves without a proper respect for the consequences. The other one, from the *Laws*, posits that the wrong kind of rhetorical performance (of which tragedy is a part) can badly influence both women and men. But this comes within a discussion about the types of drama to be permitted in the hypothetical Magnesian state and there attended by members of both sexes. The other passage from the *Laws* mentioned above (658d) might not refer to a performance context at all. The Athenian Stranger's comments, in saying that educated women enjoyed tragedy, may not refer to a theatrical audience at all but to a much smaller category of 'reading (female) public'.[65] We cannot say with certainty that women were allowed to attend the theatre based on the material available. However, if Plato was in fact making reference to a 'reading (female) public', then that would at least seem to presuppose a level of education available to some women.

It is tempting to propose that, in Classical Athens, most women whose education rivalled or surpassed that of men were foreigners to the city.[66] But this is, as indicated above, not provable at present. But it does open a window into the Athenian *ethos*. Foreigners are seen as having different customs especially in regard to women. Xenophon's idealised account of the Spartan system envisions a type of institutionalised, physical training to have existed for women—but evidently not training in the arts and sciences.[67] His reports, although perhaps more the product of imagination than fact, suggest that it might have been easier for the Athenians to deal with such a revolutionary topic as the education of women, however limited, if it took place outside of Athens.[68] Examples of highly educated foreign-women such as Aspasia, Diotima and later Phanostrate seem to have been especially singled-out as exceptions rather than the norm.

Xenophon's *Oikonomikos*, an idealised vision of aristocratic domesticity, offers an indication of the level of learning available to Athenian citizen-women—at least those of the upper-middle to upper classes—of the late 5th and early/middle 4th centuries. In this treatise on the proper execution of household affairs, the characters of Ischomachos and his fifteen-year-old wife are both assumed to possess a degree of literacy such as would at least be sufficient to administer the matters of the *oikos*. His unnamed wife, in particular, seems to have had some type of education prior to her marriage. Ischomachos gives her his accounts and lists to manage thus indicating that her level of literacy was sufficient to cope with these.[69] Did she learn her letters (and presumably numbers as well) at home at the hands of her mother or father? Did a private tutor teach her or did she go to school? It is difficult to say for certain but there is no definitive indication that Athenian females attended schools at all.[70]

If we conclude anything about the education of women in Classical Athens from the example presented by Ischomachos' wife,[71] then there is reason to suspect that citizen-women of the highest property classes may have had some limited education that prepared them for a life of domesticity in the *oikos* rather than participation in the public sphere of the *polis*—the domain of men.[72] As will be presently discussed, the role of Spartan women somewhat bent this rule in comparison to other city-states.[73] But their unique status appears to have been only a partial exception.

Ancient Athenian women participating openly in the public sphere (who were not of the lower classes and doing menial labour or engaged in prostitution) tended to be found mainly in works of fiction, myth and speculative philosophy.

Post-secondary education was available to certain male individuals in the democratic period. A youth or adult could pursue academic subjects such as political science and rhetoric, assuming his or his family's finances allowed, through attending lectures by sophists and *symposia* with philosophers. Some special few could have learned the finer points of philosophy by becoming part of the elite circles of such notables as Parmenides and Sokrates. Plato's Academy and, later in the fourth century (335 B.C.E.), Aristotle's Lykeion were more comprehensive venues for post-secondary education. The sophists continued to provide another avenue of study.[74] Some youths also had the option of becoming medical doctors. Hippocratic institutions of medical training existed in the Classical era (outside Athens) at Knidos and Kos.[75] In Athens and abroad the arts of rhetoric, history and literature could be learned from the likes of Isokrates and the sophists whilst mathematics, science, astronomy and philosophy were generally covered in the *curricula* of the Academy and Lykeion.[76]

The Athenian education was not comprehensive and, except perhaps for the advent of the *ephēbeia* in the 4th century, not particularly structured. This was probably the norm for most ancient Greek city-states—with one notable exception. The Spartans appear to have been amongst the first to make education compulsory and to organise it in a thorough manner.[77] As Cartledge indicates, it was 'compulsory for all boys from the age of seven until they attained their socio-political majority (as opposed to physical maturity) at age eighteen'.[78] The potential education of Spartan females is a subject of some debate and is discussed below in relation to Plato's approach in the *Laws*.[79]

The Spartan education was a proper institution of the *polis*. They referred to it as the *agōgē*, which means a 'leading' or 'raising'. The *agōgē*, in keeping with their national character, appears to have been quite rigid and hierarchical. It consisted of letters and the building of endurance through sport and martial activities. Above and beyond all other known educational institutions in ancient Greece, the Spartan perhaps bears closest similarity to the Magnesian system in Plato's *Laws*. Due to the numerous similarities between them, it is perhaps best discussed point by point in relation to the *Laws*. The fact that the Athenian Stranger borrows so heavily from Spartan institutions is perhaps not striking. Thucydides says that 'they from childhood seek after manliness through laborious training' and this seems to have impressed Plato.[80] Magnesia's educational programme, like that of Sparta, strives to inculcate qualities of virtue and manliness in her citizens. Both systems appear designed to promote these virtues along specifically sexual lines. But the Magnesian system takes this to another level.

Certain thinkers in the fourth century (e.g. Xenophon, Isokrates, Plato and Aristotle) perhaps felt that the democratic system had failed to offer a substantive education in the appropriate civic virtues.[81] In each case the particular author, as Ober says, 'was concerned with establishing (in theory) a formal educational system that would ensure that experts were responsible for inculcating the youth with the "right" ethical and political values'.[82] Plato's version is the most comprehensive and probably the most renowned—then as now. His narrators have outlined a *curriculum* for learning, with especial emphasis on morality, which undergoes development throughout his works. It is in the *Laws* that they provide the most details about the Platonic course of study. We are told in the *Republic* (and elsewhere) that it is difficult to find a better system than the one that entails 'gymnastics for the body and, for the soul, music' (376e1–3). This 'mantra' echoes the paradigm of the idealised Old Education of Athenian elites but evinces characteristically 'democratic' qualities in terms of the breadth of subjects covered and the range of students to be taught.

In both the *Republic* and the *Laws* the musical education comes first. 'Music' includes many subcategories such as poetry, literature and lyrical recitation. The fictional Sokrates indicates that great effort must be undertaken to screen the 'musical' material. He perceives it as having a profound influence on young minds.[83] A proper 'musical' education is seen as making children more 'civilised' and 'balanced' through their desire to imitate the good deeds represented by the paradigms represented in fictional stories.[84] The mimetic theory of learning applies as well in the *Laws* as elsewhere.[85] Gymnastics, as with 'music', has the quality of imparting temperance and other beneficial characteristics to the *psychē* along with its important role in strengthening the body.[86] The *psychē* is targeted as the first to be put into a state of (Platonic) order.[87] The health of the body is, at best, considered secondary to this—although, both body and mind must work together toward the *telos* of *aretē*. The Magnesians continue to study music and gymnastics at later stages in their tutelage.

A fundamental tenet of pedagogical theory in the *Republic* is that a child should be educated from the earliest possible age when the mind is 'best moulded and takes well the form (τύπος) that one wishes to impress upon it'.[88] This aphorism introduces Sokrates' argument against the 'damaging' effects of poets such as Homer and Hesiod who tell 'false' tales that may impair an impressionable *psychē*. Despite its literary prejudices, the theory points to an understanding of the processes of learning and developmental psychology. Plato expands his overall theory of education in adapting it to the second-best state in his final *opus*. Magnesia must be 'free, enjoy inner concord (literally "be a friend to itself"), and possess intelligence'.[89] The educational system is to be the primary means of imparting all of these aspects to the citizens.[90] The importance of early education is stressed here, as elsewhere, as are the value of its content and the quality of the subject matter to be studied. The Athenian Stranger stresses the need for engaging in both physical exercise and intellectual pursuits in concert. He, as with Sokrates, is more interested in the 'musical' aspects of education and the official paradigms there represented for imitation.

The aims of Magnesia's system of education, as Beck says, lie 'in the production of civic efficiency and political leadership, qualities which demanded the power to judge wisely and to make right decisions'.[91] Like Sparta, the Magnesian education is provided at the expense of the *polis* and is compulsory for all citizens (804d). This will be accomplished, in a characteristically un-Spartan manner, with recourse to the Athenian practice of written law.[92] The Athenian Stranger unequivocally states that 'every man and child according to their ability must of necessity be educated since they belong more to the state than to those who begat them'.[93] The Athenian Stranger's comments seem to reverse Sokrates' pronouncements in the *Republic* that compulsory education leads to a type of 'slavishness' in character and that only those who are willing should therefore be taught (536d–537a). There are, necessarily, some inherent restrictions upon one's liberty entailed by living in the *second-best* state.

Magnesia's educational programme is to be implemented at the earliest possible stage in order to achieve the best possible results. This "get 'em while they're young" approach in the *Laws* goes beyond previous Platonic expressions of the same theory. The Athenian Stranger maintains that the education and preparation of future Magnesians should be initiated whilst they are still within the womb. It suggests that Plato may have thought of an embryo, at some stage in its development, as capable of learning. This is a strikingly modern stance and would appear to go beyond other ancient theories on the development of the foetus.[94] His awareness of its educational potential may stem, as Rankin suggests, from Demokritean influences identifiable in the creation myths of the *Timaeus*.[95] In Magnesia, a child will be 'educated' from the point at which its mother is identified as pregnant.

The Athenian Stranger, having invoked some curious analogies on the benefits of motion in the raising of birds (789b5–d8), postulates the rules on pre- and postnatal care. He proposes that pregnant women should not engage in excessive sexual pleasures (792e2–6). 'A woman with child', says he, 'ought to go for walks, and when a child is born she should mould it like wax, while it is still supple, and through the first two years of life keep it wrapped up' (789d8–e3). This metaphor of 'moulding' applies to body as well as mind.[96] The mandatory prescription of exercise for pregnant women, as well as the theme of female athletics, may represent a borrowing from the Spartan system.[97] As is to be the case with Magnesia, Spartan eugenics were also concerned with maximising the efficiency of 'offspring production' or *teknopoiia*.[98] They allegedly encouraged pregnant women to exercise and eat healthy foods.[99]

During the early stages of development, a Magnesian child must not be exposed to the damaging effects of excessive luxury or be 'spoilt' by too much pleasure. The Athenian Stranger insists that 'luxury makes the characters (τὰ ἤθη)[100] of the youth fretful, bad-tempered and inclined toward overreacting to trifles whilst the opposite extreme, excessive savagery, makes them slavish' (791d5–8). He cites the Persian King Kyros as an example of one who had received a proper and well-disciplined education.[101] He, however, paradoxically neglected the upbringing of his own children in turn. Plato's narrator says that Kyros, overly busy with his military campaigns, let his children be reared in luxury by 'women and eunuchs' who pampered them and left them bereft of discipline.[102] He indicates that this led to disaster for the Persian court.[103] Such a view probably reveals a particularly Greek bias rather than actual ethnographic fact.[104]

The Magnesians will be compelled to eschew luxury and all other excesses. The Athenian Stranger favours a tough, 'manly' educational regimen like that of his idealised Persians of old (e.g. Kyros but not Kambyses), 'a hard method', he says, 'one capable of producing shepherds who are absolutely robust and capable of sleeping out in the open, even passing the night without sleep, and of fighting a campaign'.[105] A Magnesian child must not be brought up with a mindset of habitual complaining. Their education encourages them to maintain a sort of emotional *middle ground* that avoids all extreme states of mind.[106] Their upbringing cannot aim only for 'money-making or physical prowess, or even some mental accomplishment devoid of reason and justice', since it is 'vulgar and illiberal, and utterly undeserving of the name "education."'[107] As Nightingale indicates, one who is 'servile and illiberal is, by definition, not free'.[108]

The Athenian Stranger's theoretical approach to education in the *Laws* is, in many ways, more developed than any equivalents in previous texts. An innovative strategy involves the use of structured play as part of the educational process. In order to be 'good at any pursuit', the Athenian Stranger says, 'one must practice that pursuit from infancy' (643b4–6). He offers hypothetical examples of future builders getting their start with toy houses, future farmers playing at tilling the soil with toy tools, future carpenters playing with rules and measures and future soldiers learning the art of riding at an early age.[109] In this way, a child's future role in society may be type-cast and reinforced along specified lines of development.

A child's natural enthusiasm for amusement is to be routed down productive channels. This is a way to get them actively involved in learning from an early age since, as Plato's Sokrates has said, 'a free man ought not learn anything under duress . . . compulsory learning never sticks in the mind'.[110] The games that Magnesian children play are to remain unaltered from generation to generation, like those of the Egyptians, unless the city's rulers deem otherwise.[111] The Athenian Stranger discusses some specific games that Magnesian children should be encouraged to play as part of their education. These include the sorting of fruits and other items such as garlands, boxers and wrestlers (these presumably by sight only), and bowls made of bronze, silver and gold into their appropriate groups based on likeness and difference.[112] The purpose of these is to acquaint the children with basic rules of order and arithmetic.

There is also the strong possibility that these games may be used to test a child's aptitude for various tasks and thereby determine his/her role later in life within the hierarchy of Magnesian society.[113] The philosophical underpinnings of this innovative theory remain the idealised goal of *aretē*.[114]

Magnesian boys and girls from the age of three up to the age of six are to congregate at their respective tribe's temples and engage in some kind of playful but structured interaction intensely supervised by their nurses.[115] The Athenian Stranger almost appears to us as 'a modern functionalist—an anthropologist king—he', as Golden suggests, 'identifies certain qualities and consequences of children's play and then prescribes accordingly'.[116] Structured play is similarly employed by modern educationalists as an expedient means of inducing mental growth at an early age and to develop and refine important learning skills.[117] A modern type of directed play, for example, involving the sorting of objects into categories of 'like' and 'unlike' (e.g. shells, leaves, buttons and geometric shapes), may be employed to help children improve their reading and arithmetical abilities and, as Gilpatrick indicates, to promote a more 'perfect attention to details'.[118]

The law will compel a Magnesian child's nurses to carry it about all the time until it can stand on its own or until it reaches the age of three (789e3–9).[119] The nurses and children will be observed altogether 'by the twelve women appointed for this purpose' who each serve a one-year term allocated by the Guardians of the Laws (οἱ νομοφύλακες) for each of the twelve tribes.[120] The Athenian Stranger says that 'all children, especially the little ones, benefit both mentally and physically by being nursed and by being in motion all night and all day and they should live, if it were possible, as if they were always sailing'.[121]

The Magnesians will build structures for public *gymnasia* as well as schools in three districts within the city.[122] There will also be training-grounds, "courses for horses" and land set aside for an archery range.[123] Teachers will be hired from abroad and paid out of the city's treasury.[124] These must be non-citizens since Magnesians are forbidden from taking up any labour other than that which encourages the pursuit of *aretē*. The job of managing and administrating the city-state is counted as a 'virtuous' profession and there will be a Magnesian *archōn* (ἄρχων) of Education, a citizen, to oversee the programme of learning.[125] His role appears to be more managerial than labour-intensive and comes with considerable prestige. Attendance in schools for both sexes is compulsory since the future of the state depends heavily on the education of *all* its populace.[126] The Athenian Stranger outlines the selection process for various citizen-educational officials (including athletic officials) to this end.[127] Citizen-women may occupy some of the supervisory positions mentioned above but the teachers, as was the case amongst the Spartans, must be non-citizens. Since there were foreigners amongst whom were educated women, there is every indication that they too will teach in Magnesian schools.[128]

Competitions and performances of many types are to involve Magnesian youths of both sexes in extra-curricular activities that further the cause of their education and advance their stereotyped sex roles. The Athenian Stranger proposes that young people should dance together in the nude with a view to choosing their future marriage partners.[129] Plutarch (whether truthfully or wishfully) describes a similar procedure amongst the Spartans whereby young people danced and exercised in the nude as 'incitements to marriage (παρορμητικὰ πρὸς γάμου)', and these 'urged them on not with mathematics but with love (ἐρωτικαῖς) and, as Plato says, with necessity'.[130] The Athenian Stranger does not state the requisite ages of the participants in such affairs but one assumes that they would have at least reached puberty by the time they partake of the nude dances. These are not to be *polis*-sponsored orgies. The Athenian Stranger asserts that the performances should remain within the limitations of propriety and, to that end, appoints state officials to supervise them.[131] The practice of socially sanctioned (and state enforced) nude dances for the youth, in order to encourage marriage and reproduction, reveals a somewhat manipulative quality. This underscores their significance to the system of education: they will promote the official ideal of mixed-sex coupling from an early age.

Such events are designed to bind the community socially and religiously as well as being educational. Like their Spartan and other equivalents, these Magnesian dances will mimic actual warfare in a dramatic context.[132] Other activities follow along similar lines. The Athenian Stranger describes the rules for racing competitions and indicates that 'prepubescent girls will compete unclothed in the double-race, the "horse-race" and the long distance race; those from thirteen up to those awaiting marriage may compete until at least eighteen but not beyond the age of twenty', and significantly he adds, 'let these matters regarding races both for men and for women be the same'.[133] The necessity for females to engage in the generation of offspring dictates the legal ages of their participation in athletic and martial activities.[134]

When at leisure, Magnesian youths of either sex are exhorted to pursue the 'best possible pastimes'.[135] In all activities, both sexes are carefully supervised and regulated.[136] The Athenian Stranger posits a policy of equal education and physical training. He says that 'my law applies to matters concerning women as well as men, and women must be trained equally; and without reservation would I make this same argument that neither the practice of horsemanship nor of gymnastics would be suitable for men but unsuitable for women'.[137] He cites the example of the Sauromatian women who reside around the Pontus as evidence of the benefits of (limited) sexual equality in the martial arts and other aspects of daily life.[138]

His deliberate and particular inclusion of females in the public sphere of Magnesia deviates markedly from known standards of practice in most of ancient Greece. It suggests the revolutionary notion that women possess the same (or a very similar) capacity for learning as men. The Athenian Stranger's primary argument for equal education may be largely described as utilitarian. He is *not* subscribing to the same notions as those represented by 19th century Utilitarianism. There are clear similarities to be seen in Plato's second-best *polis* with regard to the principles of women's suffrage and state-supported education for all. But Mill had also 'argued on Utilitarian grounds for freedom of speech and expression and for the non-interference of government or society in individual behaviour that did not harm anyone else'.[139] These libertarian aspects of Utilitarianism are altogether incompatible with, if not inimical to, Magnesian values. The relative status of the sexes is not equal and women's 'suffrage', what there is of it, is designed to serve the greater purposes of the city-state's efficient functionality.[140] Since teachers are already being paid to educate males, the Athenian Stranger decides that, for nearly the same cost, females should also be educated. Society will reap a double benefit. This economic use of the sexes, here called 'utilitarian', hedges on universal suffrage but falls rather short of the mark.

Magnesia will save resources through another form of sexual 'equality' by mandating that its women dine alongside men at the communal messes (συσσίτια) rather than each household preparing individual meals at home.[141] The Athenian Stranger finds the common meal to be a useful means of training his hypothetical citizens in the inculcation of civic virtues. While most notably found amongst the Spartans, common meals took place in many ancient Greek and other city-states as well. Communal dining appears to have existed on Krete, from which the Spartan version was possibly derived, and in Miletos, Thurii, Megara, Thebes, Oinotria, Carthage and on the island of Lipara.[142] While it is clear that this institution served a civic role of binding the community through shared meals, it also had an educational quality. The Spartan *syssition,* as Michell indicates, 'was looked upon as a school of manners and deportment' as well as a means of induction into publicly accepted modes of discourse.[143]

The Magnesian equivalent takes full advantage of this—with certain modifications. During such common messes, one might expect fellow-citizens to 'quiz' one another on various subjects relevant to civic ideology, encouraging them by repetition and the force of peer pressure. They will be under especially heavy scrutiny whilst they dine and 'train'. Magnesian *syssitia* have at least one major difference from their Spartan counterparts. These were a form of 'institutionalised pederasty', according to Singor, and inducted youths as *erastai* from the age of twelve.[144] The educational programme incorporated into Magnesian *syssitia* will advance the official mixed-sex ethic. Same-sex intercourse is to be strongly discouraged.[145]

From the age of six, Magnesian boys and girls are to be separated during their respective educations.[146] This is designed to promote the ideal differences between the sexes and their officially approved sex roles from an early age.[147] It highlights the Athenian Stranger's plan of 'sex-role training' through controlled social interaction.[148]

But his method differs markedly from other systems. The practice of separating the sexes was also found at Athens when some upper-class boys might have gone to be taught music and the arts at about the age of six whereas the girls' 'education' from that age appears to have consisted largely of domestic duties (see above).[149] Xenophon's idealised Spartan system provides perhaps the best example of institutionalised training of women outside Plato's works—but not in the arts and sciences. The Magnesian system again appears to be more similar to that of Sparta where, according to Hodkinson, 'all girls, rich or poor, underwent a uniform, public physical training'.[150] It should be noted, however, that the precise nature of this training is a subject of debate.[151] In Magnesia, women will partake much more of the public sphere than in Athens or Sparta but they still must perform their mandated task of *teknopoiia*.

Like both the Spartan and Athenian upper-class citizenry, the Magnesians undertake their specialised pursuits and training whilst slaves perform the necessary labour. An organised regime is laid out for the Magnesian citizens including not only a comprehensive survey of the arts and sciences (πρὸς δὲ τὰ μαθήματα) but also, *mirabile dictu,* the use of weapons for both sexes.[152] The Athenian Stranger considers traditional Greek customs of education to have been largely misunderstood and therefore poorly developed. When Kleinias the Kretan inquires about these 'misunderstood customs', he explains that he is referring specifically to the training of young people of either sex in the use of weapons and their methods of practice.

In Magnesia, all youths are to be trained to use weapons ambidextrously.[153] The Athenian Stranger seems to think that ambidexterity can be taught if encouraged from an early enough age. The children's nurses are under orders to ensure 'that all the boys and all the girls will have feet and hands that are ambidextrous'.[154] This is thought to give them an advantage in fighting. 'If someone should grow up', says the Athenian Stranger, 'possessing the nature of a Geryon or a Briareus, such a one should be able to hurl a hundred javelins with his hundred hands'.[155] Male and female officials are to be appointed to keep watch over children's studies and to observe their games. These 'war games' and other martial practices figure prominently as an essential feature of young Magnesians' psychosexual development. In addition to physical training, they also serve to define many of the characteristics of their respective sex roles.

While there can be little doubt that the social systems of Sparta and Krete left a positive impression on Plato, he seems to have regarded them as being, as Rawson says, 'on the right lines but too obsessed with war'.[156] Magnesia will not be obsessed with conquest, as we have seen, but military training figures prominently into its pedagogical regimen. Women of the second-best *polis,* similar to Spartan women, will not neglect the arts of war in their education.[157] However, unlike most women in the ancient world, they are to have the opportunity to be taught on an equal footing with men. Those female Magnesians who display an aptitude for these subjects will be singled out for training 'while still girls and when grown to womanhood' (except during their mandatory childbearing years), at state expense, for military service. This is for their own educational benefit and the common defence of the *polis*.[158]

Their training includes military drills, forming marching ranks and the bearing of arms. These and other practices add elements perceived to be 'masculine', in the traditional sense, to the sex-role that has been reformulated for Magnesian women. It comes at the loss of other, more traditionally 'feminine' traits deemed undesirable.[159] This plan (though radical in its outcome) is clearly predicated on traditional stereotypes that are revealed in the Athenians Stranger's use of language. If they were not so educated then, he says, whenever danger threatens 'they would flee to the temples, massing around every altar and shrine, and drown the race of humankind in the disgrace of being the most craven of all creatures in nature'.[160] This is intolerable for the female citizens of the second-best state. Its women must be equipped to defend their homeland.

The education afforded Magnesian women is remarkable. In addition to the spear and javelin, they may also practice the art of horseracing if they choose.[161] The Athenian Stranger envisages *en masse* military manoeuvres involving 'men, women, and children'.[162] Magnesian women may celebrate martial deeds in song and will be eligible to receive state honours on the same footing as men.[163] This is not insignificant. The military plays a key part in terms of indoctrination, social control and scrutiny. Again, we need to bear in mind that Magnesia is not meant to pursue military conquests.[164] Despite the pacifist foreign policy, there will be numerous soldiers in the second-best state. Many of them also serve the efficient function of policing the civilian populace. At once these engines of social control afford some degrees of sexual equality whilst at once limiting individual freedoms for both sexes. The Magnesians will be subject to many controls and regulatory influences. The Athenian Stranger's deliberate inclusion of women in the military, especially in terms of its educational aspect, is more economical than egalitarian.

The Magnesian education is the principal instrument of social conditioning and it is designed to undertake this role with uncanny sophistication. It places much greater emphasis on the scrutiny and management of its youths during the course of their education than was apparently the case in any other ancient Greek city-state including Sparta. The Athenian Stranger's methods are, nonetheless, compatible with Spartan customs in terms of dealing with the high-spiritedness of youth through agencies of socialisation. 'The Spartans', as Powell says, 'recognise the intense wilfulness of that age, its particular tendency to commit *hybris* and its especially strong craving of pleasure; least leisure is allowed and the greatest number of strenuous activities is imposed'.[165] Magnesia's policy of holding the wilfulness of youth in check, as with the communal messes, is designed to promote harmony within the city amongst its citizens.[166] This peaceful state of affairs should furnish sufficient leisure for the adult citizen populace (and especially older citizens) to engage in those pursuits that the Athenian Stranger has deemed virtuous. Activities such as 'sham fights' and other martial training promote physical development whilst suppressing *hybris* through keeping the youths busy. They will also be ready for invasion if necessary.

There is a clear division of the sexes observable in the martial realm. Elements of choice and compulsion apply in different ways to both sexes. Certain educational activities are to be compulsory for males but, to some degree, optional for females. It is a point of inequality that underlines Magnesia's basic ideology. Citizen males are to be sent to 'the teachers of horsemanship, archery, javelin throwing and slinging' whether they particularly want to go or not—and they will be encouraged from an early age that it is virtuous and manly to desire to do so. Magnesian females are to learn all the arts and sciences, just as their male counterparts. However, as we have seen, they have a choice in terms of their military training.[167] The line appears to be drawn roughly around the age of the *ephēbeia* where young Magnesian men must perform their military service and women must begin considering the prospects of *teknopoiia* (760b). Female citizens will have the right to undertake a similar *ephēbeia* 'if they are at all agreeable to it', but they are required to spend at least a whole decade of their lives in the act of producing and rearing children before embarking on any potential military career. That option does appear to be open to them after having birthed the requisite number of offspring.

This disparity between the compulsory military education of male citizens and the optional one for females is clearly due to the fact that women are the ones who necessarily bear children. Since 'the age limit of marriage for a girl is to be from sixteen to twenty years of age' and for men thirty to thirty-five (752b2–9), it stands to reason that a Magnesian female might be getting married and starting a family at the same time as her male age-mates would be out learning the javelin and horsemanship. Despite the degrees of equality extended to Magnesian women, the 'products' of their labour, as Rosaldo says, 'tend to be directed to the family and the home'.[168] Since they will be prepared for their role as 'mother' from an early age, one expects that the significance of *teknopoiia* will comprise a major portion in their socialisation. It defines many of the limits of their femininity and imposes implicit and explicit assumptions that accompany their sex.[169] That is, their role in society will almost always be contingent on their maternal function. A major portion of a man's idealised sex-role, in turn, stands in relation to this as the paternal counterpart.

A Magnesian woman could perhaps postpone her wedding at least until the age of twenty and use that time to learn more than the rudiments of warcraft. Thereafter she would be pressed into the service of producing children. The Marriage Supervisors and Guardians of the Laws will enforce this. These women will have an especially potent influence on young brides.[170] Their role is also educational. In addition to monitoring and extolling the accepted feminine virtues, the Marriage Supervisors—

themselves mothers—will also provide them with an experiential model for imitation.[171] Being young and impressionable, they may develop relationships of emotional attachment to them and will probably identify their own roles through them.

Whilst pregnant or busy with the work of rearing children, a Magnesian woman would be in no physical condition to partake of a military career. However, after having given her mandatory ten years of service to the city-state as a mother of children, she could then potentially choose to learn more martial skills if she so wished. This might be the Athenian Stranger's intent since the Guardians of the Laws, who should theoretically have the most intense military training, must be over the age of fifty (755a), and therefore in the particular case of women would be beyond the age of mandatory childbearing. There is every indication that the only Magnesian women who will be able to participate in the public sphere of military and state activity would be either un-wed heiresses and, perhaps more likely, women who have passed the childbearing age. This is a profound statement of the importance of *teknopoiia* as the defining factor of a Magnesian woman's sexual identity and role in society.

Something further needs to be said about Magnesian 'music'. As part of their *curriculum* in the 'arts and sciences' (πρὸς δὲ τὰ μαθήματα) introduced above, Magnesians will study music, poetry and literature. This increased emphasis on letters varies considerably from the approach espoused by Xenophon's Sokrates who favoured only the most cursory exposure to these subjects.[172] The Athenian Stranger deems them to be essential to education especially in its early stages. Magnesia's state and religious officials will regulate all subject matter. He has indicated that the types of music to be taught must be carefully chosen according to their moral value as they provide paradigms for the citizens to imitate.[173] This concurs with a similar Isokratean pedagogical view expressed when he, as Beck says, 'adjures Demonicus to acquaint himself with the best things in the poets, should he aspire to nobility of character'.[174] Magnesia's system, although its aims are comparable, is less inclined toward rhetoric than that of Isokrates.[175] As Nightingale indicates, the imitation of 'good' models represents the first stage of Platonic education and is compatible with similar Athenian ideals. At secondary and post-secondary levels however, as will be shortly considered, Plato's approach aims to detach the capable student from the material realm and to train him/her in logic and abstract thinking along specific lines.[176]

The musical regimen of Magnesia ought to be, as Bury says, 'used as an ennobling educational instrument, promoting self-control'; it must not excite 'vulgar sentiment and passion'.[177] Different songs and dances will be chosen according to their rhythm, meter and content so as to properly correspond with the sex of the individuals learning them. The songs for men must embody characteristics such as 'magnificence and that which inclines toward courage' (ἀνδρεία).[178] They will impart appropriately masculine values.[179] The ones for women will favour 'that which is orderly and moderate'.[180] Both types of song denote the ideal modes of behaviour that the Athenian Stranger prefers to associate with either sex respectively.[181] In modern terms, these sanctioned paradigms expose the Magnesians to psychodynamically experiential forces, through the media of public performance, which are designed to shape their sexual roles from an early age.[182]

Magnesian boys and girls put on armour and perform choral dances both to entertain the public as well as to hone their individual fighting skills.[183] These armed performances appear to have been derived in part from the Kretan 'games of armour' of the Kuretes, the games of the Spartan Dioskuri (Kastor and Pollux), and those of Athena the Virgin at Athens.[184] There are two kinds of dances identified in the *Laws* as beautiful: the warlike *Pyrrhic* and the peaceful *Emmeleia*. The *Pyrrhic* which represents the 'motion of fighting, and . . . of fair bodies and brave souls engaged in violent effort', is specifically devised to impart courage. The *Emmeleia*, or pacific dances, signify 'the motion of a temperate soul living in a state of prosperity and moderate pleasures' and, as such, they represent the underlying the morality of Magnesia.[185] Indecent dances are identified as those that concern ugly bodies and reflect negative mentalities along with those that incline one toward comic laughter.[186] This compares well with the musical education in the Republic and generally follows Sokrates' discussion there.[187] The Athenian Stranger has addressed regulations for female performances and male performances, necessarily based on their sexual differences. Idealised masculine and feminine characteristics are identified. The rhythms and modes of musical accompaniment are designed to impart these characteristics through the process of imitative learning.

The initial music of Magnesia's official canon will be chosen by a select group of citizen-men over fifty who may consult with the composers but hold the final say themselves.[188] Once the songs and dances have been chosen, they must remain rigidly unchanged unless the Vigilance Committee decides it is appropriate to alter them. New ones may be introduced only if they adhere to the established doctrines and gain official recognition. Those that somehow attain inclusion later must bear considerable resemblance to the accepted musical canon. Strong restrictions are placed on those who compose music, poetry and literature to ensure that they do so according to state's high standards. No composer or author will be allowed to show their works to other citizens until these have met with the approval of the appointed musical judges, the *archōn* of Education and the Guardians of the Laws.[189] The Athenian Stranger indicates that he will employ a technique developed by the Egyptians in order to prevent novel and harmful types of music from corrupting the prescribed regimen.[190] The rules of music and dances, as with all of Magnesia's laws, will be consecrated to the gods and divine spirits. Altering them in any way without the sanction of the state and its religious leaders may result in the offender being excluded from ceremonies. If the malcontent persists in this subversive enterprise, he or she will run the risk throughout their whole life of being prosecuted for an act of impiety.[191]

Magnesian children of both sexes learn music from an early age through their mandatory attendance at religious festivals with parents and nurses. Later, they will be taught letters for three years from the age of ten and lyre playing from the ages of thirteen to sixteen (809e8–810a3).[192] The Athenian Stranger says that, 'as regards letters, they must work to become sufficiently able both to read and to write', but those whose progress is slower will not be required to learn to read swiftly or to write beautifully (810b1–5). This is consistent with his policy of keeping track of citizens' capacities to learn, mentioned above, and educating each according to his/her perceived abilities.

Some of the subject matter for Magnesia's schools will include philosophical discourses along with other poetry and prose that is similar in character.[193] Magnesia's canon of pedagogical texts would appear to have all of the works in the Platonic *corpus,* excluding perhaps his personal correspondences, but including the *Laws* itself. One assumes that such works as the *Apology, Crito* and *Euthyphro* would comprise one level of education, according to the students' capacity or degree, whereas the *Republic, Statesman* and *Timaeus* would probably make up another, higher level. If the teachers do not happen to approve of these literary choices and do not make an effort to learn them, they will not be permitted to teach. But one expects that they would have been carefully screened before being allowed to practice their craft in Magnesia. The canon of texts is to be vigilantly monitored along with all material that students read in general. They are not to memorise and recite a wide variety of material lest it imbue them with conflicting and potentially dangerous ideas inured by contradictory poets.[194]

Plato has apparently recognised, long before Chomsky, that institutions of learning may serve as an effective 'filtering system for alternative truths'.[195] The inclusion or exclusion of given ideas in accredited schools allows the *polis* a powerful lever with which to affect public control. This power of censorship applies to all media and would appear to be especially true in terms of the presentation of sexuality in its officially accepted form—as seen in the types of song mentioned above. The Athenian Stranger applies this principle of ideological censorship to most aspects of his educational regimen. Potentially 'dangerous' subjects merit close regulation by the Magnesian legislators in a manner strikingly similar to that of the *Republic.* In both it and the *Laws,* according to Golden, 'aesthetics subordinates itself to a morality that is itself the handmaiden of a rigidly defined ontological conception of the universe'.[196]

Dramatic performances in particular that come from outside Magnesia are to be highly suspect and safeguards will be employed against the threat of foreign artistic influences that could 'damage' the Magnesians' *psychai.* There is a notable difference here inasmuch as some dramatic modes are to be granted a degree of legitimacy in the second-best state that was altogether absent from the *Kallipolis*.[197] The Magnesians will study their own laws as a means of improving civic virtue and their ability to discern the various *logoi* with the aid of philosophical reason (957c–d). This will provide them with an 'antidote' (*alexipharmakon*) against alien discourses and it recollects Sokrates' statements on the nature of written texts as 'drugs' (*pharmaka*) that influence the *psychē* in the *Phaedrus*.[198] The Magnesians will memorise the lawcode and study the official canon of literature, as Nightingale says, so that they 'can serve as an ever-present standard for measuring all other modes of discourse and thought'.[199]

As part of their education, it will be necessary for the citizens to learn about comedy so that they know to avoid imitating such ludicrous behaviour themselves.[200] The rationale is scrupulously didactic and, as Golden says, comedy is permitted only due to 'the necessity of learning the nature of the noble through the nature of its opposite, the ridiculous'.[201] As with other types of employment, citizens will not be allowed to become actors since this is deemed to be harmful to their pursuit of *aretē*. Slaves and foreigners will be hired to perform in this capacity. Anyone who writes a comedy for Magnesia (and he appears to be referring to citizens here) must be over the age of fifty and gain the approval of the *archōn* for Education (829c–d, 936a–b). Aspiring authors must also have attained some esteem in the eyes of the city before they will be permitted to undertake the writing of a Magnesian comedy (829c–d). 'Only the "good" may write comedies', as Nightingale says, 'presumably because they alone will use ridicule correctly'.[202]

As concerns the genre of drama in general, 'no serious attention should be granted to it nor should any free man or woman be seen learning it' for purposes of imitation (816e8–11). One wonders whether any of the Magnesians would have the encouragement or the inclination to compose drama. Any citizen who chooses to do so must be mindful of public scrutiny. They would probably not be expected to take their dramatic interests too seriously except insofar as they produce an officially acceptable script. Their particular style of dramatic writing must be particularly virtuous.[203] While the Athenian Stranger does allow for this eventuality, he is insistent that the comedies must 'never be allowed to ridicule any of the citizens, either in words or by way of *mimēsis*, whether it be with or without passion' (μήτε θυμῷ).[204] Neither should the audience derive too much pleasure from these productions.[205] Only non-citizens or purely fictional characters that have no discernable analogues in Magnesia may be subject to comedy's piquant wit. These must be moderate and there is every indication that mockery will not be permitted at all in Magnesian comedies.[206]

As Nuttal says, 'Plato feared poets because it seemed to him that they told lies and whipped up irrational emotions'.[207] He appears to have somewhat revised his views in the *Laws*—this time keeping the poets tightly on a leash. The Athenian Stranger, in significant shift from the stance of Sokrates in the *Republic*, indicates that some poetic works of tragedy and serious drama may be acceptable so long as they do not teach harmful lessons that might destabilise the Magnesian peace.[208] He has composed some lines to address any would-be dramatic performers who seek a stage in Magnesia, saying:

> Most excellent of strangers, we ourselves, to the best of our ability produce tragedy altogether the fairest and the best; indeed all our constitution has been framed as a representation of the most beautiful and best life that, in reality, we assert to be the truest tragedy (817a9–b6).

This preamble to the law may be just another 'fable', a *paramyth* designed to back up state policy as being for the benefit of the populace.[209] But it appears to serve more than a propagandistic function. It may be read as a statement of belief that holds Magnesia and its laws to be the paradigmatic expression of aesthetic and philosophical virtue—a paradigm compared to which and with regard to which all other (lesser) works of art must be judged. Nightingale favours such a proposition. 'Here', as she writes, 'Plato not only denies that tragedy is truly "serious," but confers on his own creation the title of serious tragedy'.[210] Platonic 'tragedy', as Golden indicates, 'represents a triumph over the traditional tragedy of pity and fear', rather, it points 'toward what is true and good'.[211] In a political respect, a comparison may be drawn between the Athenian Stranger's speech and Perikles' funeral oration in which the Athenian constitution was referred to as both a model for (as well as an 'education' to) all the Greeks.[212]

Magnesia, unlike Athens, has sterner safeguards to protect its 'truest tragedy' of a constitution. Before a dramatic piece may be performed, it must first meet with the approval of Magnesia's rulers. To do so, it must not challenge any of the city's laws, institutions, ideals or values.[213] This suggests that only select tragedies composed for Magnesia by Magnesians could be performed. When it portrays human sexual relations, the drama and literature that is permitted must uphold officially sanctioned mores along with officially permitted expressions of 'cultural fantasy' and erotic ideals. Since mixed-sex coupling within the legitimate bonds of marriage is the preferred form of sexual expression, the accepted literary and dramatic canon must encourage this model. This will influence the psychological development of the Magnesian citizens so that they, as Chodorow says, 'are likely to build such norms (directly or indirectly, positively or negatively) into their sexual orientation and object choice'.[214]

The dramatic and literary arts are not the only ones to be carefully regulated by the Magnesian state. The Athenian Stranger indicates that some sciences may be suitable for certain students, but an in-depth study of them would be unsuitable for others. This higher learning entails the intensive study of logic, arithmetic, measuring the length and surface of solids and the motions and courses of the stars (817e6–818a1).[215] These subjects will be studied to some degree by all students during their time in Magnesia's schools and, as such, fit into the overall *curriculum* of the

Magnesian education. However, their intensive study is limited only to those students who demonstrate a natural aptitude for them. This will be identified at an early age and encouraged along specific lines of development. 'Indeed', says the Athenian Stranger, 'the majority should not labour to grasp all these subjects with precision, rather, only a certain few' (818a1–3). Later we learn that these special students are the ones being groomed to serve as Guardians of the Laws and members of the Vigilance Committee (962c, 965a sq.). They alone have the fullest and most complete education over and above their fellow Magnesians.

The Athenian Stranger proposes a revised version of the aristocratic *symposion* for the second-best *polis*.[216] The Magnesians are not permitted to partake of alcohol until the age of eighteen and are encouraged to drink only in moderation until old age.[217] The controlled drinking party is an institution designed to train them in proper modes of behaviour. It will educate the citizens into being courageous in the face of physical danger and to discourage them from illicit pleasures.[218] A good legislator is thought to be able to make a person proof against all manner of things (of the first kind, i.e. of dangerous people and things), says the Athenian Stranger 'by putting him into a state of fear within the strictures of law' (647c3–4). This is half the battle. They may overcome cowardice when faced with peril but must also learn to be moderate (σώφρων—647d3–4) and have self-control sufficient to stave off the desires for activities deemed shameless.[219] The primary purposes of the educational *symposia* are to promote the official values associated with *sōphrosynē* and to encourage *andreia*. Three powerful forces will be brought to bear in achieving this end: fear, shame and calculation.[220] Shame, through dishonour (or the threat thereof), figures prominently in the equation.[221] The Athenian Stranger notes that drunken individuals sometimes require strong negative reinforcement such as the threat of displeasure from officials who have some control over their daily lives along with the public reproach that this accrues.

The Athenian Stranger's method has particular recourse to the socially influential forces of shame and fear. In Magnesia, the 'best people' are said to hold 'φόβος in the greatest esteem, calling it αἰδώς'.[222] This reflects both Spartan and traditionally Homeric values associated with accepted social behaviour.[223] It is perhaps another example of the ongoing programme of *Lakonisation* in Magnesia. Xenophon wrote of Sparta that 'there, great *aidōs* stands beside great obedience'.[224] A kind of 'shame-culture' featured prominently in Spartan civic ideology. *Aidōs* entails the fear of public censure for breaching accepted protocols. It served in many Greek *poleis*, as Richer says, as an 'embedded means' of controlling citizens' behaviour.[225] In Sparta, the privileged relationship of *phobos* with the authoritative *ephors* is underscored, as Mactoux indicates, by 'the spatial contiguity of the place where ephoric power was exercised' and the temple of deified *Phobos*.[226] The Athenian Stranger recognises how potent a force such as shame/modesty can be when yoked with religious and state authority. '*Aidōs/aischunē* are here persistently related to fear of the external sanction of disgrace', as Cairns says, 'but the creation of a sense of *aidōs* which can withstand the influence of alcohol also suggests the acquisition of an instinctive disposition towards self-control'.[227] This, in concert with carefully administered calculation, will advance the Magnesian ethic of *sōphrosynē*.[228]

In order to achieve complete courage (ἀνδρεία), according to the Athenian Stranger, the citizens should be exposed to temptations in a controlled context similar to military training. They must overcome 'the manifold pleasures and desires that exhort one to behave shamelessly (ἀναισχυντεῖν) and to do injustice' (ἀδικεῖν— 647d4–5). This recalls the equation between the excessive partaking of pleasure and the sort of negativity perceived in femininity.[229] The desire to engage in same-sex intercourse, for example, is particularly identified as both shameless and immoderate.[230] The supervised *symposion* provides an ideal venue for inculcating appropriate values and discouraging behaviour deemed inappropriate.

The Athenian Stranger maintains that, when they have practised sufficiently, they will build up resistance to the effects of drink. Learning self-discipline under these constraints is thought, by extension, to reduce the likelihood of their indulging in excesses under normal circumstances. Having suffered together through the *symposion,* the Magnesians are seen to benefit from an increased concord: they will all be 'drinking buddies' with a firm foundation of friendship. They will have proven themselves to be good citizens too if 'they were interacting through the entire party according to the rules (κατὰ νόμους), and were obedient whenever the sober directed the drunk' (671e9–672a3).

An official observes the interactions of his subjects who are exposed to the fear-causing *pharmakon.*[231] He engages in 'encouraging, admonishing, rewarding and punishing' them until they behave appropriately. The sober *symposiarch* deploys the forces of fear, shame (modesty—fear of censure) and calculation at his disposal. He/ she has the authority of both age and position from which to dole out either rewards to those who behave properly or punishments (through dishonour and the resulting shame of public reproach) for those who refuse to submit to authority. 'Disobeying his orders', as Lissarrague says, 'results in exclusion from the banquets, hence social isolation'.[232] This sort of psychologically harsh penalty is typical of Magnesian policy.

Immoderate sexual pleasures are especially targeted. These must be tightly controlled. The only officially acceptable form of sexual expression is that between a man and a woman within the sanctioned bonds of matrimony. There is every indication that male participants in the *symposia* will be encouraged to recognise women as the appropriate objects of legitimate sexual desire on which to focus their moderated desire for pleasure.[233] It is not stated, but female participants will probably experience comparable sex role instruction in their separate *symposia*. They will all be strongly discouraged from choosing partners of the same sex.[234] Those who fail to do so will be identified and presumably dealt with. Both Kleinias and the Athenian Stranger agree that this process could serve as an 'acid test' that would benefit the *polis*. Megillus the Spartan is notably laconic throughout the discussion and drops out altogether from lines 642d4, in Book I, to the middle of Book III—including all the discussions that take place on controlled drinking parties and same-sex intercourse.[235]

The Magnesian *symposia* are perceived as a benefit to citizens that will help them hone and improve their skills of moderation—providing they succeed in meeting the criteria that have been established for judging their courage and self-control (or likewise their 'cowardliness/unmanliness quotient'). As a test, they will also identify and catalogue those with cowardly natures and thus provide a sort of index of courage/manliness, and the lack of such qualities, that also tracks those who reveal signs of 'inappropriate' sexual desire. It will provide a handy compendium of psychological profiles of the subjects involved and this presumably includes all citizens.

The Athenian Stranger maintains that the test could work on groups of people of different numbers from 'one to a few to as many as one might desire' (648c8–d1). It will be like a normal *symposion* or *andron*—but with a twist. He has taken a traditional cultural practice, which doubtless served its own purposes of socialisation, and turned it into a proper 'engine' of social control and induction into the political community of Magnesia.[236] '*Symposia* were not in themselves political;' as Murray states, 'indeed they are connected with politics only in the sense that the *hetaireia* begins from the drinking group, and is based on relations formed in the *symposion*'.[237]

The Athenian Stranger points out some of the effects of drunkenness with great accuracy.[238] His account focuses particularly on the loss of inhibition under the influence and how this can reveal the participants' true nature. As Lissarrague indicates, Plato's narrator 'claims that wine can disclose another's character'.[239] A keen observer may perhaps note certain motivations and desires present—hitherto submerged by the harnesses of sober self-restraint. A drunken individual, with inhibitions lessened by the effects of alcohol, might act out such illicit inclinations in the presence of others and so reveal his or her hidden qualities. (Hence the later Roman axiom: *in vino veritas*.) The Athenian Stranger suggests that an untested person who secretly harbours excessive desires might wait for an opportune and clandestine moment to act on them. Such a person might cheat, steal or rape secretly away from the condemning eyes of society, and is thus regarded as shameless.[240] The controlled drinking party is seen as a way of preventing this.

Plato's narrator anticipates that a broader approach, akin to the supervised *symposion,* could be implemented on his hypothetical populace at large.[241] He has introduced a means of psychological manipulation that is embedded in state institutions and designed to enforce the official value system. Many of Magnesia's laws and customs, not unlike their Spartan equivalents, deploy elements of shame and the fear of shame as negative reinforcements to ensure obedience.[242] As Cairns indicates, 'we are dealing with a concept of *aidōs* that is comprehensive in its scope, covering both respect for one's fellows and one's superiors and consciousness of one's own status as affected by the opinions of fellows and superiors'.[243] The controlled drinking party provides a venue in which Magnesia's citizens may be educated (or inculcated) into a particular mode of discourse and ideology. The fact that this is to be accomplished largely through the employment of powerful psychological pressures of a potentially insidious nature does not seem to concern Plato's narrator.

The Athenian Stranger may have anticipated George Orwell by two and a half millennia in terms of their mutual agreement that there will arise those in society who tend to be 'more equal' than others.[244] He sometimes refers to this as the 'rule of symmetrical inequality'[245] and it applies to many things.[246] The 'best of the best' in Magnesia occupy the highest offices in the land. It is they who will be afforded the most comprehensive form of education available. This class of rulers includes the Guardians of the Laws and the members of the *nukterinos* council. The education of the former is the same as that of the latter up to a point. They, however, will be expected to continue their studies in greater depth. Their preparation closely parallels that of the Guardians of the Laws and the Philosopher Kings/Queens of the *Republic*. As with these, the Magnesians are not limited by sex in the choice of officials for duties of state administration.[247]

The σύλλογος νυκτερῖνός, or 'Vigilance Committee' as Luc Brisson has called it, will be made up of ten of the most senior Guardians of the Laws and the *archōns* of Education past and present.[248] Magnesia is a gerontocracy, comparable in many ways to Classical Sparta, and its elderly leadership exert considerable regulatory power over all state institutions such as education, choruses, music, educational drinking parties and others that inculcate morality.[249] This synod of Magnesia's elders has a more intense and deeper education than the majority of their peers (965a7–9). The ranks from which they are chosen constitute a class unto itself having been especially trained from birth for their future role in government.

The Athenian Stranger indicates that a list must be kept of the intellectual and moral capacities of eligible citizens from whom to draw the Guardians of the Laws and thence the *nukterinos* council (968c9–d3). Part of their special educational regime requires them to travel abroad in order to observe the laws and customs of other peoples. They will return and make their reports to the sitting Vigilance Committee. On reflection, some of these foreign practices may be applied to Magnesia as is deemed appropriate (951a sq.). This freedom to travel and learn will be granted only to senior Guardians of the Laws and magistrates.[250]

Many aspects of the Vigilance Committee's education are omitted from the *Laws*. We are told some of it and may deduce much of the rest. Their command of the arts of statecraft must necessarily be excellent since they must be better versed in the letter and spirit of Magnesia's laws than most. The members of the *nukterinos* council are to 'posses a more accurate grasp of *aretē*, both in word and deed, than the majority of people' (964d4–5). It follows that they, above and beyond all others, should uphold Magnesia's sexual mores in exemplary manner. They must be paragons of civic virtue. In order to achieve this extraordinary status, they undergo intense training and scrutiny for at least five decades. One of their primary subjects of study will be dialectics. They have to understand that the four virtues of Reason, Courage, Moderation and Justice are truly one virtue and 'how this is so'.[251] They must pay attention to the many, but always strive for the 'One'. Although the word 'dialectic' is not actually employed in the Athenian Stranger's discussions here or elsewhere in the text, the method of practice that he has outlined is unmistakable.[252]

The rulers of Magnesia must also be able to relate their philosophical insights on 'the Beautiful and the Good' to the practice of governance.[253] This represents one of the more esoteric aspects of their education and clearly distinguishes them from the rest of the citizenry who, we are told, 'follow only the pronouncements of the laws'.[254] The Vigilance Committee's candidates undertake a thorough study of divine matters so that they might come to an understanding of the mysteries of philosophy. Some of these the Athenian Stranger has discussed in Book X, but it appears likely that they will utilise other Platonic resources as well.[255] None of the representatives of the upper classes of Magnesian society may serve even as a Guardian of the Laws unless he/she has first learned the basics of cosmology and metaphysics.

The Athenian Stranger mentions several subcategories of this education in 'divine matters' that will bring about a superior skill of governing for the members of the Vigilance Committee and, to a lesser degree, the Guardians of the Laws. A primary feature is *psychical* metaphysics, or the nature of souls. They must learn that the soul is the most ancient and divine (πρεσβύτατόν τε καὶ θειότατον) of things whose motion (κίνησις) is engaged in 'perpetually providing being'.[256] They should understand that the soul is immortal, reincarnates and 'rules over all bodies'.[257] Since the motions of celestial objects are caused by Soul and governed by Reason, they also undertake a rigorous study of astronomy, geometry and other such sciences that demonstrate this divine principle.[258] Finally, they must attain a intense comprehension of musical theory and then be able to 'apply it harmoniously to the institutions and rules of ethics'.[259] This esoteric learning of metaphysical matters appears to be a primary dividing point between the upper and lower echelons of the Magnesian government since any who cannot grasp these deeper things will be limited, at best, to lower-level bureaucratic positions.

In conclusion, the Magnesian education is designed to be fairly comprehensive—even by modern standards. It begins earlier than virtually any other known educational system available in Plato's era and includes subjects that would be both familiar and unfamiliar to his contemporaries. Plato's pedagogical approach in the *Laws* places considerable emphasis on the sciences and those subjects that today we might designate as the 'liberal arts'. The Magnesian education comes at state expense and, whatever else its goals may be, it is designed to promote literacy and numeracy for all citizens.[260] This is a remarkable proposition given the era in which it originated. Primary education is to be available to members of both sexes at all levels and includes, for those with the aptitude for it, the option of post-secondary training in many subjects. Arguably, the Magnesian education favours males over females by way of the limitations imposed on the latter through the state-mandated necessity of childbearing. More or less equal educational opportunities are ultimately afforded both sexes—even if the women who want to do so may have take up their advanced military training up to ten years later than the men.

The educational system of Magnesia appears to have its roots in the earlier values of the idealised, aristocratic Old Education. There are numerous aspects of the Athenian democratic education and especially of the systems of Sparta and Krete. Magnesia is, in many ways, a selective synthesis of all these with the added element of Platonic philosophy. The sum is greater than its parts. The Athenian Stranger includes many subjects outside the aristocratic, democratic, Spartan and other *curricula*. In a sense, he has 'democratised' the idealised and aristocratic Old Education and 'aristocratised' the democratic equivalent. This also entails making all of his citizens into a 'virtuous' elite and educating them along Spartan regulatory lines.

There is a discernable stratification to the levels of the educated in Magnesia. Common citizens obtain a basic grasp of letters and arithmetic as well as a broad, if somewhat cursory, understanding of all subjects taught in schools. These comprise the largest single group. The Guardians of the Laws (including upper and lower echelon magistrates) comprise the next degree with the more thorough studies of their advanced *curriculum*. The third and highest degree of education belongs to the members of the *nukterinos* council who possess the most complex level in preparation for their important role as rulers of the second-best state. The aims of this education overall, as with most of Plato's dialogues, is to produce rational and virtuous souls whose existence will be metaphysically harmonious and spread divine virtue on Earth.

The Magnesian education takes full advantage of a range of psychological influences, such as shame and fear, which it can exert on the developing minds of its subjects. It also strives to inculcate the value of mixed-sex coupling within legitimate marriages. Many institutions of the *polis* target sexual mores and punish those who deviate. Their means are intrusive and thorough. Above and beyond his numerous innovations in pedagogy, the Athenian Stranger seems to have presaged Victorian/Judeo-Christian values of heterosexuality—without, that is, possessing the same concept. As was discussed in chapter I, the ancient Greeks behaved in a 'bisexual' manner in terms of erotic choice. Plato's Magnesian education will be one of several agencies that seek to alter this through such sophisticated techniques as performative modelling, threat of public censure and numerous other forms of psychological coercion. The legacy of Victorian pseudo-science has demonstrated the effects of a comparable practice beyond Plato's wildest dreams (although, as I will demonstrate in a later chapter, Plato did anticipate some problems with such a plan). We are now living in a culture produced by such deliberate attempts at the direct social engineering of sex and we have yet to fully comprehend the consequences.

Chapter IV
ΑΝΔΡΕΙΑ
A Special Definition for Magnesia

I deny that confidence and courage are the same thing, and it follows that those who are courageous are confident but not all the confident are courageous. Confidence, like power, may be born of skill, or equally of madness or passion. But courage is a matter of nature and of the proper nurture of the soul.

—(Plato's) Sokrates[1]

. . . in all the human societies we have ever reviewed, in every age and every state, there has seldom if ever been a shortage of eager young males prepared to kill and die to preserve the security, comfort and prejudices of their elders, and what you call heroism is just an expression of this simple fact: there is never a scarcity of idiots.

—Iain M. Banks[2]

It is the purpose of this chapter to consider the idea (and ideal) of 'manliness', as it emerges in the *Laws,* and to contrast it with relevant historical material. I will demonstrate how the concept of manliness (ἀνδρεία) is fundamental to Plato's Magnesia in many significant respects. This is a traditional Greek value, but the Athenian Stranger's definition represents a unique modification of existing cultural norms. His conceptualisation of ἀνδρεία is, as in the Greek world, strongly connected with the broader notion of ἀρετή (goodness/virtue/excellence). The versions of ἀνδρεία and ἀρετή in the *Laws,* while grounded in cultural context, are peculiar to the Athenian Stranger. As was explored in the previous chapter, Magnesia utilises sophisticated means of psychological manipulation, on a mass scale, to inculcate its accepted values. Its methodologies entail such features as, in today's terminology, sex-role stereotyping and performative modelling. Official opprobrium and the force of law enforce and promote these. Magnesia's interest in policing the sphere of civic ideas applies particularly to Platonic 'manliness'.

In the modern, industrialised West such terms as 'masculine' and 'manly' may be seen as referring to a certain psychological/physical state meant to comply with identifiable, albeit widely contested, standards. Whilst members of the female sex may sometimes be construed as 'manly' or 'masculine' (e.g. perhaps female athletes, businesswomen and world leaders), these adjectives are normatively linked with the male sex. This is part of our linguistic construction of sexuality. Numerous such sexually delineated characteristics present the males and females of a given culture with accepted paradigms for emulation. The ancient Greeks placed a somewhat greater emphasis on a naturally assumed sexual association between courage and proper modes of masculine behaviour. There were, then as now, particular and largely unwritten rules of custom that encouraged sexually specific conformity.

In the *Laws,* as in ancient Greek in general, the word for 'courage' and the word for 'manliness' are frequently one and the same. The ancient Greek word for courage (ἀνδρεία) likewise denotes manliness. The adjective (ἀνδρεῖος) can also mean 'manly' or 'masculine' in addition to such things as 'vigorous' or 'courageous'. The terms used for either concept signify accepted modes of sexual behaviour.[3] The Athenian Stranger's definition of ἀνδρεία in the *Laws* carries with it implicitly sexual characteristics in concert with the usual Platonic prescription of moderation, self-mastery, resistance to pleasures and, as such, connects with the broader concept of ἀρετή. It may be further clarified with recourse to the cultural backdrop that informed these notions.

The *Laws* proposes a society that places severe limitations on the sort of things that today we would consider essential freedoms. Magnesia's citizens, in addition to exemplifying the ideals of 'self-harmony' and 'intelligence', must also epitomise the virtue of 'freedom' as well.[4] The concept of freedom, for the ancient Greeks as for Plato, should be regarded contextually in contrast to the state of slavery.[5] Such values have been represented in ancient art, literature, history and philosophy. The ethic of manliness/courage has a high degree of consistency amongst surviving texts. Such socially accepted ideals amongst the ancient Greeks appear to have resulted in no small part from the constraints necessitated by the political circumstances of the era. 'The continued existence of a Greek city-state', as Dover says, 'depended ultimately on the military qualities of its adult male citizens'.[6] A military defeat could (and often did) result in the physical destruction of the fabric of the city itself and sometimes, in consequence, the mass slaughter of all adult male citizens and the enslavement of the women and children. Occasionally such a defeat entailed the extermination of all male children as in the mythical account of the fall of Troy.[7]

The wretchedness associated with this fate, and especially that of being enslaved, is highlighted numerous times by Hekuba in Euripides' play of the same name.[8] In his *Andromache,* considerable grief accompanies the heroines' imposed state of servitude.[9] Since these plays were performed for fifth-century audiences, we can assume that the prospect of a citizen-woman becoming a slave through conquest was regarded as one of the more horrible possibilities that could ensue from warfare—for the survivors. While women could be regarded as a type of commodity amongst the 'spoils of war', men and male children were seen as potential threats to the victors. Menelaos, about to slaughter Hektor's son Astyanax in the *Andromache*, declares that 'it is folly to let enemies born from enemies live, when it is possible to kill them and remove the fear from one's house'.[10] He, as with all of the other male offspring of Troy, must be destroyed because, as Anderson says, 'according to Menelaos' wicked logic this second child of Andromache is an enemy and a threat'.[11] Greeks of the 5th century appear to have followed this tradition to varying degrees. In war, one city-state might visit considerable violence on a conquered enemy. They would have expected no less to be visited on them if conquered. Harsh necessity demanded much in the preparation for combat and defence of the homeland.

Athens alone was at war no less than three out of every four years between 500–322bc.e.[12] One can extrapolate a comparable state of affairs in many Hellenic *poleis*. Encouragements for young men to become manly warriors must have been intense. A man's courage might especially be judged according to the state of his physical prowess and readiness for combat. His skill with weapons and his ability for wise council in those subjects that might help to ensure the state's continued survival would be highly prized.[13] A good citizen-soldier was meant to be prepared to sacrifice not only his own life, if necessary, but also to be proof against cold, heat, hunger and thirst as well as enduring without sleep or extended respite.[14] A man might have been encouraged from an early age to pattern his life after the likes of a Menelaos or a Herakles (who allegedly never shed a tear despite his misfortunes).[15] Manly men were tough and did not cry or bemoan their occasional ill fate. Living a 'soft' or luxurious lifestyle, or being brought up without the painful experiences that resulted in increased endurance could be seen as opposed to the manly ideal.[16]

It would be erroneous to speak generally of 'the ancient Greeks' as if they were a single nation-state with common values (if indeed modern nation-states may be said to share a unified value system).[17] The differences between Athens and Sparta alone reveal two quite diverse societies.[18] However, a common self-image of manliness appears to have been a unifying factor in the special relationship between the Greeks and their non-Greek, 'barbarian' neighbours. Certainly Greeks fought against Greeks in the Hellenic world and one city-state probably reckoned the manliness of its men with regard to that of its rivals.[19] If the enemy could be counted amongst the 'sons of Hellas', that was one matter. Barbarians seem to have represented a different and more intense level of *otherness*. Herodotos' account of a speech by the Athenians to a Spartan envoy, who feared that Athens would ally with Persia, encourages Greek unity against the enemy on the grounds that 'there is a Greek nation—our shared blood and language, our common temples and rituals, our similar way of life'.[20]

Aristotle provides an insight into this view in the altered political landscape of the fourth century. He asserts that 'it is right that the Greeks should rule over barbarians' since it is right for superiors to rule inferiors.[21] This has a decidedly propagandistic tone and similar expressions may have served as rallying-points for nationalistic sentiment. As Hall says, 'Greek writing about barbarians is usually an exercise in self-definition, for the barbarian is often portrayed as the opposite of the ideal Greek'.[22] Many so-called barbarians existed from which the ancient Greeks might draw their self-definition through *otherness*. However, a particular group of them seems to have been most prominent to this end. It was the wars with Persia in the early 5th century that provided the Greeks with a common foe against which to measure their collective martial (and masculine) worth. As Dover indicates, the Persian king had become 'within the space of a single generation, the heir to *all* the monarchies of the Near East'.[23] The threat of 'barbarian hordes' overrunning Greece and destroying Greek ways of life was deployed propagandistically after these conflicts were concluded.[24] This negative image of the Persians, found in Attic literature and drama in the second half of the 5th century, served to bolster support for the Athenian democracy/empire, as Nippel says, 'based upon victories in the Persian wars'.[25]

One level of this propaganda involved the assimilation of the barbarians into an effeminate abstraction that stood in sharp contrast to the opposite, masculine abstraction reserved for Greeks. It played on views about the superiority of manly self-mastery over the 'effeminate' and 'slavish' failure to be a master of self. Although the Barbarian-Greek polarity was certainly not restricted to Athens, it reveals a particularly Athenian bias.[26] The banished tyrant Hippias had brought the Persians to Marathon in 490 in an attempt to retake his lost power. 'The subsequent rise of the barbarian in the Athenian imagination', as Harrison says, 'occurred in tandem with the demonisation of Athens' sixth-century tyrants, the Peisistratids, and the development of a self-conscious democratic ideology'.[27] In this respect, perceived barbarian/aristocratic decadence is conceptually related to both the alleged crimes of Timarkhos and the Athenian Stranger's formulation against same-sex intercourse in the *Laws*.[28] Attitudes of this kind figured into the imperial and post-imperial political landscape of Athens and were therefore present in popular discourse.[29] The Persians are often represented in Greek literature of this era as being 'soft' and given to excessive luxury.[30] 'Certainly', as Briant indicates, 'the idea of the oriental courts, ruined by luxuriousness and women, formed a convenient "philosophy of history" for the Greeks, who knew that they were incapable of conquering that vast empire on their own'.[31]

The Persian barbarians were the recognised enemy of Hellas in the 5th century and that alone may have constituted sufficient cause to represent them as an inferior type. However, the actual reasons behind such a view are deeper and more complex.[32] It is clearly present in influential media such as art and literature. For example, the famous Eurymedon vase portrays, on one side, a Persian soldier leaning over with hands upraised in an expression of fear. He is shown in flowery, Asian attire. On the other side, a manly Greek approaches in plain, democratic clothes. He is reaching out with one hand apparently to grab the enemy whilst the other hand holds his half-erect penis. The inscription reads 'I am Eurymedon. I stand bent over'.[33] The viewer seems invited to understand that the Greek is about to penetrate the Persian who is displayed in a comically receptive position. One may readily draw a broader political significance from this graphic scene. 'This expresses the exultation of the "manly" Athenians at their victory over the "womanish" Persians,' as Dover says, 'it proclaims, "We've buggered the Persians!"'[34]

They were often represented in Athenian literature as having a characteristically tyrannical government that, as a consequence, made them slavish. Euripides reflects this negative portrayal (perhaps echoing the beliefs of many Greeks) with the dramatic expression that 'amongst the barbarians all are slaves but a single man'.[35] A particularly potent formula emerged as means of rallying people in support of the Athenian democracy/empire in its opposition to Persia. If the barbarians allowed themselves to be ruled by tyranny, as slaves,[36] then it was a small imaginary step to the notion that the Greeks ought to be in charge of these 'slaves'.[37] A contributing factor to this attitude was that, in Greece, many of the slaves were non-Greeks.[38]

The author of the *Dissoi Logoi*, one of the few surviving sophistic texts, argues that the different and sometimes shocking customs of other *ethnē* do not support the proposition that there are universal rules of human behaviour.[39] This insight appears to have been largely ignored. Many other sources contributed to the propagandistic discourse on Asian inferiority with sweeping generalisations based on perceived Greek norms. When Demosthenes in the 4th century pleaded for Athenian assistance for the Rhodians who were trying to liberate themselves from the Karian satrapy, he refers to them as 'slaves of barbarians, slaves of slaves'.[40] Slavery of the sort perceived to be characteristic of barbarian tyranny was essentially opposed to the dominant Athenian democratic ideology. An important claim, as Hall says, 'with which the Athenians authorised their democracy was that it ensured freedom for all, instead of the slavery they believed other political constitutions inflicted on all but the ruling elite'.[41]

The fact that the free male citizens of Athens themselves amounted to another type of ruling elite, with an abundance of slaves, both foreign and domestic, under their own subjugation, concerned them to a significantly lesser degree. Since female Athenians of the citizen class had no acceptable means of directly participating in the affairs of the *polis*, being limited to the roles of wife and mother in the *oikos*, their ability to partake of the politics reserved for the 'vigorous elite' was, in some ways, on a par with that of the resident aliens and slaves. This seems to be an integral feature to the formulation that 'effeminacy' somehow equals 'slavishness', since being like a woman in Athens also meant severely limited enfranchisement.

Homer, widely regarded by Greeks of the Classical era as a teacher of proper morals and values, upholds this connection between slavery and unmanliness.[42] 'For Zeus', says Odysseus' swineherd Eumaios, 'who views the wide world, takes away half the manhood of a man that day he goes into captivity and slavery'.[43] The fifth-century, Athenian association between barbarity, slavishness and effeminacy reveals an important set of binary oppositions.[44] The imaginary attraction of the perceived barbarian into the same subordinate sphere as women and slaves may, at one level, be regarded in terms of their mutual status as the *other* in respect to Athenian citizen-men.[45] Presumably, it was the class of Athens' ruling male elites to whom the antithesis of barbarian slavish effeminacy (e.g. ἀνδρεία) would have been a primary value.

Other works of literature illuminate this particularly Athenian mindset. The *Persians*, as Harrison says, 'provides not only a guide to the parameters of the political culture of Aeschylus' day, but also to some of the most potent themes in fifth-century Athenian self-definition'.[46] The play may be regarded as representing the struggle between democratic ideology vs. the threat of tyranny.[47] Queen Atossa's dialogue, at lines 230–45, speaks glibly of her son's plan to conquer and subjugate 'that Athens'.[48] The Greeks could imagine the sort of catastrophic changes that a Persian victory might entail. Freedom of speech, an important democratic value of the Athenians,[49] would not be possible under a Persian monarchy.[50] Their form of government was perceived as inimical to the Athenian value of *isonomia*.[51] Aeschylus' play, amongst others, represents Persian citizens as slavish presumably in consequence of their being subject to tyrannical rule.[52]

The cultural interplay between Athens and the East went significantly beyond politics, drama and history. Interestingly, Asian fashions appear to have been popular amongst certain of the Athenian elites.[53] Those who favoured them were sometimes subjected to popular scorn. As Geddes indicates, negative assumptions about 'the character of Ionian and Phrygian people were transferred to styles of architecture and music as well'.[54] Oriental products were sufficiently visible to provoke opinionated responses.[55] Plutarch tells us that the Odeon was 'said to be an exact reproduction of the King of Persia's pavilion' and, on account of this, the comic playwright Kratinos chided Perikles who had directed its construction.[56] The Spartan Pausanias, at the beginning of the 5th century, was accused of Medism in part because he had adopted a Persian style of dress and other manners. Although acquitted, he was not allowed to return to his previously high level of social standing.[57]

Standards of acceptable clothing, as with music and architecture, amount to a kind of rhetoric that, in the eye of the beholder, upholds or decries a given value system. In Athens during the 5th century, the dominant styles reflected the democratic principle of *isonomia*. This manifested through a common plainness of garb.[58]

It and other phenomena, such as the similar plainness of fifth-century funerary ornamentation, seem to reflect popular attitudes in favour of equality and against the
unequal ostentation perceived in tyrannical *poleis*.[59] Even Athenian aristocrats tended
to dress plainly when not performing ritual functions.[60] Wearing luxurious attire
in Athens might have been, at times, tantamount to loudly broadcasting an anti-
democratic protest.

The perceived negative influences of Asian music, as with clothing, relate particularly to the *Laws*. Plato, who at times shows great respect for certain Persian
traditions, seems to favour a pro-Hellenic hard-line on the matter regarding *andreia*.
As we saw in the previous chapter, the songs for Magnesian men must exemplify
'magnificence and that which inclines toward courage' (ἀνδρεία).[61] They are seen to
impart appropriately manly values by way of imitation.[62] Those for women should
characterise 'that which is orderly and moderate'.[63] They will expressly *not* be like
those found amongst Asian peoples. Rather, the music of Magnesia will probably
reflect Spartan tradition more so than any other type.[64]

In fifth-century Sparta, as Marrou indicates, 'Tyrtaeus' elegies were still the
most popular songs in the repertoire, but that was because of their moral tone and
because they made good marching songs'.[65] This type of music was designed to make
a powerful impression. 'It was a dreadful but inspiring sight', says Plutarch, 'to see the
Spartan army marching off for an attack to the sound of the oboe'.[66] Plato's musical
preferences for Magnesia least resemble the Persian styles (and evidently much of the
Athenian as well), since his narrator locates the quality of *andreia* particularly with
the Spartan tradition. It seems somehow fitting that an idealised view of the Spartans
should represent, for some, the epitome of Hellenic manliness.

We saw some of the associations in the democratic era with same-sex intercourse as a cause/product of tyranny in chapter I. As indicated earlier, something
similar seems to have happened with regard to Persian 'effeminacy'. The sort of luxurious lifestyle perceived amongst Persian elites perhaps too readily recalled the 'bad
old days' of kingships in Athens. The democratic response was to demonise things
that advertised such blatant inequality. Conveniently, it also happened to make good
propaganda for the democracy and its successors. A popular view of the Persians
seems to have resulted that portrayed them as paradigmatically opposed to Athenian
democratic values. Their perceived effeminacy was only one aspect of the equation,
but it was an important one.

The Athenian Stranger seems to be expressing the same formulation that associates Persians (barbarians) with perceived feminine characteristics in order to indicate the slavish antithesis of his ethic of ἀνδρεία. He indicates that the Persians failed
to halt their downward spiral into decadence and that they are 'currently tainted by
an excess of servitude among the populace and an excess of despotism amongst their
masters'.[67] Much of this, he maintains, has happened on account of poor education.

Isokrates agrees on this point and Xenophon corroborates the ethnographic view of Persian 'decadence' and 'slavishness' due to excessive luxury.[68]

The Athenian Stranger cites an example of the 'bad' form of upbringing as evidenced by Kyros' children who were reared in a life of luxury with disastrous consequences (694d1–8). 'It was a womanish education', says he, that made his children 'soft' and given to excesses. This stands in stark contrast to the upbringing of Kyros himself which the Athenian Stranger regards as having been sufficiently 'manly' due to the hardships that he had to endure whilst growing up under military conditions (694e1–4). Kyros, being busy with state affairs and military campaigns, 'failed to notice the corrupted education of his children by women and eunuchs'.[69] Such an unruly condition must not come to pass in Magnesia. The laws and institutions of the state prefer that all its citizenry receive an appropriately 'manly' upbringing.[70]

One can only derive so much of a context for Plato's version of *andreia* in the *Laws* from cultural sources at large. In many ways, this task is more improbable than that of simply expressing the Athenian Stranger's definition. Whilst the Athenian Stranger's attitude toward the Persians is positive at times, his definition of *andreia* draws them into a typically Athenian association between un-manliness excessive pleasure, and luxury.[71] These things are said to make a person's character 'soft' and slavish and are thus inimical to Magnesian values.[72] Plato's definition of *andreia* in the *Laws* is clearly rooted in the contemporary values of his culture and times.

There is an ancient philosophical context out of which the Athenian Stranger's approach to sexuality is partially derived. It concerns a perceived, binary opposition regarding masculine unity vs. feminine indeterminacy. This may be found in Aristotle's *Metaphysics* where he provides a review of earlier theories. There he (or his editor) has set down a 'Table of Opposites' that was allegedly advanced by the Pythagoreans and which may have found its way into the later philosophy of Plato and others.[73] It represents a paradigm that is particularly reflected in the *Laws*.[74] This table contains ten pairs of universal principles arranged in the following manner:

Limit	(πέρας)		Unlimited	(ἄπειρων)
Odd	(περιττόν)		Even	(ἄρτιον)
One	(ἕν)		Many	(πλῆθος)
Right	(δεξιόν)		Left	(ἀριστερόν)
Male	(ἄρρεν)		Female	(θῆλυ)
Resting	(ἠρεμοῦν)		Moving	(κινούμενον)
Straight	(εὐθύ)		Curved	(καμπύλον)
Light	(φῶς)		Darkness	(σκότος)
Good	(ἀγαθόν)		Bad	(κακόν)
Square	(τετράγωνον)		Oblong	(ἑτερόμηκες)

The polar relationship between 'female' and 'male', as with the other attributes listed in the columns of the Table, is not coincidental. Other aspects of this formulation regarded sexual characteristics as also being metaphysically projected onto the mathematical qualities of number.[75] Ancient numerology posited odd numbers as naturally *masculine* and even numbers as *feminine*. Plutarch (c.46–c.126 C.E.) provides further insights into this subject in his treatise *On the Letter E at Delphi*.[76] While he was writing considerably after the time of Plato and Aristotle, his numerological reasoning appears consistent with the line of thought implicit in the Table of Opposites. It is altogether possible that much of the contemporary numerology of his era was derived in no small part from it and other Pythagorean formulations. According to the Table, odd numbers share a common likeness with the male reproductive principle and even numbers the female.[77]

The placement of 'female' in the same column as the 'unlimited' (ἄπειρων), as with 'male' in the 'limited' (πέρας) column, is significant. In ancient Greek philosophy, as Lovibond indicates, the 'unlimited' can signify not only that which is indeterminate in a numerical sense (e.g. that to which no definite number has been assigned) 'but also that which is undetermined in a more general sense of being *formless*, of not possessing a definite character'.[78] If we interpret the first pair of principles in the Pythagorean Table in such a way, the qualities listed in each column take on a theme established by the initial opposition. The category of 'male' is affiliated with form and order whereas the category of 'female' is associated with the opposite tendencies—lack of order and formlessness. Femininity, thus construed, is relegated to a negative condition in the sense that it stands opposed to the characteristics of purposive, orderly activity.

This sort of mentality considers women to be *naturally* disinclined toward order. A comparable notion appears in the *Laws*. The Athenian Stranger indicates that:

> . . . not only is the disorganised supervision of women half the problem, as one might presume, indeed this female nature, as far as we're concerned, is inferior toward the pursuit of virtue to that of the male sex—in this much it differs twofold.[79]

But this notion about the 'natural' inferiority of women is introduced, seemingly, to invite its refutation. He realises that citizen-women have been severely limited in their participation in the public sphere, saying that 'the species (γένος) of our human race naturally more secretive and cunning, the female sex, because it is weak, has been wrongly left behind in a state of disorder due to the misguided concessions of the legislator'.[80] He seems to be suggesting here that the character of women is primarily due to the socialising aspects of custom (νόμος). Women are still seen as more 'naturally' inclined toward a disorderly state of the *psychē* than men but this is evidently not a terminal condition. It may be overcome through the effective instantiation of Reason's rule. Women are thought to have the ability to become virtuous on a par with men but they are perceived to have greater difficulty due to their innate femininity. Perhaps, as Lovibond claims, 'a successful outcome is equated in Plato's imagination with a successful establishment of the *male* principle in its proper position of command'.[81]

Other potentially Platonic connections with the Pythagorean Table of Opposites can be observed in both the *Republic* and the *Laws*. A prime example occurs in artistic representation.[82] Dramatic performances that might portray a woman in a state of misfortune, grief, sickness, weeping or demonstrating the 'love of childbirth' were banned from the *Republic*. They were seen as representing certain destabilising qualities that would be inappropriate for the citizenry of the *Kallipolis* (395d5–e3). Such states of mind as excessive emotionality, instability and unpredictability are considered ignoble and analogous to 'inferior types such as women, slaves and worthless mobs of men' (431b9–c3). Poetry in general is similarly targeted as dangerous since it introduces instability through vicarious experiences of excessive emotionality (605c–607a). Sokrates pointedly indicates that rationality 'is the part of a man, while the other [emotionality] is the part of a woman' (605e1). All citizens of the ideal *polis* are exhorted to guard against the lure of strong feelings.

This theme is taken up along similar lines in the *Laws*. Such emotive tragedies, of which the Athenian Stranger says 'educated' women were especially fond, along with ridiculing comedies, are banned outright from Magnesia.[83] He supports the idea of his hypothetical citizenry learning about the imitative arts of both comedy and tragedy but only inasmuch as to avoid the *mimēsis* of either. They are perceived to constitute a severe obstacle in the pursuit of *aretē* for those who are meant to be seeking wisdom.[84] The imitation of these variegated and contradictory subjects is forbidden to male and female citizens alike. They may view them with some degree of propriety, moderation and a heavy degree of state supervision. Acting in all Magnesian dramas is limited exclusively to 'slaves and strangers who do work for hire' (816e5–6). Free citizens may learn about the imitative arts, but they are strictly forbidden from engaging in their practice (816e). Perhaps it is in respect to their diversity (associated on the Table of Opposites with femininity) that dramatic performances and emotional poetry are at odds with an ideal of 'masculine' unity. The quality of ποικιλία, which makes women's experience and behaviour an interesting subject for drama, is deemed a potentially hazardous moral example for the Magnesians.[85]

The masculine norm that the Athenian Stranger espouses is expressed in terms of unity and determinacy. It may be construed as the formative force that constructs Order out of Chaos, converting a body of diverse material into a unified whole and thus representing the positive ideal. By contrast, the concept of femininity is perceived as steeped in plurality, incoherence and indeterminacy. 'Singleness' (ἁπλότης) of purpose—as with dialectics—encourages the mind to proceed from diversity to unity. Magnesia's citizens have as their mandated goal the achievement of just such a unified state of mind, with Reason ruling over the appetites and desires. Recall that slaves and metics will perform the menial tasks forbidden to citizens for whom leisure and the pursuit of *aretē* are compulsory.[86] They are to be educated into a state of 'doxastic' *enkrateia* that, as Lovibond says, is 'the practical self-mastery which is the mark of the virtuous man as such'.[87] Doxastic self-mastery is a state in which one does not readily yield to the sway of any arbitrary opinion or judgement (δόξα) that happens to occur. Impressions, intuitive judgement and appetites that easily persuade an individual are all regarded as dangerous. This condition, sometimes characterised as feminine, is seen as being opposed to self-mastery and thought to result largely from an improper upbringing.

Courage (ἀνδρεία) is a 'good' (ἀγαθός) that the Athenian Stranger claims can be generated in the human sphere by the proper application of 'divinely inspired' laws. There are 'human' goods and 'divine' ones and the former are perceived as being wholly dependent on the latter for their existence. Whoever has the greater or 'divine' goods likewise has the lesser or 'human' goods. Whoever is bereft of one of these must also lack both. 'Wisdom (φρόνησις)', he says, 'has the first place of those that are divine and rational, temperance of soul (σώφρων ψυχῆς) comes second; from these two, yoked with courage (μετ᾽ ἀνδρίας) there issues justice (δικαιοσύνη) as the third, and the fourth is courage (τέταρτον δὲ ἀνδρία—631c6–d1). A similar arrangement may be seen in the four 'cardinal virtues' of the *Republic* and elsewhere.[88] The Athenian Stranger says much about what sort of behaviour he considers 'manly' or 'courageous' and we shall presently consider this. In order to understand the concept better, however, it is worthwhile first to examine its identified opposites.

The word for unmanliness, the opposite of ἀνδρεία, may be construed as ἀνανδρία—or one of its cognates—which Liddell and Scott define as 'want of manhood', 'unmanliness' and, also, 'cowardice'.[89] There are two instances in the *Laws* where the Athenian Stranger mentions cowardice or unmanliness in passing and employs the term ἀνανδρία. Both are revealing. At 659a, he urges the hypothetical Magnesian magistrates always to make fair judgements and never to render a careless judgement 'through unmanliness and cowardice' (δι᾽ ἀνανδρίαν καὶ δειλίαν) thereby invalidating their sacred oaths.[90] It seems right here to construe this passage in this way rather than, as the Loeb edition prefers, 'cowardice and lack of spirit'.[91] Since δειλία effectively conveys the sense of 'cowardice', 'unmanliness' is a better rendering of ἀνανδρία. The connotations of 'unmanliness' are implicitly present in the Greek. We may observe, then, that Plato's narrator in the *Laws* considers the keeping of oaths and the delivering of sound judgements to be 'manly'.

This is not the only occasion where unmanliness has been directly linked to cowardice. In Book IX, the Athenian Stranger condemns those who commit suicide without the compulsion of the state or some unfortunate circumstance such as illness or extreme decrepitude.[92] The Magnesians will be told that anyone who should commit suicide for such reasons as 'laziness and the cowardice of unmanliness' (ἀργία δὲ καὶ ἀνανδρίας δειλίᾳ—873c7) is both a disgrace to his/her people and an effrontery to the gods.[93] A purification ritual will be necessary to cleanse the state of the *miasma* produced by such an act. So not only is taking one's own life without 'legitimate' cause deemed unmanly, but here unmanliness is linked again with cowardice *and,* in this instance, also with sloth.

The above two are the only instances of some derivation of ἀνανδρία in the *Laws*. Yet there are a number of other significant examples to be found throughout the Platonic *corpus* appropriate to this discussion. We can never assume with certainty that Plato ever held any of the beliefs posited by his narrators or that he did not change his view from time to time. However, there is some continuity to be found amongst the *corpus* and the case of unmanliness is no exception.[94] In the *Symposium,* Apollodoros says that a man would most fear the shame of seeming unmanly in the eyes of his beloved (178c–e).[95] In the *Crito,* the eponymous narrator states that he and his friends might seem 'unmanly' for not being more effective at saving Sokrates' life both in and out of court (45c–46a). At *Theaetetus* 176c, Sokrates indicates that all the affairs pertaining to one's soul (including ἀνανδρία) are clearly visible to the all-seeing, all-knowing divinity. At 177b4, he suggests that those who do not stand up to his dialectical interrogations are unmanly. At 203e7–8, Sokrates says that it is 'unmanly' to abandon a theory just because it is imposing or difficult.

Even more revealing passages may be found in the *Phaedrus*. The main instance occurs—not surprisingly—in the midst of a discussion on pleasure.[96] Sokrates says that a man who compulsively pursues pleasure will seek out boys for sexual liaisons who are inclined toward a 'soft (μαλακός), unmanly (ἄνανδρος) life instead of the toil and sweat of manly (ἀνδρεῖος) exercise' (239d1). The 'unmanly' boys in the *Phaedrus* are also described as putting on makeup and taking advantage of their 'natural charms' in order to appear as attractive as possible (239d sq.). Here the contrast is readily visible. It is 'manly' to sweat a lot and do hard, bodily exercises in order to keep fit. It is 'unmanly' to be 'soft' from lack of exercise and to apply cosmetics similar to a woman. This is not only true in the physical sense. One should ideally seek to impose an orderly state on the body as well as soul. The Sokratic formulation in the *Republic,* as Hobbs indicates, posits that physical, 'sensible beauty . . . is the outer expression of inner harmony and grace, and beauty and moral goodness are thus "akin" (401a8)'.[97]

The physical state of 'softness' is perceived to be a manifestation of the disorderly state of the boy's soul. The beloved in the *Phaedrus* is identified as soft and therefore not as physically well ordered as his pleasure-seeking lover. Softness of body may be regarded as the by-product of a psychological condition inclined toward sloth (with which unmanliness has been connected in the *Laws*). This 'unmanly' youth also uses cosmetics and is described possessing 'feminine' characteristics both in terms of body and mind. Being physically unfit—physiologically and psychologically feminine—means being unsuitable for battle or partaking of the vigorous affairs of the *polis*. If the pleasure-seeking lover is physically fit, then he, at least, has an advantage in this capacity. The effeminate boy is characterised as being both physically unfit as well as psychologically unprepared for the manly rigours of life. The leap from 'softness', by way of effeminacy and unmanliness, to cowardliness seems to have spanned no great gulfs for Plato or many of his contemporaries.

A similar formulation of softness=unmanliness is found within the *Laws*. As with the above example from the *Phaedrus*, those who engage in same-sex intercourse are also identified as losing virtue and becoming 'soft'. The *erōmenos* fails the test of *sōphrosynē* and both he and the consenting *erastēs* acquire softness (*malakia*) in exchange for their diminished virtue.[98] The former is accused of intemperance, and of submitting to excessive desire for pleasures because he was too 'soft' in character to be sufficiently virtuous.[99] 'Softness' within the soul is seen as utterly inimical to *aretē*. 'Manly' individuals, as Hobbs indicates, should 'not falter through softness of the soul'.[100]

Not all instances of unmanliness point to same-sex desires as the cause. Other passages throughout the Platonic *corpus* also bear brief mention. At *Gorgias* 485c–d, Sokrates criticises those grown men who lisp and play like children (and especially philosophers who do this) as unmanly. Softness of the soul is far more dangerous than that of the body; although, the sorts of habit that encourage physical softness are also perceived to incur its psychical counterpart within the soul. In the same dialogue, Kallikles (492b) condemns men who, because they are 'slaves of pleasure' and cannot attain all that they desire, hypocritically praise justice and temperance in order to advance their lot. These men are considered to be unmanly (ἄνανδροί). Only 'manly' men, Kallikles maintains, 'are wise and *andreioi* in affairs of state: such men have the strength of character to carry out their plans to completion, and not falter through softness (*malakia*) of soul'.[101]

At *Gorgias* 522d–e, Sokrates indicates that the only ones who fear dying are those who are unreasonable and unmanly. In the *Republic*, Sokrates says that no one willingly condemns justice unless they are irrational or unmanly (ἄνανδρίας—366d2). In discussing the origin of the timocratic youth, Sokrates suggests that a significant influence comes from the mother who repeatedly nags him and calls the boy's embattled father 'unmanly' (ἄνανδρος—549d–550b). In his discussion of the rise of the democratic state from oligarchy, Sokrates tells his audience that, under such conditions, temperance is erroneously considered to be 'unmanly' or to indicate a 'lack of manhood'.[102] Finally, still discussing the evils of 'democracy', Sokrates states that this degenerate form of government suffers from a malady of discontent.

This, we are told, is at least in part due to the fact that the few vigorous individuals in society come to rule over the 'less manly' (ἀνανδρότερον) who comprise the vast majority (564b).[103]

All of these examples suggest a high degree of relative continuity between the early, middle and late dialogues (and even amongst Plato's private correspondences) on the subject of unmanliness. As a negative quality, it is generally associated with such things as disorder, a lack of control over the desire for pleasure, being submissive and a follower, and sometimes effeminacy. Whether refusing to engage Sokrates in a dialectical duel, declining to approach an imposing theory, being unready for battle, forswearing sacred oaths and rendering bad judgements, or fearing to face one's inevitable demise—in all cases there is the implicit presence of a sense of cowardliness, lack of vigour, order, 'right' reason and a deficit of manliness.

The Magnesian definition of manliness is may be seen to function more directly in the context of a discussion on pleasure and pain. Groundwork for this line of thought has been laid in the *Republic* and elsewhere.[104] As a prelude to his discussion of the educational uses of the *symposion,* mentioned in the previous chapter, the Athenian Stranger examines the connections between courage (ἀνδρεία), self-control (ἐγκρα-τεία) and pleasure (ἡδονή). That which we might designate as moral courage is not to be defined merely as 'a struggle against (διαμάχην) fears and pains alone' (633c9–d1). It must also be proof against 'both yearnings (πόθους) and pleasures (ἡδονὰς)' that are 'powerful cajoling flatterers'.[105]

Again, it becomes necessary to consider counter-examples in order to approach the Athenian Stranger's intentions. Unmanly, effeminate 'softness' that evidently arises in an individual from the yielding to excessive pleasure must be avoided. Being 'soft' is an unacceptable state for Magnesian men and boys. The Athenian Stranger regards the submission to the desire for pleasures to be most unmanly. Perceived as inimical to *aretē,* this sort of behaviour is thought to assimilate one into a slavish role unsuitable for the citizens of Magnesia to emulate. The Athenian Stranger indicates that no one will credit the act of giving in to excess as a means of achieving excellence:

> On the contrary, shall all men not blame the softness (τὴν μαλακίαν) of the man who yields to pleasure and is unable to endure, and shall they not find fault with him who imitates a woman when he turns out to be most like his model?[106]

This recalls the association between luxurious living, 'softness' and effeminacy. This sort of association was, as indicated earlier, propagandistically aimed at the perceived barbarian enemies of Greece such as the Persians. The Athenian Stranger seems to have employed a fairly commonplace connection to build toward his greater discussion on pleasure. An ideal individual in Magnesia should be the opposite of 'soft' and effeminate. The ideal citizen should in no ways be a slave—except, that is, willingly subservient to Reason and the rule of Reason-based law.[107]

The theory that one should become courageous, and therefore manly, through calculated exposure to pleasure is rather striking to the Athenian Stranger's interlocutors. Megillus and Kleinias appear mystified by it. The concept of self-mastery, as integral to courage, would not have been alien to the Spartans, Kretans or Athenians.[108] The Spartans in particular were known for seeking the improvement of *aretē* through self-imposed hardship. What is unusual is the proposition that one should improve the resistance to pleasure through being exposed to it in a controlled manner. The Athenian Stranger regards pleasures as a dangerous and insidious threat to one who is striving to be virtuous. He sees it as analogous to the experience of being seized by an unconquerable fear in the midst of battle. Pleasures are perceived to have the power 'to make the spirits (θυμοὺς) waxen' in even those who consider themselves to be wise (633d2–3).

This is the basic flaw, as he describes it, in the education of citizens everywhere. In both Sparta and Krete, as well as in most Greek cities of the day, there were many and varied forms of exercise and military training (frequently compulsory) that served to toughen the youths and build up their resistances to both naturally and artificially induced pains.[109] But there seems to have existed no such system for building up their resistances to pleasures and yearnings of desire apart from the conventions of popular morality discussed above. 'Base' (κακὸν) is the man who is defeated by or yields to pain, says the Athenian Stranger, but he is also 'base' who yields to pleasures (ἡδονῶν).[110] Kleinias the Kretan, with the Athenian Stranger's approval, adds the point that 'the one ruled by pleasures' has in fact been 'shamefully (ἐπονειδίστως) conquered by himself' (633e4–5). Magnesia will employ his plan (through supervised drinking parties and other means) in order to test and hone its citizens' abilities in terms of the resistance to pleasure. This is perceived to encourage them in developing their individual *andreia*.

Pleasures, says the Athenian Stranger, are 'one's nearest (ἐγγύτατα) and most dangerous (χαλεπωτάτων) enemies' (634b5–6). He criticises the systems in Sparta and Krete that compel their citizens 'to keep away from and not to taste of the greatest pleasures and entertainments'.[111] Failure to do so leaves them unprepared for the temptations represented by such pleasures when encountered and therefore they are more inclined toward defeat. The Athenian Stranger likens one who has no training in pleasures to one who has equally poor resistance to pain. Such a one is therefore easily defeated in a conflict by those who have been better equipped against the same adversities. The one untrained against pain is perceived as becoming the slave (δουλεύσειν) of those who are better equipped in this way (635c3). Being unschooled in withstanding pleasure results in a similar state of servitude for 'they will be slaves, of a different and yet more shameful kind, to those who are able to endure manfully (καρτερεῖν) against pleasures and especially to those who have gained mastery over (κεκτημένος) them' (635d2–4). The insidiousness of succumbing to pleasure, of not having been adequately prepared against it, is said to result in an unhealthy and contradictory psycho-ethical state. Such people, he says, 'will have a soul that is in one way slave and in another way free' and this is a state deemed intolerable for citizens who are meant to be both 'manly and free' as completely as possible.[112]

The Athenian Stranger's plan for testing his Magnesian subjects' resistance to pleasure will, as we have seen in the previous chapter, incorporate supervised drinking parties. He divides the concept of courage into the standard type of fearlessness in the face of danger, etc. and into a category of self-control against indulgence in pleasures. The supervised *symposion,* like military training, involves exposure to fear that, under controlled circumstances, is thought to strengthen one's *andreia.* The *symposiarch* keenly observes the subjects reactions and strives to promote the acceptable standards of self-mastery. Weakened and reduced to a 'child-like' state by drink, they learn the appropriate responses whilst improving their capacity to resist the pleasures that are heightened by the consumption of alcohol. As we have seen, the Athenian Stranger incorporates the element of modesty/shame as a psychological reinforcement. The anticipation of disgrace and shame resulting from potentially failing the test of self-control serves to indoctrinate a set of values through psychological manipulation. The fear of reprobation thus begets conformity—although the Magnesians should ideally *be* good rather than only seem to be so.[113]

To reinforce their cooperation, the Athenian Stranger has linked drinking, through an association between the gods Dionysos and Apollo, with the *topos* of education.[114] This may represent another Spartan element, in the case of their use of the deified *Phobos,* grafted onto Magnesia.[115] Establishing a metaphysical link with moral rectitude and correct behaviour provides considerable encouragement for citizens to display the proper responses to situations officially requiring self-control. The divine connection reinforces the perceived educational aspects of social wine drinking and brings into play both psychological and religious influences on the subjects of Magnesian *symposia* in terms of their special relationship with *andreia.*

The Athenian Stranger maintains that his plan of utilising the controlled drinking party will produce stronger, more excellent and superior citizens. At least, we may surmise that they will be well versed and rehearsed in all the appropriate responses. These 'proper' responses consist of actively and successfully resisting the temptations of the flesh and to remain orderly and polite in the company of the other drunken subjects whilst being obedient to the instructions of authority. The *symposiarch,* typically one of the Guardians of the Laws, is a representative of both divine and secular power. For those who fail to excel at the proper virtues, the *symposion* functions as an 'acid-test' (βάσανος) against wrongthinking and wrongfeeling—especially as regards the accepted values of manliness and courage.

The importance of testing these traits in the Magnesians is highlighted by a fear, as we have seen, that the unmanly *psychē* of someone who is dominated by sexual pleasures (τὰφροδίσια) could make them unfit to be placed 'in charge of one's daughters and sons and wife, thus, exposing one's loved ones to risk' (650a2–4). The controlled drinking parties will provide the Magnesian government with a convenient index of psychological profiles (*andreia* quotient? *aretē* score?) to help deal with the potential problems posed by identifiably undesirable individuals. However fanciful such a proposition may seem, the Athenian Stranger means to go through with it. The ideological policing of Magnesia's special definition of *andreia,* along with its other sexual values, will be comprehensive.

As we have seen, the Pythagorean Table of Opposites, or a comparable philosophical outlook, may have informed the Platonic concept that a virtuous soul should be ruled by reason and masterful self-control. The latter, integral to understanding ἀνδρεία in the *Laws,* falls on the same side as Man, Order, Good etc. Indeterminacy, in part through the Unlimited as we have seen, is associated with Woman. It is identified as an undesirable quality in a Platonically just soul and it falls on the same side as those categories in binary opposition to Order. Magnesian women are encouraged to adopt elements that are opposed to their perceived 'nature' to overcome the indeterminacy associated with femininity. As we shall see in chapter VI, Magnesian women must become more masculine. Although the particulars of this plan are never fully explained, the Athenian Stranger's particular definition of ἀνδρεία entails *manly* self-control being asserted over *feminine* emotionality.

Ancient philosophy, as indicated above, had formulated a correspondence between sex and the perceived metaphysical attributes of arithmetical principles. However, defining such complex concepts as 'the masculine', 'the feminine' and 'the effeminate', in Plato's era as today, is no easy thing. Modern philosophy, following Hegel or Derrida, maintains that binary oppositions (such as masculine and feminine, self and other) integrally depend on their opposites for individual self-definition. The notion that the Same partakes of the Other is not modern.[116] When confronting a set of oppositions, it is often revealing to consider each in turn as fundamentally linked in terms of self-definition. Studying the identified opposite of a thing tends to achieve a greater understanding of it.

Perhaps Loraux's theory of the Feminine Operator is applicable here to an extent. This is a curious psychological phenomenon that, according to her, functioned within the ancient Greek (especially male) *psychē* in order to actualise an accepted state of masculinity. She considers this to be a driving element within the *psychē* of a man that allowed him to take on certain culturally prescribed, albeit arbitrary, characteristics that were defined as manly. What makes the operator 'feminine' is that these traits, in turn, paradoxically contain certain implicitly feminine features or perform feminine functions. Some relevant examples of this will shortly be examined.

A specific vocabulary dealing with the ideological construction of sexuality had already been developed in the pre-philosophical era of Homer. It seems to have functioned largely with reference to the behaviour of gods and heroes.[117] An ancient philosophical debate, as we have seen, later ensued concerning the importance of 'nature' (*physis*) and culture/tradition/law (*nomos*).[118] It progressed throughout the Classical era and beyond. In Classical discourse, a new civic-oriented definition began to characterise the sphere of sexuality. One 'result', according to Elshtain, 'of the Greek division and classification of cultural phenomena was the *polis,* the concept and reality of a structured body politic set off in contrast to the *oikos,* or private household'.[119]

Part of the expected duties of an Athenian citizen-male, being a representative member of the 'vigorous elite', was to play an active role in the affairs of the *polis.* For some, this would have meant the preparation for and the undertaking of warfare. For others, it meant guiding the course of the 'ship of state', in the assembly, through the hazardous waters of international and domestic politics. Many citizen-males did both. Women were, as a rule, not afforded the opportunity to do either and were not expected to be actively involved in such matters at all outside of their roles as mothers, wives and wedable heiresses. Given the circumstances, it is perhaps not surprising that the ideal traits of a citizen-male, as with masculinity in general, favoured activity, dominance, control and self-control.

Loraux's theory applies especially to politics where men who, in order to be manly, potentially take on certain 'feminine' qualities or act in 'feminine' ways. This included participation in the business of the *polis,* debating and voting in the assembly and engaging in various power struggles with other men. There were internal conflicts, competitions for status and games of dominance. This represents at least one essential side of politics, even though politics in the form of *stasis* (sedition) is endlessly refused and rejected from the city even while it took place in its midst.[120] One cannot go far in politics in any era without making enemies and this fact tends to produce conflict. There are also the interests of diverse groups to consider and where their goals may be incompatible. In short, politics is wrought with strife, discord (*eris*), *stasis* and indeterminacy (the Unlimited) on a regular basis.

Democratic governments tend to generate a venue that encourages such conflict. For an Athenian citizen-male to actualise his masculinity fully in the public sphere, he had to readily embrace chaos and discord almost on a daily basis. Plato has written a fair amount about the defects of systems of government that entail inner turmoil, such as democratic Athens, and one recurring theme is that they are considered to be altogether too disorderly.[121] He preferred to actualise his *andreia* by influencing politics indirectly either through advice (as in the case of his involvement in the affairs of Syracuse and elsewhere) or through his writings and teaching rather than by directly engaging in the chaotic fray.[122] This was an alternative route than was taken by most of his contemporaries.

'Ideally', as Loraux says, 'the exemplary *anēr* is the model of virility'.[123] Virility is the male counterpart to fertility. While virility is implicit in all external expressions of manliness, a man exhibiting ἀνδρεία outside the reproductive confines of the *oikos* may be seen as becoming somehow unsexed or sterile. When his mind and body serve only the purposes of the state, he becomes like a sexless automaton. Athens produced exemplars of ideal masculine behaviour, as Loraux indicates, such as 'the disincarnated male model exalted by the Athenian funeral oration . . . a simple support for civic behaviour, the *soma* was the city's due, and the debt was paid with the combatant's death'.[124] Achieving 'true' manliness might entail divesting oneself not only of all things seemingly feminine but masculinity as well and also of basic humanity itself. Can a man's role in politics be 'unsexed' (as she suggests) and, at the same time, reveal a Feminine Operator (as she also suggests)? This demonstrates the complexity of ancient sexuality and the dangers of attempting its explication with theories that are problematic and too narrow in scope. But Loraux appears to be on to something at least in part.

There are other places where masculinity and femininity become conflated in interesting ways. Certain myths seem to value feminine elements embedded in a masculine form and *vice versa*. There is the curious birth of the goddess Athena, fully armed, from the 'maternal' head of her father, Zeus.[125] Add to this the fact that Athena embodies the strategic and cunning qualities of warcraft as opposed to Ares' brutal carnage. An ancient Greek male should ideally be clever, like Odysseus, in order to demonstrate true *andreia*. That is, he should paradoxically imitate the characteristics of the female goddess Athena. A parallel may also be drawn here between Athena's virginity and the sterility (e.g. particularly in terms of non-productive warfare) of the public sphere of men.

The infant Dionysos being born from Zeus' manly thigh parallels the myth of his sister's birth.[126] In either of these deities' *genēsis*, we have a male god (the quintessential male god) manifesting feminine qualities in order to advance his masculine goals. Similarly, his father Kronos had held his children in his belly before Zeus freed them with the aid of the *hekatoncheires* and *kyklopes*.[127] Thus the Olympian gods (except for Zeus) were born twice—once from their mother Rhea and again from the prison/'womb' of their father's hoary flesh. This feminine birth-imagery curiously associated with males perhaps represents an insight into ancient male thinking and may reveal an unconscious desire to embrace the feminine feature of fertility.

Suffering through intense pains like those of childbirth was also seen as a sign of manliness. Perhaps the only thing that comes close to this experience, and therefore an approximate equivalent that a man might suffer, is the carnage of the battlefield—although it is by many accounts a pale substitute. '*Andreia*', as Loraux says, 'requires the heroic test of pain, and childbirth, not war is the cause of the most intense pain'.[128] Birth and death, being mirror images, must have much in common. These two poles represent points of transcendence between the feminine and masculine, through paradox, by way of the human imagination. Yet, again we run into a similar situation as with seeking a Feminine Operator in Athenian politics. The man who suffers pain or death in war is not actually giving birth. This may be metaphorical fertility, but it is arguably closer to the 'unsexed automaton' image in terms of its sterility.

Instances of masculine/feminine conflation, akin to the one above, are to be found in the works of Plato. Variously he has appropriated the metaphor of pregnancy to signify the philosopher's creative mental processes. At *Symposium* 206e, we are told that philosophical 'conception' instantiates itself, exchanging physical sexual union for sublime metaphor, within the philosopher's soul. It is still a physically sterile experience, unlike actual childbirth, but this time the metaphorical process does beget 'offspring'. Plato's narrator expresses this condition that the soul experiences in terms of a 'seed' that grows in it until it is ready to be 'born' as if from a womb.[129] The word employed here to describe the process is ὠδίς and, while it can mean something as general as anguish, it also carries as its principal signification the 'pains of childbirth' or 'the pangs and throes of labour'.[130] Philosophical illumination requires a feminine modality. The philosopher's *psychē* is like the woman mentioned in the *Republic* who, before finding a respite from the pains of childbirth, wanders about like Io made pregnant by Zeus and hounded by Hera's gadflies.[131]

Similar sexually conflated characteristics may be observed in the presentations of manliness in the *Laws*. In the first instance there is the preparation (against pain and pleasure) for all things martial. Imperial ambitions are identified as incompatible with the pursuit of *aretē*; however, the citizens of Magnesia will all be prepared to defend their *polis* successfully against an invader. Women and men alike are to be trained from an early age in all manner of weapons and arts of fighting. The type of orderliness of body favoured by Plato's narrators is that which is to be found in the toned muscles of an athlete or a warrior. Athletics may be considered as a type of preparation for war—even if war never comes. Being physically fit is perceived as healthy both for one's self and for the *polis*.[132] A firm physique, as we have seen, is preferable to 'softness' of body—especially in men—and therefore this becomes a key characteristic of the Athenian Stranger's definition of manliness. If war is disorderly and chaotic, then it would seem to posses the quality of *poikilia*. Loraux suggests that it therefore must be somehow intrinsically *feminine*.[133] Perhaps, then, Magnesia's perpetual preparation for war may be construed as the advancement toward a feminine goal. It is possible too that, as with the Athenians, *andreia* here reveals a more unsexed modality than any other.

Certainly the sort of manly, agonistic interaction in which many ancient Greeks engaged might be seen as embodying feminine qualities. That is, interpersonal conflict = lack of order = femininity (following the Table of Opposites). Emotionally charged agonistic interaction would appear to especially qualify. The idiom of personal contest in Hellenic cities may have been a microcosmic manifestation of life perpetually under the threat of war. It was present in the works of orators and dramatists, at one level, and in everyday social interactions at another.[134] As Ober says, 'the standard ethical code exemplified by the canon of Greek literary culture may be roughly summed up as reciprocal and agonistic'.[135] This mode of behaviour profoundly affected individual interactions as well as those between city-states. The ancient Athenians, according to Dover, 'were, after all, fiercely and deliberately competitive, believing that the whole community gains if it makes a fuss of those who excel and spurs the mediocre into doing their best by the threat of humiliation'.[136] The verbally agonistic mode of 'flyting' in particular, as Hesk suggests, was probably a prevalent theme in their daily lives.[137] It, as now, could be levelled against friend or foe depending on context and intent.

If the emotionally charged *agōn* is a feminine mode of expression, then one may apply the Feminine Operator theory to it and observe the sexual paradox that this entails (e.g. masculinity is somehow actualised through participation in a feminine medium). This may work for ancient Greeks in general but Magnesia is a different place. Plato appears to have anticipated the sexually hazardous nature of the *agōn* and has established precautions in order to prevent it, in whatever form, in his second-best *polis*. The Athenian Stranger recognises that even verbal 'flyting', on account of its disorderly nature, is counter-productive toward the pursuit of *aretē* and thereby *andreia*. In the previous chapter, we saw that comedies are not to be permitted if they verbally ridicule Magnesian citizens.[138] Those that do so with *thymos* are especially singled out for exclusion. This is to discourage citizens from imitating such disorderly activities in their daily lives. The only sort of *agōn* allowed in Magnesia will be that which promotes official values and/or physical exercise in a controlled context. Perhaps there may be "friendly" contests in virtue; however, no Feminine Operators of the emotionally agonistic variety, at any rate, will be allowed.

In other respects, Platonic definitions of manliness in the *Laws* may be regarded as perhaps more self-subverting or, at least, more sexually conflated. To observe this, one must consider the experiment of Magnesia in the holistic sense. The Magnesian state, along with all its institutions, laws and conventions, has been engineered by its creator for the primary purpose of instilling as much virtue/excellence/*aretē* in its human subjects as possible—each according to his/her abilities. The Athenian Stranger declares: 'if a native should stray to some other craft rather than the cultivation of *aretē* then the city wardens will engage in chastising him with reproaches and dishonours until they restore him to his proper course' (847a5–b2).

The *Kallipolis* of the *Republic* was meant to generate Justice (= the state of Reason's rule) in the soul of every citizen. The second-best *polis* of Magnesia will not be so ambitious in its aim but nonetheless strives toward a similar goal. Not every citizen will become a philosopher king/queen—but some of them will and must do so if the city is to survive. As I discussed in the previous chapter, Magnesia's Guardians of the Laws are to be inducted into the 'lesser mysteries' of Reason's rule more so than the ordinary citizen, but they will be deprived of the deeper metaphysics underpinning these.[139] It is the *nukterinos* council (or Vigilance Committee) that comes closest to philosopher kings/queens. They are to have a broader education in which nothing of the 'greater mysteries' of philosophy will be omitted.[140] They, much as their *Kallipolitan* counterparts, are to be schooled in mathematics, geometry, astronomy, music, dialectics, philosophy etc.

Although it is never actually stated in such terms, there is every indication that these Magnesian luminaries will ultimately strive to experience the Form of the Good and thereby attain an enlightened state not different from that discussed in the *Republic*'s 'Parable of the Cave', or, perhaps more aptly, that state referred to by Diotima in the *Symposium* as 'Birth in Beauty'.[141] There she maintained that all *erōs* is really a desire for the perpetual possession of the Beautiful/Good (206a11–12). She asserted that only through the illuminating effects of 'Birth in Beauty' might this aim be achieved (206b–c).[142]

Knowing the Form of the Good amounts to a kind of psychic rebirth. The change is meant to be dramatic and profound. It is significant that this process is described in terms of labour and birth. The philosopher, after fifty years or more of intense study, 'gives birth' to a new and marvellous state of being that is characterised by Justice and Reason's rule along with the lesser, though not insignificant quality of *andreia*. The laws and conventions of Magnesia are intended to yield a consistent supply of virtuous/excellent souls—and, we may surmise, a regular if somewhat smaller number of 'Births in Beauty'. The procreative act (physically or metaphysically) is one that requires both the masculine and the feminine. After insemination, the generative act is the realm of woman alone. It may be considered that all the strictures of manliness constructed and enforced in Plato's Magnesia paradoxically serve to realise a decidedly 'feminine' goal: the gestation and generation of a new and ostensibly higher form of consciousness. This metaphysical formulation, metaphorically construed, subverts manliness—one of its express goals—through its recourse to a feminine abstraction in terms of its own generation.

In conclusion, first, it should be evident from the material presented here that the Athenian Stranger is formulating (constructing) a mode of socially acceptable masculine behaviour for his citizens. It appears clear that many of his opinions (as perhaps with Plato's) are derived out of a specific cultural context. His view of ἀνδρεία as the state of being proof not only against pains but pleasures is not new to philosophy. Its foundations are clearly present, in some form, in the ideological discourses available at the time. It is like these, in some ways, but subtly different in others. Megillus' and Kleinias' astonishment perhaps serves to represent how other Greeks of the time might have responded to the Athenian Stranger's formulation that one must 'train' one's resistance to pleasures, as with pains, by being exposed to them in a controlled manner.

His interpretation of ἀνδρεία is clearly reminiscent of those in Athens that placed the *other* (barbarians, women, effeminate males) in stark opposition to manliness and freedom. It can be observed that 'manly' and 'free' Greeks derived their self-definition from this perception of a negatively identified *other*. A comparable formulation is especially apparent in terms of the nationalistic propaganda of Plato's era. The Athenian Stranger's particular notions on ἀνδρεία are intended to become a social imperative in Magnesia and will contribute to the accepted mode of discourse on the subject. He has borrowed from contemporary propagandistic methods and adapted them for his attempt to engineer a particular cultural *ethos* about sexuality.

The Athenian Stranger's particular formulation of ἀνδρεία appears to be no less unique to Plato. The idea that a truly courageous (manly) individual must be equipped to cope with pains *and* pleasures alike is certainly interesting and influential.[143] We can observe this notion arising, again and again, in history after Plato's era. It surfaces in the Stoic values of self-abnegation and moderation and again in later Christian ideas of mortification of the flesh. It may be observed in many later manifestations of philosophical and religious asceticism that are, directly or indirectly, linked to Plato's Academy. This particular slant on courage closely connects it with the other essential virtue of moderation.

It is also relatively novel that the Athenian Stranger insists that ἀνδρεία is only one of four key virtues that obtain enlightenment only when all are fully actualised together and bound by Reason's rule. However draconian such a programme of social regulation may seem to us in this age, its author had the noblest of goals in mind. The purpose of being proof against pleasure and pain (as with any of the prescribed modes of life laid out in the *Laws*) is ostensibly to prepare humankind for ascendance to a higher, transcendent level of philosophical being. 'Birth in Beauty', despite paradoxically manifesting itself through a feminine modality, is portrayed as the height of human achievement. That end, as far as Plato's narrator is concerned, appears to justify fully the means required to achieve it.

Chapter V
Sex, the Myth of the Family and Plato's Stepchildren

The grouping of fellow tribesmen into kin of various categories, some of whom one can marry and some of whom one cannot, is central to the social organisation of most . . . peoples.

—Frederick Engels[1]

And, I presume we should mention the . . . judge who is the best in regard to aretē—if, indeed, there be such a one—who in dealing with a family in conflict will destroy none of them but reconcile them and succeed through enacting laws for them and securing amongst them for all time a permanent state of friendliness.

—The Athenian Stranger[2]

Every society, past and present, has sought to manage sex in one way or another through laws on marriage, divorce, inheritance, rape, ages of eligibility and many other matters relating to sexuality, society and the individual. As a social entity, the family actively imposes limitations on its members' choice of sexual partners and binds them inextricably with the ownership and transference of property. In addition to its real-world manifestations, there are also other more subtle ideological means through which society exercises control over families and families do the same with their members. This comes about largely through accepted modes of discourse and signifies what I am calling the 'myth' of the family.

The conceptualisation of 'family' is constructed in the sphere of ideas through speech, 'spin' and *mythos*. As we have seen, Plato's narrators are particularly concerned with the construction of such social features. The Athenian *oikos* represents a paradigm of family life contemporary with Plato that largely, but not exclusively, informs his theoretical approach in the *Laws*. 'The *oikos*', as Pomeroy says, 'includes not only human beings, but property, and therefore, according to its size and to the context, it may be translated as "family," "household," or "estate."[3] The regulation of sex in relation to the *oikos* is a particular concern for Plato's second-best *polis*. As we have seen, there are many factors that separate Magnesia from the *Kallipolis* of the *Republic*. Even so, both take considerable interest in the sex-lives of their subjects.[4] One of the most striking differences may be seen in terms of the second-best state's special relationship with the *oikos* and the men and women that comprise it.

The patriarchal family is integral to achieving Magnesia's officially sanctioned civic goals. It is a fundamental component of the overall structure of the city-state. This fact ultimately dictates that a significant portion of the *Laws* be devoted to coping with the sexual politics that families entail. There will be no communal breeding facilities as in the *Kallipolis*. Neither will Magnesian property be shared communally by all of its citizens; although, it is owned by the community at large. Offspring will be reared both by their parents, and by the *polis*, but not solely by state-appointed officials as in the more idealistic *Republic*.[5] In their stead is the semi-private institution of the *oikos*. It is *semi*-private in the sense that, while in the stewardship of an individual family, much of its affairs are regulated directly or indirectly by agencies of the Magnesian government and it is ultimately the property of the *polis*. This emended version will suffice for the second-best state to rear and induct new citizens into the community. It requires a host of legal arrangements spanning the whole range of familial affairs along with considerable state-sponsored scrutiny.

The style and manner of the Athenian Stranger's statutes strongly echo aspects of other systems, as we understand them, that had evolved in the ancient world. It combines elements of Sparta, Krete and particularly his own Athens. Other ideas recollect themes developed in the *Republic* and elsewhere. The Athenian Stranger makes it clear that these laws have been prepared for a second-best state with a view toward the inculcation of specific philosophical tenets and modes of sexual behaviour.[6] An ideal society, he says, is one where there is communal sharing of wives, children, properties, 'and all that is called private is everywhere and by every means' expunged from our lives' (739c5–7). This ideal scenario is characterised as being 'as unified as possible'. He indicates that no other will ever be laid down that is 'truer or better' in overall excellence.[7] But the Athenian Stranger admits that the citizens of this state would have to be gods or children of gods for it to prosper. For a more realistic scenario of constitution building, a paler likeness of the best city-state has to suffice. This likeness 'would be as near to immortality as possible', and it would be next to immortality in regard to its honour.[8] It is Magnesia. There, the system of human relationships second-best to total sexual communism (albeit tightly regulated) is that of the semi-private household unit (also highly regulated)—at once seemingly detached from the state, yet paramount to the continued functioning of this society: The Magnesian *oikos* will form an image of the state in microcosm.

The Magnesian *oikos* serves as an integrally functioning unit of a greater whole. The Athenian Stranger's revised version of the household has much in common with real-world analogues. The *oikos* at Sparta, as at Athens, preceded the *polis,* and perhaps served as a model for it.[9] Unlike these, however, the Magnesian *oikos'* artificiality makes it coeval with the (equally artificial) *polis.* They will be different from real social systems in terms of Magnesia's 'engineered' creation as opposed to its social evolution. The connection between the household and the state is observable in terms of the degree of social preparation that the former instils in its members in respect to the latter.

This connection is also observable in other familial relationships that mimic similar relationships between citizens and the state. In the *Republic,* Sokrates has indicated that a strong analogy can be drawn between the soul of an individual and the constitution of a *polis.*[10] The one is analogous to the other. Both the citizens and the abstract civic entity of Magnesia are intended to possess *aretē.* The primary task of Magnesia's government is to maintain a number of just souls sufficient to sustain a just state. The *oikos* in Magnesia is designed to maximise the 'production' of virtuous citizens.

In book III, the Athenian Stranger posits some theories on the history and development of civilisation that aid in his mythologizing. He says that the first advanced social unit to emerge was that of the family. Such 'constitutions' he calls 'patriarchal laws'.[11] He regards this as an essential step toward the more complicated constitutional systems of the Greeks that existed in Classical times. He also indicates that the 'patriarchal' household now serves as a kind of universal criterion that a people must obtain in order to advance.[12] This, he feels, holds true for Greeks and barbarians alike.[13] Under such a system as the 'patriarchal constitution', the father (or rarely the mother) retains supreme authority over the family unit and directs its affairs. The household may then flourish, within limits dictated by the size of the family, and the extended family tends to be dynastic.[14] But subjects of such a 'constitution' as this can only grow so numerous or so powerful before they reach the next identified phase of development. One dynastic *gens* must reach supremacy over others and attain kingship. From there, it may evolve into more sophisticated governmental systems. The household, according to the Athenian Stranger's views, may be regarded as fundamental to the development of all larger governmental entities and, since they are built on them, vital to their continuation.[15]

The importance of the *oikos* to the Magnesian state is reinforced through numerous laws that assert the primacy of parents and the honours due to them. In a speech composed for the benefit of his hypothetical populace, the Athenian Stranger lays down the Magnesian order of authorities and ranks them according to importance. In this hierarchy, 'the better are superior to the worse, parents are superior to their offspring, men to women and children, rulers to the ruled'.[16] According to the 'hierarchy of betters', the patriarchal rulership of the family is significantly placed just below the position occupied by the authority of the state.

In an earlier discussion with Kleinias and Megillus, the Athenian Stranger asserted that the condition of ruling and being ruled extends into the private sphere as much as it does into the public. Expecting nothing but an affirmative response (which he gets), he asks 'and on the whole, would the claim not be universally correct that parents rule over their offspring?'[17] Within the Magnesian household, the father and mother retain authority subordinate to that of the laws, their guardians, magistrates and the *nukterinos* council. Here the Athenian Stranger seems to be exploiting a patriotic link, drawn from the real world, between *patrios* and *patēr*, which will support his version of family values. Attic orators have also employed this type of useful rhetorical device.[18] In public discourse, as Strauss points out, 'any connotation of "father" . . . is likely to have been strong and evocative'.[19] The members of a Magnesian household must learn to respect parental authority and particularly the authority of the *patēr*. They are then expected to extend this sense of respect, by means of something akin to psychological transference, to the authority represented by the *polis*. The *oikos*, Magnesian or otherwise, establishes patterns of obedience to authority along similar lines amongst its members and mandates an ethic of respect.

The Magnesian laws, their enforcers, instruments of propaganda, councils and courts, as we have seen, will strive to impress specific societal values on the populace as a whole. All members of any Magnesian household are subject to the Athenian Stranger's proposed social conditioning. First is the universal mandate for the pursuit of the positively identified values associated with *aretē*. Those who stray from this path will be chastened and reproached.[20] This, in part, consists of carefully meted-out applications of public shame and official censure that have been psychologically calculated to maintain order.[21] The household in Magnesia will be the first agent of an individual's induction into *aretē*. It will be expected to support all tenets of the state's official ideology. To ensure this, the *oikoi* are subject to an intense degree of scrutiny by the agents of the *polis*. If any citizens should be found to have faltered from the official course, they will have swift correction at the hands of the Guardians of the Laws and their subsidiaries.

The Magnesian *oikos* plays a role similar to that of its Athenian counterpart, but in several ways it is strikingly different. At Athens, the central *oikos* deity was Hestia, the goddess of the hearth.[22] Through the cult of Hestia, as Humphreys says, 'the city was a macrocosm of the household—it too had its sacred hearth'.[23] Her presence focused inward and permeated the home. Hermes, god of thresholds, faced outward, like an apotropaic device, as if to challenge the wide world. His image provided the clear demarcation of boundaries between the private sphere of the *oikos* and the public sphere of the *polis*. Neither Hermes nor Hestia will defend their usual boundaries in

Magnesia. The situation there significantly de-emphasises the separation of private and public.

The Magnesian *polis* encroaches on the *oikos* in a number of ways. It interweaves them together almost as a single entity. This inevitably necessitates some concessions from the 'lesser partner' in this union. A Magnesian home will not be allowed to keep private shrines of any sort (909d–910b). Those familiar icons that would otherwise mark the symbolic division between the inside and the outside throughout ancient Greece will be altogether absent from Magnesia. It will be a *polis* in which the word 'private' is to have as little significance as possible (739a–740a). All shrines are to be public. There will be temples of worship by the community as a whole rather than by individuals privately.[24] These public shrines will provide a convenient means of education and mass indoctrination. The exclusion of private religious ceremonies and icons of worship represents one of several radical revisions that appear to have little or no parallel in real *poleis* of Plato's era.[25]

Private and public are further collapsed and conflated in regard to property and the family. The patriarchal household is the basic unit of the Magnesian state but, as Lacey points out, the arrangement of it leaves 'the family far short of its position in Athens'.[26] Remarkably, the Magnesian *klēros,* or household estate, is neither wholly private nor public. It cannot be sold or given away but the state will not directly manage it.[27] The citizen-holder (*kyrios*) of the lot (*klēros*) has the power, under the constraints of law and subject to the recommendations of officials, to designate its heir. A public list of *klēros*-holders is to be kept so that everyone knows who has which property at all times (741c). The *polis* keeps close contact with families to observe the manner in which they conduct their domestic affairs. This is to be accomplished in part through the offices of the Marriage Supervisors who will observe a married couple for the first ten years of their life together in order to ensure that they produce the appropriate number of offspring and rear them in a suitable way (783b–784b).[28]

The Magnesian *oikos* necessitates a division of labour along sexual lines. If a woman has just wedded the heir of one of the 5040 *kleroi,* then she and her husband will move into the other of the two parts of the estate, where the heir's father and mother do not live, and begin producing offspring (776a–b). One reason given for this is that close proximity to their parents/in-laws might provoke undue conflict (776a).[29] The paternal; estate consists of both lots of land with houses and are be located in separate parts of the city. The second house is used as a sort of nursery for the rearing of children along with being the venue for testing the newlywed couple's parenting skills. Other children may continue to live at home but also may be subject to forced emigration. Women play a much more significant role in the domestic tasks of childcare than do men—although, it would appear that their (female) slaves and servants will undertake much of the actual work.[30]

In time, the legitimate heirs will ascend to the status of *kyrioi* of the double estate. They will take up residency in the main house and manage its affairs. This process will replicate itself when their heirs marry. Nothing is said about where surviving parents/in-laws might live during this time (presumably, but not necessarily, in the main house as before). The notion of a double property may seem novel but there is some indication that this may not have been uncommon amongst upper class Athenians.[31] As Snodgrass indicates, we should not 'exclude the possibility of second homes, expressly recommended by Plato in the *Laws* (745e4–5) and later disparaged by Aristotle in the *Politics* (1265b25–6) on the grounds that they made life awkward'.[32] Both passages date from the same general period and each, in different ways, perhaps suggests that its author was familiar with the idea of keeping a double residence as a practice amongst the higher classes. If so, then this represents another level of democratisation through 'aristocratification' in the laws.[33]

Aside from the rearing of their children (which, as we saw in chapter III, turns out to be both a private and public business), what will Magnesian citizen-women do with their time on the double *klēros?* The possibility that they might spin or weave is discussed at 805e–806a. The Athenian Stranger does not make it expressly clear if they will do this or whether all such menial tasks are to be undertaken by servants and slaves. He may be taking it for granted that all women must know something of these arts. The recommended dedication of 'something woven that does not constitute more than a month's work for one woman' to the city's temples suggests that citizen-women might engage in weaving and spinning for ritualistic purposes (956a).

Weaving was a 'rite of femininity', associated with religious duties, undertaken by Athenian girls of the aristocratic classes. They wove the sacred robes that were presented to Athena annually at the Panathenaia. A similar practice was performed involving the robes offered to Artemis at Brauron.[34] These 'samples of clothing', as Cole says, 'dedicated by the women are described as *polutelestata*, "expensive", or "completely finished"'.[35] Women in the Panathenaic procession, as depicted on the Eastern section of the Parthenon frieze, attend the priest and priestess carrying the sacred *peplos* as a gift to the goddess.[36] 'As *arrhephoroi* or *ergastinai*', according to Blundell, 'they would have been initiated into the art of wool-working, seen by Greek men as the quintessential activity of the married woman in the home'.[37] A few citizen-women may only have woven fine garments for ritual or special occasions whereas many more will have engaged in the everyday tasks of making and mending clothes for common use. Nonetheless, all Athenian citizen-women were expected to know this art at an expert level.[38] Other Greek societies seem to have held similar views—with the possible exception of Sparta.[39]

The symbolic and ritualistic associations between women and weaving in Classical Athens seem to clarify the Athenian Stranger's statements about his hypothetical subjects. The designation 'a month's work for one woman' could be regarded as a fairly standard unit of value. It need not necessarily imply that Magnesian citizen-women of any class would have to undertake such work themselves on a regular basis. However, if aristocratic women in Athens made fine articles of clothing as part of their religious duties, then this lends support to the proposition that the Magnesians will do the same. The act of producing clothing for general use might be considered too banausic for citizens as it could limit their pursuit of *aretē*. Magnesia's slaves and *metics* will likely undertake most spinning and weaving for practical purposes. But liberation has its boundaries. Female citizens will probably still be initiated into these traditionally feminine mysteries even if only for the sake of ritual and public ceremony. It may be regarded as a necessary feature of their particular *aretē*.

The Athenian Stranger discusses some of the other duties that a citizen-woman will perform within the *oikos*.[40] These include the necessary care of children and, as indicated above, weaving. Another domestic role that she will be expected to undertake is that of acting as steward (ταμιεία) of the household. In this capacity, she will oversee and assign the work of domestic slaves and servants and, presumably, manage many of the economic aspects of the *klēros*. The Athenian Stranger is not especially specific in regard to all aspects of her 'stewardship', but there is reason to believe that she might exert considerable authority.

There is evidence for domestic management by women in ancient Athens and elsewhere. Xenophon's fictional husband Ischomachos, for example, makes the interesting anthropological observation that women—being softer, more tender and anxious than men—are better suited to indoor tasks. A good wife, he reasons, should be like a queen bee managing her hive. Ischomachos' model wife dispatches the servants and slaves to do their jobs and supervises all those who work inside. Her tasks are meant to include storing, administering and distributing the goods brought into the house along with the finances that affect them.[41] The comedic character Lysistrata similarly contends, in a scene with no small amount of dramatic conceit, that women are quite capable of controlling the Athenian treasury since they have been in charge of housekeeping budgets for years.[42] The comedic context does not undercut the value entailed by such a remark.

We hear of other instances where Athenian women display competence in managing household economics through the orators. They are anecdotal and perhaps should not be considered indicative of the norm, but no less revealing. In one such example from Lysias, a family meeting is described where a mother challenged that her son's guardian (her father) had mismanaged the household finances.[43] This implies that she had more than a little understanding of such matters. Athenian women, consequently, could be present in legal discussions about a household member's will and could sometimes represent their husbands on these occasions (with the aid of a male relative as intermediary).[44] Aiskhines refers to wealthy young men whose fathers were deceased and whose mothers administered their property.[45]

Many or all of these may represent exceptions rather than the norm. Xenophon's *Oikonomikos* should be regarded as an idealised vision in ways not unlike Plato's *Laws*. But there is also the indication that Spartan women had a comparable (if greater) control over their domestic affairs, in part, as Millender says, because 'the average Spartiate husband spent less time at home than other Greek males'.[46] Magnesian women, perhaps more like their Lakonian counterparts, will have greater access to the public sphere than any citizen-woman of Classical Athens.[47] Is there reason to think that they would have less authority in the Magnesian private sphere (especially as 'stewards' of the household) than they presumably did in real life? The Athenian Stranger has not told us. One is inclined to suspect that they would have at least as much authority in their 'stewardship' of the *oikos* as their Athenian counterparts.

In other domestic/economic respects, they are somewhat more limited and these same limitations are, at least, extended to both sexes. The Magnesians will not be allowed to engage in retail trading of any kind or to use the *oikos* as a means for acquiring profit. The Athenian Stranger discusses some of the iniquities of the retail trade and the manner in which innkeepers treat their guests as 'prisoners' to be ransomed at a high price.[48] He also says that such a situation need not be the case if the 'best possible' people were in charge of these exchanges.[49] In his hypothetical digression on the subject, he indicates that the 'best possible' women who might engage in it would be like 'mothers and nurses'.

The banausic retail trade is exclusively limited in Magnesia to a separate sphere of the *polis* encapsulating resident-aliens and foreign visitors (920a3–4). Citizens must not engage in mercantile ventures.[50] Those who defy this rule stand to suffer public shame and potential imprisonment. A citizen-man or woman might entertain guests at home. Perhaps the guests might offer to return the favour of hospitality to their hosts someday in kind, but neither of them would be permitted to charge any type of fee or to earn profit for these services. The matriarch of the household would act as 'mother and nurse' to the visitors as to her own family. Her role in this context indicates the sort of sexual typecasting, apart from their other masculine adaptations, to which Magnesian women will be subject.

It is forbidden for any Magnesian to carry on any kind of trade in woven goods produced in the home. It would seem that this restriction also applies to goods produced by slaves or servants. These economic regulations are designed to prevent any harsh necessity that might compel citizens of any class to engage in trading to maintain themselves. Perhaps Plato recalled the time in his youth when hardship affected Athenian citizen-women in the aftermath of the Peloponnesian War. Many became nurses, wool-workers and grape-pickers as a consequence of the general economic misfortunes. This is attested to in a speech of Demosthenes where the citizen-speaker remarks that, under such circumstances, 'we confess that we sell ribbons and do not live in the way we would like'.[51] This was regarded pejoratively by the upper classes who eschewed such banausic activities. It was not forbidden for citizen-women to engage in trade but it seems to have been preferred that they should not do so. The fact that Euxitheos, in the above speech by Demosthenes, could have his citizenship questioned on account of his mother working as a nurse and selling her 'homespun' lace ribbons underscores this status-oriented prejudice.

None of Magnesia's citizens (male or female) should have to engage in base commerce of any kind. The nurses who look after citizen-children must come from somewhere other than Magnesia. They are meant to be slaves or foreign women, hired in this capacity, under the strictest supervision and are required to be physically fit to promote healthy activities for citizen-youths (789e–a). It is typical of Magnesian policy that children's nurses are to be supervised by specially appointed citizen-women whenever they undertake their duties outside the *oikos* (794b). While citizens are subject to considerable scrutiny in public and private life, non-citizens are highly suspect and thus bear even more intense supervision by the *polis*.

Derrida has asserted that Plato's works are highly logocentric. That is, they focus on 'presence as opposed to absence', the 'living voice' as opposed to the written word, life opposed to death and soul to body.[52] He also calls them phallocentric saying that the principal goal of Platonic writing is the philosophically symbolic 'production of the son after the father's death'.[53] Dubois has criticised Derrida's argument on the grounds that it too is overly phallocentric, saying that 'it fails to acknowledge Plato's desire to appropriate maternity to the male philosopher'.[54] It is not within the scope of this chapter to confirm or deny such claims;[55] however, Magnesia's hypothetical constitution and its particular interest in the continuance of patriarchy seem to support them to no small extent.

The second-best state regulates its citizens' sexual congress to a considerable degree. Marriage is the foundation of the *oikos* and one of marriage's express purposes is reproduction.[56] Once Magnesian youths have attained the appropriate age, the laws outline a process by which potential mates are to become engaged. There is no question that designated heirs will be expected to marry and assume the roles of mother and father to a new generation. Sex-roles, as we have seen, are inculcated from an early age and girls will be especially encouraged to imitate their mothers' model as much as sons are encouraged to idolise and imitate that of their fathers.[57]

The Athenian Stranger's law says that the marriage pledge (*engyēses*) is to be 'under the authority of the father first, in the second instance of the [paternal] grandfather, in the third instance of the brothers by the same father, and after this it is under the authority of those on the mother's side in like manner' (774e4–6). This is similar to Athenian law in which, as Pomeroy says, the 'hierarchy of those who may inherit mimics the hierarchy of family relationships, with priority accorded to males within the same degree of relationship and to collaterals on the father's side (i.e. agnates), starting with brothers'.[58] There are at least two significant points in which Magnesian law differs from that given by pseudo-Demosthenes: first, that it characteristically admits relatives on the female side and, secondly, that it posits the grandfather, in keeping with Magnesia's gerontocratic character, as having precedence over brothers.[59]

This system would seem to limit the choice of one's future marriage partner but, on the whole, such limitations appear to have been common across a range of Greek *poleis*. The 'rights' of a woman in marriage were, at best, secondary. 'In wedding procession scenes on pottery', as Stears says, 'the groom grasps the bride by the wrist, a symbol of his dominance and of the inequality of the relationship; a ritual rape'.[60] While symbolic in character, such scenes imply the fact that the marriage might not necessarily be of the bride's own choosing. Herodotos indicates that freedom of choice by women of their prospective partners was unusual.[61] It was not altogether unknown. An amazed Plutarch reported that Kimon's sister, Elpinike, chose her husband freely and, likewise, he indicates that Peisistratos' daughter also married for love.[62] Xenophon's account of the Spartans suggests that their system allowed more freedom of choice for both partners (with limited contact after marriage) and, in some particular circumstances, allowed husbands to share their wives with other men.[63] There is also some evidence for women's limited influence over their betrothals at ancient Gortyn (whose legal codes appear to have interested Plato) where, as Sealey says, 'by the time the laws were written down . . . [i.e. probably early/middle 5th century B.C.E.] the woman had acquired some voice in choosing her husband'.[64]

At Athens, it was the bride's *kyrios* who generally had the authority to make a valid betrothal.[65] The legitimacy of the offspring depended on the efficacy of this. In contrast to Athens, Magnesian policy seems to be less concerned with legitimacy than stability. The *kyrioi* are recommended (but not compelled) by law to make their choices of betrothal based on the precept that 'the natural tropism of like to mate with like should be avoided'.[66] Members of the highest of the four property classes should therefore be matched with members of lower classes, and so on, in order for the state to remain vigorous and avoid decay.[67] This represents a significant change from the eugenic policies found in the *Republic* that placed little value on the family as an institution. In *Kallipolis* the different 'metals' of the three classes were not to intermingle; rather, the 'best' only bred with the 'best' etc., according to a calculated scheme, in temporary marriages mechanistically designed to produce offspring in a consistent manner.[68] Balance is to be maintained in Magnesia through permanent marriages with an economic basis in land-division.[69] No citizen may have more land than any other and, as we saw above, a single, patriarchal household occupies and tends to the allocated *klēros*.[70]

Magnesian betrothals bear a striking resemblance to those in ancient Athens. This is especially so, as Rankin indicates, in terms of 'a customary limitation of erotic "choice"' such that the particular feelings of the betrothed would seem not to figure as prominently into the equation as do other more material concerns.[71] Magnesia's methods reflect Spartan elements as well. Plato's narrator has provided some specialised social programmes to encourage young people in the choosing of an 'appropriate' mate. He outlines a scheme whereby they might become better acquainted with one another before marriage. Potential mates must know as much as possible about each other's respective family and background (771e1–5). As discussed in chapter III, they will dance together naked, observing some degree of propriety, so that they get a good look at one another.[72] This represents an institutionalised form of sex-role stereotyping from an early age. However, this pre-betrothal mingling envisaged by the Athenian Stranger for his model society suggests that, even with the betrothals being arranged by the bride and bridegroom's *kyrioi*, there would be some element of choice on the part of the participants. It is a directed 'freedom'. However, the degree to which women might influence their betrothals, through expressing favour for one individual over another, should not be discounted.[73] Perhaps even marriages of love, in the modern sense of the word, could come to pass in Plato's second-best *polis*.

The reality of 5th–4th century Athens appears to have been somewhat less than sympathetic to those who might have wanted to marry for the sake of *erōs* alone as opposed to civic duty or familial obligations. Relationships of passion could be regarded as potentially quite dangerous.[74] Athenian society required of its free male citizens that they arrange marriages for their daughters and sometimes sisters and more distant female relations. This duty to the *oikos* and the *polis* was taken very seriously.[75] As mentioned above, the *kyrios* was responsible for making the match and we have already seen that Plato's narrator, in dealing with the matter of authority over betrothals (774e4–6), has favoured a similar procedure for Magnesia. There, a male child will be designated as heir (κληρονόμος). The chosen heir is recorded in a written will and he then inherits the title to the estate on the death of the testator.

Any excess children may be married off, adopted (posthumously or otherwise) into another household or, alternatively, dispatched to an allied city or colony.[76] The Athenian Stranger provides a provision that allows a testator to leave any quantity of property deemed fit (excepting the actual, immovable Magnesian estate and its associated equipment) to children other than the heir unless they already have their own household (923d6–7). He indicates that daughters should be treated in like manner as sons, in terms of inheritance, inasmuch as they too may inherit movable property—providing they are not married or engaged to be married (923d8–e1). It follows, therefore, that the only children to inherit any movable property or money would be either any who remain in Magnesia but never gain their own household or those who have been dispatched to a colony (assuming they are eligible). The law here allows for unmarried individuals to inherit movable property but the system that the Athenian Stranger envisages does not strongly favour anyone being unmarried for very long.

A Magnesian man who has no sons will 'adopt' an heir to marry a chosen daughter. The adopted heir thereby becomes his legitimate 'son' in the eyes of the law. In the event that 'the testator should leave no male offspring, but only daughters', says the Athenian Stranger, 'let him bequeath for whichever of his daughters he may wish a husband, a son for himself, recorded as his legal heir'.[77] The posthumously appointed heir would then marry the designated heiress, when she comes of age, and become legal master of the estate and will be responsible for providing it with an heir and the city with future citizens. The fact that a brotherless heiress must be wedded to an heir for the estate to pass on to the next generation, although indicative of patriarchal control, emphasises a woman's social and legal importance in Magnesia.

There is a comparable legal emphasis on the female side of the family for purposes of inheritance present in Athenian law, in terms of the *anchisteia*.[78] This phenomenon has been considered by some to be a Classical 'shadow' of more ancient customs of matrilineal descent.[79] The Greeks do not appear to confirm this. Herodotos and others wrote about barbarian cultures that allegedly practised such a tradition.[80] The purpose of the prehistoric 'goddess' figurines dating from around or before 2,600 B.C.E., speculation about which had been used in support of the earlier conclusions on ancient matriarchy, currently remains a subject of lively debate.[81] As Pembroke states, 'it is no longer believed that the tracing of descent through women was ever universal, or that it is essentially an older phenomenon than that which is traced through males'.[82] Outside the *Laws,* some of Plato's characters have regarded autochthony as a matriarchal phenomenon. As Loraux says, in this respect 'Plato resolutely places the emphasis on the mother'.[83] Autochthony, rooted in myth, is by no means an indication about the structure of early human societies. Neither, as we have seen, is Plato bound to be consistent on every point between dialogues. The Athenian Stranger shows no sign of belief in an ancient M*utterrecht* when he discusses the patriarchal family as the foundation of civilisation.[84] The fact that certain nineteenth-century German scholars imagined such a thing probably reveals more about them than the ancient Greeks.[85]

Nonetheless, property and inheritance *are* intrinsically connected with Magnesian women in comparable ways to their real-world analogues. Legally providing for a 'son' and heir to marry the heiress and inherit the immovable estate underscores this.[86] The policy of supplying heirs to sonless patriarchs echoes similar Athenian litigation where, under these same circumstances, the 'nearest male relative succeeded to the estate' having been appointed by the *polis* through the process of *epidikasia.*[87] In Magnesia, the eldest relatives take precedence and preference is given to the eligible heirs who are in the household of male relatives more than female ones.[88] Anyone may be excluded from inheriting the estate and from marrying the heiress should he already have inherited an estate and married an heiress, or should he be otherwise unavailable.

The 'correctness' of the heir and heiress' respective ages is to be discerned by state marriage inspectors who will make a determination, in part, by viewing the males naked and the females stripped down to the navel.[89] Judging by the list of heirs, the chosen bridegroom's age could be significantly greater than that of his bride (924e6). He could also conceivably be much younger. If there happened to be several orphaned daughters, then it follows that only one, most likely the oldest, would be the designated heiress since there is only one immovable estate. The other daughters should theoretically be married to the heirs of other families if possible. Their betrothals would appear to fall under the authority of their eldest sister's husband since he would be the new *de facto* master of the household and *kyrios* of the estate.

The Magnesian system of selecting heirs and betrothals for both men and women may be seen as having a rather perfunctory or mechanical character. This would appear to accentuate the primacy of the needs of the *polis* over those of the individual as regards the generation of offspring and the population of the immovable estates. However, there is some indication that an heiress might possess some limited control over her eventual betrothal. Having described the order of succession at length, Plato's narrator grants her an interesting degree of freedom. He proposes that, when a man dies both intestate and leaving only daughters, and if the family lacks all of the relatives described in the list, then 'the girl, along with her guardians, may freely choose a willing man from the city . . . [who will become] the legal heir of the deceased and husband of the daughter' (925a5–b2). It appears to be only a slight liberty but, as England says of this statute, 'the amount of choice allowed by Plato to the bride was probably much in advance of Attic custom'.[90]

The Athenian Stranger allows a further degree of freedom of choice for women in marriage. He offers another potential situation in which an heiress might exert some control over her future bridegroom. If the city is suffering from a lack of heirs, the heiress (who has no brothers and whose father has left no will) may then recall someone who has been dispatched to a colony. If he is a family member (not an immediate relative such as brother), however distant, he then automatically becomes heir and 'son' to the deceased and betrothed to the heiress (925b7). In this case, no permission would be required from the heiress' guardians since the heir is the nearest eligible relative. However, if the man chosen is from outside the heiress' household,[91] then he may only marry her on the condition that her guardians give permission (925b6–c3).

It is uncertain how often such circumstances might arise under which an heiress could exercise direct control over her future husband. She would only be able to make a fairly resolute, binding and unchallenged choice when there happens to be nobody within the state who qualifies as the legal heir, a relative has been dispatched to a colony *and* the heiress happens to choose him. There is a difference between a selection subject to many rules and scrutiny and a completely free one. Even as an exception, these situations do not grant the sort of freedom of choice to a woman that a Magnesian father or guardian may exercise (although they too are limited to endogamous betrothals with citizens and colonials—as well as being bound by the state's policies and supervision). The daughter always has the option to agree with whomever the law, her father or her guardians say she must marry.

Let us consider Magnesian marriages and their implicit role in *teknopoiia*. The duties expected of ancient women, whether by law or custom, generally yoked them to the *oikos*. It is impossible to indicate with certainty the precise extent to which sexual segregation actually took place amongst all classes of women.[92] However, as Schaps says, 'large areas of male culture were in fact entirely closed to women: the assembly, the lawcourts and the gymnasia, and even the normal daily social encounters with Athenian men'.[93] When Lysistrata complains of the women's lateness to her meeting, Kleonike says 'dearie, they'll come; it's difficult for women to leave the house, they're always rushing about after their men, or waking up the servants, putting the baby to bed, washing or feeding it'.[94] While this is clearly a comedic description, it would appear to denote an underlying truth about real women's lives. Perhaps an Athenian marriage was not as bleak as Hooper suggests when he describes it as 'a matter of good family, good dowry, and good health . . . bearing children and managing a household were all that would ordinarily have been asked of a wife'.[95]

Magnesian women, as we have seen, reflect their Athenian counterparts in many ways. This seems particularly true in regard to women's role in the patriarchal family. As Cartledge, says, the 'making of children . . . [*teknopoiia*] could be accounted a form of state liturgy or public service elsewhere in ancient Greece too'.[96] Marriage and childbearing are identified (and will be culturally enforced) as essential parts of a woman's life in Magnesia. The one is the intended product of the other, in the Athenian Stranger's reckoning, and so they are intrinsically interconnected.[97] The relationship between a child and its household will impress a pattern for imitation from the earliest age.[98]

The stability of Magnesia's population must be assured by offspring in the appropriate numbers. Perhaps more urgent is the perceived necessity that the appropriate psychological conditions be encouraged amongst citizen families. The *polis* exerts strict supervision over marital affairs at most every level involving *oikos*, phratry and *phylē*. This may be read as an historically prevalent type of an institutionalised sexual subjugation of women based on the act of reproduction as is often cited by modern feminists.[99] But Magnesia would not be alone in this respect. The practice of regulating the institution of matrimony has not been exclusively limited to Plato's hypothetical cities. Significant portions of extant legal codes and recorded customs on marriage survive from the Classical world and especially from Sparta, Krete and Athens.

Magnesian law specifies that 'the age limit of marriage for a young woman is to be from her sixteenth to her twentieth year', and for men, around the ages of thirty to thirty-five (752b2–9). These are not merely suggested guidelines but prescriptive legislation to be obeyed by all. The statutes provide pecuniary fines and psychological penalties, through a sort of automatic social stigmatisation, for those who choose to remain single.[100] This differs somewhat from our understanding of Athenian customs in the 5th–4th century B.C.E. and may have more in common with Spartan practices. Magnesia, as we have seen, incorporates many aspects of both. Even so, the potential gap between the marriage ages of the respective sexes in Magnesia shares some similarity with practices in Athens.

Many Athenian males over thirty appear to have preferred to wed significantly younger brides.[101] This practice seems to have been structured around the age at which an heir might be expected to take on greater responsibility in the affairs of the *klēros*. Married at the age of thirty, he would be about sixty when his son (assuming he had one) might wed. On his retirement, his heir could take over the affairs of the property.[102] During the thirty or more years in which a man would most actively partake of public life appropriate to his class, perhaps his wife could better serve her husband in a domestic capacity (thanks, in part, to the vigorous and impressionable qualities of youth) were she ten to fifteen years his junior. This may have been a popular ideal, but it did not always occur in reality.[103]

As will be the case in Magnesia, an Athenian father, or the legal guardian of the *epiklēros*, makes the marriage pledge. The physical union of man and wife would then follow quite possibly in rapid succession.[104] Although such a marriage would be accompanied by private celebrations, as Lambert indicates, 'it was not marked by any legal ceremony'.[105] The legal aspects appear to have been handled by the father (through *engyesis* and *engye*) and by the husband through his phratry.[106] The new brides' names were presented to these civic kinship-groups on the third day of the *apatouria*, when their husbands made a ritual sacrifice at a ceremony called the *gamelia*.[107]

Whether this was done solely for *epikleroi* or for everybody remains uncertain. Since this ceremony took place when the bride-to-be reached puberty, we may infer that a typical age at which citizen-females might undertake their first marriage would not likely be much beyond that of sixteen and, given the ancient Athenian disposition toward virginity, it was possibly younger.[108] The laws of Gortyn are more straightforward on the subject of her age. They indicate that, prior to twelve, a Kretan *patroiokos* was considered a 'minor' (ἄνορος or ἀνέβος). Thirteen appears to have been quite acceptable. She would have come 'of age' (ἤβιονσα or ὁρίμα) and was therefore considered ready for marriage.[109]

The Spartan customs on the legal age of a *patroukhos*, as we have them, are somewhat unclear and few in number. However, they make an interesting point of contrast with what we understand of those in Athens and Krete.[110] Xenophon's ide-alised account of the Spartan constitution indicates that Spartan men often wedded 'older' women. Lykourgos allegedly forbade women to marry until they were 'in the period of physical prime',[111] but some older men still preferred younger brides.[112] Xenophon does not say precisely what age 'period of physical prime' entailed. Plu-tarch gives evidence for a comparable 'minimum age' but also does not specify what it might be.[113] As Cartledge suggests, however, these laws 'almost certainly applied only to men'.[114] That preferred by the Spartans for females could easily be the ages of six-teen to twenty. It could just as easily have been ages twelve to sixteen as was typically the case in many Greek *poleis*. The allegedly superior Spartan diet may have helped their girls mature faster and wed earlier or, alternatively, the rigorous athletics might have delayed the onset of menstruation and, thereby, their weddings.[115]

It is possible to hypothesise that having younger wives to look after their do-mestic affairs must have been rather convenient for retired husbands. But a woman who remarried after her initial husband's demise (e.g. for purposes of inheritance) might be much older than the new husband. This does not discount the fact that both in the *Laws* of Plato and in the reality of his time, at some point in her marriage a wife could be half her husband's age. The legal and traditional institutions that supported such a system were concerned with the survival and continuance of generation in a world without the benefits of modern medicine. The numerous laws and traditions governing matrimony suggest that ancient societies were actively interested in casting individuals in sex-roles from an early age with the express purpose of encouraging reproduction. These, however, seem amateurish compared to the Athenian Stranger and his arsenal of social engineering.

In framing his constitution as he has done, the Athenian Stranger has had to structure inheritance laws under the constraints imposed by his indivisible properties. The law must encourage families to produce sufficient heirs to inherit estates lest the number of households change from a stable 5040. Aristotle, in the *Politics,* criticises Plato for suggesting such a large number of citizens, saying that 'we cannot overlook the fact that such a number would require the territory of Babylon' or some other comparably large country.[116] As Nixon and Price suggest, perhaps Aristotle felt that a population centre of this magnitude could 'hardly be counted as a real *polis*'.[117]

The scope of Magnesia is impressive by ancient standards. The system for employing the controlled allocation of land units, necessitated by the population limit, appears to have very little precedent in the known constitutions of Plato's era. 'Moreover', as Hodkinson says, 'Magnesia's system of "single heir" inheritance (745b; 923c) never existed in Classical Sparta outside the retrospective fictional account of Plutarch, *Agis* 5'.[118] If this is not Plato's own invention, then it may have been part of the *mythos* of that era associated with Sparta. The plan of controlled inheritance and the indivisibility of the land units are both designed to eliminate any threat of under- or overpopulation that might hinder Magnesia's stability (cf. 740b–c). This necessitates a proactive stance toward sustaining the family unit.

If a Magnesian man should die intestate, leaving no heirs whatsoever, a couple will be chosen from surviving, estate-less relatives of appropriate age in order to assume the roles of heir and heiress on the vacant estate. The heiress will be selected from a list of relations including the deceased's sister, his brother's daughter, his sister's son, the sister of the deceased's father, the daughter of the father's brother and the daughter of the father's sister (925c3–d5). The heir is then chosen from the same list of relations as at 924e2–925a2 (discussed above). The Athenian Stranger does not say whether this new couple, designated to people the barren estate, are to have any control over the matter of their subsequent marriage. Their respective kinship-groups, presumably, would give considerable attention to the choices allowed them by law with a view toward the future couple's happiness. There is every reason to think that any such potential couple will possess an embedded ethic toward marriage that is likely to cast the prospects afforded them in a desirable light.

However agreeable the notion of matrimony may be to the Magnesians, if the actual marriage should prove too disagreeable, the couple will have a legal recourse readily at hand. In the event that married partners should want a divorce, says the Athenian Stranger:

> . . . because they are beset by a mishap of temperaments, the case must come under the care of ten men of the Guardians of the Laws who are middle-aged, and ten women of the Marriage Guardians in like manner . . . [and] if they are able to reconcile the couple, then let those arrangements stand; but if emotions seethe to a greater degree than this, then they will strive to find someone for each divorcee.[119]

These Guardians will act first as marriage counsellors and then, failing that, as matchmakers. Note that he appoints male Guardians, presumably, to counsel the husband and female Guardians, again presumably, for the wife. It seems correct to think that some members of an ancient Greek family or kinship-group would, in reality, have acted as marriage counsellors and matchmakers as needed—just as they do in the modern world. The Athenian Stranger seems to be devaluing the effectiveness of a pre-existing custom and replacing it with state agencies. He has suggested the establishment of marriage counselling, in an official capacity, in order to help maintain the state's stability. This represents a significant innovation and it appears to be out of character with ancient Greek customs as we understand them.

Another innovation is a special 'divorce clause' reserved by the state. According to this clause, a Magnesian divorce may happen automatically when a couple has failed to produce children after ten years of marriage (784c2–4). This and other such rules of divorce and remarriage emphasise the Athenian Stranger's concern that his populace should be busy 'getting children to set up new households' (930a8–b1). England suggested that the method proposed in the *Laws* would not only make the process of divorce more elaborate and complex than in Attic law, but that the additional deterrent of a forced union with a potentially unsympathetic partner would seem to discourage the Magnesians from 'swamping' the courts with divorce cases.[120] The psychological threat of remarriage, as well as the ministrations of the marriage counsellors, might deter many from making a hasty decision about separation. The passages on divorce provide much room for speculation and there is no real indication as to how much freedom of choice might be granted to potential partners for remarriage. As with many points of Magnesian law, this too will have to be sorted out by later enlightened legislators.

Magnesia places a high value on the sanctity of marriage as integral to the state's stability and prosperity. There is every sign that the ancient Athenians felt similarly but their divorce laws provide a point of contrast to Magnesia's. In Athens, a man could dissolve his marriage merely by sending his wife from the house and restoring her dowry. Few if any legal proceedings were required.[121] An Athenian woman could initiate a divorce by returning to the home of her *kyrios*. This had to be officially finalised by registration with the appropriate *archōn*, as Sealey says, 'with the help of her nearest male relative'.[122] It was not unusual for Athenian husbands to betroth their wives to wed someone else after getting a divorce.[123] Perikles, for example, made arrangements for his divorced wife's remarriage and we are told that Pasio likewise betrothed his soon-to-be ex-wife to Phormio, his manager.[124] Magnesian procedures veer away from this tradition and grant somewhat more freedom to women seeking divorces than the laws of Athens—although, it should be noted that the city-state will have the final say in any given divorce above and beyond the wishes of the individual litigants.

Kretan divorce laws, again by contrast, appear to have allowed much more latitude to women than at Athens. If a married couple should become divorced, then the wife was 'to have her own property which she came with to her husband and half of the produce, if there be any from her property, and half of whatever she has woven within, plus five staters if the husband is the cause of the divorce'.[125] If a divorced Kretan woman had borne any children, she was to receive a share of the household property and could then be remarried, with considerable say in the matter, to another man of her *phylē*.[126] Plato seems to have employed aspects of Athenian and Kretan legal codes in composing his Magnesian divorce laws but, again, with a greater emphasis on state controls and a view toward artificially maintaining a stable population. We are not told if there will be any type of movable property settlement for Magnesian divorcees. It seems unlikely. There will be no dowry to return and the *klēros* is indivisible so there might be little property to depart with an ex-wife other than her clothes and personal effects.

The Magnesian constitution provides many regulations that govern household affairs to a very precise degree with the promotion of harmony as one of their primary goals. Another example of this may be observed in the legality surrounding remarriage in the event that a spouse should die. The Athenian Stranger says that 'if a wife in death leaves behind both male and female offspring, the law we are establishing would encourage, but not compel, the widower to rear the children without bringing in a stepmother'.[127] It is worth noting here that this statement of the Athenian Stranger's appears to reflect certain observable Athenian attitudes on this matter. The sentiment appears to have been that, since a stepmother's adopted children are not her own, she would be inclined to regard them in a lesser capacity.[128] Ancient orators, playwrights and philosophers seem to concur. A client of Isaios once claimed that conflicts were especially common between a stepmother and her stepdaughter.[129] In a speech of Lysias, Diogeiton's daughter has charged that her father has been more generous with the children of his new wife.[130] In Euripides' *Alkestis*, the dying heroine begs her husband Admetos not to bring in a stepmother for their children lest she beat them.[131] Herodotos and Euripides both recount stories in which a second wife proves to be 'a real stepmother' by plotting against her husband's children—and especially against his daughters by previous wives.[132] We also have Aristotle's compelling assertion that all creatures with offspring are chiefly concerned for those that they consider their own.[133] The Athenian Stranger's preference that a father should rear his own children as a single parent rather than introduce the potentially destabilising element of a stepmother seems rather charitable, given popular views, and ultimately geared toward the children's overall well being. But it would also appear that he is indifferent as to whether one or two parents should rear the children. That there be sufficient children to inherit the *klēros* and assume the duties of citizens seems to be the more pressing concern.

Assurance of consistent and controlled reproduction is a central issue in the Athenian Stranger's approach to family law. The minimum, legally accepted number of children to be produced by marriage is one of each sex per Magnesian household (930c8–d1). The rules governing remarriage hinge largely on whether or not this quota of offspring has been filled. If there are no children, then the widower must remarry so that 'he beget sufficient children for both his household and the city-state'.[134] In the event that a husband dies leaving a widow with sufficient children, then she may rear them alone—providing she's old enough. Otherwise, her relatives are to report the matter to the 'women in charge of marriages' (the Marriage Supervisors).[135] Both they and the relatives together, having considered the details of the case, will render a decision on the issue of remarriage (930c1–7). It is unclear whether or not a young widow might have any say in her remarriage (see above). The fact that her relatives (προσήκοντες) are involved at least suggests that her wishes might be taken into account. But this is by no means certain since they too are interested parties.

Some kind of synthesis between Athenian and Kretan marriage customs appears to be taking place in the *Laws*. The Athenian Stranger's statutes on the death of a spouse are, in fact, nearly identical to those in the *Code of Gortyn*.[136] They differ primarily in terms of the rules that he provides for remarriage being characteristically stricter. A significant point of departure from both Athenian and Kretan tradition involves the diminished importance of legitimate offspring. In Athens, as Pomeroy states, 'an unattached widow had the potential to dishonour her family, and even inspire doubts about the parentage of her children'.[137] In contrast to this, the position taken by Plato's narrator on the remarriage of widows and widowers in the *Laws* is not particularly concerned with legitimacy of offspring—or, rather, a child's 'legitimacy' is less dependent on who its biological parents happened to be as opposed to its position in relation to the law.[138] Legal status, then, takes precedence over the circumstances of birth. Marriage and remarriage in Magnesia are meant to be smooth, almost mechanical processes whereby a controlled number of children will be produced in order to inherit a controlled number of properties and thus preserve the unity, harmony and functions of Magnesia.

Any inquiry into the Athenian Stranger's conception of the family in the hypothetical city-state of Magnesia must include the subject of dowries. In addition to the sort of restrictions of romantic choice discussed above, constraints are also to be placed on the amount of wealth expended when a woman weds. At 742c2–5, the Athenian Stranger says that 'when a man marries or gives someone in marriage, he must neither impart nor obtain any dowry (προίξ) whatsoever'. It turns out that a minimal amount of money may be given as something like a dowry but the figures are rather small by comparison to known Athenian practices.

There, a girl's future might depend heavily on her dowry. Without one, she could end up an 'old maid' as early as the age of fifteen.[139] The removal of dowries from Magnesia is striking. Since, at Athens, the father of the family had 'legal control of . . . his wife's dowry even after his son's majority', there may be something 'liberating' about their excision.[140] This restriction, amongst others, appears to fall under the state's fiscal policies designed to assert a kind of stratified equality within the Magnesian economy. It is part of the Athenian Stranger's plan to eliminate gaps between property classes (as is the policy of citizens being encouraged to wed outside their property class) and so help Magnesia to achieve its goal of being a 'friend unto itself' (701d). Perhaps having no dowry to provoke a domestic dispute would work to the benefit of the *oikos*.

This economic policy, of which these limitations are a part, influences many aspects of Magnesian life. The Athenian Stranger has forbidden such things as the loaning of money and charging of interest (742c sq.). These are deemed harmful to the city's concord. Magnesians are prohibited from possessing gold or silver (except on foreign expeditions) and, for their day-to-day purposes, they are meant to use a currency that is 'honoured amongst themselves but valueless to other people' (742a6). He favours what he perceives to be a Spartan custom on the matter.[141]

This is the policy outlined in Xenophon's account of Spartan currency after Lykourgos' reforms 'such that even ten *minae* could not be brought into the house without the master and servants knowing as it would take up a lot of space and require a wagon to move it; there were also searches for gold and silver, and if any was found, the possessor was punished'.[142] However, as Hodkinson says, 'contrary to the programmatic statements in literary sources, a range of evidence indicates official possession and use of precious metal currency before 404'.[143] It appears that some kind of iron-ingot currency was actually in circulation in ancient Sparta even if it was not the only kind available.[144] Again, Plato seems to be drawing upon idealised representations of Sparta for his second-best *polis*.

In keeping with this these, the Magnesian prohibition against dowries appears to be consistent with the spirit of Lakonian ideals if not actual practice. The third-century claim that this was also the ancient Spartan tradition is probably a later 'invention of revolutionary propaganda'.[145] The reasons given by Plutarch for the alleged removal of dowries from Sparta were, in characteristically egalitarian tones, 'so that none may be left unmarried because of poverty or sought eagerly because of affluence'.[146] This bears similarity to Magnesian ideology and again one is inclined to wonder, as with the *ephēbeia* (discussed in my chapter III), if Plato's writings did not exert some influence on the later tradition.[147] His version, however, is designed to correct the errors that he perceived in reality. Property is specifically targeted. A transfer of material goods seems to have accompanied Spartan brides from the 6th and 5th centuries onwards and Aristotle's reference to this as a *proix* may be a 'loose' way of describing the practice as analogous to the Athenian one.[148] He says that Spartan women had 'large dowries', loaned money at interest and were able to own and inherit property.[149] These particular Lakonian elements, if true, have been carefully excluded from the second-best *polis*.

Also in keeping with later *Lykourgan* sentiments, the Athenian Stranger indicates that 'to be exceedingly wealthy and at the same time to be good is impossible' (742e6–7). To this end, the Magnesian constitution is geared toward encouraging a state of socialised moderation amongst the populace. The prohibition against dowries is expounded on in more detail at 774c–e. In theory, members of the poorest property class have an equal opportunity to make a good marriage since no dowry will necessarily limit either their choice of potential partners or their future economic or social prospects. The Athenian Stranger adds that this problem will be eliminated since 'the necessities of life are to be available to all of the citizens within the *polis*' (774c5–6).

Another reason given for the exclusion of dowries in Magnesia is that it will make women less *hybristic* and help their husbands to avoid humiliating servility (δουλεία) on account of money (774c7).[150] As Saunders has said, 'a wife with a large dowry enjoyed a certain edge in domestic arguments'.[151] There is some indication that this may have presented a point of concern for certain ancient Greek husbands. 'When talking about the correctness of the decision not to have dowries', says Fisher, 'he seems to speak the traditional language of Greek males'.[152]

There was the possibility that a wife might 'lord' their dowry over her husband as leverage for a position of power. As Gardner says, 'marriage to a woman of greater wealth could be viewed as a loss of freedom'.[153] One way that a woman could possess and control wealth (and therefore freedom), to an extent, was through her dowry. It is possible that the Athenian Stranger, in making his rules on this subject, is trying to prevent Magnesian women from having such an option. Only a limited amount of money may be committed to a Magnesian bride's apparel without incurring a fine equal in value to the sum illegally spent. The legal amounts are up to 50 drachmae (½ *minae*) for the lowest property class, up to 100 (one *mina*) for the third, up to 150 (one and ½ *minae*) for the second and up to 200 (two *minae*) for the first propertied class (774d1–5).

These figures can be better understood when compared to actual dowries of which we have some knowledge. Isaios says that twenty *minae* would be insufficient if offered by a man of property and he asks if ten *minae* are suitable for the dowry of a freeborn girl given in marriage to a bridegroom worth three talents.[154] Demosthenes mentions a dowry of two talents and eighty *minae* put forth by a wealthy citizen when his daughter wed.[155] Plato himself reported a planned expenditure of thirty *minae* for his niece's marriage to Speusippos.[156] Ancient Kretan dowries seem to have been limited to about one hundred staters, but this is not clearly delineated and there were probably ways around it.[157] Moreover, both in Classical Athens and on Krete, the dowry remained the property of the bride for her upkeep but under a kind of administration by her husband. It had to be returned to her in the event of separation.[158] It follows, therefore, that a wife with a large dowry could potentially have used it to influence her husband. She could conceivably employ the threat of divorce that, if undertaken, might then result in his having to render the appointed sum almost immediately. No text explicitly states that the dowry had to be returned on divorce, but, as Sealey indicates, 'the coherence of principles in the Athenian law of marriage suggests that it did have to be refunded in that event'.[159] If she had a very large dowry, a divorce could be rather costly for an ex-husband. It was, as Lacey says, 'deemed to be her share of her paternal estate, a share set apart for her maintenance'.[160]

There is some indication that there was a type of inheritance similar to dowries whereby a Spartan daughter might receive part or all of her household estate when she married.[161] Although their constitution supposedly forbade the buying and selling of estates (as with Magnesia), it permitted anyone who wished to transfer land through gifts and bequests (unlike Magnesia). As a result, according to

Aristotle, nearly two-fifths of Spartan land seems to have come into the possession of citizen-women by the time of the Battle of Leuktra.[162] This may be a typically misogynistic exaggeration. Aristotle criticised this policy suggesting that a firmer regulation of dowries would have been preferable and he alleges that that such states where women dominate financially tend to be warlike and aggressive towards their neighbours.[163]

The Athenian Stranger seems to be seeking to prevent any instability amongst his 5040 land allotments and evidently was aware of some of the 'flaws' in constitutions of his era regarding such matters. By prohibiting dowries and strictly limiting a bride's trousseaux, he has excluded from Magnesian women a measure of power that many other ancient Greek women apparently enjoyed. This is ostensibly done with the intent of preserving concord, encouraging economic stability and to limit expenditures on frivolous purchases not conducive to the pursuit of virtue. In the next chapter, we shall see what kind of exchange women obtain for the loss of such liberty.

As we know by now, major *telos* of Magnesia's policies is the maximum degree of happiness for all citizens of the state as a whole. The *oikos* is crucial for the achievement of this. In addition to being semi-independent 'engines' of socialisation ('indoctrination') into Magnesian ethics such as *andreia* and *aretē*, the family must also serve the obvious function of producing new citizens to populate the city. The people will be told that the generation of offspring is like the divine act of creation. The Athenian Stranger has prepared a speech for his hypothetical colonists that is calculated to drive home the notion that every γένεσις fashions an instrument for helping to secure the happiness of the universe as a whole (903c). They are encouraged, in a manner of speaking, to 'be fruitful and multiply', granted that their population must not exceed 5040 household units.[164] The state will take measures to ensure a stable population according to the Athenian Stranger's prescriptions. These include, but are not limited to methods of contraception and abortion, along with such 'fertility treatments' as were available.[165] Excess offspring, as we have seen, may be dispatched to a colony.[166]

The Athenian Stranger's speech contains the exhortation, appealing to basic human nature, that they 'must naturally hold onto the Everlasting by always leaving behind children and grandchildren that they may render service unto the God'.[167] The subject of the procreative act itself is primary factor in the Athenian Stranger's comprehensive approach to the Magnesian household. He has provided some constitutional guidelines on correct procreation for married couples that have the force of law. Both marital partners are exhorted to engage in the act of procreation with a full sense of responsibility and propriety 'especially when no children have been born to them' (783d8–784a1). He urges that no procreation should take place when either parent is intoxicated in order to prevent damage to the foetus (775b4–e3). Sexual congress in Magnesia is to be a relatively sober affair.

To ensure that the correct procedures are followed by married couples, several Magnesian women will be chosen as Marriage Supervisors to observe them for up to ten years—providing that children come in suitable numbers (784a sq.). If a couple does not produce their quota of offspring, then they have two options. Either they may immediately divorce or receive counselling at the hands of government officials. If, having been duly counselled, they still are unable to fulfil their marital duties regarding *teknopoiia,* then 'the female officials will go into the home of the young people and admonish and threaten them to cease their error and ignorance' (784c2–4). Failure to comply may result in deprivation of the privilege of attending weddings and parties celebrating births (with stringent penalties for defying the ban—784d1–5). The Magnesian state officials use the fear of shame as a preventative measure to ensure obedience. If they continue in their disobedience, more public forms of shame may be deployed against them.[168]

Drawing an analogy from the behaviour of animals, the Athenian Stranger suggests an ideal mode of conduct for his hypothetical populace in terms of marital fidelity. He asserts that the citizens' standards should not be lower than those of the beasts and birds that are apparently monogamous.[169] Whether this analogy reflects true conditions in nature, or even common beliefs on the matter, is not really the point.[170] It is a 'pharmacological' model propagandistically embraced by Magnesia's authorities.[171] Citizens are expected to engage in proper sexual relations only within state-approved marriages between members of the opposite sex. 'Ideally no man', says the Athenian Stranger, 'would dare to have sexual relations with a respectable free-woman other than his wedded wife, nor would he dare to sow unacceptable and bastard seed among concubines, nor sterile seed in males contrary to nature' (841d1–5).[172]

This may, in part, reflect Plato's disapproval of Athenian customs, especially after 414, that permitted men to entertain 'legitimate' relations with concubines.[173] The Magnesians are clearly intended to follow a higher standard of marital behaviour. Yet there is some indication that they might not always live up to the ideal. Plato's narrator speculates on making a law in the event that some citizens' virtue should happen to fall short. He says:

> If a man should have sexual intercourse with anyone, whether she be hired or procured by some other means, other than the woman he led into his household before the gods in sacred matrimony, *except he keep it secret from all other men and women,* I think we would do rightly in passing a law excluding him from state honours since he is in fact no better than a foreigner [emphasis mine].[174]

Magnesia's policies on legal intercourse, while similar to those at Athens, promote a different emphasis and, perhaps to some extent, reflect more Lakonian ideals. No penalty is mentioned for Magnesian women caught in adultery but a comparable sort of limited social disenfranchisement would seem to apply to them as well. The punishments that breaking this law would incur act largely as psychological deterrents—but one imagines that they will be especially effective on the socialised populace. Anyone actually caught and penalised (i.e. for not having the propriety to keep an affair secret) would serve as a powerful, shame-based warning to others. Given the scrutiny under which all Magnesians live, one is inclined to wonder when or if they would ever have the opportunity to undertake such activities. Even so, there seems to be some uncertainty on Plato's narrator's part as to how far the state may infringe on the bedroom.

Adultery is one thing but rape is quite another. The latter is to receive no quarter in the second-best *polis*. If a Magnesian man should use force in a sexual manner against either a free woman or a youth, says the Athenian Stranger, then he will be slain with impunity by the individual who has been forcefully 'outraged' or by members of that one's immediate, male kinship-group.[175] As Fisher observes, this law is very similar to that at Athens in terms of the punishment of the rapist.[176] It is not known how often rapists were actually put to death in this manner and Lysias I may not be paradigmatic.[177] The Magnesian penalty, however, will apply in almost every case and seems harsher as a result. If a male citizen of the second-best state should commit rape, then he would have proven himself lacking in *sōphrosynē*, not to mention *aretē* and *andreia*. How can he be said to have achieved wisdom? Such an individual would be regarded as an enemy to Magnesia, her laws and citizens. Rapists are to be treated with contempt equal to that afforded parricides.

The harshness of Magnesia's penalty for rape and the somewhat lessened emphasis on adultery both represent a notable shift in values from those of Athens—if not necessarily in legality. In the case of the latter, an ideological distinction existed between rape and adultery that especially reflected the concerns of men. Adultery implied seduction and possibly some consent on the part of the woman while rape denoted neither.[178] Both Dover and Pomeroy see the speaker in Lysias I (*against Eratosthenes*) as responding to the fact that adultery was more of a potential threat to the husband's status than was rape.[179] It is another matter whether or not such sentiments were reflected in law. As Harrison says, 'the speaker in this case may be disingenuous, and his "sociological justification" may reflect the fact that he knows that he is being disingenuous'.[180] The idea that adultery deserved greater emphasis may have appealed to the men that comprised Lysias' audience. Seduction and passion were perceived to play greater roles in luring a woman into adultery than free will. Herodotos does not utilise such terms as 'force' or 'consent' in reference to Alexandros' sexual liaisons with Helen. Instead, the character Proteos condemns him for having seduced her, for 'exciting her passion' and then violating the hospitality of his host.[181] As Harrison suggests, 'it appears that arousing passion or excitement in a woman is actually a worse crime than mere rape. (The fact that he arouses her passion only after the initial seduction might suggest that their first liaison was non-consensual.)'[182]

The Athenian concept of *moicheia* applied to both the woman seduced and the man who was seducing her. A woman taken in adultery, as Sealey says, 'was not treated as criminally guilty or legally liable; for she was not tried . . . she was a passive object in adultery, as in the conclusion of marriage'.[183] Her reputation, however, accrued public shame.[184] She would experience, as Todd aptly calls it, 'the female equivalent to *atimia*'.[185] The woman's perceived passivity connects, in some ways, with the Dover/Foucault construction of ancient Greek sexuality along penetrator/penetrated lines; but, it is perhaps more revealing about the way that men viewed women in regard to sex rather than how women viewed sex or themselves.[186] This active/passive dichotomy is highlighted in the sophist Gorgias' *Encomium of Helen*. He argues that, if she was in fact seduced by Paris, then 'the persuader, because he compelled, is guilty; but the persuaded, because she was compelled by his speech, is wrongly reproached'.[187] In Euripides' *Trojan Women*, however, she is not so easily acquitted despite her clever use of Gorgias' suggested arguments.[188] Hekuba relentlessly presses her case against Helen. This, as Croally says, is 'an extreme rhetorical move of generalizing her attack into one of irrationality, sexuality, desire and woman (Helen and Aphrodite are taken as representative of these disturbing factors)'.[189]

Matching perhaps the Athenian perception of the crime, there were severe social and psychological penalties for women found guilty of being seduced. It was compulsory for her to be swiftly divorced.[190] Thereafter she could be kept permanently in an unwed state,[191] with an additional psychological penalty (as in Magnesia) of being deprived of the right to attend public festivals.[192] 'The ban on marriage', as Ogden says, '(a thing regarded as a woman's due and *raison d'être*) and the ban on religious participation (the basis of a woman's social life) would have been devastating'.[193] This seems quite harsh but many would have considered her corrupted through seduction.[194] Aiskhines supports the idea of seduced women being banned from public sacrifices on the grounds that they might corrupt other women present. He adds that, as part of their penalty, it was forbidden for them to be adorned with jewellery or fine clothes. If she defied this, then her garments could be publicly stripped from her on condition that, in doing so, no one cause her bodily harm. Not only might she not be allowed to remarry but she would also have to bear the public shame of her crime for the remainder of her life.[195]

The law in Athens urged the shunning of such women along with proactive 'self-help' on the part of their husbands. It could impose a loss of civic rights (*atimia*) on a man who failed to divorce his wife after winning the case against her adulterer.[196] Demosthenes and Aristotle tell us that a male citizen could kill with impunity an adulterer (or seducer) caught *in flagrante* with his mother, sister, daughter or wife.[197] This practice seems to have been seldom employed in the Classical era but was not altogether unheard of. The Athenians preferred a type of public humiliation inflicted on a male adulterer by the husband rather than the more barbarous act of murder with its attendant *miasma*.[198] This shaming might take the form of a public beating by the cuckolded husband and his friends or the offending party could, as Ogden says, 'also be subjected to *raphanidōsis*, which involved the singeing off of their pubic hair with hot ash, and the insertion of a radish or fish (a *skorpios* or a mullet) into their anus'.[199] It is possibly indicative of their androcentric character that neither Magnesia nor Athens seems to be quite so concerned about seductresses—unless perhaps they were foreigners.[200]

The Athenian Stranger's proposed law on adultery, as with many of his laws, necessitates state intervention in areas where Athens preferred self-help. This is one significant aspect in which Magnesia's mores might be seen as rather alien to those of Athens. However, not unlike Athens, the laws appear to place more importance on penalising the male seducer than the female. Nussbaum has suggested that Plato had a 'special worry about the loss of male bodily fluids that are important for reproduction, in connection with his persistent worries about population'.[201] Whether this is an accurate statement of Plato's thinking or not is impossible to say. His narrator does appear somewhat less concerned over the chastity of women and legitimacy of offspring than was apparently the case amongst the ancient Athenians.[202]

The Magnesian government is designed to take an active interest in maintaining the stable populace of 5040. Marital sex would appear to have less moral emphasis than practical necessity. This is demonstrated by the Athenian Stranger's support for methods of contraception, abortion and 'fertility treatments'. As we have seen, a loophole has been provided by which some men might engage in adultery with women who are other than citizens—in spite of being strongly discouraged from doing so. In the *Laws*, as Field says, 'strict monogamy is the rule, and Plato expresses strong disapproval of all extra-marital intercourse, though he does not think it practicable to forbid it by law'.[203] The strictness of the rule of monogamy in Magnesia is upheld less by the legal code and more through psychological influences involving shame and fear.[204]

Notwithstanding a lessened significance on legitimacy, the Athenian Stranger does not propose the sort of sexual license that Xenophon and Plutarch suggest was the case amongst the Spartans. Plutarch indicates that they regarded adultery as hardly a crime at all.[205] Xenophon does not mention adultery and Plutarch goes out of his way to deny that it existed. 'Plutarch seems to have been technically correct', as Cartledge says, 'and this is a remarkable comment on the emphasis laid on the extra-marital maintenance of the male citizen population at Sparta'.[206] It may have been the case that there was no law on adultery in Sparta except amongst the royal families.[207] Our lack of knowledge about rape and adultery in the lower classes may be due to the small number of non-Spartans that had the chance to hear about them.[208] Polybios and

Strabo both suggest that the Ephors had encouraged sexual license amongst citizens and *helots* as a means of survival in times of conflict when legitimate fathers were few and this precedent may have discouraged the criminalisation of extra-marital intercourse.[209] The Athenian Stranger does not borrow the Spartans' allegedly lax sexual mores for Magnesia, but his greater interest in population stability over legitimacy of offspring appears to favour their values somewhat more than Athenian ones.

The ancient Kretans, in contrast, appear to have preferred an elaborate system of fines for various degrees of adultery according to the economic and social status of the participants (nominal fines were stipulated for adultery with slaves).[210] Kretan law, like Athenian, refers to the 'seduction' of the woman in cases of adultery. This was sometimes called the 'sins of a wife'.[211] The Athenian Stranger is not particularly concerned with women being seduced. It goes without saying that a female citizen of the second-best *polis* ought to have better self control. But he does not penalise them in the same way as the Athenians.

The Magnesian regulations impose no fines, trifling or otherwise, for adultery and against it stands the psychological threat of public shame along with partial (and presumably temporary) disenfranchisement—only if caught. Rape earns the discouraging penalty of a violent death. Magnesia's moral imperative of *aretē* would ideally preclude engaging in such sexual acts that are deemed shameful, immoderate and/or criminal. Lacey theorises that Plato's narrator is reacting against Athenian attitudes that permitted men extra-marital relations providing that they were not with women of some other citizen's immediate family.[212] But is he? Theoretically, the Magnesian citizens should not partake of extra-marital affairs but, in practice, they could do so with relative impunity. The laws do not forbid such things but societal values strongly discourage them. The rule of moderation is intended to control the passions of Magnesia's citizen-elite, in order to facilitate their pursuit of *aretē*, but leaves some legal space for a more 'human equation'.

The Magnesian family hierarchy is primarily patriarchal. Men play an active role in terms of their authority within the household. The Athenian Stranger's 'hierarchy of betters', as we have seen, posits that 'parents are the superiors of children, and men (ἄνδρες) of both women and children, since rulers are superior to the ruled'.[213] One may deduce from this that the father is meant to hold the highest position of authority within the household. Magnesian mothers likewise appear to have some authority (second to fathers) but their essential role remains that of bearing offspring. As Chodorow indicates, women have been traditionally 'defined as wives and mothers, thus in particularistic relation to someone else, whereas men are defined primarily in universalistic occupational terms'.[214] The father is *kyrios* of the Magnesian estate and his male heir (by blood or adoption) then becomes the next *kyrios*. It is the Magnesian father who makes out the will and it is to his line of relatives to which primacy is accorded (for the purpose of designating the new male heir to be *kyrios*) in the event that he should die intestate (924e2–925a1).

Very little is said about the actual relationship between Magnesian fathers and their offspring. The role of the father will be to direct the household. It is fair to say that the model of masculinity that he is exhorted to follow is 'idealised or accorded superiority' and this makes it desirable for male youths to imitate by example.[215] Yet there are limits to the powers that a father may exercise over others in his household. All the members of the *oikos*, it should be recalled, are first and foremost subjects of Magnesia and 'belong more to the state than to those who begat them' (804d4–6).

In order to assure a peaceful concord, the Athenian Stranger has established legal protocols to cope with potential problems that might arise between parents and their offspring. These rules are not comprehensive in their coverage but, presumably, the *nukterinos* council and the Magnesian magistrates will provide more detailed guidelines later. The Athenian Stranger's outlines will be paradigmatic for dealing with a broad range of familial problems. He indicates that the sort of difficulties that his laws encompass should be quite uncommon in a virtuous city like Magnesia. They are more likely, he says, 'to occur amongst men who are wholly evil'.[216] Even so, as if anticipating that there might be exceptions to the norm, he provides statutes to regulate disinheritance of sons by fathers and indictments of senility against fathers by sons.

If a Magnesian father wishes to disinherit a son, he may not do so without due process.[217] Potentially this law may apply to daughters as well but the Athenian Stranger has not said so and his language here suggests that sons might be the primary ones to suffer disinheritance. The word υἱός literally means 'son', but, in later Greek examples, can also convey the more general sense of 'child' much as ἄνθρωπος can indicate all of humanity.[218] Here it probably does mean 'son'. Even so, there is no reason to assume that daughters might not also be subject to the same law. The crucial point appears to be whether or not the offspring in question is due to inherit the indivisible estate.

The state of being legally 'fatherless' is regarded as a weighty matter in Magnesia. It is a condition that carries with it an implicit sentence of eventual exile (928e7–929a1). An estranged father must call together an assembly 'of his own kinfolk as far as cousins and likewise his son's kinsfolk on the mother's side'.[219] The parent and child are both given equal opportunity to present their respective cases before a family gathering. If the assembled members vote (excluding the father, mother and child in question) in favour of the father by more than half, then the child is disinherited (929b7–c3). He is not without recourse, however, since any citizen of Magnesia may adopt the outcast within a ten-year grace period specified by law (929c3–d3). Otherwise, after that span of time the disinherited will be compelled to emigrate.

Certain legal procedures apply if a Magnesian child (again, the word used is υἱός) should wish to have a parent indicted for senility. The situation discussed by the Athenian Stranger is one in which a *kyrios* has become seriously demented and is no longer capable of his managerial role over the *klēros*. This legislation may not apply in the same manner to a senile mother unless she happens also to be the head of the household. Such a situation seems likely to be a rare occurrence given both the 'hierarchy of betters' and the strong social convention that all Magnesian citizens of the appropriate ages should be married with the man in a dominant role—but it is not beyond the realm of possibility that a woman could be a single parent at effectively *kyrios* of the household. A son who seeks to have his father declared senile 'must first go before the eldest of the Guardians of the Laws and report to them his father's condition and they, after a full enquiry, will advise whether or not he should bring an indictment' (929d9–e4). If after their investigations they advise in favour of an indictment, then these same Guardians will act as advocates and witnesses for the son's case before a magistrate (929e4–6). If the father in question is deemed senile by the court, then the son (if he is next in line) will assume the role of *kyrios* and the senile father 'thereafter will have no power to administer even the smallest title of his property and he will be considered as a child in the household for the remainder of his life' (929e6–9).

These procedures for dealing with disinheritance and indictments of senility also have their analogues in ancient Athens. However, it is fair to say that the Athenian Stranger's system represents a significant revision of any ideas borrowed from there. We are told that an Athenian father could legally disown his son, even after paternity had been acknowledged, by a formal rejection (*apokeryxis*) if evidence was brought to light proving the child was not his own.[220] 'Some scholars', says Mac-Dowell, 'have taken *apokeryxis* to mean "disinherision;" but the Athenian evidence is against the view that it was legally permitted for a father to disinherit one who was actually his son, except by having him adopted by someone else'.[221]

More is known about indictments of senility brought against their fathers by Athenian sons. There were a significant number of such cases. Golden suggests that this might have been due to mounting tensions between fathers and sons over inheritance plus having recourse to a ready means of addressing the problem through established legal tradition.[222] An Athenian son might indict his father with a *graphē paranoias,* 'a lawsuit asserting that his father was no longer competent to manage his affairs'.[223] Attesting perhaps to the unfairness of some of these proceedings, there is the famous (but dubious) case of the playwright Sophokles who successfully defended himself against an indictment of senility by reputedly reciting aloud lengthy passages from his *Oedipus at Kolonos.*[224] The Athenian Stranger clearly expects fewer such conflicts to occur between Magnesian fathers and sons. His legal proceedings on the issue appear fairer and more sophisticated than those at Athens.

Firstborn offspring of Magnesian families will remain within their respective households until they become married, ideally inheriting a title to a land unit, and begin a household of their own. Most will remain in Magnesia and be throughout much of their lives, in some form or another, subject to their parents.[225] The interplay between the integrity of the household unit and the stability of the *polis* is a special aspect of the myth of the family. A process of transference directs the mandated respect for elders into a sublimated respect for the state. He says that 'the view which should be held by everyone, both amongst gods and men, is that the older is considerably more revered than the younger' (879b7–c1). The citizens will be told that 'injurious treatment (αἰκία) of an older person by a younger one is a shameful thing (αἰσχρὸν) to see occurring within the state and is hateful to the god' (979c1–3).

The religious sentiments that he is associating with proper behaviour toward one's parents are not unique to Plato but partake of a broader cultural *ethos*. The ancient Athenians appear to have maintained similar views. In Athens, as in Magnesia, 'anyone, and not merely a wronged father', as Strauss indicates, 'could file a special lawsuit against a son for alleged mistreatment of parents (*graphê goneôn kakôseôs*), including neglect or physical violence'.[226] The religious implications of parental respect may also be seen, as Golden says, by virtue of 'the interest in the subject they [the Athenians] attributed to the gods'.[227] The gods themselves were thought to take an active interest in the treatment of parents by their offspring and this was an influential factor in the ever-present background of traditionally perceived norms that dictated Athenian custom. Whether they adhered to this virtue in real life or not, it affected their moral outlook. Lykourgos the orator, in his attempt to prosecute Leokrates on a charge of treason, indicates that the gods preside most of all over the duties to 'parents, the dead and themselves'.[228] There is every indication that, at least ideally, disrespect for one's parents could be viewed as an effrontery to the gods and therefore as an act of impiety.[229]

The official virtue of respecting one's elders in Magnesia also displays certain Spartan leanings but should not be considered as 'wholesale' borrowing from their culture. 'Honours given to the old at Sparta', as Powell states, 'represented the culmination of an elaborate hierarchy based on age and beginning in early schooldays'.[230] Magnesia, as we have seen, will be a sort of gerontocracy like Sparta—with its Guardians of the Laws over the age of fifty and the Vigilance Committee made up of the eldest of these.[231] The Athenian Stranger's preference for 'Spartan-style' institutionalised reverence for elders may be taken as a criticism of Athenian society in terms of practice if not theory. According to Xenophon, in contrast to his idealised Spartans, the Athenians tended to show their elders considerable disrespect in spite of the official religious sentiments.[232]

The ethic of revering one's parents was as deeply rooted in myth and religion as in culture. Its social function in Magnesia, as elsewhere, may be seen as serving to maintain a kind of harmony amongst families and the state at large. The Athenian Stranger's particular approach to the problem of encouraging all of his citizens to respect their elders is at least threefold in nature. First, there is the all-encompassing Magnesian moral imperative for the pursuit of *aretē*. The educational system of Magnesia (not unlike that of Sparta) indoctrinates this ideology into its subjects. But, since this is to be a second-best state, something more is perceived as necessary to ensure the maximum net result of proper behaviour for all. The second method employed by the Athenian Stranger's involves propaganda. This includes such axioms as those mentioned above, the use of *paramyth* or 'fables' to convince the masses as well as other examples of this information-based tactic.[233] The third and, perhaps, the most powerful weapon in his arsenal is the law itself, which works in concert with moral imperatives and elements of propaganda. Such a law is introduced in book IX. It mandates that Magnesian youths must regard all citizens over a certain age as parental figures with all of the incipient authority that such status entails.[234]

His method is designed to promote stability of the *polis, phylē* and *oikos* by reinforcing the 'hierarchy of betters' and extending it communally outside one's immediate family group.[235] Most people in positions of authority will be over the age of fifty and will thus be able to demand a high degree of socially conditioned and legally mandated respect from younger citizens. The latter are recognised as perhaps the most likely ones to resist authority. Magnesian law will provide a number of discouragements for any potentially irreverent youths. In most circumstances, a youth will have no choice but to submit to virtually any type of treatment by an elder. 'When a young man is beaten by an old man', says the Athenian Stranger, 'it is appropriate that, in every case, he should quietly endure his anger, and thus store up honour for his own old age' (when he may then beat younger men who are behaving badly—879c3–5). Alternatively, if a young person should beat their parents (and presumably this would include all metaphorical 'parents' as well), and the assailant is not afflicted with madness, then they will be exiled on pain of death should they attempt to return.[236] Perhaps out of a concern for fairness, those Magnesian magistrates who judge children that have committed such crimes against their parents must themselves have children who are not adopted (878e).

One of the worst crimes that a Magnesian citizen might conceivably commit is that of parricide. This sort of outrage is considered to be on par with temple robbery and rape.[237] It is seen to deserve the heaviest of penalties. There might be some small consideration for the perpetrator if they 'should dare to slay a parent in the madness of rage' *and* if the dying parent should happen, perhaps as their final act, to acquit the offender (869a4–b2).[238] They would be permitted to undergo rites of purification like those who commit involuntary homicide. However, if there are no such mitigating circumstances, then the law will be most severe. The Athenian Stranger says that if it were possible for the un-acquitted parricide 'to die many deaths', then this would be an appropriate punishment to fit the magnitude of the crime (869b5–8). The penalties for a parent who slays a child in anger (868c7 sq.), along with husbands and wives who kill each other in rage (868d7 sq.) and siblings who kill each other under the same circumstances are considerably less severe and usually involve ritual purifications and sometimes temporary suspension of certain privileges (869c8 sq.). Underscoring its significance, even in the 'madness of rage', to slay a parent in Magnesia can incur the ultimate penalty of death by execution (869c5–7).

Only under extreme circumstances might a child prevail over the will of his or her parent and virtually never by force.[239] However, as we have seen, parents are not given total supremacy over their own affairs or their children's. They are all subject to a higher authority that is intent on its own goals and its self-preservation. The state casts parents and children in specific roles within a hierarchy designed to promote respect and obedience. The connection between respect for parents/elders and the sanctity of the state is made clear in book III. There, the Athenian Stranger indicates that a lack of the proper reverence for parents is like the condition of anarchy. He and Megillus have been discussing how 'excesses' and 'liberties' (manifested in such things as poetry, music, drama and democracy) lead to the deterioration of a state. Music and the theatre, improperly managed, are seen to have the potential to make men 'without fear' such that their 'audacity begets effrontery'.[240] After this condition has festered for a while, the audacious subjects then refuse to obey their rulers. The next phase of deterioration, closest to pure anarchy, is arrived at when children 'flee submission to their parents and elders and their admonitions'.[241] The final phase of decadence comes when people lose all respect for the gods and thereby revert to a pitiful state.[242]

In order to avoid this spiral of decay and promote civic stability on the whole, the Athenian Stranger indicates that respect for parents and other elders is compulsory and supported by force of law. People's attitudes toward their superiors are regarded as a sort of barometer for indicating a society's overall health. The microcosmic authority represented by parents and elders symbolises the greater authority of the macrocosmic *polis*.

A significant means by which this hypothetical society will support the myth of the family (and thereby the solvency of the *polis*) may be observed in the honours extended to the dead. These rituals strengthen family unity and reaffirm the sexed hierarchy of the *oikos*. Parents are to be buried by their families in a manner that preserves the general rules of moderation and *aretē*. There will be yearly ceremonies in honour of deceased relations.[243] These, much like similar honours later paid to the Roman dead, will encourage shame/modesty and respect (*aidōs*).[244] As Flower indicates, 'Shame is often an important ingredient in cultures which are small-scale like city-states . . . [these] societies depend on personal rather than on abstract obligations, as citizens regularly came face-to-face with one another'.[245] The Athenian Stranger, in one of his prepared speeches to his subjects, says that if these rites associated with the dead are followed properly, then 'we shall win rewards from the gods and from all that are mightier than ourselves and we shall pass the greatest part of our lives enjoying hopes of happiness'.[246] The opposite will be the case if they are not followed.

Religious sentiments bind the Magnesian *oikos* to the *polis,* much as in the real world of Plato's era, through a process of transferring reverence from a deceased relative to the state as a whole. This is consistent with contemporary modes of 'death and memorialisation' in the Classical world that, as Stears says, 'appear to have provided an avenue for the expression of a number of social norms and ideologies'.[247] In Magnesia, as in the real world, there will be the added incentive that, if one performs the correct honours to the dead, then the gods will favour the individual doing so, his/her family and Magnesia. It is also implied, but not actually stated in the *Laws,* that the neglect of these honours due to the dead could cause severe damage to the state and thereby any negligent families.

The theme of persuasion present throughout the *Laws,* as with other elements of propaganda, recollects Perikles' famous 'Funeral Oration'.[248] But Magnesia's ideological foundations are profoundly different from those of imperial Athens.[249] Similar rhetorical techniques to those of Perikles will nonetheless be employed. They will urge the Magnesians that 'the degradation of cowardice must be immeasurably more grievous to a man of spirit than the unfelt death which strikes him in the midst of his strength and patriotism'.[250] Also, the quality of *andreia* will be particularly extolled at Magnesian funerals.[251] These and other notions indicate no small degree of comparable attitudes in both Plato and Perikles.[252] *Andreia,* as previously discussed, has a different meaning for the Athenian Stranger and Magnesia will not be a *polis* that praises imperial values—in death or otherwise.[253] Different virtues take their stead.

Magnesian funerals will be expressions of familial and societal reverence. They are subject to many restrictions and, as with everything else, Lakonian-style scrutiny. It was not unusual for the ancient *polis* to dictate the parameters of funerals conducted by private families.[254] Magnesia is to be more comprehensive in this capacity than any real *polis.* The appropriate religious interpreters will expand the Athenian Stranger's outline of the particular customs of burial, 'whether the deceased be either a man or a woman' (958d3–6). Different sorts of ceremonies will be fashioned according to their sex.[255] The Athenian Stranger does not spell out every detail, but he is willing to provide some guidelines for Magnesia's future theologians to follow in making their individual interpretations.

Graves are to be situated, pragmatically, in ground that has no use for cultivation so that the dead do not deprive the living of the necessities of life. The burial mound can be no larger than that which can be completed by the work of five men in five days. The grave markers, on the whole, must be kept simple in design.[256] For most citizens, the undertaker 'will make the stone grave-markers not larger than as much as will contain no more than four heroic lines of *encomia* on the life of the deceased'.[257] I will return to this point in relation to the role Magnesian women in the following chapter.

The family of the deceased is admonished 'to spend a measured amount as is appropriate for a soul-less altar of the ones beneath the earth'.[258] The Athenian Stranger says that it would not be unseemly for the legislator to define the 'measured' expenditure as five *minae* for the funeral of one of the highest property class, three for the second class, two the third and one *mina* for an individual of the lowest property class.[259] There are to be no elaborate funerary devices (none of the archaic *kouroi* or *korai*, nor any of the familial sculpture—even plain, democratic ornamentation—associated with Athenian tombstones from c.500 B.C.E. onwards) as this de-emphasises the importance of personal expression in terms of wealth and class.[260] The Athenian Stranger's restrictions on funeral expenditures appear to reflect a similar desire for a kind of equality (or near-equality) in death as those allegedly introduced by the democratic reforms of Solon at Athens.[261] Unlike Athens, however, Magnesia will ensure that its funerary practices are scrutinised by one of the Guardians of the Laws to ensure that the rule of moderation is strictly upheld.[262]

Like Solon, the Athenian Stranger seeks to avoid excessive emotionality at funerals. As will be discussed more in the next chapter, it must be checked with 'manly' austerity and women have been particularly singled out by this injunction. In part, such a position is predicated by the rule of moderation. It may also reflect the Athenian Stranger's views (and possibly Plato's) on the nature of the soul, its immortality and its importance above and beyond that of the flesh.[263] As time passes in Magnesia, its cemeteries will fill with the virtuous dead whose souls have gone beyond. The plain memorials left to them seem to be a psychological mechanism for the transference of adoration poured on them by individuals and families. They become a monument to the *aretē* of the city-state as a whole.

Magnesian funerals are events of importance for the family but the glorification of the *polis* clearly overshadows the individual's significance. The yearly ceremonies to be held by family members to honour their deceased relatives serve both to unify the citizens of the state through the common practice of mourning as well as to strengthen the bonds of respect for their ancestors. These also reinforce societal views of sexuality. They honour Magnesia's collective dead and bind the community through the participation of families evincing a common reverence for their ancestors and, as with Periklean funerary rhetoric, they propagandistically advertise the civic virtues that these are seen to represent. The *oikos* meets the *polis* at a Magnesian funeral and the yearly memorial ceremonies. The one draws on the other for strength, comfort and exaltation. The ideals of the *polis* and the role of the *oikos* within it are mutually forwarded in these celebrations of death and remembrance.

In conclusion, there are many and subtle ways in which the Athenian Stranger is constructing the myth of the family for Magnesia. These include, but are not limited to law, calculated rhetoric, imposed custom, educational indoctrination, censorship and mythologizing. It is fair to say that the Magnesian household is significantly different from its analogues in ancient Athens, Krete, Sparta or anywhere else. This difference is underlined by such distinguishing characteristics as the participation of Magnesian women in and outside the *oikos,* frequent supervision by the state and the rules governing marriage and the inheritance of property. The indivisible 5040 land units may be seen, at least in part, as limiting upward (and downward) social mobility but also functioning to stabilise the socio-economic foundations of the *polis.* As with the level of supervision, this recollects idealised representations of Sparta. The Magnesian state is an active agent that regulates many more activities in the private sphere of the populace, policing the sphere of ideas, more so than most real governments at the time would have considered possible.

The structure of the Magnesian family, as Plato's narrator has outlined it, is patriarchal and appears fairly traditional on the surface—especially by Athenian norms. The 'hierarchy of betters' and other such passages suggest that greater authority is to be granted to fathers than to mothers. More emphasis also seems be placed on the importance of sons as heirs and future *kyrioi* than on daughters. Their role in inheritance, while ultimately no less significant, is portrayed as having somewhat less emphasis than that of males. Sometimes it seems that the Athenian Stranger wants Magnesian women to be independent and active citizens in the same way as their male counterparts. He has granted them no small role in both the *oikos* and the state. The Athenian Stranger's statements to the effect that women are somehow naturally 'inferior toward the pursuit of *aretē*' seem to devalue and relegate mothers and daughters to subordinate and secondary position compared to those of Magnesian fathers and sons. More on the issue of Magnesian women's 'liberation', and the costs thereof, will be explored in the next chapter.

Plato's decision to utilise the institution of the patriarchal household in his hypothetical Magnesia seems ultimately based on utilitarian efficiency in fulfilling the perceived needs of the second-best *polis.* In the *Kallipolis* of the *Republic,* all property is held in common and the state-sponsored breeding facilities perfunctorily perform their tasks with the sureness of well-oiled machines. These were designed for an ideal society. Magnesia employs a more de-centralised approach with the semi-private household conscripted to perform the work of a breeding facility with less expense and supervision. It may represent a practice not unlike like the modern, Western approach to socialism in which the state provides the means for independent, corporate entities to thrive so long as they perform a specified socio-economic role according to specific regulations. One may construe the Magnesian *oikos* as a semi-independent, corporate entity that indirectly exercises the will of a centralised authority. Its main purposes are to ensure the continuation of the populace and to prepare citizens for their future place in society. This includes carefully moulding their modes of thought and promoting their ideal sex roles from an early age. The myth of the family works together with the greater myth of the *polis* in order to achieve these ends.

Chapter VI
A Brave New Femininity

Go into the house and see to your tasks, the loom and the distaff, and bid your handmaidens go about their work. War will concern men, all those born at Troy and me especially.

—Hektor[1]

To allow the female to live in luxury, spend money, and follow disorderly pursuits, while supervising the male, is to grant only half of a totally happy life—instead of double that for the city.

—The Athenian Stranger[2]

Then card wool and work it delicately whilst munching beans. War will be women's business.

—Lysistrata[3]

As discussed in earlier chapters, Magnesian women have an unparalleled status in their society. Yet they are constrained in particular ways. Their status stands in contrast to the state-mandated necessity of *teknopoiia*. In addition to this, they will be encouraged to modify their femininity by subordinating certain perceived negative aspects of it to the rule of orderly, manly Reason. How is this 'new femininity' defined for Magnesian women? This chapter proceeds from the assumption of contemporary philosophical thought to the effect that 'male, like female, is an idea about sex . . . to say that male-ness is "absence of female-ness," or vice versa, is a matter of definition and metaphysically arbitrary'.[4] Plato's narrator is no stranger to metaphysical arbitration in the sphere of sexual ideas.

The second-best society significantly revises the traditional dichotomy between *oikos* and *polis* by allowing women unprecedented access to participation in the affairs of the latter (along with the state's encroachment on the former). This freedom comes at the cost of some characteristics here expressly associated with women. The Athenian Stranger seeks to obtain part of his 'masculinisation' of Magnesian women through a Lakonisation and/or Kretanisation (it could likewise be termed 'Sauroma-tianisation', or maybe even 'Amazonisation') of essentially Athenian feminine norms.[5] Members of either sex in Magnesia will be thoroughly supervised throughout their entire lives and both the state and the family will inculcate their accepted sex-roles from an early age. The ideal role for a Magnesian woman emerges as a synthesis of traditionally 'manly' qualities (such as warcraft and politics) together with tradition-ally feminine qualities (e.g. housewife and mother), both norms of ancient Greek life, to bridge the gap between public and private spheres. The result is revolutionary.

There are a number of ways in which Magnesian women directly participate in the *polis*. They must necessarily devote a significant amount of time and effort to the bearing and rearing of children. In this capacity, Magnesians enjoy a freely available system of nurses, teachers and state-subsidised slaves to take many of the responsi-bilities entailed in their children's upbringing. Apart from the necessity of generating offspring to populate the city-state, a Magnesian woman will be groomed from youth to participate in the public realm alongside men—if not entirely on an equal footing with them.

Institutions such as phratries and the mixed-sex communal dining tables take women outside the household and place them squarely in the sphere of the *polis*. The system of education outlined for both sexes allows for the sort of preparation needed not only for the pursuit of *aretē* but also for participation in public life.[6] Magnesian women's military involvement heightens their capacity to interact on a similar stand-ing as men. There is to be some sexual segregation in religious ceremonies but even this places women together in a civic capacity. The situation of Magnesian women in the public sphere seems to be derived more out of a utilitarian urge for efficiency than any modern ethic of sexual egalitarianism.

The potential range of 'civil liberties' allowed to female Magnesian citizens remains unclear in many respects but future legislators will work out the fine details. The Athenian Stranger's account, as with all of his other laws, provides a fundamental framework that leaves many of the particulars for others to supply. He has, however, provided a great deal of information on the lives of women in the public sphere. He constructs their place in society with recourse to some of the different parts that women in other cultures of his day are perceived to have played and then formulates a role for his second-best state. Reductively speaking, what he intends a sort of merging of traditional feminine attributes with specifically identified masculine ones.

Are Magnesian citizen-women going to work on a farm, herd sheep and cattle and serve the household like slaves? Or will they be completely shut off from the outside world and tend exclusively to household matters such as weaving, cooking and cleaning (805d–e)? Will they follow a Spartan example (however idealised) and partake of gymnastics and music,[7] weave and spin little,[8] and exist in a sort of middle ground between taking care of others, acting as stewards of property and rearing children? If Magnesian women lived in a manner such as Lakonian women or, that is, the way that the Athenian Stranger seems to think they lived, then he says that they could learn both gymnastics and wool-working but:

> They would not partake of warlike things, so they would not be able, if at some point fate should compel them, to fight for the sake of their city and their children; nor would they be able to shoot arrows, like certain Amazons, nor could they be acquainted with the skill of any other missile, or to take up spear and shield in imitation of the goddess, so as to nobly oppose the ravaging of their fatherland[9]—nor indeed could they produce fear in the enemy, if nothing more, by being seen arrayed in martial order. Living in such a way, they would not dare to imitate the Sauromatians, whose women would seem like men compared to these.[10]

Magnesian women, as we shall shortly see, will have the opportunity to become well versed in the arts of war and fighting. The Athenian Stranger has decided not to imitate precisely any of the customs, mentioned in the above passage, in formulating a role for Magnesian women. Rather, he borrows something from each of them in order to achieve a synthesis of sexual characteristics that he deems desirable for women of the second-best *polis*.

Ancient Greek women's participation in the public sphere, as we have seen, could be described as limited at best.[11] Plato's utopia, however 'second-best', demands a greater degree of equality and this entails some socio-sexual re-programming. The masculinisation of women in Magnesia is perhaps most evident in terms of their involvement in the military. It may also be observed in their apparently more limited role in city politics. Some of the 'manly' ideals that the Athenian Stranger plans for his female subjects to adopt are indicated in the selection from the text above and elsewhere. Repeated references are made to the model of the Amazons, Spartan and Sauromatian women. His choice of images reveals a complex network of relationships in the final product.

The concept of Sauromatian women, one of the examples cited in support of military training for female Magnesians, would have evoked an immediate association with the *other*, less 'civilised' peoples of the world and their apparently 'topsy-turvy' modes of existence. Sauromatia, the Athenian Stranger says, is a culture in which women are instructed to handle horses, the bow and other weapons on equal terms with men.[12] According to Herodotos, the Sauromatians were a people who lived East of the Skythians.[13] They were allegedly descended from an intermingling of Skythian men with a band of marauding Amazons who were raiding villages and generally 'misbehaving' in that region. According to the story, a band of Greeks had defeated these women in Themiskyra and, whilst captives aboard ship, they successfully overtook and slew their male captors. Knowing nothing of the art of sailing (since they were women), they roamed aimlessly until they reached Lake Maeotis (Sea of Azov) where they encountered the Skythians. Herodotos' audience had long been fascinated with these warrior women. Characteristic of the relationship between the Greeks and Asians (real or imagined), there was intense fascination for the Amazons—this, mingled with the usual degree of scorn reserved for foreigners and their ways.[14]

Herodotos' account of the Amazons reveals, as Gould says, 'his open-eyed acknowledgement that human experience is multiform and that the role of women is culturally determined'.[15] This would seem to be true inasmuch as Herodotos can imagine that foreign cultures differed in remarkable ways.[16] Amazons are barbarians by Athenian standards but they are still considered European, although they are situated at the periphery.[17] As Romm says, they 'dressed, according to the usual Greek depictions of them, in leather clothing that gave them a distinctly Asian appearance'.[18] These women, imagined or otherwise, who take up arms like men stand in stark contrast to the vast majority of their Greek counterparts.[19]

All versions of the myth contain curious distortions of normal Greek customs. In response to the Amazonian invasion, Herodotos tells us that the Skythians decided to send their youngest men, of *ephēbic* age, to live amongst the Amazons, to live like them and, ideally, to seduce them into marriage. The Amazons eventually agree to take the young men as husbands—but only on condition that they go and fetch whatever movable property they would inherit from their fathers. This represents one level of an inversion of the 'normal' that tends to be present in the myth at large. 'So here', as Hartog indicates, 'it is the husband—not, as is customary, the bride—who brings the dowry'.[20] In this way, according to Herodotos, was the wild Sauromatian race born.

Amazons were a popular *topos* for Athenian art and literature from the 6th century B.C.E. onwards.[21] Representations of them had been present in ancient Greek culture at least since the time of Homer and Hesiod and probably earlier. Portrayed from the outset as barbarians, they are abstractly localised in a realm that belies the societal norms of Greek society.[22] Their images on the Parthenon, as Blundell says, 'like the other mythical opponents on the metopes, can be seen on one level as an example of the "defeated barbarian" type'.[23] Their 'barbarous' reversal of norms also made them attractive objects of erotic curiosity.[24] They reverse a polarity whose paragon is the adult male hoplite-cum-father and *kyrios*. The psychological implications that they appear to have signified to Greek men are complex. It is possible that, as counter-examples, they represent subversive elements present in the Classical mindset toward women.[25]

The Amazons provide revealing insights into the modes of thought on sex at the time. They upset the boundaries that were clearly defined for the public and private spheres in many Greek *poleis* and especially Athens.[26] Amazons attained a peculiar status through the negation of these traditional norms.[27] 'Imagining an inversion of roles', as Hartog writes, 'meant transferring women from the sphere of marriage into that of war and excluding men from the latter'.[28] Their mythical representations paint an interesting picture of Greek male psychology. Strabo indicates that the Amazons would engage in physical relations with men from a neighbouring people, the Gargarians, once a year in order to 'top up' their female population.[29] In contrast, Diodorus' version says that they did marry but that their menfolk meekly performed that which would have traditionally been 'women's work'.[30]

Another inversion of Athenian norms may be seen in Diodorus' account of the myth. He says that they remained virgins whilst pursuing their military activities but ceased to fight when married. Thereafter they become magistrates and went about Amazonian civic affairs.[31] War then, according to this particular representation, is the business of virgin-Amazons. These would appear to constitute an age group that experiences the equivalent of a period of *ephēbeia,* comparable to the male equivalent and likewise brought to its conclusion by marriage.[32] This bears more than a passing resemblance to the Athenian Stranger's plan for Magnesia's female citizens. It is not a complete reversal of norms, as in the case of fictionalised Amazonian culture—male Magnesians also undergo this training and do not undertake 'women's work'—but the inclusion of women in traditionally male roles is quite remarkable.

In the same passage of Diodorus mentioned above, he also says that the Amazons seared the breasts of their female children shortly after birth since these, if fully developed, would hinder them in combat. Thus they could be said to resemble beardless, athletic (male) youths with long hair. The image that this evokes is that of muscled, armoured and flat-chested figure, who is androgynous but still clearly female.[33] She retains the potential for the sort of sexual liaison that is possible between a man and a woman. In some sense, this type of attraction is that which we would today call 'homoerotic'. The androgynous Amazon is comparable to Spartan imagery found in bronze figurines, mirror-handles and *kylix* interiors that, as Cartledge says, often 'portray girls and young women with underdeveloped or de-emphasised secondary sex characteristics'.[34] As with Spartan representations, the image of the Amazon seems to present an idealised 'receptive' male, untamed, but with feminine qualities.[35] These are, after all, women who unabashedly undertake 'men's business' with remarkable zeal if not always with success.

It was perhaps important that they were seen as having been defeated by men. Amazons fought in vain on the Trojan side against the Greeks, led by Queen Penthesilea, whom Achilles slew.[36] They stormed Athens either to retrieve Hippolyte/Antiope's girdle (or to rescue the queen herself) and were either defeated or bargained with.[37] They fought Bellerophon, Herakles and Theseus with little or no success.[38] They were represented on Athenian temple friezes amongst vanquished foes.[39] Their greatness was propagandistically transferred to their conquerors. Lysias wrote that the defeat of the Amazons 'made the memory of the city's valour imperishable, and rendered their own country nameless on account of the disaster that they suffered in our land'.[40] This is one of a long line of victories named as preceding (and 'spun' as presaging) the defeat of Persia at Marathon, Salamis and Plataea.[41]

The Amazons are martial heroes who are recognisably feminine.[42] When they have been conquered, as Hardwick says, the 'defeated individual Amazons are presented as assimilated to the property- and power-oriented framework of exclusive citizenship and *oikos,* by displaying qualities of submission and loyalty valued in Greek families'.[43] Their place in Athenian ideology and identity seems clear if perhaps a bit strange.[44] They were 'women behaving badly' who have the potential to be 'rehabilitated'. Their reversal of normal values made them attractive to more men than those in ancient Athens and, especially for the latter, it seems to have invited their conquest and reform—if only in artistic representation and myth.[45]

This contextual backdrop helps inform our understanding of the *Laws.*[46] The fact is that Plato's narrator wants his Magnesian women to be like the Amazons. But 'like' is not 'the same as'. He too displays the particularly Athenian inclination toward their reform. His will be 'tame' Amazons who marry and rear offspring of both sexes. They will not sear their breasts but, departing from Athenian custom, they will engage in exercise and military training. This will make them more muscular and martial than was the norm. The sort of heroic qualities associated with the warrior-women of myth will be encouraged and refined in Magnesian women as they put on armour, train and fight, if necessary, like men.[47] The mythical Amazons were imagined as retaining their peculiar psychosocial/psychosexual identity through selective inculcation and education. The Athenian Stranger is certainly proposing something akin to this in the production of his new femininity.[48] Magnesian women are to be 'manly' and heroic yet, at the same time, fertile and motherly.

There is not a great deal to be found in the *Laws* detailing the social lives of Magnesian women but what there is bears scrutiny. All social activities, and especially those involving women, are to be subject to intense supervision and regulation by forces of the *polis.* One such Magnesian social function is that of the public messes (*syssitia*).[49] These are meant to unite the Magnesian people through their participation in a common event (i.e. eating). As with the Spartans, these meals offer a diet especially formulated for the promotion of the citizens' health.[50] Like many other communal activities in Magnesia, they seek to preserve and reinforce the harmony of the *polis* through calculated ideological influences.

The Athenian Stranger has a high regard for the Kretan institution of communal meals (625c). This custom is described by Athenaios who indicates that each dining hall accommodated the citizens of a single *hetaireia* (similar to phratries).[51]

We are told that every citizen contributed one tenth of his produce and almost every participant was served an equal share (except for young boys who received slightly less). A woman presided over the meal and assigned the best portions to citizens who had earned distinctions of merit. Aristotle's account of Kretan communal meals differs somewhat from that of Athenaios on the extent of female participation, as does Plato's in the *Laws*.[52]

The Spartan practice of communal dining, which evidently did not include women together with men, provides a contrasting model for Plato's narrator. Xenophon says that Lykourgos instituted public messes (*andreia*) as a preventative measure against neglect of duty and disobedience. They were maintained by a specified quantity of food donated by each citizen.[53] By contrast, Athens had no such tradition of communal dining. Their formal banquets were sexually segregated with citizen women dining apart from the men.[54] These were held by individuals of the upper classes and could not be considered communal dining in the same sense as that implied by Magnesia's *syssitia*—although they are similar in some ways. The closest Athenian equivalent to this Spartan or Magnesian practice comes in the form of dining certain (male) individuals of public distinction at state expense.[55]

In Magnesia, both sexes partake of communal meals and seem to do so together. Newlyweds are to be exhorted and probably compelled, to continue their prescribed daily practice of attending the common messes just as before marriage (780a8–b2).[56] The Athenian Stranger uses this subject to launch into a larger discussion on the role of women in both his hypothetical *polis* and perhaps society in general. Note that he does not seem to think that women were included either in Spartan or Kretan *syssitia:*

> For your benefit, Kleinias and Megillus, the custom of communal meals for men has been beautifully established by some divine necessity, but a legal provision concerning women is in no ways rightly neglected and the practice of communal dining by women has not come to light,[57] but the species of our human race naturally more secretive and cunning,[58] the female sex, because it is weak, has been wrongly left behind in a state of disorder due to the misguided concessions of the legislator.[59] But because of this neglect, many things are thoroughly absent from your institutions that could be considerably better than they are now, if women were thus administered under law. For not only is the disorganised supervision of women half the problem, as one might presume, indeed this female nature, as far as we're concerned, is inferior toward the pursuit of virtue to that of the male sex, in this much it differs twofold.[60]

Such points as women's perceived 'weakness', along with his clichéd statements of their 'natural' inferiority, seem contradictory to his plans for reforming them through training and education.[61] This may be an indication of the persistence of traditional conceptions in Plato. The Athenian Stranger's solution to the problem that he has identified is innovative. He continues in the same passage, saying:

> And so, to take this matter up and amend it, the organisation of all prac-
> tices in common for both women and men is better for the happiness of the state;
> but just now the race of humankind has, as it happens, not yet arrived at that
> point (780d9–781b6).

The Athenian Stranger goes into great detail here (and also at 806e2–807a3 sq.) in developing a clearer picture of this major feature of Magnesian life.

The inclusion of both sexes in the public communal messes emphasises a radi-cal difference between the roles of Magnesian women and their real-world coun-terparts. It may also represent a cunning strategic manoeuvre on the part of Plato's narrator. The fact that the state feeds its citizens communally would appear to grant it a powerful force for influence in terms of implanting its values and ideology. Citizens come together each day for their meals under the scrutiny of authority. Since women participate in the Magnesian government and throughout the city in various official and other capacities (not to mention their important role as mothers of future citi-zens), it stands to reason that they should be included amongst the city's communal tables. Their induction into the official ideology would be at least as important as that of men if not more so since they represent the 'first round' of influence to which future citizens (their children) will be exposed.

His comments about the 'secretive' and 'cunning' nature of women should perhaps be read less as an expression of Plato's own opinions and more a statement of the dominant sentiments of his era.[62] The view that women are the more 'secretive' and 'cunning' sex is not unique to the *Laws*.[63] It is not unreasonable to suggest that such an attitude developed as a result of women's segregation in the private sphere. Xenophon's idealised portrayal of domesticity within an upper/middle class, citizen family, for example, provides a model of behaviour that severely limits a woman's public access. His narrator, Ischomachos, indicates that 'it is seemly for a woman to remain at home and not to be out of doors; but for a man to remain inside is a disgrace'.[64]

If an Athenian woman was observed outside at parties with men, it could be seen as proof that she was a courtesan and not a lawful wife.[65] When citizen-women in Athens were crouching in doorways asking those passing by on the streets about news of their husbands, fathers and brothers after the disastrous naval defeat at Chae-ronea, one speaker described this as 'degrading both to them and the city'.[66] The simple act of talking to men other than her husband or male relatives (in the presence of her husband) could be taken as affront to a woman's modesty and a potential threat to her chastity.[67] Even mentioning her name in a public context such as the lawcourts could be scandalous.[68]

If women's 'weaknesses' were a purely natural deficiency instead of the product of socialisation, then why would the Athenian Stranger feel that he could educate them at all and allow them to serve in the government and armed forces? His language suggests that he does in fact regard them as inferior in some vague way. He seems to think that there is something intrinsic in female 'nature' that inclines them to be less orderly and more emotional.[69] This condition is perceived to be surmountable to a great extent, though, through the 'proper' psychic alignment toward 'manly' order. Either he is being contradictory or the above statements on 'natural inferiority' should not be taken as a wholly accurate commentary on women's innate characteristics.

Sexually integrated *syssitia* will promote the official paradigms of male and female behaviour. They will also be integral in granting Magnesian women wider admission to the public sphere. But Plato appears conscious of his readers' sensibilities. Since the rest of the world is not as philosophically advanced as the Athenian Stranger and his companions (or the hypothetical Magnesians), he admonishes Megillus and Kleinias saying 'therefore bear in mind not to mention this in other places and city-states' where they would find such progressive ideas disturbing.[70]

There will be phratries in Magnesia, as well as twelve tribes (*phylai*), and there is every reason to expect that women will play an active role in all of them.[71] Plato perhaps assumed that his audience would be acquainted with these institutions but, to his modern readers, they are somewhat obscure. A phratry was a kind of kinship-group. It was closely affiliated with the *oikos* but consisted of a wider range of individuals. Such civic groups may not have been indicative of actual family relations, although there appears to have been a perceived connection of kinship amongst their members.[72] The phratry was interested in property and its inheritance and arguably held greater sovereignty over these than did the *oikos*. It played an active role, in connection with that of the *oikos*, which related more broadly to matters of the *polis*.[73]

In order to understand the significance of potentially admitting women into phratries in Magnesia, recourse must be made to the cultural context out of which the practice derives. Membership in an Athenian phratry was crucial for determining a male's legitimacy as citizen and heir. Kinship-groups perhaps comparable to phratries date back at least to the era of Homer.[74] No consensus has yet been reached on whether a single system of such groups ever existed in Classical Athens to which all male citizens belonged (e.g. the Kleisthenic *demos*, *trittys* and *phylē*) or whether they particularly had to be members of phratries, in addition to these others, to be considered true citizens. The evidence points to the latter. Athenian sons, especially those who were heirs, were first introduced into their fathers' phratries and later became full members themselves.[75]

As Lambert suggests 'both deme and phratry were conceived of as intimately associated with citizenship and . . . the character of the link, subtly different in each case, can be explained in terms of the nature and functions of each institution with respect to the qualifications and to the other criteria for citizenship'.[76] The special relationship between kinship-group and individual status may be observed from the late 5th century onwards in the granting of Athenian citizenship to foreigners who had performed some outstanding service for the city-state. There are some exceptions, but generally the new citizen was assigned membership in both a deme and a phratry.[77] The intrinsic connection between these is highlighted in Aristophanes' *Birds* where he uses the word *'phratēr'* almost as a synonym for 'citizen'.[78]

In the Athens of Plato's era, citizenship was dependent on the legitimacy of both parents.[79] Female children possibly played a greater role in their fathers' phratries after Perikles' citizenship law (451/0). Since the mother's descent had to be valid, phratries appear to have exercised a kind of oversight in regard to the daughters and wives of their male members. Isaios provides us with some evidence that female children might have been introduced to their father's phratry as part of determining their ability to inherit. The speaker is seeking to demonstrate that one Phile was not the legitimate offspring of Pyrrhos, whose estate was in dispute, and a sister of Nikodemos; the speaker says that 'he (Pyrrhos) had the option, if he had really married the sister of Nikodemos, of introducing the daughter who is allegedly hers to his *phratēres* as his own legitimate child, and of leaving her as heiress of his whole estate'.[80]

This speech alone, however, is not necessarily indicative of actual practices in all phratries. It is possible to deduce from the sources, as Lambert has done, that a.) in some phratries (but not necessarily all), daughters intended to become *epikleroi* were introduced to their fathers' *phratēres,* b.) in some phratries, daughters other than intended *epikleroi* were introduced to their fathers' *phratēres,* and c.) in some phratries, daughters who were not *epikleroi* were not introduced by their fathers.[81] But were they 'introduced' to the *phratēres* in person at the phratry's official meeting or through some other means? The speaker in Isaios III is contentiously describing an event that did not happen and might have never happened under normal circumstances. Classical sources, which should be regarded as the most accurate on this matter, specifically describe the enrolment of males only. A decree of the Demotionid phratry, as Pomeroy says, 'the only extant complete decree describing admission, describes the introduction of a son and does not mention daughters'.[82]

Byzantine writers refer to Greek girls being personally introduced to phratries at the *gamelia* seemingly as a matter of legal registration.[83] Pollux and the scholiast's statements cannot be taken to indicate that they were admitted as members of phratries in fifth- to fourth-century Athens—although this may have been the case significantly later.[84] In his edition of the Scholia to Aristophanes' *Acharn.* 146, Dindorf cited the 10th century Suda (s.v. *meiagogein*) and embellished the Greek text to give the impression that both boys' and girls' names were inscribed on phratry lists.[85] This emendation, which had been regarded as important evidence for the registration of girls, is now omitted in the current edition of the Scholia.[86] After betrothal and marriage, a Greek husband in the Hellenistic age may have personally introduced his wife to his fellow *phratēres*. A sacrifice and a ceremonial meal would follow as in the Classical tradition.[87]

Both Isaios[88] and Demosthenes[89] speak of presenting a marriage feast to the phratry, as part of the *gamelia*, 'on behalf of' (ὑπέρ) a wife. This suggests that a man presented *the name* of his newly wedded wife to his *phratēres* and they, perhaps having done some discreet investigation into her background, effectively accepted her as capable of bearing male children whom they would eventually receive as phratry members and citizens. Their official acknowledgement of female children who could bear legitimate offspring was apparently a prerequisite.[90] In this capacity, an aspect of the public sphere profoundly influenced the private. The connection between this scrutiny and the transferral of property should be especially noted along with the female participant's relatively passive role in the proceedings. If an Athenian father did not personally introduce his daughter to his *phratēres*, why then should we expect a husband to have personally introduced his newlywed-wife? The Classical phratry was, after all, a 'brotherhood'. Whatever else it may have implied to an Athenian woman's status, the *gamelia* did not, as Lambert says, 'bestow actual phratry membership on her'.[91]

Do the Magnesian phratries represent a significant shift from Athenian practices? From their first year of life, every Magnesian citizens of either sex will have their names inscribed on the register of their respective family's phratry.[92] Does this mean that women will be full members in the same sense as the men? The Athenian Stranger has not told us. It may be that the Magnesian phratry is merely acting as its Athenian counterpart in terms of providing a record of official births and deaths. It is nonetheless possible to speculate that phratry-oriented functions would constitute some of a citizen woman's social interaction in the public sphere. It is also a likely possibility that women's role in these, if any, would extend to the Marriage Guardians in their capacity of undertaking the scrutiny of married couples. Other than registrars of citizenship status, the precise activities to be undertaken in Magnesian phratries remain uncertain. Presumably there would be banquets, sacrifices, plus ceremonies and business meetings.

Through traditional phratries, male family members and the local community undertook a similar sort of 'supervision' in Athens and elsewhere. I would like to be able to draw the conclusion here, as elsewhere, that he has metamorphosed another existing cultural institutions into a more formalised agency of the government thereby allowing women a greater degree of participation in phratries. If so, then he has presaged future practices of Greek phratries. However, it is not possible to say that this is so based upon the information available. It does seem probable that Magnesian women would play a greater role in phratries of some kind or another—but it is unclear what that role would be.

Magnesian women have the right to be chosen for state duties. The Athenian Stranger has stated that the Magnesian legislator will not be limited by sex in his choice of officials for duties of civic administration, saying that 'the law has already granted him permission, and still gives him permission, to choose whomever he wishes of the men and women of the state for public commissions' (813c6–9). There is every indication that Magnesian women, when they have passed the childbearing age, will be included amongst the Guardians of the Laws and therefore the *nukterinos* council. However, their numbers amongst these will probably be fewer than men and it appears that most citizen-women in positions of authority will be Marriage Supervisors and Supervisors of Children's nurses.[93]

Magnesian women are also allowed to participate in courtroom affairs both in terms of prosecuting a case and being prosecuted themselves should they be accused of committing a crime. For example, if someone has been slain by another with forethought, the Athenian Stranger indicates that it is the duty of anyone related to the deceased 'on either the male or female side' to bring the matter to court and prosecute the alleged murderer (871a–c). If a woman should kill her husband out of rage, she is to suffer the same penalty as a man who slays his wife under the same emotional circumstances.[94] There will be a trial and, if found guilty, the murderer can be banished from the city for three years (868e). Citizen women are to be granted the same legal footing as anyone else with regard to attacks on their person (882c). However, one thing will not be permitted for women (or anyone else) to do in terms of the legal sphere. A trial must be a sober and austere occasion. No one is allowed to speak with oaths for the purposes of persuasion, or to curse themselves or their families, or to employ unseemly supplication or 'womanly wailings' to sway a legal case.[95]

This degree of freedom allowed Magnesian women stands in stark contrast to the reality of Plato's era. Only a few ancient Athenian women were known to have actively participated in court.[96] There is the example is the wife of Megakles of the Alkmeonid clan who seems to have upheld her civic virtue in testifying—but the case was an extraordinary one and she a woman of foreign birth.[97] Agariste was one of the three witnesses who gave evidence that Alkibiades illicitly celebrated the mysteries in the house of Charmides in connection with the Sicilian disaster.[98] If a citizen- or metic-woman needed to initiate legal proceedings, then a male relative or sponsor would undertake the case on her behalf.[99] Men were the only ones who brought cases to trial and who sat on the juries. When women are mentioned in a courtroom setting, their names are frequently avoided unless they were being disparaged. An Athenian woman who was sufficiently visible in the public eye could accrue shame. 'The most respectful way to refer to a woman', as Schaps states, 'was not to say what her name was, but to indicate whose wife, or daughter, or sister she was: for indeed, if she was a proper woman, the jurors would not be expected to know her, but would be expected to know her *kyrios*'.[100]

Magnesian women, in sharp contrast, have the right to become highly visible and publicly known by name. The law allows women full access to the courts. They also appear to be entitled to vote and stand for ministerial positions.[101] The right to do so is extended to all the *kyrioi*, to individuals who possess heavy weapons (including members of the cavalry and infantry) and to veterans of wartime activities.[102] A large number of men would qualify having been trained to fight with the requisite arms or by simply being *kyrioi*. As we have seen, female Magnesians also have the opportunity to be trained in the use of heavy weapons and the art of horsemanship.[103] It follows that some women could nominate someone as well as be nominated themselves—providing they meet the requirements of possessing certain arms and/or having fought in a war. The restriction of participation based on possession of heavy weapons would appear to be more of a limiting factor for Magnesia's lower property classes than for the female sex in general. However, the number of women standing for election would be significantly lower than that of men.

In addition to including women in governmental activities, albeit to a clearly limited extent, Plato's narrator has also admitted an uncharacteristically high degree of democracy into the second-best state. Magnesia's partially democratic election system is modified by this society's peculiar attributes. As Bobonich says, this political activity on the part of the Magnesians, 'that is, participation in the social institutions of the just city aimed at furthering the common good, is good in itself and forms an important part of each citizen's happiness'.[104] All citizens, engaged as they are in the pursuit of *aretē*, should posses a better *technē* for political decisions than the populace of the average Greek democracy. This utopianisation of democracy is part of the reason why Magnesian women are granted such an unprecedented political status.

Counsellors in the *boulē* of 360 are chosen according to property class (90 from each) and, while all citizen males of the first and second classes are compelled to vote under penalty of fine, the right to vote is afforded to 'anyone who wishes'.[105] This statement, echoing Solonian values, would also appear to include certain Magnesian women as well—if not all of them. There are thirty-seven special officials of the state apart from the elected *boulē* and the unelected *nukterinos* council. The list of nominees for 'ministers of the laws', military commanders, *hipparchs, phylarchs* and *taxiarchs* is to be placed in public for thirty days and 'anyone who thinks it fit' may remove any name they wish.[106] This feature demonstrates some the limitations imposed on democracy inasmuch as certain people might always tend to be excluded or included by the time of election. The *nukterinos* council, Guardians and sitting officials will scrutinise these undertakings with care. The ministers already in office take the first three hundred of the remaining names (in alphabetical order?) and place them on a ballot for the citizens to cast a second round of votes again by deletion.

The magistrates choose a hundred names from the second short-listing and then 'anyone who wishes' may cast their actual votes. The thirty-seven who receive the most votes will be examined by the sitting magistrates and, if they pass, are installed in office (753c–d). It is unclear whether or not the 'anyone who wishes' who are permitted to strike names from the list of candidates and then to vote on them refers to those who possess heavy weapons or are from the citizen-populace at large. The Athenian Stranger appears to mean that the selection of candidates for nomination is to be limited to those who possess the requisite arms. The actual short-listing and voting would seem to be the privilege of the citizen populace as a whole including many men and as many women who wish to do so. It is unclear whether women will sit on the supreme *nukterinos* council.[107] Since its members are appointed from the eldest of the Guardians of the Laws, it is possible to assume that they might be included—although this is never explicitly specified.[108] Women's role in higher Magnesian politics is clearly marginal, but their implied potential emphasises the contrast between the ideal world of a second-best utopia and the realities of ancient Greece.

The case of the Marriage Supervisors is perhaps the clearest example of Magnesian women in the public sphere. These are citizen-women who work for the *polis* yet regularly enter the *oikos* to make certain that state policies are properly adhered to in the private lives of married individuals. This important office is ranked highly in the value-system of Magnesia. Its agents serve an implicitly civic role through the infiltration of the private household with the express purposes of ideological manipulation and behaviour modification.

Bearing children who will eventually become heirs and heiresses of their parents' immobile estate is the desired goal of a Magnesian marriage. The Athenian Stranger stresses the necessity of *teknopoiia* to replenish the state in a proposed lecture to his hypothetical populace.[109] His persuasive exhortation, as we saw in the last chapter, states that one 'must naturally hold onto the Everlasting by always leaving behind children and grandchildren after one that they may render service unto the God'.[110] He follows this preamble with binding constitutional guidelines on correct procreation in marriage.[111] These and other activities come under intense scrutiny. The supervision of married couples may be taken as an example of Magnesia's official efforts to reduce privacy to a minimum (739a–740a). In this way, a link is established to allow direct intervention in the *oikos* on behalf of the *polis*. Magnesian women's labour of *teknopoiia* (that which is most essentially 'their own') is to be subordinated to the will of the state and their lives directed, along with those of the men, toward the aims of the state's approved ideology.[112]

The Magnesian women chosen as Marriage Supervisors observe their assigned couples for up to ten years—providing that children come in suitable numbers and the marriage remains solvent (784a sq.). An intimate relationship is suggested between them and the couples being observed. Regular contact to scrutinise their private affairs will be the norm. If a couple does not produce the appropriate amount of offspring or rear them properly, then they may either divorce or, as we have seen, 'the female officials will go into the home of the young people and admonish and threaten them to cease their error and ignorance' (784c2–4). The preferred solution is that they be reconciled, through counselling, avoid divorce, and continue to promote the official myth of family concord.[113]

Marriage Supervisors are chosen by the rulers of the city and will meet in committee each day at the Temple of Eileithuia (Artemis of Childbirth)[114] to discuss, amongst other matters, those couples whose activities do not seem to be inclined toward 'what was enjoined upon them at the marriage sacrifices and sacred rites' (namely the proper manner of begetting and rearing children).[115] They will make regular reports to the 'women magistrates' and Guardians of the Laws who have the necessary legal authority to intervene directly, as they deem appropriate, in the lives of members of a citizen-*oikos*. Failure to comply with the Guardians of the Laws may result in deprivation of the privilege of attending weddings and parties that are celebrating births (with strict penalties for defying the punishment).[116] The Marriage Supervisors, therefore, may be construed as serving both as observers of families and as agents of state influence. A married couple in Magnesia will not only have the rules of procreation with which to contend. The Marriage Supervisors will 'advertise' the official doctrines in close quarters for at least ten years of their charges' lives.

Akin to these, the Supervisors of Children's Nurses oversee all those to whom the care of the young is entrusted (including nurses, tutors and slaves—794b sq.). Twelve women are to be chosen by the female Guardians of the Laws who oversee the Marriage Supervisors (vaguely implying that such upper-echelon female Guardians will in fact exist) to keep order over a particular 'herd' of children for a one-year term.[117] During their tenure of office, they have the authority to command the city's servants or slaves and to punish both male and female slaves along with strangers to the city (e.g. hired teachers) who violate Magnesian strictures.

These women even have the mandate to exert their authority over a Magnesian citizen—subject to specific conditions. If one of them does so, she must have a clear case in order for her indictment to hold. Being a citizen, the accused has the right to dispute her claim through due legal process. If this happens, then she must take up the matter with one of the City Wardens (ἀστυνόμοι) and if he/she upholds her claim against the accused, then the law will 'let her punish even a citizen' on her own authority (794b7–c2). It seems correct to anticipate that more Magnesian women will become Marriage Supervisors and Supervisors of Nurses than will make up the higher ranks of the Guardians of the Laws, the city's magistrates or the *nukterinos* council. However, there is every reason to believe that a minority of women will occupy even these lofty positions in Magnesian society.

There are further limitations imposed particularly on women's activities within and without the *oikos*. Prostitution of any sort is to have no official legal status in Magnesia. The Athenian Stranger is fearful that there might be instances of it nonetheless. He has framed some legislation to deal with its possible occurrence. What he does not say about this issue may speak louder than his words (which are relatively few). This specific segment of the Magnesian population is notorious not so much in its presence, but in its absence. Their position in this society is marginal in the extreme but their potential, so disturbing to the Athenian Stranger, readily informs this examination of sex and society.

Plato's narrator has made regulations on the subject of extra-marital intercourse that contain implicit indications that there might be individuals who hire themselves out for sexual favours amongst the citizenry of the second-best state.[118] As we have seen, this sort of thing is not the ideal marital behaviour that Magnesians are intended to follow. However, the Athenian Stranger seems to anticipate that, even in the second-best state, not everyone will pursue *aretē* with equal vigour. This may be said, at least, to lend a dimension of realism to Magnesia. He provides a law in the event that some men cannot uphold the ideal, saying that there will be harsh psychological penalties for anyone who does so 'except he keep it secret from all other men and women'.[119] The inclusion of such a 'secrecy clause' in this law admits the possibility that some Magnesian men might engage in sexual intercourse with someone in the *polis* other than their wives. There is a special concern that this might include hired or un-hired liaisons with young boys or male youths.[120] Aside from any doubts that this might cast on the practicalities of the pursuit of *aretē*, a further question is raised: who, in all Magnesia, would be the prostitutes?

By virtue of their status and the expectations that it entails, it is clear that citizen-women are not expected to fall even loosely into the category of prostitute. Magnesia is meant to be a society where almost every citizen is either married, engaged to be married, too young to be engaged or too old. The official myth of family, as we have seen, does not favour the single lifestyle. All citizens are held to a high standard that carries with it certain legal restrictions as to what types of sexual and other activities they may undertake without incurring public shame and official injunction.

There is the law, for example, that precludes both male and female Magnesian citizens from running a business.[121] Such base commerce would interfere with their compulsory pursuit of *aretē*. Therefore the running of any business of prostitution would be prohibited in the extreme for any citizen. All citizens (including spinsters, unwed maidens and boys) would be excluded from the role of 'sex-worker' on the same grounds. The overriding mandate for the pursuit of virtue forbids all citizens, regardless of their sex, from being a prostitute or running a procurement service for others.[122]

There will be resident aliens in the city-state who are permitted to run businesses. Such individuals must possess some relevant craft to provide their livelihood and are allowed to stay no longer than twenty years without special dispensation (850b–c). Whoever engages in the retail trade must be either one of these *metics* or a stranger to the city (920a). Resident foreigners pay no special alien tax, as they would have in Athens and elsewhere, 'except that of being moderate'.[123] Slaves and other foreigners who educate or rear children, as previously indicated, will be held to a high standard and are forced to bear considerable scrutiny. There is little or no indication that the rest of the resident-alien population is to be so closely supervised. It may be the case that they will be permitted to abide by Magnesia's morality of temperance to a lesser degree than citizens.

They appear to represent a possibility for the sex-trade in Magnesia if only inasmuch as they alone can provide retail goods and services. However, the prescription that they must be 'moderate' in order to be allowed to remain in the city suggests that any resident aliens who might hire out prostitutes could only do so under the constraints of extreme secrecy and the appearance of propriety. A resident alien man or woman might engage in prostitution him/herself or serve as a procurer for others. There is also the possibility that some amongst the ubiquitous slave population of Magnesia could serve as certain citizens' personal concubines—albeit perhaps at great risk to both master and slave. Resident aliens might also hire out slaves, again potentially at great risk, as prostitutes.

They appear to be the likeliest choice, of necessity having to be subtle to avoid the Guardians of the Laws and City Wardens, but their being subject to somewhat less supervised than Magnesian citizens or their slaves, teachers and nurses allows the possibility. It is reasonable to posit that, if they keep it quiet, the use of prostitutes could be a common state of affairs amongst them. They might also be hired out discreetly to citizens. However, they will be familiar with the Athenian Stranger's decree of 'abstaining from any female field in which you would not want your seed to spring forth' (839a1–3). If a citizen should 'dare to sow unhallowed and bastard seed in concubines' or other prostitutes, then she (or he) would probably have to be purchased through the mercantile class of resident aliens.

The issue of 'prostitution' in the ancient world is complex, but the Athenian Stranger's brief mention of the subject is revealing. It points to a 'two-type' model that may have been a prominent feature of ancient views on sex. The distinction that he makes is between the kinds of woman with whom citizen men may have legitimate sexual intercourse (citizen-wives) and the type with whom they may not (the rest).[124] The terms given to designate a Magnesian man's proper sexual partner describe her as the 'women who entered into his household under the sanction of the gods and the sacred marriage ceremony' or, more simply, his legally wedded wife. The ancient Athenians appear to have followed a similar formula in distinguishing a legally 'married wife' or 'a wife married according to the laws' from the mass of other women.[125]

The distinction between a lawful wife and 'the rest' is important in determining the role of a citizen-woman in Magnesian society. Anyone other than one's 'lawfully wedded' spouse is automatically excluded from the list of sanctioned erotic choices for men and women. However, the Athenian Stranger does suggest a couple of the possibilities (namely other men and *pallakai*, 'whether hired or procured by some other means') with whom a citizen should not have sex—but theoretically could.

The restrictions against Magnesian citizens undertaking prostitution echo conservative Athenian values. The law quoted by Aiskhines, in his case against Timarkhos, reads 'because the legislator considered that one who had been a vendor of his own body for others to treat as they pleased, [they] would have no hesitation in selling the interests of the community as a whole'.[126] The prostitutes who, as Dover says, 'plied their trade in brothels and paid the tax levied on their profession . . . were presumably for the most part foreigners'.[127] A similar philosophical position seems to be operating in Magnesia. Unlike Athens, there is no legal permission for prostitution of any sort. The Athenian Stranger, however, seems to recognise the fact that the complete prohibition of something desirable is ultimately impossible.[128] He instead, as we have seen, focuses his efforts on other discouragements of a more psychological nature to this end. If the citizens choose to do such things, then they had better not get caught.

Something more needs to be said about religious life and death than was discussed in the previous chapter. As we saw, there are to be annual festivals for both the men and women of Magnesia. They take part in these sometimes together as a community and sometimes separated by sex (828c5–6). Sexually integrated public ceremonies did occur in the ancient Greek world (e.g. funerals), but there is also some indication that they could be stressful to the normal boundaries of sexual decorum.[129] Magnesia goes beyond Athens in these matters. All shrines are public and all religious events will be highly civic in character. The Athenian Stranger is adamant that Magnesian shrines are to be exclusively public institutions. He appears to be concerned that anyone attempting private religious ceremonies might undermine official doctrines. His warning against the establishment of private shrines is especially aimed at women who, he indicates, are more likely to do so than men.[130]

The religious ceremonies to be performed consist of a series of hymns, *encomia* and prayers to the various gods, heroes and spirits that meet with the approval of the Magnesian authorities (801e). Plato's narrator insists that no one will be permitted to sing such praises in honour of notable citizens while they still live. When they have passed on, they may be officially deemed worthy of public displays of adoration and only then will it be appropriate to add their names to the consecrated lists. Sacred songs constitute a major component of Magnesia's religious ceremonies. Different songs will be chosen according to rhythm, meter and content, relative to the particular religious occasions, in order to correspond properly with the sex of the individuals who partake of them. There are certain types of songs specific to men's religious events, others specific to women's and some deemed suitable for both when the occasion requires them to be together.[131]

As we saw in the previous chapter, the right to be honoured in sacred songs for living a virtuous and noble life is extended equally to both sexes. The Athenian Stranger says 'let all these things be in common amongst us for both men and women and those of either sex who are conspicuously good' (802a3–5). This process of state-sanctioned apotheosis would appear to provide exemplars for ordinary citizens to emulate through their pursuit of *aretē*. It also provides an incentive for good behaviour as well as a tremendous honour for the family to whom the heroic deceased belonged. Perhaps the Athenian Stranger intends that most families will have at least one relative amongst the ranks of 'city heroes' thus democratically spreading the honours.

Twelve festivals for the twelve Olympian gods, who will give their names to the same number of Magnesian *phylai,* will be undertaken annually. These consist of monthly sacrifices held explicitly in the public sphere and accompanied by other festivities.[132] Gymnastic events, musical contests and choruses figure prominently in these. Magnesia's priests and priestesses 'will distribute the women's festivals, as many as it is appropriate to celebrate, apart from men and as many as are not' (828c5–6). Little is actually said about those religious festivals specific to women except for the passage that deals with the offering of woven goods to temples on special occasions (mentioned above—956a–b) and the 'moderate' type of music they are permitted to perform.[133] As with many aspects of his hypothetical constitution, the fine details will be ironed out by the Magnesian officials working in their offices rather than by the Athenian Stranger with his companions on the road to Mt. Ida.

The burial of the dead and its accompanying funerary affairs provides a significant religious context in which Magnesian citizen-women partake of both the public and private spheres—yet act in a largely civic capacity. The Magnesia cemetery is, amongst other things, an area for the public display of familial descent. This places its political ends alongside those of its Athenian counterpart amongst others. But the differences even in this single respect are striking.

The Athenian cemetery was a place to display patrilineal kinship-groupings in which women played a largely secondary role. The monuments were constructed, as Stears says, 'with emphasis in the diachronic and agnatic affiliations, the *oikos* and perhaps the *genos*'.[134] Athenian women, she goes on to say, 'were important for the construction and cohesion of the cognatic kin-group the *anchisteia*, a limited bilateral grouping centred on an individual, through which ran the line of inheritance'.[135] Women's importance granted them a permanent place in funerary monuments as members of the cognatic kinship-group, but this 'memorial' was more figurative than physical.[136] The *anchisteia* was considerably less prominent than the *oikos* or *genos* in terms of funerary representation. Its function was no less significant. Athenian women's tombs, as is also to be the case in Magnesia, served a particularly political role. They were important to the *oikos, genos, demos,* phratry and *polis* as a means of claiming, demonstrating or countering refutations to one's inheritance.[137] They functioned as a kind of official notice of legitimacy.

The Athenian Stranger has insisted that later religious legislators give equal consideration 'whether the deceased be either a man or a woman' (958d3–6). He advises that plain grave markers (*stelai*) of a simple type will be erected in common style for all deceased citizens with only a few exceptions.[138] As discussed in the previous chapter, the undertaker will 'make the stone grave-markers no larger than as much as will contain not more than four heroic lines of *encomia* on the life of the deceased' (958e8–959a1). The simplicity of these grave-markers highlights a degree of equality between men and women—just as the limitations on expenditure for funerals and tombs serve to equalise most Magnesians—in death.

The honouring of women in death through symbolic representation and inscribed commemoration echoes traditional Athenian practices to an extent but definitely steps beyond them. As Osborne says, 'women had a major place in the symbolization of relations between humanity and the gods in archaic Athens, but virtually no place at all in the symbolic language in which the loss of human life was marked'.[139] They were only infrequently represented in funeral monuments before c.500 B.C.E.; however, from the middle of the 5th century onwards they appear in symbolic representation virtually as often as men. The archaic Athenian *stelai* are not unlike those to be used in Magnesia except that they were more elaborate in terms of carving and embellishment.[140]

The equality of Magnesian men and women in death is emphasised by their inscribed commemoration on the burial monuments. Both sexes will receive an equal number (and presumably quality) of lines of heroic *encomia* on their respective *stelai*. This is a marked difference from the real world. 'Although women were depicted in [Athenian] funerary monument images as frequently as men', according to Stears, 'they were not recorded in inscriptions as often'.[141] The simplicity of Magnesia's grave-markers, their placement on graves without regard to the sex of the deceased and the limitations on funerary expenditure all emphasise a point of equality between all Magnesians in death. However, this democratic 'equality' is nonetheless moderated by economic class and social status.[142]

The Athenian Stranger's plans at once reflect Athenian funerary practices and, to a lesser extent, Spartan while, at the same time, going beyond them. Unlike Magnesia, the Spartans evidently buried their citizen-dead within the city and placed tombs for their kings outside.[143] Michell suggests that this was to prevent the angry spirits of vengeful duarchs from entering the city and bringing their *miasma* on the people.[144] The only names inscribed on their ceremonial *stelai* were those of warriors who had died in battle or women who had died whilst performing sacred offices. This was perhaps because they believed that spirits of the dead could not find their tombs unless their names were inscribed on them. By thus limiting the inscriptions, according to Mitchell, they sought to ensure that only 'virtuous' souls would return to influence the living.[145] Plato's narrator may have borrowed somewhat from these Spartan traditions but he democratically extends essentially the same privileges in death to all of his virtuous elite.

One of the Guardians of the Laws will administer a final duty of supervision in the act of overseeing the funeral preparations undertaken by the deceased's family.[146] He/she does so to make sure that the rule of moderation is upheld. The Guardian's authority is backed by official sanction and the threat of shame.[147] The funeral procession is to be highly regulated and a sober attitude of *sōphrosynē* must accompany all funerary events. 'To command that that there be weeping for the deceased or that there be no weeping', says the Athenian Stranger, 'is unseemly, but the singing of threnodies and the raising of voices outside of the household (ἔξω τῆς οἰκίας) is forbidden'.[148] The deceased's remains will be prepared for burial (*prothesis*), as was the tradition in Athens, at home by women and probably slaves.[149] The Athenian Stranger does not say whether a religious ceremony might take place in the *oikos* as in the case of an Athenian *prothesis*.[150] The prohibition against establishing private shrines would seem to apply here, although he has not specified it in detail.

The Athenian Stranger's guidelines are designed to make the Magnesian funeral a reserved and dignified affair. The corpse must not be carried 'open to sight' on the roads and the *ekphora* has to be out of the city before daybreak. Crying aloud is forbidden whilst the remains are being borne through the Magnesian streets to the city's cemetery.[151] There will be a yearly ritual in honour of all Magnesia's deceased at which a similar 'orderliness' (κόσμος) is to be maintained by the participants.[152] Overt expressions of grief are strictly confined to the *oikos* alone and, as with unseemly behaviour in court, women have been specifically singled out as the ones who run the greatest risk of breaking this taboo.

An exception to the general rule of equality in funerals arises in regard to the burial of deceased 'priests of Apollo and the Sun'. The assembly of the entire citizen population will choose these revered individuals each year (946a–b). It may be based on a similar practice of honouring deceased priests in Classical Sparta but this is questionable.[153] The Magnesian connection with Apollo, here as elsewhere a major deity, has more obvious *Lakonian* overtones.[154] The Athenian Stranger indicates that the assembly is to make its choices from the citizens over the age of fifty and to 'present three men from amongst their number to the god'.[155] This dedicatory service, possibly as with the Spartans, seems designed to produce a propagandistic effect. He does not specifically indicate whether women might be chosen for these positions. It could be the case that they are eligible and that the Athenian Stranger is simply generalising with the term 'men' to include both sexes; yet, the specification of 'men' in particular suggests the stronger possibility that women might be excluded.

The funerals of those elected priests of Apollo and the Sun will be elaborate affairs of Magnesian patriotism. They entail lengthy celebrations with choruses of boys and girls singing poetic hymns during the entire day before the burial. As with ordinary citizens, no dirges or overt lamentations will be permitted (947b5–6). At dawn the bier is to be carried by a hundred young men from the *gymnasion* who are chosen by the deceased's relatives. The procession consists of unmarried youths in light armour along with cavalry and infantry in heavy armour. Boys singing the national anthem go in front and 'girls will follow behind along with any women who have passed the childbearing age, and after these the city's priests and priestesses'.[156] As with ordinary citizens, their crypts are to be constructed underground and made of porous stone for endurance. These are considered extraordinary citizens and they merit special attention in the commemoration of their virtuous lives. A sacred grove of trees will be planted around the site of their tombs. Each year musical, gymnastic and equestrian contests will be performed by the citizen body in honour of the city's heroic dead and attended by the populace at large.[157]

Even in the case of the funerary events for priests (and possibly the priest- esses) of Apollo and the Sun, moderation and propriety must be maintained. In any Magnesian funeral, as we have seen, there can be no outpouring of public grief, no manifestation of excessive emotion outside the *oikos*. In these respects, it seems that the Athenian Stranger's plan is related more to Athenian ideals than any other. Mag- nesian funerals bear considerable resemblance to those that were supposed to occur in Athens after the reforms of Plato's famous ancestor Solon.[158] Strict rules were meant to govern the displays of wealth and public grief that could be acted out by Athenian citizens on such occasions. Solonian funeral legislation has been considered as an ef- fort to promote democratisation. It was designed, in part, to limit 'the participation of women in funerals', as Pomeroy says, 'for mourning by large numbers of women had been a means for ostentatious families to parade their wealth'.[159]

Solon's funerary laws, like Plato's, forbade the singing of dirges during the *ekphora*. Apart from women over the age of sixty, those who were not members of the deceased's *anchisteia* could not attend. In Athens, as in Magnesia, there appear to have been no limitations to the number of men who could be present at the *ekphora*. The Athenian Stranger's statutes permit young women to follow behind young men in the funeral processions of notables although he does not specify whether they could do so in an ordinary citizen's funeral.

As MacDowell says, the strictures of Solon's legislation, in terms of who may or may not participate in funerals, seem 'to have been to ensure that a funeral was a discreet family event, not an occasion for extravagant displays of feminine grief to disturb the general public'.[160] But a primary goal was probably the prevention of inter-kinship-group conflict. Wealthy families might flaunt their status with 'professional' mourners (many of whom would be women) who would weep very loudly and lacerate their flesh for pay. This could provoke social unrest and possibly rouse old clan rivalries. As Stears indicates, 'the legislation was directed at excessively disruptive and even socially dangerous displays by kin-groups and not at women *per se*'.[161] This theme is compatible with Magnesia's goal of self-harmony and these borrowings from Solon may also represent a form of homage to Plato's famous ancestor.

Some of the specific restrictions placed on the participation of women in Magnesian funerary rituals may reveal a cultural disposition toward childbearing, death and pollution (*miasma*). Note that in both the cases of an ordinary citizen's *ekphora*, as well as that of the priests and priestesses of Apollo and the sun, the only women allowed who are of childbearing age are those immediate members of the deceased's *anchisteia* (prepubescent girls are permitted at the priests' *ekphorai* and women past childbearing age at both). As indicated, this is basically in keeping with the spirit of Athenian custom. The exclusion of women not of the *anchisteia* along with those who were of childbearing age seems to have been designed to avoid *miasma*.

Athenian mothers who had just given birth did not take an active role in the religious rites involved in incorporating her offspring into the family. This was, as Stears says, 'most notably because she was thought to be still polluted by birth, perhaps until the cessation of post-partum bleeding'.[162] The association between blood (whether menstrual or post-partum) and pollution, as well as that with death, perhaps came into active psychological play in the context of public burial.[163] There appears to be some perceived connection between women and the realm of the supernatural in both Athens and Magnesia. This sets limits for the roles that they play in transcending both public and private spheres through the celebration of death. It is, after all, they who greet mourners coming into the *oikos* and they who help prepare the body of the dead during its *prothesis*. It is they who uphold the public *philotimia* of their *oikos*, *anchisteia*, *genos*, deme and husband's phratry in performing the ritual lamentations correctly and honourably during the *ekphora*.[164] Women are uniquely integral to the rites of death and burial and this point has not been lost on Plato's narrator in the *Laws*.

Mourning cuts off some of the perhaps more feminine aspects of the Magnesian household from public life as much as it provides a venue for public and private spheres to interact. Magnesia, in this respect, reveals a number of the ideals of post-Solonian Athens, as Humphreys indicates, such that 'in the privacy of the *oikos* grief could be given full expression; but its public manifestations had to be controlled'.[165] The degree of moderation and sobriety in the funerary customs of Magnesia may be seen in terms of the controlled public displays of emotion and the clear segregation of the private expression of grief from the public. This indicates a conscious attempt to impose a 'manly' quality of discipline on affairs that could otherwise deteriorate into a state of 'feminine' emotionality. Otherwise, the latter could threaten Magnesia's harmony and potentially provoke civil unrest. The societal norms of behaviour regarding funerals and the dead in Magnesia indicate the Athenian Stranger's desire for his hypothetical citizenry to maintain 'masculine' self-mastery over their emotions even at times of severe emotional duress such as when a loved one has passed away. The participation of women in the public sphere through funerals appears constrained both in terms of the number and type, according to age and kinship, allowed by the Athenian Stranger's rules as well as the degree of emotional expression that they are permitted to exhibit. This is somewhat ameliorated by the general equality of funerary monuments allowed both sexes. Perhaps well-socialised Magnesian women would have no inclination to show the kind of excessive emotionality expressed by their real-world counterparts.

In conclusion, the role of citizen-women in Plato's Magnesia contrasts markedly with that of their analogues in Athens, Sparta and elsewhere. At the beginning I mentioned the Athenian Stranger's 'Lakonisation' and 'Sauromatianisation' of his hypothetical female citizenry—but the 'masculinisation' of Magnesian citizen-women goes beyond this. They have been granted all manner of legally supported degrees of enfranchisement including equal or nearly equal education in both martial and scholastic subjects,[166] legally sanctioned participation in government and law at almost every level (if not at all levels) as well as partaking of other traditionally male institutions.

Magnesian women's assimilation into the sphere of the *polis* entails a loss of certain aspects traditionally associated with femininity. Many of the negative traits that the Athenian Stranger seeks to purge from his hypothetical citizen-women are regarded as the detritus of improperly managed societies. He sees no reason why, through proper supervision, women should not be 'led into the light'. In order to do this, the Athenian Stranger seeks to limit all forms of emotional expression as much as possible that have been identified as feminine and, in their place, to instil certain 'manly' virtues. Part of Magnesian women's masculinisation may be observed in their wearing armour (like Pallas Athena) and being trained to fight (like Amazons, Sauromatian and allegedly Spartan women) along with the general rule of keeping their excessive inclinations for emotionality to a minimum—especially in public.[167] They will not remain at home as much as Athenian women, but when they are out in the public sphere they will have a specific reason to be there.

Emancipation is a modern notion with modern implications. The Athenian Stranger's 'new femininity' is not liberation; rather, it is a demand of efficiency imposed by his utopian plan. Everyone in Magnesia is in some way constrained by the unique directives of that society. The greater degree of equality (although it is by no means true equality) between the sexes is, paradoxically, a consequence of these constraints. There still remains the unresolved issue of women's perceived 'inferiority' but this seems to be an issue that is considered to be surmountable through the application of philosophy and psychology. Plato certainly contemplated the question of what should be the appropriate role for women enough to frame the statutes and write the discussions that deal with this matter in his final *opus*. It is clear that, in order to fulfil the requirements of this somewhat idealised role, Magnesian citizen-women will have to behave and become more like (similarly idealised) men.

Chapter VII
Magnesian Moral Hygiene
Same-Sex Relations, Pleasure and Madness

And alien tears will fill for him
Pity's long-broken urn,
For his mourners will be outcast men,
And outcasts always mourn.
—Oscar Wilde[1]

Are those who would partake of same-sex intercourse to be banished from the second-best state of Magnesia and, if so, why? Has Plato changed his mind on the matter? As concerns the second question, it seems fitting to point out that nowhere in the extant *corpus* of Plato's works is there a comprehensive statement of his philosophy, as it stood at any given period of his life, detailing its axioms or systematically explaining its methods or offering proof of its conclusions. It would appear fair to deduce that there was an ongoing evolution in his thinking that took place exterior to, but reflected in, his writings at various stages. The fact that we do not know the exact dates of the composition of each text (although the *Laws* is generally thought to have been his final work) heightens the difficulty of forming a comprehensive picture of his thoughts. To say that he has changed his mind on the issue of same-sex relations is dangerous if not utterly ludicrous: we don't know what he ever thought about it at any given point in time.[2] There are only the words of his speakers in the surviving texts that provide a clue to the philosopher's perceptions.

Plato's narrator is less than clear on the evocative subject of same-sex intercourse but he has nonetheless delineated a hypothetical process by which the calculated use of language (with the aid of fear, shame and the authority of the state) may be employed to influence people's thinking, and therefore their actions, with regard to that which we would today designate as sexuality.[3] The primary means by which values are to be transmitted in Plato's Magnesia, as with most anywhere else, is through the medium of words and speech. The official philosophical position, designated as 'correct argument', maintains that one who is to be wise must avoid becoming a slave to fleshly passion and thus become a master of one's self.[4] Same-sex intercourse is particularly associated with a state of the soul characterised by a lack of self-mastery over pleasure.

In order to gain a thorough insight into the subject, this chapter goes through the principal passages in books I and VIII and examines them with regard to their relevant textual, cultural and philosophical contexts. Some of the linguistic issues that arise are problematic and complex, but they are essential to this analysis of the subject. Recourse will be made also to other Platonic ideas on love and desire as expressed in the *Symposium, Phaedrus* and elsewhere and their connection with the *Laws*. Finally, this chapter will analyse the Athenian Stranger's ultimate summation of the law on sex and some difficulties and ambiguities that arise from it. Taking all these things into account, it I will attempt to determine what sort of resolution (if any) is to be made about same-sex relations in the second-best *polis*.

This section will focus on the relevant passages found in Book I. In terms of the over-all narrative structure of the *Laws,* the first several books have a decidedly theoretical inclination. The subject of conversation tends to wander broadly over many related topics in which some general issues are perused. Later, the narrative becomes more of a monologue dealing mostly with the many fine details of hypothetical legal ar-rangements. The opening books, by contrast, provide fertile ground for the narrator's philosophical expositions on social theory and practice. Beginning with his discus-sion of the Greek customs of gymnastics and common meals, the Athenian Stranger proceeds to a seemingly tangential argument that becomes his initial thesis opposing same-sex intercourse. He levels his criticism chiefly against Sparta and Krete as city-states that he perceives to have legitimised same-sex behaviour.[5] He maintains that these practices have yielded not only civil discord but also an institutionalised form of sexual indulgence that is 'contrary to nature'. He says:

> Whereas these *gymnasia* and common meals now benefit your cities in many other ways, they are harmful in the event of civil strife (πρὸς δὲ τὰς στάσεις)—as the example of the youths of Miletos, Boeotia and Thurii demonstrates—ad-ditionally this practice seems to have corrupted an ancient custom[6] according to nature (κατὰ φύσιν) concerning sexual pleasures (περὶ τὰ ἀφροδίσια ἡδονὰς)[7] not only of human beings but of beasts as well. And someone might first accuse your cities of these things along with as many of the others that avidly utilise the *gymnasia.*[8]

I shall examine these points severally and return to some of them later in the chap-ter. First, whether *gymnasia* and common meals might have been major causes of factionalism and civil discord in these cities is difficult to demonstrate; although, it is not without plausibility. Perhaps it is precisely 'in the event of civil strife' that one might expect them to play a significant role for both physical training and conspiratorial plotting. But the Athenian Stranger is still at the theoretical stage of constitution-building since, later, he outlines the legislation for common meals and *gymnasia* despite having alluded to some of the dangers that they might represent. In book VI, common meals are considered to be so useful a civic institution that attendance at them by both men and women is to be compulsory as we have seen.[9] Perhaps his criticism of existing institutions of a similar nature might have more to do with their lack of regulation by the stabilising powers of philosophical Reason.

In the world of Plato's time, the events mentioned by the Athenian Stranger in the above passage were not insignificant in the shaping of history and thus bear some closer inspection. The Ionian city of Miletos, on the coast of Asia Minor, experienced an oligarchic revolt in 405 B.C.E. that was allegedly instigated by the Spartan admiral Lysander.[10] In Thebes, the principal city of the region of Boeotia, an oligarchic faction that was opposed to Sparta arose in the years following the Peloponnesian War and eventually gained superiority over the pro-Spartan (also oligarchic) faction that had dominated for many years.[11] Thurii was a colony in southern Italy, originally founded by Perikles, which was often troubled by civil strife–especially following the Athenian naval defeat in Sicily. Thereafter it reportedly adopted Spartan customs and a pro-Spartan policy.[12] Other than the Athenian Stranger's implications, there is no indication that same-sex practices facilitated these conflicts.

The *gymnasia* appear to have provided both physical training and a context in which individuals could form bonds of association. Since the youths of the cities in question were typically well trained for physical combat, they were readily able to assist in the military action required to overthrow the governments of each region.[13] Similarly, common meals may have aided factions in forming through providing an ideal venue for the plotting of conspiracies amongst comrades whilst they dined together. This, as with the *gymnasia*, seems a possibility that may or may not come to pass, depending on social conditions at the time, but is not necessarily the fault of the institution itself.[14] Any state should be concerned with the diet, health and fitness of its populace and Plato's Magnesia is certainly no exception.[15] *Gymnasia* are institutions that have a decidedly oligarchic/aristocratic quality (as with Spartan common meals). But their long relationship with same-sex intercourse is the precise point that the Athenian Stranger has here pointedly associated with the notion that they have likewise urged civil strife.[16] A real connection between same-sex practices and factionalism is not particularly overt, but it is implicit nonetheless and provides a springboard for him to launch into a discussion on the malefactions of the negatively identified indulgence.

As we can observe, a sort of public discourse on the subject of sexuality was underway in ancient Greek culture for many generations prior to and including Plato's participation in it. There were, quite naturally, many degrees of difference between the various traditions. Popular variants of myths existed with alternative interpretations and morals (usually cashed away, doubtlessly to our great benefit, in one of Aristotle's catalogues of allegedly ethnographic data). The position that Plato's narrator in the *Laws* takes with regard to myth and history represents one particular line of interpretation with its own peculiarities. In other mytho-historical traditions which he deliberately excludes, the custom of same-sex relations between men often yielded more positive consequences.

The Athenian Stranger does not mention that same-sex relationships have been associated also with the preservation of freedom from tyrants and tyrannical regimes. These are reported by later authors along with those of Plato's era. For example, Athenaios of Naukratis (2nd–3rd century c.e.), attributing his intelligence to Hieronymus the Peripatetic (of Rhodes, 3rd century b.c.e.), reported that love affairs between young men became widespread because, in the vigour of their youth, 'the mutual sympathy of their companionship brought many tyrannical governments to an end'.[17] This phenomenon was generally considered to have resulted from the fact that, when their partners were present, lovers became more willing to suffer the hardships of battle, and thereby gain victory, rather than incur a reputation for cowardice in the opinion of their favourites. Interestingly, in the *Symposium* (179a), Plato puts virtually these same words into the mouth of his Phaedrus. Athenaios also claimed that the military benefits of same-sex relationships were proven by the Sacred Band at Thebes and by the 'murderous attempt on the Peisistratidae made by Harmodios and Aristogeiton; and again in Sicily by the love of Chariton and Melanippus'.[18] In the *Symposium,* Pausanius had argued that barbarian tyrants tended to outlaw same-sex affairs because they are fearful of strong attachments arising amongst their subjects. He reformulated the unwillingness between lovers to tolerate disgrace in battle (also indicated by the character of Aristophanes at 178d4–179a2) into an unwillingness to acquiesce under threat of tyranny. Pausanias, again, cites the instance of Harmodios and his lover Aristogeiton who, according to popular lore, overthrew the tyranny of the Peisistratids at Athens and thereby cleared the way for democracy (182b6–c7). Aristotle indicates that Harmodios attacked the Peisistratids for an offence done by them to his sister.[19] Even so, Harmodios' lover Aristogeiton is said to have joined in the attack due to the strong affection between them.[20]

Conversely, a tyranny could be overthrown due to the overindulgent sexual forays of the tyrant himself. Aristotle cites several examples in the *Politics* where certain tyrants' erotic relationships with members of the same sex, or their indirect participation in such things, became harmful to them in the long term. A conspiracy is purported to have arisen against Periander, the tyrant of Ambrakia, because he jokingly inquired of his male favourite, 'Aren't you yet with child by me?' (1311a16). Pausanias made an attack against Philip of Macedon reportedly due to the fact that Philip had allowed him to be sexually outraged (ὑβρίζειν) by Attalos and his friends. An attack against the tyrant Amyntas by Derdas was said to be due to the boasting of the former that he had enjoyed the 'youthful favours' of the latter (a17).

Hellanokrates of Larissa was reported to have joined with Krataios in making an attack against the tyrant Archelaos of Macedonia. Hellanokrates' complaint against Archelaos was allegedly that, despite having enjoyed his sexual favours, the tyrant refused to uphold his promise to restore him to his native city. Krataios had been carrying on a stormy sexual liaison with Archelaos and, developing resentment for his lover, nurtured a yearning for revenge (Aristotle suggests that another cause of this conflict was due to Archelaos breaking his promise to let Krataios marry one of his daughters—a17–18). It could be argued that same-sex activities were more or less incidental, though connected, to this and other such potential tyrannicides. Aristotle suggests that 'living luxurious lives, they [tyrants] make themselves contemptible, and offer their assailants plenty of opportunities' (1312b33). All of these examples are anecdotal. However, they demonstrate some means by which those within same-sex relationships may, to their credit, resist a tyranny and/or bring about its demise. This would seem to cast same-sex acts in a positive light.

Plato's narrator in the *Laws* does not seem to favour such a line of mytho-cultural tradition that would promote the potential benefits of same-sex relationships as indicated by the above examples. Same-sex practices by the citizens of Magnesia are to be subject to some kind of potentially aggressive legislative restrictions along with moral and social reprobation. The Athenian Stranger aims his argument (first in Book I) against the Spartan and Kretan acceptance of same-sex activity as part of everyday life. His claim that the myth of Ganymede and Zeus is a false invention of the Kretans (636d) is unique to Plato and ought to be read alongside the denunciation of myths about the sexual exploits of the gods found at *Republic* 390b–392c.[21] Same-sex intercourse, the Athenian Stranger asserts, is both a corruption of ancient *nomos* and constitutes an indulgence in excessive desires. He elaborates on the situation in a general condemnation of it in a tone that echoes the sentiments of many modern opponents:[22]

> And whether one ought to regard these things *in a playful way or seriously* (παίζοντα εἴτε σπουδάζοντα), one must bear in mind that this [sexual] pleasure seems to have been naturally (κατὰ φύσιν) granted to male and female for the act of mutual procreation; but [sexual pleasure] between men and men, as well as that between women and women,[23] seems contrary to nature (παρὰ φύσιν)[24] and the *audacity* seems to have come about *prominently* (τῶν πρώτων) due to a lack of control over pleasure (τὸ τόλμημ᾽ εἶναι δι᾽ ἀκράτειαν ἡδονῆς
> —636c1–6, emphasis mine).[25]

There are certain semantic issues in this passage that demand attention. We shall return to 'prominently' and 'audacity' in a moment—but it is absolutely crucial whether the Athenian Stranger is speaking 'in a playful way' or 'seriously'. Dover suggests that the correct way to consider this matter is not so much as a contrast between the humorous and the solemn, but as 'playing an intellectual game' and 'saying what one really thinks'.[26]

If he is just 'playing an intellectual game', then what follows on the subject of same-sex relationships, here or elsewhere, should not *necessarily* be regarded as having any real legislative potential.[27] It could be little more than philosophical speculation. The discussion is hypothetical in character (much of the passage is dependent upon δοκεῖ), yet a distinction is made and this question of 'naturalness' is a central factor in determining the exact quality of the argument.

Nussbaum favours a radical position saying that 'same-sex conduct is not singled out for special blame', and that 'there is no evidence that Plato regarded same-sex conduct as morally worse than other forms of sexual conduct'.[28] This is a curious proposition. In response to Nussbaum's allegation, Rist maintains that her statements are 'highly misleading if not simply false', since 'even in the *Phaedrus* Plato condemns *most* same-sex intercourse, only in a few special circumstances giving it limited approval'.[29] It appears clear that the act of same-sex intercourse *has* been singled out, as Rist says. Whether this represents Plato's opinion is another matter beyond the scope of modern discourse. His narrator disapproves of it on moral grounds.

A piece of evidence in support of the Athenian Stranger's seriousness on this subject occurs in book VIII, to be considered later, where he is framing laws against sexual misconduct. There he indicates that no freeborn male citizen of Magnesia should engage in 'sterile and unnatural intercourse with males' (841d4–5). The fact that there might be exceptions to the rule in both the *Laws* and the *Phaedrus* is suggestive. At the very least, nothing has been set in stone. Unfortunately the issue of the Athenian Stranger's (or Plato's own) 'seriousness' about this subject remains uncomfortably uncertain. The association between the inclination for same-sex intercourse and a lack of control over the desires meshes into the greater discussion on pleasure throughout the *Laws,* considered below.

The Athenian Stranger posits these notions about sexuality, not insignificantly, with a view toward the overall happiness of his populace. This is a state of being that he wants to encourage through the drawing of pleasures in moderate measure (636d8–e3). As Rist indicates, if citizens are willing to abstain from sexual delights for athletic victory, then 'why would they not abstain for a victory over pleasures and the acquiring of the virtue of self-restraint?'[30] Persuading the Magnesian populace that most forms of sexual activity (including perhaps same-sex intercourse) are 'fine' in private and in secret, but otherwise shameful seems to be the best alternative.[31] Perhaps it is wrong to talk about the Athenian Stranger's contemplation of same-sex desire in terms of legislation (or even as a matter of legality). He could be engaged in an experimental foray into the possibilities and moral considerations of exercising a specific psychological/sociological influence on theoretical subjects. However, there may be more 'seriousness' to it than not.

The passage at 636c1–6, quoted above, has some other difficulties beyond whether the Athenian Stranger takes the matter 'in a playful way' or otherwise. I rendered καὶ τῶν πρώτων τὸ τόλμημ' εἶναι δι' ἀκράτειαν ἡδονῆς (636c6)[32] as 'and the *audacity* seems to have come about *prominently* due to a lack of control over pleasure', following England's notes.[33] This rendition may be in error. Dover offers two alternative versions: 'a crime *of the first order*, committed through the inability to control the desire for pleasure' (italics mine), and 'a crime caused by failure to control the desire for pleasure'.[34] Nussbaum has questioned Dover's translation asking why one's weakness should cause something to be classified as a 'crime of the first order'. 'Weakness', she says, 'might, of course, cause the *commission* of a crime, but it seems implausible that weakness should cause something to be "among the first" in the ranks of crime, which is what the sentence so construed would say'.[35] She takes τῶν πρώτων to mean 'of the first people to do it', which was the rendition that England rejected.

The fact that the Athenian Stranger has been talking about the occurrence of this sexual practice in the *gymnasia* of Sparta and Krete might lend some credibility to her interpretation. Note, in passing, that the Athenian Stranger does not appear to think it strange that males will find other naked males attractive.[36] Nussbaum argues that these sorts of sexual relations cannot be a 'crime of the first order' since 'he urges his citizens to believe that this conduct is *kalon* provided that one does not do it within the cognisance of others at that time,[37] a teaching that he certainly does not promulgate for murder, theft, sacrilege, and other major crimes'.[38] The passages at 839d–842a—to be presently considered—at least appear to lend some support to Nussbaum's claim that same-sex acts do not constitute a 'crime of the first order'. Likewise, England's rendition as 'prominently' might be due to his own prejudices, or those of his era, leaking into his commentary on Plato's text. The passage could easily be rendered 'of the first ones to do it'. Even so, the ambiguity of this section is heightened as much by τῶν πρώτων as by τόλμημα.

The word τόλμημα refers to an act of daring that does not necessarily, in and of itself, constitute a state of criminal 'audacity'. Taylor's translation of the passage at 636c6–7 as 'the *crime* . . . [e.g. of same-sex intercourse] is a capital surrender to lust of pleasure'[39] (italics mine) appears at once inconsistent with τόλμημα and altogether slanted. The 9th edition of Liddell and Scott cites *Laws* 636c as an instance of this word which could be rendered as 'a daring *or* shameless act', but this only indicates that 'shameless act' was thought to be appropriate because of its use in some passage or passages between the 6th century B.C.E. and the 9th century C.E. 'Daring' is provided as a viable alternative to 'shameless'.[40] In fact, since this is the only occurrence of τόλμημα in all the works of Plato, one ought to construe this noun consistently with its originating verb τολμάω which occasionally means 'to endure' and more often 'to dare'. The un-compounded verb occurs 123 times in the Platonic *corpus*. It always indicates an action that is either bold or daring and, as Nussbaum states, 'sometimes the context will show the daring to be good, and sometimes the context will show it to be bad'.[41]

In light of these observations, Nussbaum attests that Dover has since recanted his previous rendering of τόλμημα as 'crime' and has suggested 'venture' as a correction.[42] This also lends further support to reading τῶν πρώτων as 'of the first ones to do it' rather than 'prominently' or 'of the first order' as it would be unclear what was meant by a 'venture of the first order' here. Wherever the truth may lie, same-sex intercourse as a 'crime of the first order' seems an uncalled for and heavy-handed translation at best—yet those like Taylor (and sometimes Dover) who have favoured 'crime' are certainly picking up on themes which are present in the passages under discussion. Who, then, were the 'first ones' that possessed such daring? It is difficult to say for sure but the Athenian Stranger later suggests that Laios, the father of the infamous Oedipus, may have been to blame. What is not difficult to say is that same-sex intercourse appears quite clearly to have been designated here as a thing that is 'contrary to nature'. Whether this is meant to be taken merely as *paramyth* or fable, rather than a statement of fact remains uncertain. It will be told, nonetheless, to the Magnesian populace with a persuasive intent.

This section examines the argument in Book VIII when the same topic again arises. The Athenian Stranger states at 835d2–e1 that he is concerned with how to manage a state in which the youths are in fine physical condition and 'free from the harsh labours that serve most to quench *hybris*' (οἳ μάλιστα ὕβριν σβεννύασιν). He indicates that the laws, magistrates, state institutions and system of education already have implicitly in their charge the role of checking many of these illicit desires (ἐπιθυμιῶν) that lead away from *sōphrosynē*.[43] He vehemently warns that the uncontrolled 'erotic love (τὰ δὲ τῶν ἐρώτων) of youths both male and female, and such love of men for women and women for men' have long been the bane of cities and individuals (836a6–b2). It is not just same-sex indulgences that constitute a yielding to excessive desire but lust for the opposite sex is likewise included. This comes as a prelude to the Athenian Stranger's more in-depth discussion on same-sex intercourse.

His treatment suggests its categorisation as one particular manifestation of general sexual desire—unlike a modern tendency to group same-sex relations (called homosexuality) as a separate psychosexual state alongside heterosexuality and sometimes bisexuality.[44] It is evident that the Athenian Stranger is striking out on a rather unorthodox approach when he tells Kleinias and Megillus that, whatever their other contributions to his hypothetical constitution, the Spartan and Kretan city-states are themselves opposed to his postulations about sexual desire (836b5–8). Certainly there would have been some opposition amongst the Athenians against embracing his policies with open arms. Many of Plato's contemporaries would probably have considered his ideals of sexual behaviour overly restrictive and prudish.

The Athenian Stranger brings up same-sex intercourse prior to his discussion on three types of love.[45] His tone could be taken as at once declamatory and less ambiguous than the hypothetical material in Book I. Addressing his Kretan and the Spartan interlocutors, he says:

> For if someone following nature (ἀκολουθῶν τῇ φύσει) should posit the law that existed prior to the time of Laios,[46] arguing that it was always right[47] for a man not to partake of sexual acts with a young man (νέων) as he would with a woman, presenting as evidence the nature of beasts and demonstrating in respect to such things that male does not cling closely to male because this is not natural, then he would probably pursue with an unpersuasive argument and one which is in no ways harmonious with your city-states (836b8–c7).[48]

Except for his philosophical position against excessive pleasure, the primary exemplars with which the Athenian Stranger has framed his argument would seem to be 'ancient custom' and the behaviour of animals. These seem to be the only premises on which he has based his declaration that same-sex intercourse is particularly unnatural. Later, in the same book, it is affirmed that the citizens of Magnesia should behave no worse than 'birds and many other creatures . . . [that] live in continence and unspoiled virginity' until the appropriate age when they pair off in opposite-sex units and live together 'in steadfast piety and justice' (840c11–e2). This argument from the perceived 'nature' of animals is problematic at best.[49]

Consider *Philebus* 67b, where Plato's Sokrates states that 'the many' prefer to use such arguments from the natural world as authoritative fact rather than divining deeper truths from philosophy.[50] 'The many' are seen to look on animal behaviour as in some ways paradigmatic of how they ought to behave. Plato's use of this argument from animal nature in the *Laws* is, as Nussbaum says, 'a powerful rhetorical device that will have a serious effect on his citizens' and possibly nothing more.[51] It is perhaps the Athenian Stranger's concern with the issue of excessive pleasures and desires that permits him to frame his most plausible argument against same-sex relationships. There is no indication that same-sex acts are essentially wicked or immoral. They are, however, identified as being extremely pleasurable and therein lies the rub. One of the Athenian Stranger's primary interests is, in Dover's words, 'to reduce to an unavoidable minimum all activity of which the end is physical enjoyment, in order that the irrational and appetitive element of the soul may not be encouraged and strengthened by indulgence'.[52] Same-sex intercourse is perceived as producing too much emotional and somatic enjoyment for the sober-minded Magnesians.

Aspersions have already been cast against those who give in to excessive desires back in Book I at 650a2–5, where Plato's narrator has raised concerns over the dangers of allowing such individuals to participate in the daily lives of other 'normal' citizens. A 'safe' way of testing Magnesian citizens' psychic solvency (e.g. through supervised drinking parties) is favoured over discovering their inadequacies before they actually commit a crime of passion.[53] This is preferable, he says, to making a 'test of one whose soul yields to pleasures, by placing him in charge of one's daughters and sons and wives, so, by endangering one's loved ones, the character of his soul is revealed'. The dangerous and potentially criminal characteristics associated with the lack of *enkrateia* over their desires for pleasure highlights the recurring theme of the (albeit sometimes ambiguous) declamation of same-sex intercourse as a specific type of indulgence that indicates a lack of self-mastery.

It is worthy of note that daughters, sons and wives are all included as being subject to the potential dangers posed by those whose souls are improperly aligned in this way. Again, it suggests much less differentiation between mixed- and same-sex desires than we make today. More emphasis is placed on the act of indulgence itself—resulting from the incumbent psychic disharmony that is perceived to be intrinsic to the souls of those who are ruled by their appetites. The 'one whose soul yields to pleasures' is here considered a sexual threat to both sexes. This widens the scope of condemnation to place same-sex intercourse alongside rape, albeit in an implied manner, as both being symptomatic of the same root cause. This perhaps propagandistic juxtaposition of same-sex intercourse with other criminal acts occurs not only here and in the law on rape but likewise in its associations with *hybris* that will shortly be discussed.

The Athenian Stranger, at 836b8–c7, mentioned a law 'prior to the time of Laios'. This would seem to indicate that he (or possibly Plato himself) is following a mytho-cultural convention to the effect that, as Athenaios says, 'Laios initiated such erotic acts when he was a guest of Pelops'.[54] Aroused by and enamoured with Pelops' son, prince Chrysippos, Laios reportedly stole him away to Thebes in his chariot.[55] I draw attention to the wording of the passage which refers to a 'custom' (τὸν νόμον) 'prior to the time of Laios' (πρὸ τοῦ Λαίου) because it denotes an assumption, or at least an implication, that before that time no such same-sex practices existed in Greece. Or, to be precise, it seems to be taking as fact that the dominant sexual ethic before Laios' time was contrary to same-sex intercourse, itself introduced as a custom by the deeds of the mythological king of Thebes (and possibly his son). The seriousness of such a proposition seems unlikely but not beyond possibility. The Athenian Stranger would appear to posit (whether only as a fable for the Magnesian populace or as a given fact) that there was some custom of sexual interaction, exclusively between members of the opposite sex, which dominated in the time before Laios. He has deliberately excluded other mythical possibilities that might call his statements into question.

One such alternative, maintained directly following Plato's era, is afforded by the fragmentary account of Timaios of Tauromenion (c350–c260 B.C.E.) who claims that these practices of same-sex intercourse were derived from the Kretans themselves and thence introduced to Greek culture.[56] Excluding the fable of Ganymede and Zeus as spurious, as the Athenian Stranger has done (636d), there is another fictitious Kretan to consider. In Rhadamanthys' tale there is the hint of an ongoing cultural debate being expressed through popular myth. Ibykos of Rhegion, a lyric poet of the 6th century B.C.E., informs us that Rhadamanthys engaged in *erōs* with a youthful male lover named Talos.[57] The child of Zeus and Europa, brother of King Minos of Krete, Rhadamanthys became one of the three judges in the underworld due to his having led a life on earth characterised by justice. This son of Krete and paragon of virtue is praised by the Athenian Stranger at 948b for his wise discernment in all matters judicial and for his just insights in determining the truth. If Plato was aware of the mythical tradition that portrayed Rhadamanthys as a partaker of same-sex delights, he has chosen to make his narrator ignore it.

As we have seen, one may present alternative versions of a given myth and it is certainly at Plato's discretion to do so. Perhaps we are to assume that such a myth cannot be true (to be regarded as a fiction, like that of Ganymede, concocted to justify same-sex acts) when considered in the light of Sokrates' condemnation of slanderous myths that portray an erroneous image of the sexual practices of the gods at *Republic* 390b–392c. Yet it is not unreasonable to question the assumption that 'prior to Laios' the only sexual ethic in practice allowed sexual intercourse exclusively between members of the opposite sex. The fact that the Athenian Stranger has used the phrasing 'prior to the time of Laios' to introduce his discussion on same-sex acts sets a particular tone for the argument which is perhaps more important than whether or not Plato thought Laios was the actual originator of the custom. The implications of sexual perversity associated with Oedipus and the cursed Theban royal house add fuel to the Athenian Stranger's condemnation of same-sex intercourse as 'contrary to nature'. Virtually everyone in the Greece of Plato's time would have been aware of the sexual taboos broken, albeit unwittingly, by Oedipus and his mother (not to mention the crime of, again unwittingly, slaying his father). I propose that the mere mention of Laios here in association with same-sex acts carries with it a great many weighty connotations that serve, psychologically, to bolster the Athenian Stranger's arguments against same-sex intercourse in terms of persuasion if not necessarily conventional reason.

Here I need to take a small but important diversion into the discussion of three kinds of love. Also in book VIII, Plato has provided his readers with a pithy philosophical discussion on the subjects of love, affection and desire. Through the voice of the Athenian Stranger, he has posited in the *Laws* a threefold definition of φιλία. Of its three parts, the proper expression is said to occur in a non-physical manner between individuals who are most 'like' one another in 'goodness'. This definition, postulated chiefly for individuals of the same sex who have some kind of attraction for one another, favours non-corporeal, 'soul to soul' (Platonic) love. This is said to work best toward the achievement of the ideal *telos* of *aretē*. The Athenian Stranger also suggests a procedure of sublimation,[58] functioning through 'soul to soul' love, which is meant to free the soul from the base desires that threaten to ensnare it.

On this complex issue, Field asserts that 'Plato himself always strongly disapproved of physical intercourse between individuals of the same sex', but 'he recognised the prevalence of the tendency even among men who, in other respects, had the highest potentialities for good . . . his discussion of it may be taken as an attempt to show that the desire may, in our modern phraseology, be "sublimated" into the pursuit of knowledge and goodness'.[59] Plato certainly appears to have given much consideration to the subject of the conquest of baser desires through the (proper) love of the Good—and not only in the *Laws*.[60] His concern with such matters may be largely derived from his philosophical/metaphysical interest in the immortality of the soul and the after-life in relation to the pursuit of excellence in life. In Magnesia, as we have seen, the officially favoured position is to attain a type of immortality through the generation of children (not an exclusively Platonic idea) along with the Platonically sublime passion for 'eternal realities' that represent the higher forms of 'affection' for which an individual seeking the Good must strive. The definition of φιλία in the *Laws* does not appear to be something new that is peculiar to Plato's final work. The Athenian Stranger's formulation signifies a further development of a longstanding Platonic tradition. It seems to represent a logical continuation of previous lines of thought already well developed in his works.[61]

The Athenian Stranger, at 837a–d, posits some notions on the nature of φιλία between individuals presumably (although perhaps not exclusively) of the same sex. His discussion of 'three types of *philia*' comes directly after his fairly lengthy disquisition on the inherent problems of same-sex relations (836 sq.). It appears to be the case that Plato's narrator here is employing *philia* in terms of non-sexual affection as well as in an erotic sense. He has done this before in the *Lysis* (221b7–8) where, as David Konstan says, 'Socrates casually collapses the differences between *philia*, *eros,* and *epithumia* (cf. *Laws* 8.837a1), and the discussion moves freely among cases of parental affection, erotic attraction, attachment between friends, and even the appeal of inanimate objects'.[62] Dover points out that the verb φιλεῖν (containing the same base as φιλία) may be used as easily to denote familial love—as in Aristophanes' *Clouds* 79–83, where Strepsiades demands of his son, Pheidippides, whether or not he has *philia* for his father—and also in an erotic context—as in Xenophon's *Symposium* IX.6, where a pair of dancers enact the romantic legend of Dionysos and Ariadne.[63]

The narrator of the *Laws* indicates that the subjects under examination are those of 'affection and its conjoined passion' (τῆς φιλίας τε καὶ ἐπιθυμίας ἅμα) and that of 'so-called love' (λεγομένων ἐρώτων–836e5–837a2).[64] He supposes that much confusion has resulted from a misunderstanding of the fact that these things are not really two, but three: from the two types he postulates a third category, the mixed product of both, all signified by the single term *philia*. It is possible that this apparently new division should be read in terms of the distinctions made in Pausanias' speech at *Symposium* 180d, on the subject of ἔρως πάνδημος and ἔρως οὐράνιος or in terms of Diotima's characterisation of 'birth in Beauty'. It is also possible to view this new division as a reworking of the myth of the two horses at *Phaedrus* 246b.

The Athenian Stranger's discussion of affection has some novel features about it. As Dover says, 'Plato handles *erōs* very mistrustfully in *Laws* 836e–837d, as the *philia* which amounts to need and desire and the *philia* between those who are attracted by their affinity; the passage is strikingly unlike those in his earlier works, and a stage more remote from ordinary Greek attitudes to *eros* and love'.[65] The distinctions given in the *Laws* are 1.) 'φιλία between opposites', 2.) 'φιλία between those who are similar', and finally, 3.) the mixed combination of categories 1 and 2. Furthermore, the Athenian Stranger says, 'whenever each one becomes intense, we designate it "erotic love"' (ἔρωτα ἐπονομάζομεν—837a8–9). In this respect, *philia* has not simply been conflated with *erōs* but, under certain circumstances, it has the capacity to evolve from just friendship or affection into something more erotic and, therefore, much more dangerous.[66] It is precisely this aspect of *erōs* (*philia* run amok?) that the Athenian Stranger wants his hypothetical citizens to avoid through the lofty, non-physical affection expressed between souls rather than in the customary manner between bodies.

The first of these, '*philia* between opposites' (ἐναντίων), is described as 'violent and unrestrained and most often not reciprocated'.[67] This evokes a hypothetical situation in which one individual has a strong passion for another who (perhaps because he is opposite in character, status, economic class, education, etc) does not return the same affection. Even if the beloved returns some affection, the Athenian Stranger suggests that such a relationship will always be characterised as 'violent and unrestrained', which cannot possibly encourage one to become σώφρων.[68] The corporeal lusts for ἡδονὴ must be reined in and brought into accord with 'right-thinking' in one who is to be wise (696c9). Therefore, affection between opposites amongst the Magnesians is to be avoided at all costs as a matter of course.

The second category, '*philia* between those who are similar', seems a far more promising route for one to pursue—*sans erōs*—in the daily affairs of the second-best state. Such a relationship, the Athenian Stranger says, is both 'gentle and has continuous mutual affection throughout life' (ἥμερός τε καὶ κοινὴ διὰ βίου—837b3–4). Non-physical *philia* between the souls of those who are similar in 'goodness' is considered the ideal.[69] This commonplace expression of Plato's can be found too at *Lysis* 214b3 and elsewhere.[70] The 'likeness' and 'equality' in this type of a relationship must be so only in terms of 'goodness'. The notion of non-physical love experienced in the mind/soul alone reflects similar attitudes expressed at *Philebus* 41c sq., where 'the body stands apart from the soul and has no communion with it in respect to its affections'. It also has a parallel in Xenophon's idealised account of Lykourgos' reforms, in the *Spartan Constitution*, where he reports that the love of souls—like brotherly love or the love of parents for children—was deemed more worthy than the love of bodies between men and youths which was, in consequence, allegedly discouraged.[71] However, the Athenian Stranger indicates that the most likely manifestation of *philia* in a real-life relationship is going to be some combination of categories 1 and 2 (μεικτὴ δὲ ἔκ τούτων—837b4) in which *erōs* may or may not enter the equation.

When one has been persuaded to pursue the ideal form of 'soul to soul' love, it should be ranked higher in value than any potential physical love. If this is achieved, as Vlastos says, 'mere physical beauty will now strike the lover as a "small," contemptible thing'.[72] The following is, according to the Athenian Stranger, an acceptable way for two such people to behave and so is prescribed as a paradigm which he hopes his citizens will emulate when faced with the egregious affliction of the desire to engage in excessive sexual indulgence:

> But when he holds that the desire of the body is secondary, gazing upon his beloved rather than engaging in *erōs* (ὁρῶν δὲ μᾶλλον ἢ ἐρῶν),[73] yearning for the soul of his beloved with his own soul,[74] he will believe that the act of satisfying body with body to be *hybris,* but while respecting and revering moderation (τὸ σῶφρον), and especially courage (ἀνδρεῖον)[75] and magnificence (μεγαλοπρεπὲς) and good sense (τὸ φρόνιμον), he would wish to remain chaste with a chaste beloved (837c3–d1).

In this instance, Kleinias interestingly remains silent as Megillus and the Athenian Stranger approve of the moral imperative outlined above for the benefit of the Magnesian state.[76] Through a mental process that is strikingly similar to Freudian sublimation, the lover is meant to reassign his fleshly passions for the beloved to the status of an intellectual ideal (admiration of the beloved's beauty/goodness/nobility/etc.) rather than the alternative outlet of joining in sexual union with the physical person of the beloved.

In this passage there are also some difficulties in translation and interpretation worth mentioning. Taylor's rendering of *hybris,* in c5, as 'wanton shame' seems imbued with an unnecessary degree of judgement. Pangle's version, truer to the text, posits 'wantonness' for *hybris,* appearing to follow Taylor's lead but leaving off 'shame'. It is the case that Liddell and Scott give 'wantonness' as a primary translation for *hybris,* but I recommend something along the lines of 'outrage' here as a more plausible rendering rather than 'wantonness' or 'wanton shame'.[77] Taylor also gives ἀνδρεῖον as 'manhood' and derives 'chastity' out of the litany of reverences that the Athenian Stranger lists in c6. In fact, τὸ σῶφρον may be translated as 'chastity', perhaps picking up on ἁγνεύειν (to keep pure) in c7, but it appears that 'moderation' would be a more reasonable rendition.[78] It seems more correct that 'moderation', rather than 'chastity', would be a better rendering of τὸ σῶφρον given that no Magnesian citizen is expected to be wholly chaste but they are expected to be moderate in their pursuits of pleasure. *Hybris,* however, represents another level of complexity altogether.

What is this *hybris* that concerns the Athenian Stranger so much and allegedly afflicts those who sate bodily desires with other bodies of the same sex? The word *hybris* is itself employed twenty-two times throughout the *Laws* in one form or another. It is often associated with those who break the law or who are unjust but sometimes, depending on context, the indication is not so severe. The Athenian Stranger declaims the *hybris* (ὑβρισταὶ) of mercenaries at 650b6. He warns, at 641c3, that those who win many victories run the risk of becoming too *hybristic* (ὑβριστότεροι) and that this *hybris* begets even more *hybris* (641c5). He declares (661e2) that the man who is beset by *hybris* can never be truly happy and, not insignificantly, he associates the state of being *hybristic* with injustice (662a2, 761e7). Similarly, a man with excessive wealth is said to be potentially inclined toward a type of *hybris* (ὕβρις) that can lead to injustice (679c1).

The Athenian Stranger's statute that severely limits (if not altogether banish) dowries, as we have seen, is in part framed with the intent of making wives less *hybristic* through any monetary controls that they might otherwise gain over their husbands (774c7). Magnesian masters are encouraged to be just toward their servants as this, in turn, will discourage them from committing *hybris* (ὑβρίζειν–777d4). Those who are *hybristic* toward their parents (885a3), orphans (927c2) and the laws (885a6, b2, 927c8) may be subject to fines and penalties in the second-best state. We are also told that ungoverned children, lacking in the proper guidance, become the 'most *hybristic* of beasts' (ὑβριστότατον–808d7).[79] Hard labour, of which the Magnesian citizens will be free, is just the sort of thing, the Athenian Stranger says echoing Lakonian ideals, which quenches *hybris* in the young (835e1).[80] In a *paramyth* designed to encourage his hypothetical citizens to follow the rules, he states that *hybris,* injustice and imprudence destroy while justice and moderation lead to salvation (906b). In almost all of these instances, Pangle has rendered *hybris* as 'insolence'. There is a sense of 'overstepping bounds' or 'going to excess' in these uses of *hybris.* There are fewer frames of reference for an association between *hybris* and sexual matters. Even so, it is possible to derive a context-based translation.

In discussing the benefits of shame (αἰσχος) as a means of correcting and preventing inappropriate behaviour, the Athenian Stranger cites a list of undesirable mental states, especially when they run unchecked, that are not conducive to the pursuit of virtue.[81] He says that 'vehement anger, erotic love (ἔρως), *hybris,* ignorance, the love of profit, cowardice, and even yet such things as wealth, beauty, strength, and many other similar particulars that drive a man out of his mind through the intoxication of pleasure' should each be carefully controlled and directed (649d4–7). Pangle renders *hybris* here again as 'insolence' and Taylor, somewhat curiously, gives it as 'pride'. The term is employed in juxtaposition to the Athenian Stranger's condemnation of excessive pleasures. This indicates, as Fisher says, a vice 'that must be controlled in a well-run state, and in a well-ordered soul'.[82] Plato's placement of *hybris* alongside ἔρως is telling, as are its other associations with pleasure. Here as elsewhere, it is considered to be a state of mind that can both accompany and also encourages certain types of excess. Too much of almost anything, it seems, inclines undisciplined humanity toward *hybris.*

The only other occurrence of *hybris* in a sexual or erotic context (aside from its use in describing male same-sex relations) appears during the Athenian Stranger's discussion on the penalty for rape at 874c. 'If someone should use force', says he, 'in a sexual manner (περὶ τὰ ἀφροδίσια), against either a free woman or a youth, let him then be slain with impunity by the party who has been forcefully outraged (ὑπό τε τοῦ ὑβρισθέντος βίᾳ) or by that one's father or brothers or sons'.[83] Here the sense is of a violent sexual act that constitutes *hybris,* as an outrage, insult or effrontery against the victim. The one who submits to excessive desires so much as to commit a rape *outrages* the injured party in the commission of said act. This picks up on the transitive use of *hubrizein* in the sense of an active psychosexual assertion (or physical insertion) carried out on one individual by another. In both instances of *hybris* mentioned in a sexual context (that of rape and of same-sex intercourse), the indication is one of an *outrage* arising from a lack of control over excessive desires.[84]

One may draw several conclusions, based on context, about the reference to male same-sex relations (sating body with body) as a commission of *hybris.* First, it is observable that the Athenian Stranger uses such a term with a view that same-sex intercourse amounts to a type of yielding to excessive desires. Added to this is the implication that such yielding will cause even more instances of yielding to excesses to come in the future. If the 'penetrative' partner may be construed as forcing himself (and thereby submitting to uncontrolled excess) on the 'receptive' partner, then he may be seen to have *outraged* him by the imposition.[85] That is, it is possible to draw such a conclusion if one subscribes to the active/penetrator and passive/penetrated model espoused by Dover, Foucault, Halperin *et al.*[86] Thus one could interpret the use of *hubrizein* as denoting the passive partner suffering a demotion of status by being so *outraged.*[87]

This model of penetrator/penetrated, however as we have seen, is problematic.[88] In the case of Demosthenes, in Aiskhines II, a demotion in status due to his role as an object of pleasure for others is certainly implied. But Taylor's rendering of 'wanton shame', in his version of *Laws* 837c3–d1, does not appear entirely solicited. As Cairns says of this passage, 'here, then, *aidōs* involves positive respect for standards of decency and leads one to avoid outrage or excess'.[89] Same-sex intercourse between consenting partners cannot bear the same implications as in the case of the Magnesian law on rape and, not surprisingly, there is no mention of the beloved slaying his lover due to his 'outrage'. In discussing same-sex relations in concert with *hybris,* a sense of yielding to excessive desires is surely indicated but not precisely the same sort of *hybris* as in a criminal act. Yet, by employing such terminology as the Athenian Stranger has chosen, he again conceptually attaches criminal connotations.

In terms of the Athenian Stranger's condemnation of same-sex intercourse as a type of *hybris,* the emphasis is perhaps placed more on the loss of self-control and lack of moderation than on one individual 'outraging' another through sexual penetration. Both partners in a same-sex relationship are described as becoming less 'virtuous' since the lover will have lost *sōphrosynē* and the consenting beloved will have lost courage due to his softness (*malakia*).[90] There is an external sense of dishonour in such a relationship with regard to the beloved, for whose welfare the lover allegedly gives no concern, and a quality of internal shame for the lover who has subjected himself to, as Fisher says, 'the enslavement to the worse desires, and the acceptance of madness (which is not now handled with any sympathy)'.[91] *Malakia* in the soul is perceived as a great threat to *aretē.* Only appropriately 'manly' individuals will act heroically and, as Hobbs says, 'not falter through softness of the soul'.[92] As far as the Athenian Stranger is concerned, one who submits to such *hybris* has failed to recognise that he/ she has unseated Reason (which ought to rule over his/her soul) in favour of the part that should be ruled—i.e. the appetites—for the hedonistic purposes of self-gratification. *Hybris* in this sexual context becomes a diabolical antithesis of moderation and denotes a state of psychic disharmony. It constitutes a failure of individual souls to serve Reason, the gods and the 'proper' order of the *kosmos.*[93]

Based on these passages in the *Laws* and other texts, Dover and Foucault's theoretical approach construes the 'active', male partner in a same-sex union as committing a type of *hybris* on the 'passive' partner in terms of dominance and submission and contrary to accepted sex-role stereotypes. It is not so easy to see what sort of *hybris* the 'receptive' partner commits. The answer appears to lie not so much in his supposed 'passivity' but in his perceived 'softness' (effeminacy) and, rather strikingly, his *active* insatiability for sex.[94] In the *Problemata,* attributed to Aristotle, the subject of those who are 'female-like' is discussed. The author indicates that sexual desire arises in the pelvic regions that are swollen with moisture and semen. These fluids find release through ejaculation. However, in some men the passages to the testicles are thought to have been blocked and these ensuing fluids collect instead in his anal region. As Davidson says:

This can happen to some extent to those who overindulge in sexual intercourse but with those who are by nature effeminate all moisture is secreted in this region . . . [since they are] unable to find release, their desire can never be properly assuaged 'wherefore they too become insatiable (*aplestoi,* lit. "unfillable"), just like women'.[95]

While there may be little of scientific value in such a notion, it reflects elements of public opinion at the time. Examples of women as being sexually insatiable and having a lack of self-control are certainly attested to in Classical drama and elsewhere.[96] This may point the way to the *hybris* of the receptive *erōmenos* to which the Athenian Stranger has alluded as having a 'feminine' lack of control over his desire for sexual gratification. He has already been characterised as 'soft' and therefore more like a woman. The receptive partner's quality of effeminacy represents a state regarded as inappropriate for a virtuous man (836d5–7, e1–3). But he is not alone. Interestingly, both partners in a same-sex union are construed as having fallen into a negative condition, ideologically connected with *hybris,* of 'sexual frenzy and madness'.[97]

As we have seen time and again, the Athenian Stranger seems to be aware that the citizens of his Magnesia are not always going to measure up to the standards that he would prefer.[98] Even though a man is encouraged not to sow 'unhallowed and bastard seed in concubines' (841d sq), he may enter into the bed of a woman (and the context appears to indicate only a woman) other than his legally wedded wife on the condition that he keeps the affair a secret.[99] Should the tryst be discovered, says Plato's narrator, 'we'd be right to exclude him by law from the award of state honours, as one that has proved himself a stranger indeed' (841e2–4). The prominence of social pressures for conformity is a good example, as Fisher says, of Plato's 'persistent tendency to incorporate elements from his understanding of the strengths of Spartan society'.[100] As psychologically damaging as the punishment for being caught might be, nonetheless it is very interesting that the Athenian Stranger has allowed for a kind of tightly managed legitimacy, providing it is undertaken in secret, for this particular indulgence at least between members of the opposite sex.

It remains uncertain whether or not a Magnesian might also engage in a similar sort of clandestine same-sex, extra-marital intercourse. It may be the case that some degree of excessive sexual desire for the opposite sex (albeit manifest in secrecy) is to be tolerated, perhaps because it is potentially reproductive, while *any* same-sex expression of passion whatsoever will be banned. If this is true, then the discussion of three types of *philia* along with the principles of sublimation of desire are aimed primarily, if not exclusively, at the would-be practitioners of same-sex intercourse alone. It is not clear whether there is legitimacy of any sort to be given to this kind of sexual expression except that, apparently, no physical interaction should ensue between those who have such desires. We do not have in the *Laws* a comparable discussion that specifically addresses the subject of excessive desires for members of the opposite sex to such an extent. That is, unless the three types of *philia* may also be applied to mixed-sex desires—which is a possibility. Since moderation is necessary for the achievement of wisdom, it follows that anyone who would be wise (of whatever sex) must be moderate in terms of all sexual expression and not become a slave to the gratification of excessive desires.

However, he has dealt with the subject of the regulation of the desires of citizens for members of the opposite sex. This occurs primarily in the law on rape, mentioned above, and in regard to marriage laws and rules of procreation.[101] These strictures appear to be more limiting to women than to men who pursue the opposite sex in order to gratify their desires. The implicit necessity for moderation in the case of romantic relations between members of the opposite sex has been suggested and reinforced through the myth of the family. This reflects similar philosophical tenets in the *Phaedrus* where *sōphrosynē* is considered the hallmark of a true lover.[102] Whether or not Plato means to uphold the same notions in the *Laws* is uncertain although it seems probable. Sokrates, at *Phaedrus* 250e3–251a, declares that those not recently initiated into the 'mysteries' of philosophy or whose purity has been stained cannot behold the Beautiful. They are perceived to be fixed on temporal beauty alone and so cavort, in a bestial fashion, with women and presumably also with men contrary to nature (παρὰ φύσιν).[103]

This citation from the *Phaedrus* may shed some light on the same phraseology in the *Laws*. What is actually 'contrary to nature' may not be the same-sex act itself, but the indulgence in excessive desires for pleasure that provokes one to engage in such an exceedingly pleasurable act in the first place.[104] This might seem like 'hairsplitting', but it may be the crux of the Athenian Stranger's argument that is ostensibly derived from his philosophical and metaphysical interests in the human soul. Same-sex desires are considered to possess the quality of introducing instabilities into the psychic harmony of individuals. Such instabilities are perceived to be exacerbated if they go on to actually indulge in these excessive pleasures. The Athenian Stranger has particularly singled out same-sex relations as one of the most 'dangerous' of sexual pleasures. They are, as we saw earlier, deemed to be somehow 'too' pleasurable. Whereas, in contrast, copulation between married, mixed-sex couples is evidently not so dangerous due to it perhaps being less pleasurable than same-sex intercourse.

The verbal associations between same-sex acts and other acts considered morally reproachful in the *Laws*, a standard text on Magnesia's 'required reading' list, appears to be part of the Athenian Stranger's employment of calculated language to achieve his societal ends. Appealing to his citizens with popular aphorisms and persuading fables is another level of this.[105] In the passage at 836b8–c7, the Athenian Stranger has again employed an argument from nature against same-sex intercourse.

As we saw earlier, he claims to favour the restoration of an (imagined) exclusively mixed-sex-oriented sexual *nomos* as it is perceived to have existed 'prior to Laios'.

This would evidently be 'following nature'. Likewise, we saw that he suggested that his hypothetical citizens should take an example from the 'nature' of animals since they do not engage in same-sex intercourse. He restates his assertion from Book I that sex between males is 'unnatural'.[106] It is possible to see that the very mention of Laios in connection with same-sex intercourse constitutes an association with incest that furthers the Athenian Stranger's argument. This portrays the concept of same-sex intercourse, perhaps in the mind of an impressionable listener who has heard this story throughout their lifetime, in such a way that it is supplied with unnatural, criminal and sacrilegious connotations. At 838b–c the Magnesian law against incest is framed. The Athenian Stranger indicates there that no one questions the unnaturalness of incest and the proscription against it is socially reinforced by religion, popular scorn and 'serious tragedy'. This would appear to give us an indication of Plato's understanding of the uses of socialisation and psychological persuasion through methods of repetitive indoctrination to achieve the desired ends with regard to moral hygiene.

Turning rather swiftly from the subject of incest to other sexual acts deemed 'contrary to nature', our narrator then makes the proposition, as Dover says, 'that the religious sanctions which already operate against incest, so that "not so much as a desire for such intercourse enters most people's heads" (836b), should be extended to sexual legislation in general'.[107] The Athenian Stranger states:

> For in this was the very thing that I was saying, that in regard to this law (τὸν νόμον) I might have a craft of making use of sexual intercourse, according to nature (κατὰ φύσιν), for the generation of children, on the one hand abstaining from the male, not deliberately killing the species of humankind, nor sowing seed in rocks and stones, where it will never take root and yield natural fruit,[108] and on the other hand abstaining from any female field in which you would not want your seed to spring forth. For in the first place it [this law] is laid down in accord with nature (κατὰ φύσιν), and it serves to prevent erotic frenzy and madness (λύττης δε ἐρωτικῆς καὶ μανίας), all manner of adultery, all excesses in food and drink and it makes men become friendly and dear to their own wives (838e4–839b1).

The law under discussion here (and it should be noted, again, that the Athenian Stranger is speaking hypothetically) promotes, through social indoctrination, mixed-sex intercourse only between properly married couples. This state of affairs has been defined as 'natural' or 'in accord with nature' (κατὰ φύσιν). Same-sex intercourse, masturbation and adultery have been grouped together into the opposite category.

The Athenian Stranger again associates same-sex intercourse with excessive indulgences, 'erotic frenzy', and insanity (μανίας). The relationship between same-sex intercourse and *mania* is derived from the Athenian Stranger's formulation that

Reason should rule in the souls of his subjects over their desires. Such a state of psychic disharmony in which Reason is unseated in favour of the appetites amounts to an 'unnatural' disorder according to the philosophical model that he has defined. According to Dover, his 'condemnation of same-sex acts as contrary to nature was destined to have a profound effect on the history of morality'.[109]

However, it is appropriate to stress once more that nowhere does Plato's narrator consider the *desire* to engage in sexual acts with members of the same sex to be unnatural.[110] Elsewhere he cites instances in which someone might be tempted to partake of these activities and there is no indication that such a state of attraction *per se* would itself be considered abnormal. In seeking to stifle same-sex sexual expression altogether, the Athenian Stranger here appears to have struck out on a position that is somewhat divergent from that of many of his contemporaries. One can potentially see Plato working out his own thoughts on sexuality, through the media of these discourses. His is one voice in a chorus of many. The new ethic of sexuality in the *Laws* is, in many ways, both opposed to many contemporary practices and also at once derived in no small part from them. The views that are expressed in his works may not have been taken very seriously in his own lifetime and he was probably aware of this.[111] The *Laws* (as with any Platonic text) may be regarded both as a philosophical and a rhetorical exploration of cultural ideas. This exploration takes place against the backdrop of Plato's native time and culture. Whilst he steps beyond the norm in proposing a number of radical changes as we have already seen, he still viewed his world in many ways through the 'lens' of perception necessarily imposed on him by his life and times.

Back in Book I, at 636b1–c1, the Athenian Stranger spoke of the tendency for same-sex acts to occur in the milieu of the *gymnasia* almost matter-of-factly as if it were a foregone conclusion that such attractions were commonplace. At 839b, he talks about the vehement protestations that a given youth 'bursting with seed' might make to such restrictions on same-sex intercourse as discussed in the passages cited above. However, according to the model that Plato has constructed, one who is overcome by the desire to copulate with another of the same sex, to such an extent that the desire causes them to partake of the deed, is showing a lack of control over the appetites by the rule of Reason.[112] The desire itself is not unnatural. As we have seen, it appears to have been a cultural norm taken for granted, but the submission to that desire to such a degree that it manifests in same-sex intercourse amounts to the unseating of Reason from its proper psychical position and the consequent domination of the undisciplined soul by the desires and appetites. It would seem that the same argument could be applied to the indulgence of excessive desire for, e.g. food or drink, wealth or power along with sex as means of producing this psychical disharmony—but sex has been particularly targeted as an important manifestation of the sort of excessive indulgence that is said to invite madness.

It is necessary to recall that the Athenian Stranger is theorising about a second-best *polis* for which second-best rules and regulations are being framed. His discussions of same-sex intercourse are often more theorisation than legislation. As mentioned above, he has identified a hypothetical youth, 'bursting with seed' (πολλοῦ σπέρματος μεστός), who would ridicule any legislation that places such limitations on sexual activity (especially same-sex activity) as 'foolish and impossible restrictions' (839b4–6). This protest would not necessarily stand in the way of the legislation but it does demonstrate at least one of the problems that could arise from thrusting this novel moral code on a society that would probably react strongly against it.

The muted legitimacy granted to extra-marital, mixed-sex intercourse does not seem to cover same-sex intercourse. This is only so inasmuch as no declarative statements to that effect have been made. But his ultimate position remains far from certain and the proscription of same-sex activity may not actually come to pass. There is a degree of uncertainty that the Athenian Stranger reveals (and possibly Plato as well) in terms of dealing with some of these finer points of sexual law. He is unclear over whether or not to pass legislation to limit same-sex acts or whether exclusively psychological influences might serve better for this end. In a potential reversal of his normally aggressive approach to the legal codification of *nomos*, Plato's narrator seems to be favouring 'unwritten laws' on matters of same-sex intercourse.[113]

In order to achieve this novel sexual ethic, he proposes a novel societal means by which it can be accomplished. He indicates here (as before at 835e1) that hard work serves to quench excessive desires (841a6–8) and then he hypothesises that the desired result of 'proper' sexual conduct might be achieved without legislation 'if it were not possible to undertake sexual intercourse without shame'.[114] Through shame, the act of engaging in sexual indulgence may be curtailed and the frequency of such indulgence is meant to decrease the sway of this harmful 'mistress' over them.[115] Those who fail to master their desires are said to be 'weaker than themselves' (οὓς ἥττους αὑτῶν–841b7–8), and it is hoped that they will be lured into the expected mode of behaviour through the socially inculcated mores of reverence for the gods, the love of honour and desire for the beauty in souls rather than bodies (841c4–6). However, in England's words, 'it is too much to hope that these motives would keep *all* men perfectly virtuous'.[116]

The employment of shame, along with other societal influences, as a psychological force to prevent sexual indulgences represents one key aspect of the Athenian Stranger's plan. The use of actual legal code is the other. He might choose one over the other or he could decide that both will work better together. His treatment of the issue, as we have seen, indicates a degree of indecisiveness (and perhaps discomfort) about how best to deal with matters of sexual conduct. Proof of this is observable in the apparent 'loophole' that is introduced by which one could effectively breach the normal mode of sexual conduct (again one assumes, referring to mixed-sex activities alone, but this remains un-clarified). He says:

> Let it be the rule of custom and unwritten law that it is noble for them to do these things secretly, and let the act of not doing them secretly be shameful, but not necessarily the commission of the act.[117]

This clause focuses greater emphasis on maintaining the appearance of appropriate behaviour even when that is only an illusion. As Cairns points out, the uses of shame in Magnesia are 'designed to foster concepts of honour which focus on the outward aspect of actions and encourage conformity rather than commitment'.[118] A Magnesian who breaks with the approved sexual conventions runs the risk of public censure and public shame. The added feature of public scrutiny makes getting caught, when his/her illicit gratification becomes excessive, a greater likelihood. The fear of shame may be considered a sufficient deterrent against breaking this custom of secrecy since there is the indication that the use of force (or stringent penalties) will be employed against any would-be transgressors. A type of fixed penalty is later introduced in the final statements of the (speculative) law on sex.

At 841c, the Athenian Stranger proposes two ordinances—either or both (and possibly neither) of which might ultimately be put into legal practice. It is evident that he would like to eliminate same-sex practices altogether from his second-best state but whether this can be done, or will be done, he does not say for sure. The passage begins with some uncertainty (whether only a prayer or a myth–841c), invoking the aid of a higher power, and then, somewhat paradoxically, concludes on a definitive statement that this will be the law on 'sexual matters'. There appears to be a high degree of ambiguity here inasmuch as it is never quite resolved which, if either, of the two laws will actually be enforced:

> And perhaps (τάχα δ' ἄν),[119] if God be willing, we might enforce one of two laws concerning sexual matters (περὶ ἐρωτικῶν) either [1.] no one whatsoever should dare to touch any well-born and free woman except his own wedded wife, nor is he to sow bastard and unhallowed seed in concubines, nor is he to sow fruitless seed in males contrary to nature; or [2.] we should prevent sexual intercourse between males altogether (τὸ μὲν τῶν ἀρρένων πάμπαν ἀφελοίμεθ' ἄν), and concerning women, if someone should have intercourse with anyone except the woman who entered into his household under the sanction of the gods and the sacred marriage ceremony, whether purchased or obtained in any other manner, *unless he escapes the notice of all other men and women,* we would probably (τάχ' ἄν) seem to legislate rightly by enacting that he be punished by depriving him of honours within the city since he actually is a stranger. Then let this law be established concerning sexual matters and all things erotic (περὶ ἀφροδισίων καὶ ἀπάντων τῶν ἐροτικῶν), inasmuch as we do rightly or wrongly[120] in

associating with each other because of such desires. (841c8–842a2—emphasis mine).

While Megillus the Spartan laconically nods assent, it is worth noting again that Kleinias the Kretan, as with the passage at 837c3–d1 discussed above, refrains from stating his opinion on the matter. In the first instance, the Athenian Stranger says that his regulation of sexual activity will forbid extramarital affairs (between citizen men with free-women and courtesans) and will actively discourage 'fruitless intercourse between males against nature' (παρὰ φύσιν). The second option intends 'to prevent sexual intercourse altogether between males' and then allows the discussed 'legitimacy' for extra-marital affairs (presumably) only between members of the opposite sex—provided that they are kept quiet (d1–5). I have made much of this passage in this and previous chapters, but its significance justifies its repeated reference.

The two parts of this law both deal with same-sex intercourse and mixed-sex intercourse but both parts contain clauses that would seem to ban same-sex intercourse. The Athenian Stranger is aware of the difficulty of such legislation (in practice or in theory) and he admits that perhaps his statutes on sexual behaviour may exist only in myth rather than reality (841c6). Even so, he concludes his discussion on the twofold statute of sexual behaviour saying 'let this law be established, whether we call it one or two, concerning sex and all things erotic' (841e5–842a1).

As indicated, both laws single out same-sex activity for exclusion. As England says, the 'two laws' in question are '*one* inasmuch as they try to secure the same end, but differ in that the second threatens only *dishonour*, not a definite *penalty* for the minor offence'.[121] The first law, at 841d1, states the ideal form of sexual behaviour—with no implicit penalty for those who break it. The second part allows for a kind of tightly-managed legitimacy for men who secretly have extra-marital affairs—essentially a restating of the 'loophole' which demands secrecy but not abstinence. Failure to obey (not keeping one's trysts secret) bears the penalty of public defamation and deprivation of honours (841e2–4). The first law clearly represents the Athenian Stranger's ideal and the second one, anticipating that such problems will occur, is potentially more suited to the real world of the second-best state. But can it be that same-sex intercourse will also be allowed the same 'legitimacy' if it too is undertaken in secrecy?[122] Or is it the case that, as Price says, 'homosexuality [sic] is always excess, never necessity' and therefore never to be suffered any degree of tolerance in this imperfect utopia?[123] Unfortunately, the Athenian Stranger has left us considerable room for doubt.

By the time of the *Laws*, Plato has seriously considered some philosophical grounds for forbidding certain types of sexual acts. Same-sex intercourse, in particular, has been specifically targeted as a type of behaviour to be discouraged if not banned outright. The Athenian Stranger has levelled such charges against it to the effect that it is sterile, unnatural, that it constitutes and encourages indulgence in excessive desires and, as such, that it is potentially harmful to the souls of both lover and beloved and therefore to the sanctity of the *polis*.[124] As previously discussed, the argument from the 'nature' of animals is dubious at best and ambiguous at least given the passage at *Philebus* 67b. It seems more intended to convince the populace by means of *paramyth* or 'noble lie'.[125] The 'sterile' (ἄγονος) quality attributed to same-sex intercourse (at 841d4–5) is another matter.

The importance of mixed-sex couplings for the production of offspring is not lost on Plato's narrator and it would appear that he has expended no small effort in framing his laws to govern such unions. The essential necessity of procreation is deliberately and significantly connected to divinity. The Athenian Stranger, as we saw in chapter V, exhorts his hypothetical citizenry to marry saying that 'one must naturally hold onto the everlasting by always leaving behind children and grandchildren after one that they may render services unto the gods' (773a5–774a1). It is γένεσις, the primal force of reproduction that grants humankind a necessary foothold on immortality.[126] It would therefore be a mistake for an individual to conclude that all of creation exists for them alone and not for its own purposes.[127] The Magnesian state is a microcosm mirroring the universe and the Magnesian citizenry must strive to serve the state in much the same way as cells, or organs, 'serve' the body. Ideally, proper children will be produced through proper marriages and so the institution of marriage is therefore carefully regulated to ensure a stable population within the 5040 land divisions.[128]

Since Magnesia has been designed to favour the family unit with a view toward maintaining a stable population, all acts of sexual intercourse become subject to official regulation. Non-reproductive sexual union is regarded as acceptable only under certain conditions. The fact that same-sex intercourse happens to be 'sterile' would not seem to qualify it as a special case for prohibition. The view that Price describes as 'more acceptable to Plato' should be to allow any sexual act of the non-reproductive type 'so long as they fall within a sexual relationship that as a whole is reproductive in kind'.[129] Why would the Athenian Stranger object to one's failure to be reproductive in one instance if one is successful at it in another? Not every act of sexual union need produce offspring and he is aware of this.

Elsewhere, as we have seen, he enthusiastically supports methods of contraception and abortion, as well as 'fertility treatments', in order to maintain his stable population.[130] One of the Athenian Stranger's foremost concerns, this allows for and encourages certain types of 'sterile' intercourse. Curiously, only the married and mixed-sex variety is granted any real degree of legitimacy. In Plato's Magnesia it is not the case that 'nature' requires everyone to remain open to the perpetuation of the immortality of the species in every instance of sexual union. One could arguably posit that same-sex intercourse between some people ought to be encouraged (or, at least not actively discouraged) in order to prevent overpopulation beyond the specified 5040 familial units. This particular inconsistency is never fully addressed or resolved. In addition to the difficulty of any plausible argument from the nature of animals, the 'sterile' quality of same-sex intercourse does not alone appear to provide reason enough to single it out to be expunged from the second-best state.

The Athenian Stranger's idiosyncrasies in respect to same-sex erotic expression, as indicated hypothetically or otherwise in the *Laws,* are at variance with such theoretical views that Dover and Foucault maintain were part of the ancient Greek cultural *ethos.* The point of contention lies in the fact that Plato's narrator has condemned not only the 'receptive' partner of a same-sex coupling but also the active.[131] This diverges from Dover and Foucault's presumptions about the dominant attitudes amongst Plato's contemporaries.[132] Enjoying the 'passive' (or 'receptive') sexual position, Dover argues, was not favoured for a male who would one day assume the status of Athenian citizenship (or at least one who might pursue a political career).[133] Such a one could incur the disdain of the community as well as the designation *unnatural.*[134] However, the 'active' male partner, according to Dover and Foucault's cultural reconstruction, would still be playing the dominant sex-role regarded as appropriate to manly behaviour.

Plato's narrator, in condemning the act itself as a kind of outrage, faults both lover and beloved. The active lover who has his way with another of the same sex is accused of intemperance (836d7), and of submitting to an excessive desire for pleasures against which he is too 'soft' in character to be true to the test of virtue (d9–e1, cf. 636c6–7). His 'softness' is derived from allowing his 'masculine' Reason be subverted through a 'feminine' loss of control and the tendency towards seeking excessive pleasure. The *erōmenos,* in addition to running the risk of some psychical damage (having his Reason unseated), is also charged with 'softness' (effeminacy). This state of being is construed as inappropriate for a man (836d5–7, e1–3).

According to a standard Platonic formula, both partners ultimately fall short of being 'masters of themselves'.[135] Submitting to excessive pleasure (e.g. through same-sex intercourse) amounts to the superior part of their soul being dominated by the base or appetitive part.[136] One who yields to the domination of pleasures may be thought to have succumbed to 'madness' (μανιάς),[137] and a state of 'slavery'.[138] Rather, as Konstan says, the Athenian Stranger praises laws (839b1) that 'will teach men to despise "lustful madness" (*lutta erotikē*) and all forms of excess and make them instead "proper friends," or perhaps "dear relations" (*oikeioi philoi*), to their own wives'.[139]

It is again important to bear in mind that the Athenian Stranger has been framing his laws with a view toward the most attainable net quantity of happiness for his populace. They are ostensibly meant to undertake the pursuit of virtue through their whole lives. Happiness, he maintains, is to be reached through overcoming the 'slavery' to the desire for excessive pleasures (840c5–6 with 636d5–e1). At 733e–734b there is the firm indication that the moderate, prudent and courageous (manly—ἀνδρεῖος) life is 'healthy' and happy since it is a life that is mild, with gentle pleasures and pains, and characterised by desires that are similarly mild and loves that are not mad (καὶ ἔρωτας οὐκ ἐμμανεῖς). Opposed to this is the unhealthy life of the imprudent, the cowardly and the intemperate. Such a life is characterised as being filled with intense pains and pleasures, frenzied physical desires and loves that are as mad as possible (καὶ ἔρωτας ὡς οἷόν τε ἐμμανεστάτους). The milder life is (officially) considered to be the more pleasant, accepted and desirable goal for the Magnesians to attain.

The greatest victory is that over one's self (626e2–3). However, a rational appeal to 'nature' along with the distinguished authority of the legislator (721b7–c8) may not suffice to produce the desired result in the hypothetical populace. The various methods employed by the Athenian Stranger to support his propositions on pleasure and happiness include stories and songs to which Magnesian youths will be exposed (840c1–3), the problematic (though popularly persuasive) examples of the behaviour of birds and other animals (d2–e3), physical exercise as a distraction from sexual appetite (841a6–8), an inculcated ethic which emphasises the need for physical privacy (b2–4), religious respect, love of honour and a 'mature' passion for the beauty of mind over that of body (c4–6). In fashioning his laws for the second-best state, the Athenian Stranger has posited an ideal statute that prohibits all extra-marital affairs while at the same time he has proposed a more realistic law that requires them to be undertaken, if they should happen to occur, always in secret. Notably, such extra-marital affairs will be potentially reproductive in nature. The Athenian Stranger has anticipated that there might arise a gap in the practices and values of the hypothetical Magnesians, as tends to be the case with human nature, between the ideal and the real.

The real question is this: why does same-sex intercourse amount to an excess in pleasure and thence an indulgence of excessive desire for the gratification of such a pleasure? Some of the possible explanations have already been considered, but I believe that the answer may lie in the Platonic formulation of Reason as a type of control over the chaotic, appetitive elements identified within the soul. What has to be overcome by Reason's rule consists of intemperate appetites and emotions that are perceived to have *feminine* characteristics (recall the Pythagorean Table of Opposites). Lovibond's assessment that 'a successful outcome is equated in Plato's imagination with a successful establishment of the *male* principle in its proper position of command' seems plausible.[140] In this way, a loss of control over sexual desire, manifesting especially in same-sex intercourse, is construed as *unmanly* and therefore improper. The Athenian Stranger has indicated that same-sex intercourse amounts to an act of *hybris*—employing the term along with implied criminal connotations. This particular use of language, whether Plato's narrator believes it or not, is bound to have a powerful psychological effect on the citizens of the second-best state who read the *Laws* as part of their classroom *curriculum*.[141]

Both of the participants in same-sex intercourse (whether male and male or female and female) fail to master themselves and their appetites through the conquest of (masculine) Reason over (feminine) desires. This would appear to be the underlying complaint against the practice of same-sex intercourse. By designating same-sex acts as 'unnatural', the Athenian Stranger seems to have adopted the position that the sexual role of 'penetrator' belongs properly to the male and the role of 'penetrated' belongs properly to the female. The fact that he has done this in addition to characterising those inclined toward acts of same-sex intercourse as indulging in excessive pleasure is doubly damning. He will tell his Magnesian citizenry that these roles have been 'naturally (κατὰ φύσιν) granted to male and female for the act of mutual procreation' (636c).

It would seem fair to ask whether it is possible for two people of the same sex to consent willingly to a relationship and thus partake of sexual congress without it constituting an act of *hybris*. Why could such a thing not transpire between two individuals who are 'alike' in terms of 'goodness'? The Athenian Stranger's answer, it would appear, is that they cannot. In the first instance, such an inversion of the 'natural' sex-roles, according to his formulation, has been characterised as necessarily 'contrary to nature'—for whatever reasons.[142] Secondly, since the *act* of same-sex intercourse corresponds to what is defined as an excessive indulgence in the appetites, it becomes impossible for two people, alike in 'goodness' as it has been defined, to engage in such actions and remain alike in 'goodness'. This is so because the act is delimited as a breach of the normal rules of 'goodness', namely an excessive indulgence in the appetites which amounts to a state of 'slavery' whereby the baser elements of the soul rule the higher elements—i.e. Reason suborned by base Desire which amounts to a type of erotically induced madness.[143]

Anyone who seeks to subvert such a 'natural' state of affairs is perceived to do so as a consequence of the loss of control over excessive desire. The Athenian Stranger appears to uphold the premise that the desire for same-sex intercourse is a naturally occurring phenomenon, but that the expression of said desire through sexual acts results in an upheaval of the proper sex-roles as defined by the *ethos* that has been framed for the Magnesian populace. Lacking mastery of self, in terms of submitting to excessive desires likewise amounts to an 'unordering of the *psyche*' and this is contrary to the proper, *masculine* structure that is meant to be maintained by Reason's rule.

On these grounds, the Athenian Stranger has established that the act of same-sex intercourse, singled out as a highly and dangerously pleasurable form of sex, constitutes indulgence in excessive desire. While he reveals a degree of uncertainty or discomfort with the subject of sexuality in general, he also seems unsure as to whether a policy opposed to same-sex activity would or could be implemented on a real populace. Both of these factors are represented in the Athenian Stranger's arguments. This is evident as much in the hypothetical nature of the discussion itself (whether 'in a playful way or seriously') as also in the ambiguities throughout the wording of the laws of sexual conduct.

It is unsound to propose that Plato has changed his mind on the subject of same-sex intercourse. The erotic exploits of his mentor Sokrates, alleged in Plato's own works, must have constituted a major factor in his thinking. The fact that he considered the subject at all is evidenced by the sheer quantity of material in numerous dialogues so devoted and implied. One is inclined to wonder why a thing condoned, even favoured in the *Republic* and elsewhere may be banished from the *Laws*. It is impossible to say whether the Athenian Stranger's views are Plato's or whether any or none of the verses attributed to him actually reflect their maker's true beliefs. Yet, it remains for us to wonder if the Athenian Stranger's assertion that same-sex intercourse is in fact excessively (dangerously) pleasurable is true and, if so, how did he know?

England, in his commentary on the *Laws,* has said that the Athenian Stranger's proposed legislation on erotic matters 'amounts to a distinct recantation of many of the views expressed in the earlier erotic discourses (*Lysis, Symposium, Phaedrus*), and the inculcation of a far stricter code of sexual morality'.[144] If the subject of same-sex erotic love in the *Laws* signifies a shift from earlier positions, it would seem that the Athenian Stranger has not recanted the fundamentals of previous Platonic views. Rather, he has revised them to an observable extent.

His preference for the term φιλία, as we have seen, with regard for the three types of affection discussed in the *Laws* (as in the *Lysis*) may be an attempt to downplay any sexual elements of friendship as much as possible. It signifies a departure from the term ἔρως which appears to signify, as Gould says, 'his word for friendship in the *Symposium* and *Phaedrus*'.[145] The Athenian Stranger does employ ἔρως elsewhere in the *Laws* and it would be foolish to conclude that Plato did not distinguish between it and φιλία whatsoever. Certainly he did, but in some instances φιλία may convey sexual connotations (as in the three types of affection) and at other times it does not. Sometimes the terms φιλία and ἔρως may be treated as interchangeable.

Through her famous speech in the *Symposium,* the character Diotima has shed some light on Platonic conceptions of love that are also observable in the *Laws*.[146] She argues that love is not a god, as perhaps many might believe, but a 'great spirit' (Δαίμων μέγας).[147] What is meant by this term is somewhat unclear and (see my note below) presents difficulty in formulating a proper English paradigm.[148] At 203c5 sq., Diotima indicates that erotic love (Ἔρως) is the offspring of the deified principles known as Resource (Πόρος) and Want (Πενία) who were joined together in divine sexual union. *Erōs'* conception, she says, not surprisingly coincided with Aphrodite's miraculous birth. His state of being is described as 'neither mortal nor immortal', rather he is enigmatically somewhere in between these two (204d8). *Erōs* becomes identified as a sort of spirit that embodies infinite longing for infinite fulfilment. No corporeal resource obtainable can perpetually supply such a longing. This includes acts of sexual intercourse. Diotima maintains that all forms of *erōs* are really a desire for the perpetual possession of the Beautiful/Good (206a11–12). She asserts that only through the illuminating effects of 'birth in beauty' can this aim be attained (206b–c).

Plato's allegorical description, through Diotima's speech, characterises love as a spiritual entity 'in-between' Want and Resource. Unlike mortals, divine beings are generally described as lacking nothing. On this, we have the account from Homer's *Iliad* to the effect that the gods are generally free from the pains of mortal existence.[149] The philosopher Melissos (c.440B.C.E.) later maintained 'that which [truly] is' does not feel pain or grief because, in addition to its other metaphysical features, it is necessarily 'healthy'.[150] Xenophanes of Kolophon (2nd half of the 6th century B.C.E.), who was probably a strong influence on Melissos' thinking, had held that divine beings 'lacked nothing', which is to say that their existence is perfect.[151] It follows that divinity would be free from any sort of desire—of which love, here defined, is a specific kind. Diotima's speech seems somewhat problematic inasmuch as it posits love as a type of in-between-divine-and-base, eternal yearning and attraction for eternal fulfilment. If the gods want for nothing, and Love is divine, then how can Love be said to desire anything? The issue may not be resolvable with recourse to traditional metaphysics. Plato's conceptualisation of *erōs* defines it as 'wanting' eternal fulfilment. This is an integral aspect of its metaphysical character. Then again, he may be constructing another metaphorical 'fable' that should not be taken too seriously on theological grounds.

Plato's Sokrates has stated that mortals may strive to attain eternal fulfilment through seeking 'birth in Beauty'.[152] In this way, a chance is provided for human beings to become like the gods as much as they possibly can. The fact that something base (e.g. the part of love's nature which corresponds to Want) may desire and be attracted to something eternal and perfect (e.g. that part of its nature which corresponds to Resource) is prevalent in Plato's narrators' considerations about imitation of divinity and the immortality of the soul in the *Laws* and elsewhere. However, human beings are not gods and are subject to base desires. The Athenian Stranger is aware of this and it is clearly on his mind as he tries to delineate a hierarchical value system of those desires that are acceptable and functional to some degree (e.g. mixed-sex desires within certain limits) and those that are purely excessive (e.g. same-sex desires actualised in deeds).

In the *Phaedrus* (246b sq.) is 'the myth of the two horses' which represents another of Plato's conceptualisations of desire and sex.[153] It is noteworthy that this narrative on love comes as part of a greater discussion by Sokrates on the immortality of the soul—a concept that resurfaces at *Laws* 714a, 894b sq. and 966d–967d.[154] In the *Phaedrus* myth, the human soul is likened to two winged steeds being steered by a person in a flying chariot. The souls of gods are considered altogether good and free from any discord (perhaps this is why love must be a 'spirit' in the *Symposium*). The souls of mortals, in contrast, have two 'horses' of which one is wholly good and noble and the other possesses the opposite inclinations (246b). These two generate a sort of strife between them—one tending toward the good and the other toward its opposite. Rist, in discussing Plato's views toward same-sex relations, describes a feature of one of these two 'horses': 'When we see the "lovable vision," part of us thinks of using force [e.g. the presence of ὕβρεως at 253e3]: we want to "leap on" the beloved (254a2–3). Such urges, apparently irreducible in human beings, must be vigorously, even violently suppressed; "modest restraint" must prevail. But our darker side (typified by Plato's "black" horse) will try seduction along with force: we will be "compelled" to approach the beloved boy, reminding him of the pleasures of sex'.[155]

This dualism within the soul generates much conflict and presents a problem for the 'charioteer' trying to 'steer' his soul aright. The two principles of action that are distinguished within it, according to Price, are an innate desire for pleasures (ἐπιθυμία), and an acquired judgement (δόξα) which aims at what is best (237d6–9).[156] These two psychical forces may agree or, more often, be in dispute (d6–10). If they are in conflict, then one or the other may prevail (e1–2). When good judgement has mastery, it leads the soul toward that which is rationally 'best'. This is synonymous with self-mastery and moderation (σωφροσύνη). The rule of the opposite inclination, desire for indulgence in 'base' things, drags the soul irrationally toward the perpetual and compulsive gratification of these excessive desires (e2–238a2). A definition of *erōs* arises from the *Phaedrus* in the following words of Plato's Sokrates:

> For when Desire (ἐπιθυμία), having gained mastery in the absence of logical judgement (which urges one toward what is right), bears one toward pleasure in respect to beautiful things, and, in turn with desires kindred to itself, it then rushes on the beauty of bodies, conquering in its mode of conduct, taking its name form the force itself (ῥώμη)—this is called *erōs* (ἔρως–238b9–c4).

Erōs may thus be construed as a 'state in which a certain species of desire prevails over Reason'.[157] Rival impulses threaten to distract and confound the lover.[158]

On the one hand, says the Athenian Stranger, the lover wishes to enjoy the charms of the beloved whilst, on the other hand, his Reason forbids it. One who craves the body of his beloved 'as if he were so much ripe fruit'[159] does so 'without giving a thought to the character of his darling's soul' (837b8–c3). Here he is clearly talking about the relationship between an *erastēs* and *erōmenos*. The subject is one of bodily desire versus moderation in a same-sex context. Desire can have as its object either Beauty/the Good or something 'base' and 'bodily'. Judgement may, of course, rein in 'improper' yearnings (which encourage a state of yielding to excess) and beget wisdom in one through 'divine philosophy'.[160] However the passage at *Phaedrus* 237d4–5 suggests, without actually saying it outright, that all desire is really desire for the Beautiful—however misdirected or otherwise. The 'horse' that inclines against the Good (clearly an agent of Strife) corresponds to the mortal part of human beings that fails, through ignorance and through not surpassing its own limitations, to be attracted to the proper object—namely, the Beautiful/Good.

Any form of *erōs*, even that which desires the Good as its object, still has the dubious distinction of being a species of madness.[161] This is troubling because the definition holds not only for human love-objects but a comparable form of *mania* is also positively associated with both philosophy and mystical practices.[162] As Vlastos says, this 'convergence of μανία and νοῦς in love does not seem to intrigue commentators'.[163] Pieper objects to 'madness' as the meaning of *mania* here due to the fact that it 'suggests ties with the orgiastic Dionysian rites'.[164] He may have somewhat missed the mark, however. There is ample evidence (including the passage at *Symposium* 218b) that such orgiastic Dionysian rites were not entirely disagreeable to Plato's narrators.[165] In the *Laws*, we also have a comparable instance in which the Athenian Stranger praises 'divine erotic passion' (ἔρως θεῖος) for producing prudence and justice that, again, seems contradictory in light of the negative connotations of *mania* (711d6 sq.). We are left with a seemingly conflicting notion in which one type of 'madness' is acceptable whereas another is not. Nonetheless, it is clear in the *Phaedrus* that Plato has drawn the conclusion that the rule of the appetites in the soul amounted to a particularly malevolent variety of madness.

If we read the *Laws* with recourse to Plato's earlier works that deal with same-sex issues, a pattern emerges.[166] The Athenian Stranger discourages immoderate behaviour in favour of the rule of Reason and 'self-mastery'. Diotima's allegory of 'birth in beauty' in the *Symposium* supplies a means by which one may achieve the proper psychical alignment through the focusing of desires on their proper object, the Good. In the 'two horses' myth of the *Phaedrus*, logical judgement helps the charioteer steer toward what is rationally best. If desires are allowed to run unchecked, they then incline the charioteer away from the goal of self-mastery. Not to be master of one's self is to invite (negative) *mania* into one's soul. A gateway for this *mania* to enter is perceived to open through the impulsive pursuit and gratification of excessive pleasures.

Both the *Symposium* and *Phaedrus* provide guidelines for moral behaviour comparable to similar guidelines found in the *Laws*. Since the act of same-sex intercourse has been there defined as a pursuit of excessive pleasures, one who engages in it must not have the Good as his/her goal and likewise could be viewed as yielding to the 'dark horse' of base desires. When we read the *Laws* in the context of the Platonic *corpus*, there the clear indication of certain unifying themes. A noteworthy difference between such works as the *Phaedrus*, the *Symposium* and the *Laws*, is that the latter is a hypothetical venture constructing a society in which philosophical ideas are not merely being discussed in a purely theoretical context; rather, they may be imposed on hypothetical individuals with the force of law. The Athenian Stranger has legislated that the Magnesians, in their pursuit of *aretē*, must become resistant against yielding to their (so defined) negative or 'dark' influences. Sound judgement is to be inculcated in their souls by legal and social forces. They are taught to strive to place Reason on its proper seat as ruler over their fleshly desires for gratification. The goal for most citizens is the attainment of *aretē* with the option open to some of them for a *telos* of 'birth in Beauty'.

The fact that a kind of *erotic* love, not dissimilar from the type of erotic expression (identified negatively in the *Laws*) felt by partners in a same-sex relationship, may be (positively) felt toward philosophical enlightenment is not insignificant. It is likewise noteworthy that Plato's narrator has associated a sort of 'sublimated' erotic love with the pursuit of philosophical truths. This has a higher value above and beyond any 'base' loves experienced by his hypothetical citizenry. Elsewhere in ancient Greek literature, the language of love is frequently employed as a rhetorical metaphor in the context of politics.[167] When Perikles, in the 'Funeral Oration', indicates that citizens ought to become, as Monoson says, 'lovers (*erastai*) of the *polis*' he 'is proposing that the Athenians can—and *should*—turn to their ordinary understanding [of *erōs*] . . . for guidance in thinking about the demands of democratic citizenship'.[168] The Athenian Stranger in the *Laws* does not make a similar claim for the Magnesians (nor Sokrates for the *Kallipolis*). Philosophy (along with the 'virtue' that leads to philosophical enlightenment) is the only thing that should be the object of such erotic desire—however 'sublimated' and 'mad'.

As we have seen, the Athenian Stranger has indicated that an 'ancient custom according to nature' (*kata phusin*), regarding sexual practices, has been corrupted by those who engage in same-sex acts (636b1–c1). Again, at 636c1–6, he declared that sexual activity 'between men and men, as well as that between women and women, is contrary to nature' (*para phusin*). While no further explanation is given at that point, presumably the ancient custom (*nomos*) of which he speaks is that of purely mixed-sex behaviour (with the male engaging in sexual penetration and the female in penile reception). As I discussed in my first chapter, the ancient Greek conception of sexuality did not recognise a dichotomy between the character types of the homosexual and heterosexual (or *trichotomy* of homo-, hetero- and bisexual). Dover and Foucault assert that that which we designate by the term 'sexuality' was regarded largely as a series of hierarchical relationships consisting of active, pleasure seeking males (subjects) in contrast to receptive females, youths or men (objects).[169] This view, however, is too unilateral to be completely accurate. It was not a simple case of 'zero-sum'.[170] Both penetrator and penetrated appear to have taken pleasure in these acts of sex. While this sentiment is clearly present in the *Laws,* the role of penetrator is to be reserved for the adult male alone with the only 'natural' objects of sexual penetration by men in Magnesia being their wedded wives. This is because same-sex intercourse (presumably involving members of either sex) is deemed to be excessively and dangerously pleasurable.

The construct of penetrator and penetrated does not work so well for women who partake of same-sex intercourse. There is no 'active' and 'passive' in the sense of penetration (unless we allow for the use of prosthetic devices). Female same-sex partners are nowhere indicted for becoming 'softer' in the same way as the male receptive partner in a same-sex act. Yet they too have little place in Magnesia, opposed as they are to the official myth of the family, since they generate no offspring through their sterile sexual unions. But they must be considered 'soft' in respect to self-mastery in much the same way as men who yield to the desire for excessive pleasure. The perceived sex-role reversal comes about when women fall prey to their 'feminine' lack of 'masculine' control over the appetites.[171] This is a curious notion but seems to be what the Athenian Stranger is driving at. Women presumably fall into the same category as men in terms of their 'erotic madness'. Same-sex intercourse between women—with or without penetration of some type—must also be regarded as excessively pleasurable and therefore dangerous.

The Athenian Stranger's diatribe against same-sex relations condemns 'men and men' *and* 'women and women' in terms of seeking sexual pleasure through intercourse. If a woman is always meant to be the 'passive' object of a man's desire, then how can she have an 'active' desire for another woman? The Athenian Stranger's admission that such a state of affairs can and does take place allows that a woman might partake of a role that Dover, Foucault and Halperin's models of ancient Greek sexuality would associate exclusively with that of a man. Halperin suggests that this state of affairs is that which has been characterised here as 'contrary to nature'.[172]

A woman who seeks to perform 'active' sex with another woman, just as a man who seeks the 'passive' position in sexual acts with another man, would appear to constitute a reversal of their 'proper' sexual roles. This could be seen to hold true not only regard to 'active' and 'passive' sex roles but also in terms of psychical alignment. However, the issue again appears to be that of submitting to excessive desires for pleasure that is considered 'contrary to nature' rather than any appeal to 'active' or 'passive' modalities—although these are conceptually related to the formulation. Women in a same-sex union presumably also err only insofar as the fact that (1) they are not engaged in producing children, which is a significant part of their designated role in the Magnesian state, and (2) they may have given in to excessive pleasure. Male and female Magnesians must adopt a 'masculine' attitude toward sex in terms of self-control and mastery of their desires. This sort of reversal is not considered 'unnatural' but more like an upgrade from emotional 'femininity' to rational 'masculinity'. Nonetheless, it is the women who are meant to occupy the receptive sexual position of the penetrated—evidently denied to Magnesian men—whilst paradoxically remaining emotionally 'masculine'.[173]

The Athenian Stranger has condemned both male partners of a same-sex union for lacking mastery over their appetites for pleasure and this would appear to extend to women, in terms of same-sex relations, as well. Whatever the citizens may be led to believe about the 'naturalness' or 'unnaturalness' of same-sex intercourse, what is 'contrary to nature' appears to be only justifiable on philosophical grounds in terms of the lack of self-mastery and the absence of Reason's rule. Later authorities have picked up, whether from Plato or through other means, the notion that a loss of control over sexual desire might be the impetus for a reversal of normative sex-roles. A writer of the middle 5th century c.e., Caelius Aurelianus, translated into Latin an adaptation of an earlier Greek work on chronic diseases by Soranos (early 2nd century c.e.). By this point, Roman attitudes of dominance and submission appear to have informed Soranos' (not to mention Caelius') views.[174] Either Caelius or Soranos (or both) may have been familiar with Plato's arguments on the subject of sex in the *Laws*.

Caelius' model indicates that those males who choose the objective/receptive role, as with females who seek the subjective/active, do so out of excessive desire. Desire is perceived to defeat their sense of shame and thereby force them to use parts of their bodies for sexual acts unintended by nature. The individual so afflicted thus takes on the characteristics of an 'active' or 'passive' role contrary to their 'natural' role as defined by sex. In regard to same-sex interactions between women, Caelius says 'for just as the women called *tribades*, because they practise both kinds of sex, are more eager to have sexual intercourse with women than with men and pursue women with an almost masculine jealousy . . . so they too are afflicted by a mental disease'.[175] But 'active' or 'receptive' must have a different meaning for a same-sex relationship between women than they would for one between men. There is no real comparison to 'penetrator' and 'penetrated' present—except again, perhaps, in terms of the employment of artificial prosthesis. Even so, the employment of prostheses lacks the same quality as the penis (essentially part of a man) and the sense of physical penetration is one step removed from the user. The 'unnaturalness' of female same-sex relationships in Plato's *Laws*, as we have seen, is due to the manifestation of uncontrolled sexual appetites, unseemly in a woman as much as in a man, brought about through a lack of self-mastery. This is what is called 'contrary to nature' and 'madness' in the *Laws*. That is, it amounts to a mental disorder characterised by a reversal of the 'proper' sex-roles and spurred on by excessive desire.

The Athenian Stranger's argument against same-sex acts amongst the citizens of Magnesia comes about in consequence of both the manner in which he has structured his hypothetical society and the views on sexuality that were, to the best of our knowledge, part of the cultural *ethos* of the Greek world in Plato's time. Magnesian citizens are intended to pursue 'excellence' (*aretē*).[176] A major feature characterising this pursuit is that their appetites be ruled by Reason (644–much as in the *Republic*). We have already seen that the Athenian Stranger considers same-sex intercourse to constitute a type of *hybris* in which the one party 'outrages' both the other party and himself. This would appear to be a mutual 'outrage' rather than the sort of 'zero-sum' relationship suggested by Dover and Foucault.[177] The condemnation of same-sex acts as 'unnatural' may be seen in part as producing mutual outrage and mutual psychical damage.

'Masculine' and 'feminine', and the 'unnatural' reversal of these, seem to have different connotations for Plato's narrator than merely the 'active' and 'passive' sex-roles. Men must behave as men and women as women. Or rather, as it turns out, women must in many respects behave like men. In terms of self-mastery, they must overcome their 'emotional' and chaotically 'feminine' psychic elements in favour of the rule of Reason which is why many (including Rist above) tend to view all souls, in the Platonic context, as really 'male' souls. A major physical difference is implicit inasmuch as women only bear children. A disruption of the 'appropriate' sex-roles, especially one that constitutes a state of yielding to excessive desires over Reason, cannot be conducive to the pursuit of 'excellence'. It is not as simple as 'active' and 'receptive' corresponding to the proper roles for male and female—although just such an attitude may have informed the Athenian Stranger's (re)construction of sexuality for Magnesia. Plato has expressed, through his narrators, some novel ideas about 'the masculine' and 'the feminine', beyond sexual penetration and being penetrated.

The resolution of this issue lies in the characterisation of same-sex acts as excessive indulgences of desire. Such a state of affairs, as previously indicated, comes about in one whose soul is ruled by the appetites rather than by Reason. It is interesting and revealing that this condition of disorder in the soul has been specifically associated with unmanliness.[178] Elsewhere, at *Republic* 431b9–c3, Plato has written that emotional diversity, instability and unpredictability are ignoble. They are associated with inferior types of women, slaves and the 'worthless mass of so-called free men'. Modern models of ancient sexuality seem to express a similar sentiment. A 'real man', as Lovibond states, 'is one who successfully subordinates the multiple, fluid and contradictory demands of feeling to a single, centralised agency of control which will resolve the contradictions between them'.[179] Femininity is often expressed (by male sources) as a state of incoherence, plurality and indeterminacy. The feminine lacks the 'male' formative power and is given to excesses of emotion. By indicating that same-sex acts constitute excessive indulgence, the Athenian Stranger would seem to be proposing, as Davidson suggests, that the male who acts as *erōmenos* is not 'a sexual pathic, humiliated and made effeminate by repeated domination, he is a nymphomaniac, full of womanish desire', and repeated sexual intercourse of this type is thought to encourage his 'womanish' inclinations.[180] Effeminacy, then, may be associated somewhat less with 'passivity' in the sexual act but more in terms of a 'womanish' inclination toward sexual indulgences. An effeminate male is paradigmatic, as Davidson says, 'of the life of endless pleasure, the leaky vessel, the supreme example of the appetite unbridled'.[181] In the *Laws*, a similar case is made for the *erastēs* inasmuch as he too yields to a similar 'womanish' desire by actively pursuing same-sex relationships. Lack of self-mastery is a failing that the Athenian Stranger assigns to both lover and beloved. It is largely this lack of moderation (*sōphrosynē*) and self-control (*enkrateia*) that is said to constitute an 'unnatural' state.

Are those who engage in sexual acts with others of the same sex going to be excluded from Magnesia or not? Regardless of his uncertainty in the framing his laws on sexual conduct, the Athenian Stranger seems likely to enforce such a prohibition if he is to follow the precepts that he has established concerning the 'dangerous' character of certain types of erotic love. At the very least, he is bound by his established tenets to attempt the discouragement of same-sex intercourse. Its 'unnaturalness' may be construed less as a function of societal conceptions (perceived by Dover, Foucault and Halperin) of the proper 'active' sex-role of men and the proper 'receptive' role of women and more in terms of Plato's philosophical determinations on the nature of self-mastery—itself, as we have seen, grounded in cultural context.[182]

As discussed in my chapter I, Dover and Foucault's model of active/passive, penetrator/penetrated does not appear wholly to reflect actual ancient Greek societal views. The 'unnaturalness' of same-sex intercourse, as far as the Athenian Stranger is concerned should be considered in terms of (masculine) Reason subverted by (feminine) intemperance within the *psychē*. The beloved's character is perceived to become 'soft'. His soul is tainted through indulgence in excessively pleasurable sexual acts, deemed *hybristic*, and by the unseating of Reason in favour of chaotic nymphomania. It would appear to be difficult if not impossible for him to pursue *aretē* in Magnesia. The lover who has allowed his (feminine) excessive desires to subordinate his Reason and thus pursues intercourse with other males 'contrary to nature' is not only corrupt himself but actively corrupts others. Same-sex intercourse, it would appear, is simply too pleasurable to be granted official opprobrium.

There will be a kind of ideological 'war' against excessive pleasure in Magnesia. Official propaganda, allied with the forces of fear and shame, will condemn both male and female same-sex partners as ultimately failing at being masters of themselves through allowing their 'feminine' qualities to overrule 'masculine' Reason. Since the act of same-sex intercourse has been defined as 'contrary to nature', it can have no accepted place in a society where (masculine, orderly) Reason is meant to rule. Its participants are seen as suffering 'a lack of control over pleasure' which is incompatible with the standards of moral hygiene in Magnesia. For those unfortunates in whom Reason does not rule, and in whom there is to be found this erotic 'madness' that urges them to indulge their appetites with members of the same sex, there can be no official suffrage under Magnesia's laws. The only type of physical relationships that these outcasts might undertake would be illegitimate and therefore could only transpire in the form of furtive and clandestine liaisons. Such secret lovers must be skilful at acting their parts as ideal citizens whilst keeping their illicit activities utterly locked away in the 'closet' lest they risk public censure, religious intolerance, demotion and potential exile. There will be little quarter in Magnesia for the 'love that dare not speak its name'.

Chapter VIII
General Conclusions

Thus we shall have as an accomplished fact and waking reality that result which, but a short while ago in our discourse, we treated as a mere dream when we constructed a kind of image of the union of Reason and the head. . . .
—The Athenian Stranger[1]

Pure livers were they all, austere and grave,
And fearing God; the very children taught
Stern self-respect, a reverence for God's word,
And an habitual piety, maintained
With strictness scarcely known on English ground.
—William Wordsworth[2]

The *Laws* is a large and complex text that lends itself well to an inquiry into issues of sex and society. It describes a hypothetical experiment in the directed development of humanity. Its narrator, the Athenian Stranger, seeks to promote virtue through the careful application of philosophically informed social engineering. In many ways, Plato's work is highly revealing in terms both of its cultural context and its significance to the canon of Western historical/philosophical literature. Perhaps some of the most striking insights present in the *Laws* relate to those points of social, philosophical and sexual morality that differ (sometimes quite dramatically) from our understanding of the 'norms' of the ancient Greeks. The ultimate importance of the *Laws* may be seen in its impact on modern academia through the latter's (Hellenistic) tendency for introspection through constant re-interpretation of the significant ideas of our forebears. In this examination of the *Laws,* under the broad canvass of Cultural Studies, I have sought to scrutinise certain notions relevant to Plato's life and times that reveal much about the ways in which we view the world today through our informed re-reading of these ancient ideas.

The *Laws* clearly stands apart from the rest of the *corpus* and, at once while standing apart, may be seen as fully participating in the holistic continuum of

Platonic thought. Like the *Republic,* it proposes a hypothetical, utopian vision of a city-state whose citizens will strive for (and presumably attain) a virtuous existence. Unlike the *Kallipolis* of the *Republic,* Magnesia is to be second-best. The differences between these two idealised realms proceed accordingly. Magnesia will be ruled by a constitution of near-perfect laws (as opposed to philosopher kings/queens with absolute power) that permits a Platonically uncharacteristic degree of democratic participation on the part of the governed. Nevertheless, Magnesia is not to be an unfettered democracy as some have seen Athens to be. The citizens have a say in electing certain officials and magistrates but all their lives are governed and regulated, in a rather Lakonian manner, at almost every conceivable level by the strictures of their rigid constitution and the oligarchic agents of its enforcement. While they can have some say in the choosing of elected officials, they have little or no opportunity for altering the law itself.

The Magnesian constitution, as outlined by Plato's narrator, in particular seeks to direct numerous aspects of the citizens' social and sexual lives in such ways that may be seen as strikingly significant to us in our post-Orwellian world. The *telos* of the Athenian Stranger's approach, as we have seen, is the production of the maximum degree of human virtue (*aretē*) in his hypothetical citizenry and, thence, the maximum degree of happiness possible in a state that is second-best to the ideal. Magnesia's underlying ideology asserts that the *polis* as a whole must exemplify 'freedom', enjoy inner concord ('be a friend unto itself') and possess intelligence.[3]

The 'freedom' of Magnesia may seem somewhat problematic to the modern reader when one considers the degree of social/sexual regulation to which the Magnesians are subject. But 'freedom' should be read contextually in contrast to the (negative) state of slavery. It should also be read as a condition resulting, paradoxically, from the rational obedience to proper authority. The Magnesian education ensures that its subjects possess intelligence and, through its socialising functions encourages concord and stability. It strives to inculcate obedience to the proper authorities. In order to achieve the desired end of virtue in its citizens, Magnesia's educational system marks the beginning of the process of preparation (some might say 'indoctrination') for a citizen's appropriate participation in the second-best state.

This educational system is particularly interesting to modern students of pedagogy and it represents the nucleus of educational methodology still in use today. It is compulsory and employs imported teachers at public expense. It is designed to be thoroughly comprehensive covering such broad *topoi* as music, literature, arithmetic, geometry, astronomy, athletics and philosophy. Strikingly, it aims at basic literacy and numeracy for *all* citizens and includes the option for more advanced studies according to the relative abilities of individual students. The fact that this education is open to Magnesians of both sexes highlights a significant point of divergence from the standards of Plato's era and culture.

The system enables agents of the *polis* to track students' abilities according to performance and moral outlook. This, in turn, contributes toward determining their future place in society. The function of the Magnesian education may be regarded as a means to prepare its subjects for their future roles in life within the *polis*. Female students must take a break in their education for a mandatory decade of childbearing and child-rearing whereas their male equivalents pursue a type of *ephēbic* military career in roughly the same time period. Women have the option of taking up military training providing they perform their mandated task of *teknopoiia*. Ensuring a continuous and regular supply of offspring is a primary concern of the Magnesian state. It is mainly through the constraints of reproduction that women may be seen as subordinated by this society. It will be a culture in which the act of bearing children in accordance with the will of the law is regarded as a fundamental value. This is inculcated from birth and supported, propagandistically and otherwise, by institutions of the state.

All students in Magnesia, whatever their abilities, will be impressed with a sense of obedience and conformity to their constitution and the importance of each fulfilling his/her proper place in society. A young Magnesian may grow up to become one of the many citizens whose sole purpose is to practice virtue (but not to partake of higher political offices) or, if his/her aptitude so indicates, he/she may become a Guardian of the Laws or even a member of the powerful *nukterinos* council. The Magnesian education represents a fundamental means of social control and ideological inculcation from a very early age and thus functions as an agent for the perpetuation of such state-sanctioned ideals as obedience/freedom, intelligence and concord.

A significant social value that Plato's narrator seeks to encourage in the Magnesian men and women alike is that of *andreia*. Normally rendered as 'manliness' or 'courage', the Athenian Stranger's special definition of this concept makes it an integral socio-sexual value. Its implicitly sexed characterisation entails its embodiment to be somewhat different in a man than in a woman. More emphasis is placed on the greater difficulty (and therefore extra effort) required for women to attain manly self-mastery. In reductive terms, the virtue of *andreia* represents a state of being able effectively to resist both pleasures and pains. It may be seen as a principal component of the freedom that the Magnesians are meant to embody as a vigorous elite. The opposite mental state is characterised as a kind of 'soft' and 'effeminate' psychological slavery to excessive desires and emotions that are considered 'womanish' or 'feminine'. The Magnesians cannot achieve their goal of being 'free' if they are slaves to their baser psychical aspects. The second-best *polis* safeguards its populace and its ideals by encouraging and reinforcing the value of *andreia* through educational and civic institutions, propaganda, religion and the myth of the family.

The Platonic concept of *andreia* is employed to mould the characters of Magnesian women and men according to the characteristics represented by this ideal. As a result, the role that Magnesian women are meant to adopt is more 'manly' than that of most of their counterparts in the real world. *Andreia* is considered to be able, when properly applied according to the Athenian Stranger's formulae, to drive out certain negatively identified 'feminine' qualities such as a lack of self-control over one's desire for pleasure. Another application of this ethic occurs in the morally hygienic removal of such 'dangers' that are identified as inherent in the partaking of same-sex intercourse. The foremost identified 'danger' of this is that it is perceived to promote a state of slavery to excessive desire and, as such, it erodes psychical solvency. One with sufficient *andreia* should be able to overcome these dangers.

To be free, to possess *andreia,* is not to be a slave. For a man, being effeminate or 'soft' means that he is in some ways like a woman. In traditional ancient Greek societies, women were typically subordinate to men. Effeminacy or excessive 'womanliness' is equated with a state of yielding to excessive pleasure and this is what is meant by being 'soft'. This denotes a particular lack of freedom and thus, by transference, slavishness. The Athenian tendency to negatively portray the Persians as fulfilling their own cultural paradigms for being effeminate and slavish is a pertinent example of cultural context informing the Athenian Stranger's reasoning. In the *Laws,* being enslaved by one's own desires for pleasure considerably reduces one's *andreia*. Since this is identified as an essential 'good' intended for the benefit of Magnesia, nothing must be allowed to harm it. He uses such a line of reasoning to determine the social roles for men and women in Magnesia as well as many of the regulations governing their sexual conduct.

Magnesian women are intended to be more 'manly' (Amazonian, Sauromatian and/or Spartan) than their Athenian counterparts. In fact, the Athenian Stranger prefers them to be more like the mythical Amazons and imagined Sauromatians than even the idealised Spartans. A central feature of the concept of *andreia* in the *Laws* is that it represents order, structure and reason. There are many negative aspects associated with (unsupervised) femininity such as disorderliness, lack of reason and emotional instability. The Athenian Stranger intends for his revised ethic of *andreia* to overcome most of these negative traits linked with women (e.g. secretiveness, negatively identified cunning and disorderly emotionality). This unfortunate state of affairs, as he has indicated, comes from a lack of appropriate supervision on the part of legislators who do not understand how to deal properly with matters of sex.

Magnesia supervises its women (and its men) to ensure that they develop properly according to the Athenian Stranger's plan. Their education and degree of participation in society serves to shape these hypothetical women's characters. Socialising forces are designed to persuade them to pursue *aretē* no less than men but, sometimes, in their own special way. These forces encourage women to adopt a more orderly, 'manly' character of self-control. Granting them greater degrees of participation than one would expect to find in an ancient Greek society is integral to achieving this idealised state of mind. Magnesian women have the opportunity to be educated equally with men, according to their individual talents, in all academic subjects. They are expected to learn military skills and the option is available for them to pursue these courses of study in greater depth. Magnesian women are able to hold public offices including those of the Guardians of the Laws and the Vigilance Committee. They are also expected to bear a state-sanctioned number of offspring during a specified decade of their lives. They must, at all times, keep any excessive emotionality that they might experience down to a controlled and orderly minimum. The constraints of socio-sexual regulation appear to apply somewhat more stringently to women than to men. Or, at least it may be said that the regulation of women presents a special case to the Magnesian legislator differing, as it must, from the regulation of men.

True sexual equality as we conceive of it in the modern era is out of the question for Plato's Magnesia. It may be observed that the mandatory decade of childbearing places a real temporal restriction on a woman's participation in society in the public sphere of the *polis*. Her role as mother, however, is a major way in which she, by virtue of her sex, plays an active part in her society through the semi-private sphere of the *oikos*. As an agent of reproduction (in a sense, a state-sanctioned sex-worker), she serves in the civic capacity of ensuring a number of offspring appropriate to sustain a stable population amongst Magnesia's 5,040 citizen-family units. This sexual regulation by the state limits women's power in the household whilst other laws give them greater access to the public sphere. It cannot, however, be said that a true balance between the sexes has been struck—neither is it apparently the Athenian Stranger's plan to do so.

There are other inequalities worth noting. For example, Magnesian men appear to have the option to engage in extra-marital affairs provided that they keep them secret. No such freedom is suggested for married women. Their greater scrutiny in reference to their perceived limitations for the pursuit of virtue would seem to hinder this to a greater extent than with men. More decision-making power appears also to have been extended to men with regard to their role in both the family and the state. A Magnesian man has the potential to become the *kyrios* of a household with a considerable degree of accompanying authority in consequence. The inheritance laws appear framed to place greater significant on sons rather than daughters since sons are the ones who become *kyrioi*. Women could theoretically become *kyriai* in Magnesia as well but this possibility is not fully explored by Plato's narrator.

While they are destined to play significant roles at all levels of society, one may surmise that *teknopoiia*, that which is most their own and is taken away, limits them sufficiently to ensure that men will fill the majority of Magnesia's positions of power. The goal of a 'good' Magnesian should be neither the attainment of sexual equality nor the acquisition of high-status offices of state. It is meant to be nothing less, for all citizens, than the unhindered and orderly pursuit of *aretē*. The laws and customs will encourage this. With regard to this pursuit, Magnesian men and women appear to stand on more or less equal ground. Yet, there also remains the implication that women are regarded as possessing a poorer inclination toward this pursuit than men.

The Athenian Stranger has described a societal role for Magnesian women that stands in sharp contrast to the perceived lifestyle of Athenian citizen-women as well as that of others in the ancient Greek world. Whatever limitations a Magnesian woman may have imposed on her (e.g. a mandatory decade of bearing and rearing children), she is intended to possess much greater freedom of participation in the public sphere than her Athenian counterparts. Magnesia's approach to women stands in stark contrast to the paradigms expressed by Xenophon's *Oikonomikos,* where an idealised representation of the role of women limits them rather severely through the ideological constraints of their defined relationship with the *oikos.*

Magnesian citizen-women are granted far greater access to all levels of society. They are not to be relegated merely to domestic activities. Perhaps most striking is their education, which is virtually equivalent to that of male citizens. Their participation in military and governmental affairs widens the gap between the real world of ancient Greece and Plato's idealised Magnesia. Part of this near-sexual equality is achieved through their 'masculinisation' with recourse to the philosophical tenets of *andreia* and *aretē.* The situation of women in Magnesia represents a revolutionary departure from the norms not only of Athenian society but virtually all of ancient Greek society as we understand it.

Their state-mandated task of *teknopoiia* should not be underrated. Like Athenian citizen-women, as with most other ancient Greek women in general, they too function in the capacity of bearing offspring and ensuring familial continuity through marriage and inheritance. They also play a part in passing on citizenship through legitimate heirs. The importance of rightful parentage for defining citizenship is given less significance in Magnesia than in post-Periklean Athens. Magnesian women are not bound to the sphere of the *oikos* in the same way as their Athenian counterparts are thought to have been. They are granted considerably greater liberties of societal participation than apparently were their Spartan and Kretan counterparts. Implicit in the Athenian Stranger's formulation of a role for Magnesian women appears to be an underlying assumption that the female sex is capable of far more than just bearing children and tending to the business of the household. This is an assumption evidently not shared by the vast majority of Plato's peers.

As I have sought to demonstrate, the Athenian Stranger has been drawing on models from Spartan, Athenian and Kretan society, amongst others, in formulating his role for women in Magnesia. It is his intent that his women should surpass all of these. The degree of participation available to them outstrips even the most imaginative notions of Spartan and Kretan women by far. Magnesian women appear to have more in common with those of myth and legend such as the Amazons and idealised Sauromatians, the wives of heroes and the mortal daughters of the gods. Nowhere in the reality of Plato's time could there be found a single model for the role of women in Magnesia. Though it reveals identifiable aspects of several traditions (mythical and otherwise), it would appear to be the case that this remarkable phenomenon is a unique synthesis and one that owes much to Plato's own industrious imagination

Whilst Magnesian women are granted unparalleled degrees of participation, it should be noted that both they and Magnesian men alike are subject to considerable scrutiny and regulation. There is every indication that Athenian citizens experienced sexual 'policing' through both the agents of law, kinship groups and society at large (e.g., the cases of Timarkhos and Demosthenes), but nowhere is there the suggestion that Athens or any real *polis* did so on the same level as Magnesia—although, Sparta (idealised or otherwise) comes the closest. We hear of no 'marriage supervisors' in ancient Athens. In Magnesia, these female agents of the state will work with the Guardians of the Laws (male and female) to scrutinise and regulate the family lives of citizens.

While there is perhaps something sinister, in an Orwellian sense, about Magnesia's 'marriage supervisors' (e.g. 'Big Sister' is watching), their task of sexual scrutiny is designed for the express purpose of ensuring marital stability along with the state-prescribed number of offspring. As indicated above, the 'marriage supervisors' could be regarded as an extension of a role performed by certain family members and kinship groups in the real world in terms of their supervisory and regulatory capacity in a given familial relationship. The difference between inter-kinship-group sexual supervision and the Athenian Stranger's employment of a bureaucratic programme is notable. This may be seen inasmuch as Magnesia's 'marriage supervisors' are not only given the backing of state authority but also in terms of the fact that the state itself should take so intense and active an interest in scrutiny of its citizens.

Sexual regulation in Magnesia is not limited only to the *oikos*. Myriad slaves, tutors and their supervisors will keep vigilant watch over the sexual development and behaviour of Magnesia's youth. Her citizens are to be under intense scrutiny and subject to correction at all times. In addition to the Guardians of the Laws, ordinary citizens are encouraged to observe fellow citizens and may report them to state officials for breaching Magnesia's sexual and other codes of conduct. Couples are expected to uphold their vows of marital fidelity (with some leeway granted to men who keep their affairs secret) and even non-citizens are meant to follow similar rules of practice. While many of these situations are perhaps not especially at variance with the spirit of Greek law and custom, Magnesia represents a higher standard of conduct than we might expect from any given culture at the time. This standard is consistent with the philosophical aims of the *Laws*.

The question of same-sex intercourse in Magnesia is conceptually related to the perceived psychical characteristics of women. It has been singled out as deserving the strictest socio-sexual regulation. In part, this appears to be due to the pre-eminence of the family's role in the structure of Magnesian society. The pursuit of same-sex relationships might undermine the myth of the family and thereby threaten the stability of the *polis*. However, the official complaint against it is rooted in moral and metaphysical philosophy. The issue of *andreia* arises as a significant factor in relation to same-sex. It is especially notable in terms of the freedom/slavery construct that forms so pivotal a role in the ideological underpinnings of the second-best *polis*. The Athenian Stranger never makes it clear whether same-sex intercourse will be prohibited by law or only discouraged through official custom and persuasive rhetoric. His discussions on the subject, however, suggest that he favours reducing same-sex activity to a minimum in Magnesia. His argument falls just short of banning it outright but leaves the option open for later legislators to do so if they see fit.

The Athenian Stranger theorises that the *erōmenos* in a same-sex coupling fails to master himself by submitting to the desire for excessive pleasure gained through committing the act itself. Ruled by his appetites and repeatedly submitting to them, he is perceived to develop a 'womanish' character. This proves him to be a slave to his appetites and he is regarded as morally (physically and metaphysically) 'soft'. His manliness is reduced and he is assimilated into a role like that of a slave. Perhaps uniquely, Plato's narrator also faults the *erastēs* on similar grounds. The degree of emphasis that he places on this as a fault is more intense than was probably the norm in Greek culture. Through his engagement in same-sex intercourse, the *erastēs* is seen to have demonstrated a lack of self-mastery and a slavish submission to excessive desires. He may also be construed as criminally contributing to the delinquency of his *erōmenos*.

Very little is said about female same-sex relations except that they too evidently fit into the formula of failing to master one's self also due to the fact that they are excessively pleasurable. They too should therefore be avoided lest those who partake of them lose self-mastery and so damage their souls. Any such influences that might threaten the Magnesians in their pursuit of *aretē* will be identified and reduced if not eliminated. According to the Athenian Stranger's reasoning, same-sex intercourse of any type appears to represent a threat to the moral hygiene of his *polis*.

As stated, all of Magnesia's sexual and social regulations strive to uphold the philosophy of freedom, concord and intelligence. The aim of the second-best *polis* is virtue. The degree of intelligence amongst Magnesia's populace is secured through the state's comprehensive pedagogical methodology. The educational system also serves as a primary means of socialisation, indoctrination of sexual values and as a powerful force for encouraging obedience to the laws. Other institutions of scrutiny and management police the Magnesian citizens' public and private lives at all levels of society to ensure that citizens are properly engaged in their appropriate pursuits. The goal of *aretē* is to be achieved in no small part through the philosophical/sociological influence of the ethic of *andreia*. This fact, in turn, particularly affects sexual regulation. Men and women in Magnesia have clearly defined sex-roles. These are partially dictated by the constraints of human reproduction and the structure of the family. However, the 'programming' of the hypothetical citizens' psychosexual make-ups appears to represent one of the more subtle and influential forces at the Magnesian legislator's disposal.

Magnesian citizens are tracked from birth according their abilities, educated appropriately and guided toward the ultimate role that society chooses for them. Platonic values regarding such concepts as *andreia, sōphrosynē,* wisdom and justice are encoded into each citizen's mind from an early age and throughout their lives. A citizen should ideally be free from the external and internal slavery and psychic disharmony that negatively identified mindsets are said to induce. The sexually specific aspects of this 'programming' are abundant. Since sex is recognised to be so powerful a force, it is perceived to demand careful management. Magnesian sexual morality teaches sexually-specific modes of behaviour, sanctioned by the official religion and the state, that form the citizens' psychosexual identities. The ultimate goal seen to justify this, as we recall, is to obtain the maximum degree of *aretē,* and therefore happiness as it is defined, for all members of the Magnesian society as a whole.

While it is unclear whether or not Magnesia will prohibit same-sex acts altogether, it is appears fairly safe to suggest that they will be strongly discouraged. Religious prohibitions, about which the Athenian Stranger has theorised, figure prominently as part of this discouragement. This appears inconsistent with our understanding of ancient Greek societal norms regarding shame and respect but steps beyond them. The Athenian Stranger, condemning both the *erōmenos* and *erastēs* for failing to master their desire for excessive pleasure, seems to have taken the sort of Athenian attitude that would vilify someone like Timarkhos on account of his alleged excesses to an entirely new dimension. While this seems to uphold some contemporary Greek modalities, the vigour with which he has declaimed same-sex intercourse is atypical.

It may be observed that the Athenian Stranger's views come as part of a new ethic of sexuality. This new ethic posits that it is the 'natural' role of a man to pursue women as their only permissible sexual counterparts within the constraints of sanctioned, monogamous relationships. This is further reinforced by Magnesia's 'new femininity'. Magnesia will achieve these new ethics through a logical extension of Platonic philosophy to the effect that giving in to excessive desire for pleasure is not conducive to the pursuit of *aretē*. The alleged importance of the family, and its official 'myth', is given considerable status and legitimate sexual activity becomes confined to relationships between a man and a woman, sanctioned by religion and the state.

As with the role of Magnesian women, there is some cultural background informing such a radical view. However, Plato's narrator appears to have made a striking leap in an unexpected direction. This marks the beginning of a dominant ideology that survives (with changes) to the present day.

There can be little doubt that Plato's writings on the subject of sexuality have had an influence on many individuals and societies since the Classical era. The views expressed by the Athenian Stranger in the *Laws* can be seen as figuring prominently into this influential discourse. As I have demonstrated, the attitudes toward sexuality in the *Laws* differ—sometimes quite dramatically—from the norms expressed in other sources contemporary with Plato. This difference is particularly noteworthy with regard to matters of same-sex intercourse and the role of women. It is appropriate to consider what significance can be gleaned from Plato's narrator's ideas on these subjects. We may likewise wonder why Plato has chosen to express these views through the medium of the dramatic dialogue.

The value of the *Laws'* contribution to the history of philosophy, along with its influence on the past and future history of civilisation, is beyond question. It is possibly, and not insignificantly, the first example of a comprehensive, written constitution. Perhaps even more important is the remarkable proposition, featured prominently in the *Laws,* that the fundamental qualities of the human character may be moulded and shaped by the policies of an ideologically interested and socially interactive state. The *Laws* may be seen as an exploration of the proposition that society, for whatever reasons, can be changed by the will of Mind with the aid of philosophy and imagination. This notion has potentially affected the lives of billions of people for thousands of years after Plato's death. In this examination of the Athenian Stranger's constitutional and other methods to direct the psychosexual aspects of his hypothetical citizenry, we have also seen many other areas of related social engineering. Perhaps even more so than the *Kallipolis* of the *Republic*, Magnesia represents a kind of practical methodology for managing a state according to specifically outlined thematic goals. This model represented in the *Laws* has far-ranging applications in any era—allowing for particular extrapolations, interpretations and the advents of technology.

The particular contribution that Plato has made with his *Laws* to the ongoing advancement of the science of Sexuality, as it is currently being pursued by academics today, is worthy of note. The *Laws* demonstrates a hypothetical means by which both societies and individuals may be 'moulded' according to an ideological theme. In the case of Magnesia, this theme is set by a specific definition of virtue with recourse to a particular interpretation of the ancient Greek concept of *aretē*. The implementation of this plan involves the careful and deliberate use of language to affect the ways that people think. The emphasis on this function of language anticipates many modern philosophical trends. That which we would today call sexuality is perceived to be particularly subject to linguistic effects. Plato's narrator has demonstrated that the use of a particular type of calculated rhetoric, along with fear, shame and officially 'correct argument' amongst other forces to support it, can influence people's thinking, and therefore their actions. He has also intensively explored many hypothetical avenues of the psychological effects of this method on human sexuality in order that it might be (re)constructed according to his plan.

It is not possible for us to speculate on whether such a system as is proposed in the *Laws* would work in reality or if it would fail due to a potentially erroneous tendency to assume that human behaviour can be so completely controlled and directed. Such is beyond the scope of this inquiry and neither does it appear to have been Plato's aim in composing the *Laws*. It is possible, however, to conclude that all these considerations bear relevance to modern civilisation in its ongoing quest for self-examination. This is a mission that we have inherited from the ancients and we can benefit from the light that the author of the *Laws* has shed on matters of sex and society. His ideas and ideals will continue to influence the world so as long as we follow in the paths of Sokrates, Plato and Aristotle in our love of learning and our affirmation that the unexamined life is not worth living. The limitations of the text, as Plato was well aware, prevent us from interrogating his narrator and questioning his ideas in living discourse. Otherwise, as Megillus suggests, we would 'detain this Stranger here, and by entreaties and every possible means secure his co-operation in the task of settling the *polis*'.[4]

Notes

NOTES TO CURRENCY CONVERSION

1. These are taken from Carradice (1995), p. 10–11; cf. also Sealey (1990), p. 190.
2. (2001), p. 142, probably recollecting Marx's (1909) famous axiom: 'Property is theft'.

NOTES TO PREFACE

1. *Utopia* VII.3–8. The word 'utopia', if not the concept, appears to be More's own invention (and not Plato's). It is derived from the Greek οὐ τόπος, thus meaning, appropriately, 'no place'.
2. Cf. Robinson and Groves (2000), pp. 124–9.
3. With respect I quote Tathagata Buddha, the Father Buddha, who said, 'With our thoughts, we make the world' (Ch'êng-ên 1979).
4. *Laws* 625b6–8.

NOTES TO CHAPTER I

1. Qtd. in BBC2 interview, Sept. 2001.
2. (1996), p. 422.
3. Qtd. in Golden and Toohey (1997), p. 2.
4. (1998), p. 25. Cf. Hesk (2000), pp. 15 sq. who, having compared the trial of Oliver North to texts of Demosthenes and Plato, considers it beneficial to compare 'modern representations' with ancient equivalents—albeit with a clear understanding of the inherent differences between them.
5. Cartledge (1998), p. 26.
6. Cf. Auden (1973), p. 8.
7. Cf. Aristotle's *Nicomachean Ethics* IV, 1140a
8. E.g., as I write these very words, heated political debates are taking place in both the United States and Great Britain affecting the future of homosexuals with regard to law and society which, if anything, indicates the tensions and uncertainties felt by many on this matter.
9. (1997), p. 1.

10. In my employment of the terms 'male' and 'female', as well as 'masculine' and 'feminine' throughout this work, I attempt to uphold a convention largely used by feminist critics today (cf. such notables as L. Irigaray and H. Cixous). 'Male' and 'female' therefore indicate biological categories. 'Masculine' and 'feminine' may be seen as denoting symbolic or culturally constructed classifications within a given social or philosophical context.

11. (1986), p. 1056.

12. Cf. Hall (1992), p. 9.

13. *Ibid.*

14. Cf. Scott (1983), p. 101.

15. Butler (1995), p. 50.

16. Cf. O'Brien (1981) below.

17. *Ibid.*

18. O'Brien (1981), pp. 8–15, 46.

19. (1982), p. 518.

20. *Ibid.* p. 543.

21. It is noteworthy that the sexual subjugation of women existed prior to the advent of capitalism and later continued even under ostensibly non-capitalist regimes.

22. Cf. Scott (1986), p. 1060.

23. *Ibid.*

24. Cf. Chodorow (1978), p. 169.

25. Cf. Grosz (1990).

26. (1986), p. 1062.

27. 'To problematise the matter of bodies', as Butler (1995), p. 51 says, 'entails in the first instance a loss of epistemological certainty, but this loss of certainty does not necessarily entail political nihilism as a result'.

28. (1993), p. 223.

29. Cf. my chapters II and VI for the Solonian phrase 'anyone who wishes'.

30. E.g. the famous Kinsey Reports of the 1940s that suggested, contrary to previous conventions, that homosexuality was more than merely a *latent* biological condition. Edmund Bergler, a leading psychoanalyst in 1954, stated that 'Kinsey's erroneous conclusions pertaining to homosexuality will be politically and propagandistically used against the United States abroad, stigmatising the nation as a whole in a whisper campaign', (qtd. in Macherey (1978), pp. 59–60).

31. Cf. Foucault (1978).

32. The main reason that we have this information at all is because, at the time, the state felt compelled to torture it out of would-be offenders ostensibly lest the 'wrath of God' be brought down upon the nation such as in the biblical examples of Sodom and Gomorrah (Davidson, 2001, p. 50).

33. Bray (1992), pp. 16, 34 and 88. This provides an interesting contrast with the Athenian Stranger's condemnation of same-sex acts on the grounds that they are too pleasurable.

34. Halperin (1990), p. 15.

35. *Ibid.*

36. *Ibid.*, p. 16.

37. Foucault (1978), p. 43.

38. Sinfield (1994), p. 38.

39. Although, given the rate of technological development over the past two and a half centuries, along with the advent of numerous chemical substances to the environment and to individuals that affect hormone levels, it is difficult to say if we have changed sexually or if we may not do so in the future.

40. Examples of this abound particularly from the very influential medium of television. In a *Carry On* film from the early 1960s currently being re-aired on the BBC, when the audience fails to turn up for a beauty contest, the impresario declares 'Men not interested in girls . . . ? I can't believe it. It's unhealthy'. Is this tongue-in-cheek or subtle socialisation? An often-played advert shows scenes of men and women romantically enjoying a holiday on a tropical island, whilst a singer intones 'what the world needs now is love, sweet love . . . ' the small print indicates that the offer is valid for couples that include 'one man and one woman only'.

41. Cf. my chapter IV and below.

42. (1995), p. 41.

43. Some good examples of ancient authors who exemplify this Classical discourse on sex include, but are not limited to, the following: Plato, Aristotle (esp. *Politics* 1269b32–3 sq.), Aeschylus (*Eumenides*), Aristophanes (*Lysistrata, Ekklesiazousai*), Euripides (*Medea, Alkestis* and *Hippolytus*), Sophokles (*Antigone,* etc.), Herodotos (I.173.4, I.203, I.4.176, etc.), Thukydides (II.45, III.74.2), and Xenophon (esp. *Lak. Pol.* I.9 and the *Oikonomikos*).

44. Cf. Aghion, Barbillon and Lissarrague (1996), pp. 99–101 and 297–8.

45. (1980), pp. 515–16 n. 35.

46. The subject of continuity of change concerned the ancients from Parmenides and Herakleitos onwards; cf. Golden and Toohey (1997), p. 1.

47. For Aspasia, who was a Milesian, as the composer of Perikles' funeral oration cf. *Menex.* 236b, on her eloquence and her role as Sokrates' own mistress of rhetoric 235e. Diotima is also introduced in Plato's narrative (*Sym.* 201d) as a foreigner.

48. Cf. Pomeroy (1977), pp. 51–68, esp. p. 60.

49. Clairmont (1993), 2.890, mid fourth century Menidi; cf. Pomeroy (1997), p. 133

50. They were most likely *not* instructed in the use of weapons. Cf. my chapter III.

51. *Oik.* VII.30. If an Athenian woman was seen outside at parties with men, it appears that this could be taken as proof that she was a courtesan and not a lawful wife; Isaios III.13–14. Cf. my chapter VI.

52. My own feeling is that 'homosexuality', 'heterosexuality' and 'bisexuality' are altogether artificial constructions and that human sexuality is more like a continuum (or spectrum) between these perceived norms.

53. I hesitate to include other similar subjects may be found under the broad category of 'sexuality' since some of them are illegal and/or immoral to the current mindset, nevertheless such a list includes, but is by no means limited to bestiality, necrophilia, sadism and masochism (separately or together), dominance and submission, fetishism of all sorts, cross-dressing and masturbation. The human mind can be quite imaginative when it occupies itself with the subject of sex.

54. (1992), p. 216.

55. Cf. *GH*, p. 16, pp. 84–106 and Foucault (1984), pp. 46–7.

56. (1990), p. 30.

57. According to Foucault (1984), p.215, 'sexual relations—always conceived in terms of the model act of penetration, assuming a polarity that opposed activity and

passivity—were seen as being of the same type as the relationship between a superior and a subordinate, an individual who dominates and one who is dominated, one who commands and one who complies, one who vanquishes and one who is vanquished'.

58. *GH*, pp. 60–8.

59. *Ibid.* pp. 50–2, 123 sq.

60. In the *Phaedrus* (255d), Plato's narrator has indicated that the boy-beloved cannot reciprocate *erōs* for his lover but rather experiences a form of affection (*philia*) which can never be on equal footing with the feelings of the other. Cf. Xenophon (*Symp.* 8.21) where 'the boy does not share in the man's pleasure in intercourse, as a woman does; sober, he looks upon the other drunk with sexual desire'. These may represent the (Platonic) ideal rather than the reality; or, alternatively, they may represent accepted social conventions rather than actual emotions of individuals.

61. Xenophon (*Lak. Pol.* II.12) makes the extraordinary ethnographical claim that, amongst the Boeotians, men and boys lived together as if married, cf. *Symp.* VIII.3–4 (although there is no way to verify this). Otherwise, the notion existed elsewhere as the subject of derogatory jokes, cf. Aristotle, *Politics* 1311a16. It would appear that the Romans had a similar idea also reserved for the sake of ridicule, cf. the *Life of Antoninus Elagabalus* XI (c. 4th–5th century, a Roman text of uncertain authorship), where some of Elagabalus' male courtiers were reputed to have announced they had husbands (even if untrue, it indicates that the concept existed as a source of scorn).

62. Blundell (1995), p. 135, states that 'Nowadays, there seems little doubt that sexual segregation did at least exist as an upper-class ideal'. Cf. Xenophon (*Oikonomikos* VII.30).

63. *GH*, pp.149–51; *GPM*, pp. 209–16. Cf. Ogden (1996) on the post-Periklean concerns for legitimacy.

64. Gunderson (2000), p. 169. Cf. Aristopanes, *Ekkl.* 112–113, for the notion that same-sex intercourse could be a means to social advancement in ancient Athens.

65. Humphreys (1983), p.17.

66. *GPM*, pp. 160–7.

67. *Hiero* VII.3

68. II.150–1. An important issue raised by this passage, to be later discussed, is that of self-discipline vs. the lack thereof.

69. Davidson (2001), p. 41.

70. I will later argue that this appears to have more to do with their lack of self-control in respect to the pursuit of pleasure.

71. (1984), p. 220; cf. Davidson (1997), p. 169.

72. Halperin, Winkler and Zeitlin (1990), p. 178. Cf. too Plato, *Timaeus* 90e, where cowardly men are reincarnated as women; and cf. *GPM*, pp. 95–102.

73. (1990), p.4; cf. Laqueur (1990).

74. (2000), p. 28.

75. (1990), p. 33.

76. I.195. Attitudes on sex in Athens underwent a shift in the fourth century that Aiskhines perhaps reflects. In the fifth century, same-sex intercourse was possibly less of a perceived problem when it took place between citizens.

77. Cf. pseudo-Aristotle, *Problemata* 4.26, discussed in *GH*, pp. 168–70.

78. I.185.

79. Sexual intercourse with children under the age of twelve was apparently considered 'infamous' and deserving some kind of 'social opprobrium', Cantarella (1992), p. 42; cf. the case of Strato in *Greek Anthology* XII.228. Even so, the law against sexual violence mentioned in Lysias, *On the Murder of Eratosthenes, 32*, does not seem to include children. Cf. my chapter V.

80. Cf. Cantarella (1992), pp. 36–42, for a discussion of the sources.

81. (2001), p. 28.

82. (1991), pp. 68–9.

83. (2001), p. 23.

84. Phylarchus, *FGrH* 81, F45. *Kinaidos* may also be found in Plutarch's *Moralia* 126a, 705e, but, even though it follows a similar tack to that of Plato and Aiskhines, I shall exclude this as being outside the temporal context of our concern—albeit conceptually related.

85. *Gorgias* 493a–494e; cf. my chapter VII. Bobonich (2002), p. 354, indicates that Platonic pleasure is not 'a feeling that the experiencer perceives; rather, sensory pleasure is itself the perception of a replenishment or restoration'.

86. Hypereides (fr. 215 *DK*) summons a personification of Nature as witness against an alleged *kinaidos* who has forfeited his manliness saying 'What if we were conducting this case with Nature as judge—Nature who has distinguished male and female so that each performs its own proper duty and office—and what if I were to demonstrate that this man has misused his own body in a feminine way? Surely Nature would be shocked and astonished that any man would not think it a most blessed gift for him to have been born a man and that he had despoiled Nature's kindness to him, hastening to transform himself into a woman'.

87. Davidson (2001), p. 23; Aiskhines I.131, 171, II.99, 166.

88. *GH,* p. 23.

89. IV.26.

90. Cf. my chapter IV on *andreia.*

91. Davidson (2001), p. 22. Cf. *Timaeus,* in *FGrH* 566 F124b; Aristophanes, *Acharnians,* 106–7, *Knights* 720–1.

92. Aristophanes, *Lysistrata,* 137. Cf. Davidson (2001), p. 22.

93. *GH,* pp. 113, 142–3. He argues that, despite the word's general usage as 'lecherous', the 'original', more specific reading referring to pathics could have been adduced by an ancient Athenian.

94. Jocelyn (1980). He acknowledges Jocelyn's insights in a supplementary note to the second edition of *Greek Homosexuality* (1989), pp. 204–5, but continues to support an aggressive meaning for the verb.

95. (1983), pp. 99–100. Cf. Aristophanes *Knights* 1288–9.

96. The case of the Eurymedon vase, later discussed in chapter IV, presents a potential instance of aggressive penetration but occurs within the context of the Persian Wars and may represent a special, though no less significant, set of values.

97. Lysias I.49.

98. MacDowell (1978), p. 124. For instances of this in literary sources, cf. Aristophanes, *Clouds* 1083, *Wealth* 168; and Eubulus in *PCG,* fr. 106; cf. too Dover (1968), p. 227 and my chapter V. Also, cf. *Od.* 575–85 for the repeated (eternal) humiliation and painful torture inflicted upon Tityos in Erebus for raping Zeus' mistress Leto.

99. Cf. Davidson (2001), pp. 48–9.

100. *Mem.* II.1.30.
101. (1997) p. 5.
102. On this same passage, she says (2002), p. 36, that 'It is hubris to use men as women, even in contexts where the sexual relationship is apparently neither coercive nor mercenary. Here the points at issue must be passivity and penetrability, which normatively characterise the female in sexual relationships and which insult a man's or even a youth's sexual honour precisely because it is treating them as if they had the sexual honour appropriate to a woman.' While, in the main, I believe this has definite merits, I take issue here and in chapter VII with the unilateral view that such a model tends to uphold; cf. also my chapter V for more on *hybris* and rape.
103. *Mem.* I.3.11. Likewise, in the dialogue that Xenophon constructs between Sokrates and the pre-Epicurean Aristippos (*Mem.* II.1.1), Aristippos is charged with being 'rather undisciplined' in regard to 'practising self-mastery (*enkrateia*) over the desire for food, drink, sex, sleep, cold and heat and hard work'. He prefers to carry on in self-indulgence and personal comfort rather than uphold the city's culturally approved norms of *machismo*.
104. I.95–105.
105. *Mem.* I.5.1; *Oik.* XII.13; *Mem.* I.3.11.
106. ... πρὸς τὸν πόρνον πεπορεῦσθαι; Aiskhines I.70; cf. 41, 75, 107–8, 115; cf. too Aeschylus *Agamemnon* 1625.
107. Theopompus of Chios (b.376 B.C.E.), in *FGrH* 115 F224–5; Polybios VIII.9, 10; Xenophon *Anabasis* II.6, 28. Cf. Davidson (1997), pp. 165–6.
108. (2001), p. 31.

NOTES TO CHAPTER II

1. *Letter VII,* 326a–b.
2. Qtd. in Walters (2001), pp. 4, 12, in reference to a different but no less similar utopian scheme.
3. The *Minos* is probably later than the *Laws.* So is the *Epinomis* but these two dialogues, although clearly inspired by Platonic thought, are generally considered to be works of other hands.
4. (1970), p. 26. He is referring mainly to such passages that strongly echo Platonic formulations elsewhere. This issue will be later addressed as appropriate.
5. (1999), p. 113. Cf. Thomas (1995), pp. 33 50, for a broader discussion of this. According to Aristotle (*Pol.* 1286a9–17), writing down the laws encourages fairness and is an essential basis for democracy and (1338a15–17) that writing is useful for household management, money-making, learning and political life. Gorgias (*Palam.* DK 30, fr. 11a) declares that 'written laws are the guardians of the just'.
6. There was also, at once, a sense of distrust of the written word, cf. Thomas (1995), p. 35 sq. on Plato and his 'elitist' criticism of writing in the *Phaedrus* and elsewhere, and see below.
7. (1960), Excursus F, pp. 515–18. Taran (1975), p. 124, agrees that he was probably the *philosophos* of the *Suidas.*
8. *Com. In Euclid,* LXVII.23–68; Cf. Taran (1975), p. 126.

9. Morrow (1960), p. 515. *Ind. Herc.* Col. III.36–41. He is likewise identified as an ἀστρολόγος as well as a *parapegmatist* (one who observes both star and weather signs).

10. Alex. Aph. *In Meteor.* 151.32–152; Taran (1975), p. 118.

11. III.37; τοὺς Νόμους μετέγραφεν, ὄντας ἐν κηρῷ.

12. *Prol. In Plat. 25;* ἀδιορθώντους καὶ συγκεχυμένους; Taran (1975), pp. 128–9, indicates that the author of this text was not, as has sometimes been assumed, Olympiodorus (5th C.E.), but a Neo-Platonist from Alexandria—possibly Elias or one of his contemporaries—who misinterpreted Proclus.

13. (1975), p. 128.

14. *Ibid.* p. 130, n. 543; although, the division into chapters was a later advent.

15. *Ibid.* p. 130.

16. III.37.8–10.

17. Cf. *LSJ* s.v. μετέγραφω.

18. Taran (1975), p. 130, n. 543, gives other contextual examples of Diogenes' use of this verb.

19. (1970), p. 22; for a fuller summary of the division of Plato's dialogues cf. Crombie (1962), p. 9 sq. and, more recently, Kahn (1996), pp. 45–48. But he has not abandoned 'dramatic interest' altogether.

20. See above on the *Epinomis*.

21. Goldhill (2002), p. 61, writes that the 'studied anonymity' of the Athenian Stranger is one of Plato's more striking narrative masks that represents a 'veiled' and 'internalised' approach to philosophy.

22. 625b—possibly near or in the famous Idaean cave re-discovered in the 9th century C.E. On the age of the interlocutors in this dialogue, cf. 625b, 685a, 712b, 770a, (that they are older than Magnesia's proposed Guardians of the Laws—themselves at least fifty) 820c, 821a, 846c.

23. (2000), p. 50.

24. (1998).

25. (1972), pp.90–92. Cf. Thuc. II.35–46 and MacDonald (1959), pp. 108–9 for a criticism of Toynbee's view and cf. my chapter III on education, esp. the part about the 'Best and Truest Tragedy'.

26. (1983), p. 225; cf. *Gorgias* 515e.

27. Cf. esp. *Rep.* VIII.558c5–6, where it 'distributes a kind of equality to equal and unequal alike'. Cf. my chapters III and IV.

28. (1998), p. 49; cf. pp. 45, 143.

29. (1986), p. 83.

30. On this designation see *Laws* 739, 807b. Interestingly, the Athenian Stranger discusses the attributes of an ideal vs. a second- and third-best state not only in terms of the moral behaviour of their citizens but also in terms of private vs. communal property.

31. (1998).

32. (1960), p. 11. That is, it is hypothetically situated on Krete.

33. *Republic* 484, 519–20, 540.

34. Cf. *Rep.* Books V–VII, for the training of these philosopher-kings (-queens), esp. 473 sq.

35. *Rep.* 414 sq., 440–41.
36. *Rep.* 428,430, 537 sq.
37. ἐν οὐρανῷ ἴσως παράδειγμα ἀνάκειται—592a–b.
38. (1969), p. 74; cf. *Laws* 739a–740a, cp. 742c.
39. τὴν τοῦ νοῦ διανομὴν ἐπονομάζοντας νόμον—714a1–2.
40. Cf. Xen. *Lak. Pol.* VII.1–3, for a similar situation reputed amongst the Spartans.
41. *Laws* 772e7–e4. If the wealthy only marry the wealthy and the poor marry only the poor, in time the division between the classes will be so great as to cause tensions and possibly class conflicts which Plato rightly seeks to avoid (cf. 744a8–745b1).
42. *Rep.* 459d–460b; cf. 546a1–547a6 for the infamous 'Nuptial Number;' there are numerous works dealing with this complex passage among which include, but are not limited to, Aristotle, *Pol.* E 12. 1316a4 sq.; Macrobius *Somn. Scip.* II 11. 10 on the so-called 'Great Year' or 'Cycle'; Proclus *In. Remp.* II p. 38; cf. Adam's edition of the *Respublica* (1891), p. 79 sq.
43. Cf. *Laws* 684d for the difficulty of land distribution; there are 5040 (a number divisible by 12, 10, etc.) administrative units for land-holdings by the citizens of the city (737e); each lot supports one family, the number of families is meant to remain at more or less a constant of 5040 (740b–c): one of the male children will inherit the holding and the females are given in marriage where appropriate; excess offspring will be obliged to emigrate (740d–e, 741). Cf. Xen. *Lak. Pol.* I.9, VII.3–6 and Polyb., *Hist.* VI.45, 3–5, for a (reputedly) similar situation of land allotment in Sparta. Cf. my chapter V.
44. Cf. my chapter V for more on this curious land-division as well as Aristotle's objections to it.
45. Cf. my chapter VI.
46. (1970), pp. 5–14
47. On the selection and education of these Guardians of the Laws, cf. (for the female guardians) 783d sq. 794a sq., 930a sq., 932b–e, (and generally), 968c sq.
48. *Ath. Pol.* VIII.4; cf. Plut. *Solon* 19.2. For the Areopagos prior to Solon, see Aristotle, *Ath. Pol.* III.6; and for the reference to Ephialtes see XXV.2. Cf. Diod. XI.77.6, who adds a 'moral' to the story, saying that Ephialtes was punished for 'attempting such lawlessness . . . he was done to death by night'.
49. As has been proposed by Chase (1933), p. 135. Of course, we don't actually know whether or not this institution of guardians in the Areopagos actually existed. Cf. Morrow (1960), pp. 211–214.
50. *De Legibus* III.46.
51. Cf. Cawkwell (1997a), pp. 115–30 for a fuller discussion of this issue.
52. Cf. Hodkinson (2000), pp. 56–57 on the ephors and their role in enforcing Spartan *sōphrosynē.*
53. (1960), pp. 526. Cf. Richer (1999), pp. 99–100.
54. Cf. my chapter III and below.
55. Cf. *Laws* 908a, 909a, 951d sq., 961a sq. and 968a. For a similar 'Nocturnal Council' of Atlantis, cf. *Critias* 120a sq.
56. That is, if Aristotle and Plutarch are to be believed, cf. Aristotle, *Pol.* 1270b; Plut. *Lyk.* 26.
57. *Laws* 960–65.
58. (1998).

59. *Ibid.* On the name *nukterinos* cf. *Laws* 968a; for their meeting time cf. 951d.
60. (1960), p. 509.
61. See below.
62. Qtd. in Hamilton and Cairns (1989), p. 1225.
63. (1960), p. 12. All of which, fit the spectrum of Plato's mythologizing.
64. Homer and Hesiod apparently qualify as 'true myths' since the authors seem to have fashioned their literary works based on pre-existing myths and presumably did not originate the mythic tales themselves.
65. Qtd. in Bremmer (1987), p. 1.
66. Cf, *Phaedrus* 275b3–c2 for a discussion of this principle of veracity as a touchstone for determining the difference between *logos* and *muthos*.
67. (1995), p. 12. Cf. Brisson (1982) pp. 111–112.
68. *Rep.* 376e6–377a8.
69. Such as his modification of the myth of Ganymede at *Laws* 636d as well as Sokrates' critique of the myth of Kronos and Zeus at *Rep.* 378a2.
70. (1999), p. 261
71. *Rep.* 377d9–e3
72. (2000), p. 162.
73. (2000), p. 152; cf. pp. 153–201 on Plato's use of so-called 'noble lies' and below.
74. See below.
75. (1999), p. 257.
76. This also serves to distinguish Platonic (or philosophical) mythologizing from the methods employed by the sophists. 'The contrast', says Morgan, 'is not between truth and falsity or verifiability and non-verifiability, but between well-intentioned philosophical persuasion and sophistic browbeating' (2000), p. 166.
77. Such as Frutiger's context-driven categorisation of allegorical, genetic and parascientific myths; Cf. Morgan (2000), p. 161.
78. *Ibid.*, p. 162.
79. (2000), p. 154.
80. Powell (1994), p 284. He says that 'Spartan official deceit including not only lying to helots as to whether they would be rewarded or killed, and misleading other enemies in wartime (a practice which Xenophon commended explicitly to non-Spartans), but also lying to their own citizens about the outcome of battles involving Spartan forces'. Cf. Hesk (2000), pp. 136, 157–62 on this. Cf. Thuc. IV.80.3 sq., Xen. *Ages.* I.17, *Hell.* I.6.36 sq., IV.3.13 sq. On the 'noble lie', cf. Plato, *Rep.* 398b–d, 414b–c, 415c and 459c.
81. (1991), p. 382.
82. (1994), p. 120.
83. Cf. *LSJ*, s.v. παραμῦθία.
84. Brisson (1982), pp. 200–2.
85. 720a1–2. Cf. Bobonich (1991), p. 365 sq. for a broader discussion of many of the linguistic issues represented by this passage.
86. *Laws* 719b–c. Cf. Brisson (1994) pp. 120–21.
87. Cf. Bobonich (1991), p. 370.
88. (2000), p. 168.
89. Cf. *Laws* 887e8–888a7.
90. (2000), p. 169.

91. *Laws* 636c1–6. 'whether one ought to regard these things *in a playful way or seriously*' (παίζοντα εἴτε σπουδάζοντα); I discuss this passage in considerable detail in chapter VII.
92. Cf. e.g. *Rep.* 424e5–425a1, *Meno* 79a7, *Crito* 46d4–5.
93. Cf. Hesk (2000), pp. 151 sq.
94. (1980), p. 105.
95. Cf. Blondell (2002) who deals in greater detail with many of the literary aspects in Plato's dialogues discussed below.
96. (1973), p. 23. Cf. MacDonald (1959) for a comparison between Laws 704a–707c (later discussed) and Thuc. II.35–46.
97. Cf. Thomas (2000), pp. 88, 130–1.
98. (1978), p. 16.
99. As Thomas (1994), p. 37, indicates, 'Plato's authoritarian scheme in the Laws, intended to control every aspect of citizens' lives, does not, so far as I can see, think entirely in terms of written laws'. Cf. *Laws* 822d sq., 788b, 793a–d.
100. Kahn (1996), p. 53
101. 'Some of the most influential of those whom we now categorise as early Greek philosophers', as Murray (1996), p. 18, says, 'wrote in verse'.
102. (1996), pp. 44–5.
103. This ordering of the Platonic dialogues is given in my chapter 1; but cf. *ibid.*, pp. 37 sq. for some of the problems involved in drawing definitive dates for each dialogue.
104. Cf. Morrow (1960), p. 506 n. 12 and pp. 573–5.
105. Rutherford (1995), p. 76.
106. *Ibid.*, p 9.
107. Plato is said to be present at Sokrates' trial (*Apology* 34a) and was reported to be physically unwell at the time of his mentor's death (*Phaedo* 59b).
108. E.g. Aristotle, Cicero, Berkeley and Hume, to name a prominent few, have employed this medium in their philosophising.
109. (1995), p. 8.
110. Cf. e.g. the closing passages from the *Euthyphro* as well as the slave boy's geometry lesson in the *Meno*.
111. (1997), p. 6.
112. Murray (1996), p. 18. Such instances include, but are not limited to, *Republic* 331a, 331d, 334a–b; *Protagoras* 339a–341e, 343d–347a; *Meno* 95c–96a.
113. (1997), p. 6.
114. Cf. *Statesman* 303e–304e, rhetoric is described as a subsidiary aspect of the science of politics but it persuades 'through mythological speeches and not through instruction'. The *Laws* would seem to represent a new level to which this sort of mythologizing has been taken.
115. *Laws* 718b–723a.
116. 722d, 723c–d.
117. 722d.
118. Cf. Nightingale (1999), p, 117 for comparisons with the *Statesman* and Morrow (1960), pp. 552–60 for more on this aspect of the preambles.
119. (1996), p. 212.
120. *Laws* 691c–d, 713c, 874e–875d and see above.
121. *Laws* 822e–823a.

122. Yunis (1996), p. 214. Cf. my chapter III.
123. Cf. Nightingale (1999), pp. 117–18, Hesk (2000), p. 152–4 on Plato's 'pharmacy' and cf. my chapter III.
124. *Laws* 719e–723c. What he is actually favouring is a combination of the two. The Magnesian lawgiver will dispense justice just as surely as the slave doctor prescribes his treatments (and the populace will be equally subject to them) but, like the free doctor, the Magnesians receive some persuasive explanation as to why the 'treatment' must be undertaken.
125. (1999), p. 118.
126. 859a; cf. 923a–c for this propagandistically 'parental' theme and cf. my chapter V.
127. (1996), pp. 229–30.
128. *Laws* 715e–716b.
129. The general impression, as Yunis (1996), p. 236, indicates, is that 'religious experience was conveyed *through texts* only among esoteric groups such as Orphics and Pythagoreans'.
130. It related particularly to sex, as Cartledge (1993), p. 64, says 'in the rhetorical discussions of sexual matters there are 'explicit or implicit manipulations of the polar opposition between "nature" [*physis*] and "culture" [*nomos*]'. Cf. Pindar, fr. 169.1–4 where 'Law is the king of all, of mortals and of immortals . . . ' and Hdt. Hdt VII.101–4, where Demaratus tells Xerxes that the Greeks 'are free—yes—but not entirely free, for they have a master and that master is Law (*nomos*), which they fear much more than your subjects fear you'. Cf. my chapter I.
131. *LSJ*, s.v. νόμος. Cf. Humphreys (1987), p. 214, who says that the 'idea that *nomos* was originally connected with land division is not implausible (though a connection with division and distribution of sacrifical meat is also possible; the earliest surviving use of the term, in a fragment of Hesiod, 322 MW, refers to sacrifice) but an early association specifically with written law cannot be maintained'.
132. *Laws* 700b, 722e, 734e, 775b, 799e. Cf. Todd and Millett (1990), p. 12.
133. (1956), p. 28.
134. *Iliad* IX.99.
135. *Od.* XI.569–70: θεμιστεύοντα νέκυσσιν . . . οἱ δέ μιν ἀμφὶ δίκας εἴποντο ἄνακτα. Cf. Aghion, Barbillon and Lissarrague (1996), pp. 171–3
136. For Plato, as Goldhill (2002), p. 280, indicates, 'taking up philosophy is expressed in terms of an initiation into a mystery religion'.
137. Cf. Aristotle, *Pol.* IV.4 3–7, for a use of *nomos* that is more akin to "law".
138. I.81.
139. MacDowell (1978), p. 44. If he is correct in his assessment, then *nomos* may by symptomatic of 'the change to a democratic attitude, and implies that the validity of a law depends rather on its acceptance by the community than on the power of a ruler'. Clearly the acceptance of the 'rightness' of the laws introduced by the Athenian Stranger to the citizenry of Magnesia is of importance, but their 'rightness' is predetermined by a philosophical/metaphysical imperative. Cf. Ostwald (1969), pp. 20–54.
140. (1956), p. 33; cf. Dem. XXIII.51: νόμος Δράκοντος and *ibid.* 62: θεσμός also of Drako's laws. In a passage from Empedokles (Diels, B9), *themis* is contrasted with *nomos* to mean, perhaps not surprisingly, something equivalent to *physis*.
141. *GPM*, 75.

142. B278 (DK)
143. VIII.72.
144. Cartledge, Millett and Todd (1990), glossary p. 231.
145. Andokides I.87; cf. also 85 and Dem. XXIV.30.
146. (1969), p. 1; cf. Hignet (1952), p. 300.
147. For this legal procedure in the 4th century, cf. Dem. XXIV.20–23 and Kahrstedt (1938) pp. 1–25. Hignett's view (1952) that the decree in Andokides I.83–4 is the first instance of this procedure should be modified in light of the objections raised by Harrison (1955), pp. 33–5.
148. Cf. Nightingale (1999), p. 105 and Rhodes (1991), pp. 87–100. These events may have had an influence on Plato's *Laws* in terms of their being a written legal code.
149. (1978), p. 45. Cf. Cartledge, Millet and Todd (1990), pp. 231–2 and 237.
150. (1987), p. 217.
151. E.g., as Humphreys *ibid*, p. 218, says 'We should therefore be wary of supposing that for Herodotus the Indian *nomos* of eating the dead and the Spartan *nomos* of fighting on against overwhelming odds were different kinds of principle . . . *nomos* represents an incalculable element of human behaviour'.
152. (1999), p. 101. However, the Athenian Stranger's recourse to 'ancestral customs' in this discussion is possibly more propagandistic in intent than a statement of belief. See below on Plato's preference for political science over ancestral law.
153. See above on the preludes and their persuasive intent.
154. Cf. Rhodes (1981), pp. 115, 376–7.
155. (1986), p. 50. Although, Plato's approach to it is markedly different.
156. The Isokratean passages on the 'ancestral constitution' are assembled and examined in Jost (1936), pp. 140–45. Cf. Rhodes (1981), pp. 323, 371–2, 421, 429–30 on Plato's characterisation of Athenian politicians and views on oligarchy.
157. Aristotle, *Ath. Pol.* XXXIV.3. Cf. Rhodes (1981), pp. 375–7.
158. There are exceptions, as indicated above. E.g., Solon is mentioned eighteen times in the extant Platonic *corpus* with casual and friendly references. He was a good lawgiver, the alleged source of the Atlantis myth, a gnomic poet to be quoted and reputed to have been an honourable ancestor of Plato's mother, Periktione. His legalistic theories represent a kind of 'ancestral law' that might be seen as influencing Plato. Cf. Lambert (1993), pp. 316–17. Cf. Hartog (2002), pp. 217, 219 on the Atlantis myths and their potential historical connections with Solon.
159. The *Dissoi Logoi,* one of the only texts of the sophists to survive, also posits a hypothetical society that is antithetical to Athens (although not completely opposite), cf. Thomas (2000), pp. 130–1, 231.
160. The Magnesians will not only study law. Plato's narrator, as Nightingale (1999), p. 103, says, 'even explicates the precise goal of this activity: one "studies" the law in order to become a better person and a better judge of the other kinds of *logoi*'.
161. 293b–299a.
162. The proposed laws on medicine and navigation are to be displayed on *kyrbeis* (as laws were posted in Solon's day) and on *stelai* (as in Plato's).
163. (1986), pp. 51–52.
164. (1999), p. 102; cf. *Laws* 858a–859a.
165. As the Athenian Stranger has done in the case of Solon's laws, cf. my chapters V and VI.

166. 704b–705c. Plato's Magnesia will not build a navy. Cf. Macdonald (1959), pp. 108–9 on this as a 'conservative prejudice' against Athenian democracy and empire through naval power.

167. (1960), p. 31. There is an ancient inscription from Magnesia-on-the-Maeander (3rd B.C.E.) in Asia Minor that records its foundation by colonists from the original Kretan Magnesia, cf. Kern (1900), p. 17, lines 7 sq. This inscription is likewise discussed by Wilamowitz (1895), 177–198. For another account of this same tradition see Strabo XIV, 1.2. Also, The *Palatine Anthology* (VII.304) preserves a grave inscription of a man from Kretan Magnesia.

168. For some recent Kretan archaeology, cf. *http://www.interkriti.org/*.

169. 624a7–b3, cf. *Odyssey* XIX, 178–9.

170. 631b.

171. Cf. Polyb. VI for a more negative view of Kretan tradition.

172. Hdt. I.65.

173. *Pol.* 1274a, 25–31. This Thaletas is the Melic poet who was meant to have established the naked-boy dances (γυμνοπαιδίαι) at Sparta. Cf. *Rep.* 452c.

174. *Nik. Eth.* 1102a, 8–11.

175. Plut. *Solon* 12. Plutarch's source was likely an ancient one, possibly Theopompos; cf. Diog. I.109.

176. Cf. Halsall (1998), *http://www.fordham.edu/halsall/ancient/450-gortyn.html* for the dating of this ancient legal code's inscription to the middle of the fifth century.

177. (1960), p. 20

178. (1991) p. 347. This issue of Kretan influences is taken up later throughout.

179. *Dion* LIII.2.

180. Cf. Rawson (1969), pp. 65 sq. for more on Sparta and the *Republic.*

181. The written laws from archaic Chios (c. 600–550 B.C.E.) may have been another constitutional influence as well as those from Dreros.

182. Cf. Rawson (1969), pp. 4–6 for an outline of reforms attributed to the mytho-historical Lykourgos by the fifth century. The fact that Spartan laws were unwritten (as opposed to the Code of Gortyn or the laws of Chios or Dreros) appears to represent a degree of sophistication removed from written legal codes, but the theoretical structure of the Spartan state proved no less interesting to Plato and many other ancient Greeks.

183. *Rep.* 544c; cf. too *Crito* 52e.

184. Aristotle, *Politics* II.9.1271b1 sq., criticises the *Laws* as advancing particularly warlike virtues. However, such a claim could only be tested in terms of actual experimentation and goes against the Athenian Stranger's expressed intent.

185. Cf. Bobonich (2002), pp. 119–122.

186. E.g. *Laws* 631b3–6, 718b2–4, 743c5–6 and 806c3–7.

187. (2002), p. 120 and p. 198 n. 126. Cf. *Laws* 660d sq., 696b–697c and 742d–744a.

188. II.5 *seq.*

189. Jaeger (1923), pp. 300–301, n.1

190. Cf. Powell (1994), p279. On Spartan constitutional reforms and political history, cf. Hdt. I.65; Thuc. I.12.3, 18.1; Xen. *Lak. Pol.* X.8; Plato, *Laws* 691e–692a; Aristotle, *Pol.* 1313a; Plut. *Lyk.* II, VII, XI.

191. (2001), p. 9. It was surely a combination of these and other matters (e.g. the defeat by Argos at Hysiae c. 669—Pausanias II.24.8) that led to the changes.

192. Cf. Austin and Vidal-Naquet (1977), p. 91. A notable similarity between Sparta and Plato's Magnesia, is the implementation of a state-sponsored system of education Sparta was the only ancient Greek society of which we know that had such a system.

193. (1986), p. 136

194. *De vita Pythagorica* XXV seq. On some of the pros and cons of using Iamblichos as a viable source on the Pythagoreans, cf. de Vogel (1966), p. 20 and esp. Appendix D, *On Iamblichus,* p. 204. Also cf. Kingsley (1995) on recent archaeological data that provides stronger links between the Neopythagoreans of Iamblichos' time and the earlier Pythagoreans than had been previously supposed.

195. Cf. Burkert (1972), pp. 115–120, 141–145, 152 sq. for a more detailed discussion.

196. Cf. e.g. Burnett (1920) and Kingsley (1995).

197. Morrow (1960), pp. 8–9.

198. Cf. Bluck (1947), p. 174.

199. Cf. *ibid.* pp. 175–181 and Morrow (1962), pp. 5–16, for a breakdown of the arguments and ancient corroborative evidence. Most importantly, perhaps, is that all the Platonic letters are listed in the canon drawn up by Aristophanes of Byzantium (3rd B.C.E.) and also in the canon of Thrasyllus (1st C.E.). The *Laws* would probably have been cast out of the Platonic *corpus* by the same nineteenth century detractors had not Aristotle vouched for it (see above).

200. (1962), p. 8.

201. *Ibid.,* pp. 10–11.

202. *Ibid.,* p. 16.

203. (1984), p. 93.

204. *Adv. Col.,* 1127a.

205. *Ibid.,* 1126c–d.

206. Cf. Jaeger (1923), p. 112. He had allegedly bolstered his political successes with a title purchased from the Persians.

207. *Ibid.* pp. 112–113

208. *Letter* VI 322e.

209. *Ibid.* 322d, unlike the tyrants of Syracuse.

210. Jaeger's translation and restoration (1923), p. 114–15. From Didymus col. 5.52, Diels-Schubart.

211. Isok. *Ep.,* 7.135.

212. Cf. Dem. XX.84; on his son's name see Vatai (1984), p. 88, n. 158.

213. Athenaios XI.509 sq.

214. *Ibid.* 11.508 sq.

215. *Ibid.* 11.509 sq. Cf. Paus. VII.27.2; Athenaios 11.508d–509b. Both Chaeron and Timolaos appear to have received Macedonian assistance.

216. (1962), p. 586.

217. (1972) p. 119, esp. n. 62 and 63

218. Cf. von Fritz (1968) esp. pp. 5–62. On Plato and the Pythagoreans in Sicily etc. cf. Cicero, *Rep.* 1.10; *Fin.* 5.29.87; *Tusc. Disp.* 1.17.39. On Plato in Sicily, cf. Nepos, *Dion* 2; Plut., *Dion* 4.1–3; 5.4–5; 11.2; 13.1–4; and cf. Plato, *Letter* VII.

219. Cf. Green (1974) for the view that it was through Aristotle's friendship with Hermeias (*gratis* Plato) that the former got his introduction to the court of Macedon—given

that Aristotle and Hermeias were allegedly good friends and Hermeias and Phillip II were also good friends.

220. Migrating colonists might spread Magnesia's ideology through a form of cultural imperialism, but it seems unlikely that they would spread it far beyond their particular colonies.

221. (1888), pp. 532–3, from his *Dion*.

NOTES TO CHAPTER III

1. *Laws* 813d2–5.
2. *Republic* 377a12–b3.
3. (1964), p. 238.
4. Burnet (1930), p. 311.
5. Cf. my chapters V and VI.
6. Cf. Davies (1971), pp. 332–5, on the wealth of Plato's family and its status of Solonian heritage. Ariston, his father, claimed descent from the god Poseidon by way of Kodros, the last king of Athens, and Solon was allegedly an ancestor of Plato's mother, Periktione. Pyrilampes, his stepfather, had been an ally of Perikles and was sometime ambassador to Persia. Cf. Miller (1997) on Pyrilampes and also Lambert (1993), pp. 316–17.
7. (1999), p. 100.
8. Some of 'the Greeks were literate', as Beck (1964), p. 75, says, 'as early as the fifteenth century, but Linear B was not widely, if at all, known in the Dark Ages'. Cf. Harris (1989), pp. 45–48 for a broader discussion of pre-Classical education.
9. Hornblower (2000), p. 363, indicates that this 'nickname' appears to have originated with Gilbert Murray (1897), but he adds that 'no-one is quite sure'.
10. Pseudo Xenophon, *Ath. Pol.* I.13. This is probably best characterised as a comic/satirical or 'ludic' statement, but it may portray a kernel of the truth about older practices.
11. (2000), pp. 365–76.
12. *Ibid.* p. 379.
13. 'This was a life of leisure', according to Beck, 'in which physical activity, games and chariot-racing were the chief daytime diversions, while in the evenings their cultural life centred around the men's club, in which song played an important part', (1964), p. 79.
14. *Rep.* 376e1–3; cf. 398c sq., 522a; *Protag.* 326a sq.; *Crito* 50d, *Theaet.* 206a; *Laws* 654b sq. 660c sq. Cf. Burkert (1972), pp. 369–71, for an analysis of ancient musical theory in regard to Plato and the Pythagoreans. On the further relationship between music, number and metempsychosis, cf. also Pindar *Ol.* 2.56 sq. (fr. 133), Empedokles *Katharmoi, passim,* Hdt. II.123 and Plato *Phaedo* 81b, *Menex.* 81a, *Phaedrus* 248d, *Rep.* 614 sq., *Gorgias* 525c.
15. Castle (1961), p. 74.
16. (2001), p. 34. Cf. Graziosi (2002), pp. 18–40, on Homeric recitation.
17. 981 sq.
18. Cf. Vidal-Naquet (1977), pp. 107–8.

19. (1994), p. 35.
20. There is evidence of schools dating back to the aristocratic era and possibly even to the middle of the 7th century. The Athenian Stranger (*Laws* 629a) says that Tyrtaeus was a native Athenian who later moved to Sparta and Pausanias (IV.15.6) maintained that he taught at Athens; cf. scholia on *Laws* 629a. But this is generally not believed to be true; cf. Marrou (1982) p. 17, who indicates that 'it seems unlikely that Tyrtaeus was an Athenian'.
21. Herodotos (VI.27) describes a disaster that befell a school of the Chians in 494 B.C.E. According to Plutarch (*Themistokles* 10), the Troizenians provided schools for their Athenian guests in 480 B.C.E. Thucydides (VII.29.5) also reports that Thracian mercenaries, in the employ of the Athenians, massacred all the boys in a school at Mykalessos in 413 B.C.E. He says that 'this was a calamity inferior to none that had ever fallen upon a whole city, and beyond any other unexpected and terrible'. This passage contains the earliest use of διδασκαλεῖον to mean school; cf. Beck, 1964, p. 78.
22. Thomas (1995), pp. 150–1. Many who could not otherwise read or write could probably sign their own names as evidenced by examples on *ostraka*.
23. (1989), pp. 62–3.
24. Beck (1964), p. 81. This stands to reason given the 'capitalistic' character of democratic Athens
25. (2001), p. 189; he says that 'doing so would have had distinctly anti-democratic implications in terms of limiting the freedom of each citizen to identify and pursue somewhat different conceptions of his (individual) good'.
26. Cf. pseudo-Plato *Alkibiades I* 122a–b, where a slave of Perikles, one Zopyros the Thracian, considered too old for work, was sent to be Alkibiades' *paidagōgos*.
27. Castle (1961), p. 63.
28. Cf. *Prot.* 326. It is unclear whether these subjects were taught at the same time or in the order indicated above. Aristophanes *Clouds* (960 sq.) suggest that at the age when philosophy was being taught, gymnastics and music were being learned concurrently.
29. Cartledge (2001), p. 82.
30. Cf. Xen. *Lak. Pol.* III.1 and Plato *Laches* 179a.
31. Beck (1964), p. 95, n. 6.
32. Vidal-Naquet (1977), p. 107, indicates that 'to practice a manual craft did not disqualify citizens from enjoying their full political rights'. But it could be a propagandistic point in legal attacks by other citizens, cf. my chapters V and VI.
33. Hesk (2000), pp. 87 sq. is critical of Vidal-Naquet's assertion that the *ephēbeia* existed in the 6th and 7th centuries. However in the 5th century, as he (p. 87) says, 'this idea of an "in-between period" involving institutionalised practices and associated stories that were anti-hoplitic gain credence when we think of the deceptive behaviour of young male characters in Attic Tragedy'.
34. Aiskhines, *On the Embassy* 167.
35. (1982), p. 105; on Epikrates' law, cf. Harpokration's *Lexikon*, s.v.Epikrates.
36. (1971), pp. 123–4; he proposes, in the light of these inscriptions, that 'the ἄρχοντες to whom Aiskhines appealed as witnesses to his service (2, 167) as a frontier guard along with his συνέφηβοι, can be no other than the kosmetes, among others, and that the existence of the same organization which is attested in 361/0 must be extrapolated at least to ca. 371/0, some ten years later'.

37. *Ibid.* pp. 137–8.
38. *On the Embassy* 167. Plato, in the *Laws*, refers to the Magnesian equivalent of the *ephēbeia* (the *agronomoi*) indicating the etymological meaning of *peripolos* saying that they 'circle around' the city first in one direction and then in the other (760b); see below. Cf. Xen. *Mem.* IV, III.6.10 and *Kyr.* I.2.9–12, and Aristotle, *Rhet.* I.1360a for a similar tack on rural guardians and cf. Ober (1985), pp. 92–3 for a comparison between Plato's *agronomoi* and the *ephēbeia.*
39. Cf. De Marcellus (1994) p. 35.
40. *Ibid.* pp. 37–8.
41. *Ibid.* p. 30.
42. *Antidosis* 286–90; cf. also Xen. *Mem.* III.5.19
43. 666e sq.; cf. De Marcellus (1994), p. 30. Also at *Laches* 179a, Lysimachos expresses the wish that there should be something constructive that his teenage sons could be doing other than gambling and drinking.
44. *Ath. Pol.* 42.5.
45. Vidal-Naquet (1986), p. 107.
46. Cf. Cartledge (2001), pp. 82–3.
47. That is, that they may have served as a kind of 'hit squad' or undertaken the work of thugs. Cf. Hesk (2000), p. 87, 100–1 on these and Winkler (1990b), p. 34. But, as Vidal-Naquet (1986b), p. 142 indicates, 'What is true of the Athenian ephebe *at the level of myth* is true of the Spartan *kruptos* in practice'.
48. Although, it may be derived at least as much from the Spartan *krypteia* and the Kretan *agelai.* Cf. *Laws* 760b; and Vidal-Naquet (1986), p107 sq.
49. Cf. my chapter VI on the Amazonian *'ephēbeia'.*
50. Ober (1985), p. 92.
51. *Ibid.* p. 93. Cf. also p. 135, 223 sq. The *ephēbes* were trained at the Mounichia and Akte forts, p. 90.
52. Cf. Thuc. I.105.4, Lysias, *Funeral Oration* 50–53 when some youths (whether *ephēboi* or otherwise) were compelled to enter combat during the Peloponnesian wars. Cf. Vidal-Naquet (1986), pp. 106–8, 112–113 on similar practices in Krete and Sparta.
53. We hear of songs sung by women at the loom from Homer (*Od.* V.61, X.221). There were also funeral dirges and ritual hymns, cf. Thomas (1995), pp. 105–6.
54. Sappho, 'who presumably learned to read and write well either in Lesbos or in Sicily during the last quarter of the seventh century', as Harris says, 'should be regarded as exceptional though not unique, her family having been a privileged one' (1989), p. 48 and n. 13. Cf. Thomas (1995), pp. 102–3.
55. Cf. Pomeroy (1977), 51–68, esp. 60.
56. Foley (1985), p. 231.
57. 'Phanostrate, a midwife and physician lies here. She brought pain to no one. Dead, she is missed by all' Clairmont (1993), 2.890; cf. Pomeroy (1997), p. 133 sq. Cf. my chapter I.
58. (1975), p.80.
59. As Thomas (1995), p. 153, says 'Women with the privilege of acting without a *kyrios* or guardian are sometimes literate, sometimes not'.
60. Beck (1964), p. 85 sq., asserts that 'women attended the theatre and were expected to appreciate the plays, which require for their understanding a thorough knowledge of mythology; hence many of them must have learnt their mythology at home, and

where else but from a study of the poets?' However, Beck's conclusions are by no means definitive. See below.

61. Tragedy (*Philebus* 48a) is said to produce mingled pleasures and pains and (*Republic* 602b) therefore not to be taken seriously. Cf. *Republic* 394d sq. and *Laws* 816d sq.

62. 962–7.

63. (1994), pp. 348–9.

64. *Gorgias* 502d and *Laws* 817b–c.

65. Goldhill (1994), p. 350.

66. For Aspasia as the composer of Perikles' 'Funeral Oration' cf. *Menex.* 236b, on her eloquence and her role as Sokrates' own mistress of rhetoric 235e. Diotima is also introduced (*Sym.* 201d) as a foreigner.

67. *Lak. Pol.* I.4 sq. He tells us that the Spartan reformer Lykourgos considered motherhood to be a woman's primary function. So Lykourgos reckoned, like Plato, that they would be better suited for this purpose if they were in good shape. To this end 'he insisted on physical training for the female no less than the male sex'. As always, Xenophon's reports on Sparta are probably not an accurate representation thereof. Even he admits that its constitution has probably changed since the alleged reforms of Lykourgos (*Lak. Pol.* XIV.1–3).

68. Perhaps it is for this very reason, at least in part, that Plato has placed his two fictional texts that support the education of women sufficiently far enough away from Athens to be at a safe distance. E.g. Magnesia is to be on Krete and the *Kallipolis* is utterly imaginary—but both are clearly not in Athens.

69. *Oik.* ix.10; most of the *Oikonomikos* represents a kind of 'education' for women inasmuch as Ischomachos goes about instructing his wife on the administration of the household.

70. Cf. Harris (1989), p. 96, esp. n. 140. There are some tantalising examples from red-figure pottery (mentioned in both Harris and Beck) that seem to indicate some women were taught by tutors or were themselves tutors—but this is by no means certain.

71. The real Ischomachos was thought to have possessed an estate at one time valued at more than seventy talents, a princely sum, according to Davies (1971), pp. 265–268.

72. 'The public world of the Greeks', according to Redfield (1977–8, p. 160), 'was always restricted to men; a man's public relations were with men, and his relations with women were private relations'. Rosaldo (1974, p. 36) suggests that 'women's status will be lowest in places where there is a firm differentiation between domestic and public spheres of activity and where women are isolated from one another and placed under a single man's authority, in the home'. See my chapters IV and V.

73. Cf. Cartledge (1981), p. 85, where he discusses the extreme views of Spartan female 'liberation', along with some counter-arguments, and concludes that a balance, or synthesis, of these was probably the case. As Cartledge (2001), p. 84, also says 'a Spartan woman's primary role was not, unlike that of her Athenian sister, the performance of strictly domestic tasks—though she was expected to be able to run a home . . . rather, the goal of her life was childbearing (*teknopoiia*)'.

74. The educational potential of sophists is, of course, not highly regarded in the works of Plato. Cf. e.g. *Hipp. Maj.* 281d, 283a; *Protag.* 312a–c, 316b; *Soph.* 223b, 233c. Isokrates is likewise harshly critical of their abilities and claims as teachers in his

Against the Sophists (c. 390s B.C.E.). Xenophon too upbraids them—if only to dissociate their methods from his own (*Kynegetikos* XIII.1–7).

75. Marrou (1982), pp. 46, 192–3; the first recorded schools of medicine in ancient Greece were located at Kroton (Hdt. III.129 sq) and Kyrene (III.131).

76. Beck (1964), pp. 141–142. Post-secondary education in grammar was also taught by some of the sophists, notably Prodikos (143).

77. It should be noted that our sources on this (such as the pro-Spartan Xenophon) may have 'coloured' their representations somewhat—but there does appear to be some consistency amongst the sources to the effect that the Spartans did have an actual *system* of education. Cf. Michell (1964), pp. 165 sq.

78. Cartledge (2001), p. 83.

79. Cf. too Kennell (1995) for a broader discussion of this complex issue.

80. II.39.

81. Xen. *Kyr., Mem.*; Isok. *Areop.*; Aristotle, *Pol.* Cf. Too (2001).

82. (2001), p. 189.

83. *Rep.* 377b sq.

84. *Protag.* 325d sq.

85. On the importance of μίμησις to learning, cf. *Rep.* 395c sq., 602a and *Soph.* 267e; this principle is explained less in the *Laws* than elsewhere but appears similarly applicable (cf. *Laws* 667d. sq., 669b, 798d sq.). Interestingly, as Motluk (2001), pp. 23–26, indicates, scientific research has recently suggested that the reactions of a certain set of neurons (called 'mirror neurons') within the human brain, in response to the words/actions of other human beings, strongly favours an 'imitative' theory of learning.

86. *Rep.* 410c, *Protag.* 326c (cf. *Laws* 743e ad 839e). It is 'manly' to be physically fit, cf. my chapter IV.

87. As Nightingale (2001), p. 139, says 'they are not taught to develop their own ideas [initially] but rather to absorb and enact a specific ideology'. She discusses the importance of indoctrination in the early stages of education in the *Kallipolis*.

88. *Rep.* 377a12–b3; Cf. also *Protagoras* 326c1–3, where the best education comes to those who begin earliest in their studies; and see below on this theme in the *Laws*.

89. Yunis (1996), p. 212. Cf. *Laws* 701d and 693b–c.

90. Concord and intelligence may be obvious virtues imparted by the system of education, but 'freedom' can be regarded both in contrast to slavery as well as, somewhat paradoxically, the correct submission to proper authority (762e) and this is one area that the educational system will inevitably reinforce. Cf. Yunis (1996), p. 215–216.

91. Beck (1964), p. 255; cf. Isokrates *Panathenaikos* 30–2.

92. Cf. my chapter II.

93. 804d4–6. As Cartledge (2001), p. 84, says 'there was no State (with a capital 'S') in a post-Hobbesian sense in Classical Greece'. Rather, there was the *koinōnia* of citizens whose interests overrode those of the individual.

94. Plato's own thoughts about the development of embryos are the subject of much debate but Rankin (1968, pp. 36–37) maintains, along with Michael of Ephesus (1st century C.E.), that Plato most likely was a preformationist. If true, this would mean that he thought certain 'seed-organs', carried within a fluidic substance, assemble the embryo inside the womb. Praechter (1928, pp. 18–30) has argued in favour of a postformationist theory, similar to that of Aristotle's, whereby a 'postformed' embryo,

delivered whole from the male semen, ferments to ripeness within the womb. Cf. also Lesky (1950), p. 20, who follows Praechter's view that Plato was not a preformationist. For Aristotle's postformationist theory, cf. *Hist. Anim.* 721b11.

95.   (1968, pp. 36–37); cf. *Tim.* 18c sq., 86b sq.

96.   'According to psychoanalytic theory', as Chodorow (1974, p. 45), indicates 'personality is a result of a boy's or girl's social-relational experiences from earliest infancy'. So, early influences must be important to the development of sex roles and how they are defined.

97.   Hodkinson (2000), p. 228.

98.   Cf. my chapter V.

99.   Cartledge (2001), p. 116.

100.   On Aristotle's distinction between virtue of 'character' (*ethos*) and of 'intellect' or 'mind' (*dianoia*), see e.g. *Nik. Eth.* 1103a3–10.

101.   Cf. Hdt. III.68–88 for his rather martial representation of the traditional Persian education.

102.   Cf. Xenophon's *Kyropaideia* I. 2 seq. for the educational system developed by the Persians. But Xenophon and Plato do not cite the Persian education (as Herodotos has done) as being a major causal factor in their defeat at the hands of the Greeks. See below.

103.   *Laws* 694d1–695b1, 728e5 sq., 744d3 sq. Briant (2002), p. 193 sq. discusses Kambyses and the 'decadence' associated with his reign by the Greeks in their media. Cf. Briant (2002), p. 193

104.   Plato may have had a more direct insight into Persian affairs than many considering that his stepfather, Pyrilampes, was ambassador to Persia from about 450 (Davies, 1971, pp. 329–335); cf. *Charm.* 158a; but such close contact could also feed prejudice. Cf. my chapter IV.

105.   *Laws* 695a; cf. Briant (2002), pp. 194–5.

106.   *Laws* 792a sq.; In Aristotle's *Politics*, VIII.2.1336a35, there is the indication that 'the people in the *Laws*' are wrong for stopping their children's tears. The Athenian Stranger says that, while crying is not pleasant to the ear, its harmful quality lies in the fact that it can damage a person's character. Crying too much as a baby may, through habituation, carry over into adulthood to produce adults who are given to excessive complaint—presumably harmful to the pursuit of *aretē*.

107.   *Laws* 643e9–644a6. On the avoidance excessive wealth in order to build a good character, cf. *Republic* 422a1 sq. In Herodotos, Kroisos advises Kyros on how to make the Lydians soft and easy to rule saying that he should 'command them to educate their sons to play the *kithara*, pluck the lyre and practice retail trade' (I.155.4). Cf. Kurke (1999), p. 76 on this.

108.   Nightingale (2001), p. 141; she says that the Platonic implication that Athenian democratic elites engaged in banausic 'wage-earning' by profiting from their educations and thus 'working for the multitude, is a bold piece of rhetoric that collapses traditional hierarchies'. Cf. Hesk (2000), pp. 121, 136. The term 'banausic' is derived from metallurgy, cf. Kurke (1999), pp. 44–45 on its etymology.

109.   'So, we should try, by means of their games (διὰ τῶν παιδιῶν), to direct the pleasures and desires of children toward the state at which they should arrive as their ultimate goal. Indeed, foremost we say that education consists of the correct nurture that most strongly draws the soul of the child at play to a love of that pursuit over which,

when he becomes a man, he must have excellent mastery' (643c8–d4). Aristotle (*Pol.* VII.1336a29–34) is in agreement with the basic structure of this scheme. Cf. also *Tim.* 69c–e, 90 sq. The application of toys to encourage learning at an early age has some scientific backing in the modern age. Experiments with rodents have found that greater brain mass is developed by those rats in cages where toys have been placed as opposed to those without them, Swerdlow (1995), pp.19–20.

110. *Rep.* 336e sq.

111. 798b7–d6; Cf. Kurke (1999), p. 251, on his recourse to the Egyptians in the context of games. At *Phaedrus* 274c5–d2, Sokrates also indicates that the Egyptian god Theuth 'invented number and reckoning and geometry and astronomy and, in addition, *petteia* [a game like draughts] and *kubeia* [dice-playing], and especially writing'.

112. 819b–c. Cf. Kurke (1999), pp. 289–90, for *astragaloi* (knucklebones and/or dice), a game played by Athenian children in the Classical era that probably helped them learn rudimentary mathematics.

113. In the *Statesman* (308d), the Eleatic Stranger has suggested to Sokrates (with a positive affirmation from the latter) that children should be tested by trained educators through the use of games. Cf. *Rep.* 536d–537a, where children in the *Kallipolis* will be tested by their 'voluntary' participation in games.

114. 'The education that we are talking about would be', says the Athenian Stranger, 'that which trains them from childhood in excellence (*aretē*), making them eager and desirous to become perfect citizens, understanding how both to rule and to be ruled with justice' (μετὰ δίκης—643e5–9).

115. 794a sq. Cf. 808c–d for the analogy between a 'herd' of children and that of beasts. This recollects the Spartan 'boy herd', cf. Cartledge (2001), p. 83.

116. (1990), p. 54.

117. Belfiore (1986), pp. 426–7, discusses Plato's attitude toward education of children in the *Laws* saying that its goal is 'the production of that part of ἀρετή, correctly trained pleasures and pains, of which they are capable before they are able to reason.' Cf. too Aristotle, *Politics* VIII.5.1340a14–28 for his general agreement with the Platonic approach to early education.

118. (2000), p. 13.

119. Kleinias, the Kretan interlocutor, affirms that this and other similar rules 'were spoken reasonably' and would likely work well if they were continually enforced from the founding of the Magnesian colony (790c4); cf. *Timaeus* 89a and Aristotle,*Poetics* 1449b27.

120. 794a8–b2. The Athenian Stranger provides guidelines to ensure that every official fits into the hierarchy of authority and is always to be held accountable for her actions (794b sq.).

121. ... οἶον ἀεὶ πλέοντας—790c6–8. He also states that the best cure for a sleepless child, as well as for someone who has the 'Korybantic Condition', consists of a rocking motion and humming a type of tune (790d4–e4). This condition was cured homoeopathically by the regular music and dancing of the Korybantic ritual. For an alternative interpretation cf. Linforth (1946), pp. 121–62.

122. 804c2–7. According to Nigel Spivey (interviewed in Channel 4 2002c) the *gymnasion* was effectively one of the things that made a Greek *polis*.

123. 764c, 779d and 804c.

124. 804d . This practice too has Spartan overtones, cf. Michell (1964), pp. 40, 168 sq., 180.

125. 765d5. This official must automatically be over fifty since he or she is chosen from the Guardians of the Laws (755a) and he will later come to sit on the *nukterinos* council (951d–e, 952a, 961a).

126. Plato's apparent advocacy of compulsory education at state expense, probably derived from the Spartan model, was clearly ahead of its time. As S. Cole (qtd. in Foley 1985, p. 231) says 'subsidised education is introduced in many cities in the Hellenistic period, and it is clear from epigraphical evidence that young girls as well as boys benefited from these local schools'. The third century c.e. writer Cassius Dio (LXXXI.2) says that the emperor Marcus Aurelius (reigned 161–180 c.e.) was the first to provide a form of education completely at public cost. However, this was not compulsory and we likewise hear of no legal machinery of compulsion in Classical Athens or elsewhere except Sparta; cf. Cartledge (2001), p. 85.

127. 764c5–765d3. The Athenian Stranger's loose style of classification, with brevity of detail, is typical of the *Laws*. The author's main concern here seems not to have been to distinguish between the arts and gymnastics, but to provide a general impression of the 'Ministry of Education'. Cf. England's (1921) note on *Laws* 764e2.

128. Cf. my chapter II.

129. 771e5–772a3.

130. *Lyk.* 48b8–c2, citing *Rep.* 458d. Cf. Michell (1964), p. 46–9.

131. The magistrates in charge must be under the age of forty; cf. 764e sq.

132. Michell (1964), p. 187. We also have reports of other similar dances and 'games of armour' in which both sexes partook: e.g. the Kretan and Spartan *Hyporchēma* (Lucian, *De salt.* XVI, Athen. XIV, 630d–e), and the Spartan *Hormos* or 'String of Beads' (Lucian, *De salt.* II).

133. 833c8–d6.

134. The 'upper limit' for women getting married appears to have been around the age of twenty amongst most of the ancient Greeks, as Cartledge (2001), p. 116, indicates, cf. my chapter V.

135. 803c6–9. He is not especially specific here, aside from the activities mentioned above, but one expects that the Magnesians will be equipped with a kind of Platonic formula for gauging the relative *aretē*-value of their activities.

136. 942a6–7.

137. 804d6–805a3. Cp. *Theat.* 175a and cp. Aristophanes *Vesp.* 1010.

138. 'It is the height of folly . . . for men and women not to fall in line and engage in the same pursuits with all their might; it is the case now that, with the same expenditure, and with the same effort, almost every state turns out nigh half of what it might have been—a strange blunder for a lawmaker to make' (805a4–b3). Cf. my chapter VI.

139. British Library (2002) http://pages.britishlibrary.net/mikepymm/utilitar.html

140. Cf. Tyrrell (1984), p. 33, for a discussion of the 'suffrage' granted to Female Guardians in the *Republic*.

141. *Laws* 625c sq., 633a, 780b sq., 781c sq., 806e sq., 839d and 842b.

142. On Krete (Aristotle, *Pol.* 1272a), Miletos and Thurii (Plato, *Laws* 636 sq.), Megara (Theognis, CCCIX), Thebes (Polyaenus, II.3.2), Oinotria (Aristotle, *Pol.* 1329b), Carthage (*ibid.* 1272a) and Lipara (Diod. Sic. V.9.4).

143. (1964), p. 94.

144. (1999), pp. 78–9. Cf. Bremmer (1990), p. 137, where he indicates that Spartan boys 'were allowed, even encouraged, to visit public messes' for sexual purposes.

145. Cf. my chapter VI.

146. Cf. Hdt. I.131 sq. for a parallel here with separation of sons from fathers.

147. As Chodorow (1974), p. 53, indicates, the social construction of sex roles for women depends heavily on their relationships with other females from an early age. The same also applies to the development of masculine identity.

148. *Ibid.* p. 54.

149. Blundell (1995), p. 132.

150. (2000), p. 227; cf. Euripides' *Andromache* 597–600, for their participation in racing and wrestling; some post-Classical sources indicate other such practices as running, wrestling, discus and javelin (Plut. *Mor.* 227d; *Lyk.* XIV.2–3; Cic. *Tusc. Disp.* II.15; and Schol. in Juvenal IV.53); and even partaking of the *pankration*, boxing, hunting and warfare (Propertius III.14.1–20).

151. Xen. (*Lak. Pol.* 14, I sq,) tells us that Lykourgos regarded motherhood as a woman's primary function. He reports that Lykourgos thought, not unlike the Athenian Stranger, that they would be better suited for this purpose if they were in good shape. To this end 'he insisted on physical training for the female no less than the male sex'. Cf. Cartledge (2001), p. 83, for an account of Xenophon's idealisation of Spartan values; and Cartledge (1981), pp. 89 sq. for more on Xenophon's pro-Spartan bias.

152. 'Boys are to spend their time with boys and likewise girls with girls; each should be instructed in the arts and sciences, and the males should be sent to the teachers of horsemanship, archery, javelin throwing and slinging; likewise, if they are at all agreeable to it, the girls should be sent to the lessons—most especially in the use of weapons. Truly at present the customs concerning such matters are misunderstood by nigh everybody' (794c2–d3).

153. 794d5–795d5, along with 671d–672a. Cf. Aristotle, *Politics* II.12.1274b12 sq. on ambidexterity in the *Laws*. Aristotle does take issue specifically with Plato on this subject but expresses his own ideas at *Nicomachean Ethics* 1134b33, and *De Part. Anim.* 666b35 sq., where he says that the natural superiority of the right hand to the left is evidenced by the fact that it receives more blood; cf. also *ibid.* 684a26, and also *De An. Incessu* 705b13, where he discusses this subject at greater length.

154. 795d2–4.

155. 795c5–7.

156. Rawson (1969), pp. 65–66.

157. 753b, 814c2–4. Cf. Aristotle, *Politics* VI.1264b35–40

158. 813e–814a.

159. Inverted commas here, as elsewhere, are deployed to indicate the constructedness of these concepts.

160. 813e4–814b7.

161. 834d3–7. Spartan women, according to Plutarch (based largely upon Xenophon's idealised views), learned how to manage horses and drive chariots in procession (*Life of Agesilaus* XIX.5). Athenaios likewise reported that Spartan women raced two-horse chariots at the *Hyakinthia*, a festival to Apollo and Hyakinthos (IV.4, 139c–f). The facts were probably different, but it reveals an interesting insight to know that some men thought about women in this way.

162. 829b5–c5.

163. 829e4–5, 802a1–5 sq.

164. 'It is our object to avoid war entirely, if we can', the Athenian Stranger explains, 'so soldiers must get their training in sham-fights and the like' (829a8–b1). Might they not make pre-emptive strikes in the interest of security if a neighbouring *polis* threatened their value system? They would certainly be prepared to do so. Cf. my chapter II.

165. Powell (1994), p. 277. It is important to consider that these views on Spartan values have been largely derived from Xenophon's idealised accounts and therefore may not represent actual practices. Cf. Xen. *Lak. Pol.* III.1 sq.

166. The Athenian Stranger seeks to strengthen the Magnesian citizens' solidarity, in Kretan and Spartan fashion, through the mandatory attendance of citizens at the communal dining tables (806d–807a).

167. In the real world, rhetoric and mathematics were taught exclusively to males, cf. Foley, 1985, p. 231.

168. (1974), p. 34.

169. Cf. Butler (1995), pp. 50–1.

170. Cf. my chapters V and VI.

171. Chodorow (1974), pp. 65–6.

172. Geometry was to be studied only superficially (*Mem.* IV.vii.3), arithmetic was to be learned only to avoid difficult labour (IV.vii.8), and astronomy to know the hours, dates and seasons (IV.vii.4).

173. 654e sq, 668a, 798d–e.

174. (1964), p. 118; Isokrates *To Demon.* 51. Cf. *Phaedr.* 279a for Isokrates' favourable mention.

175. Gunderson (2000), pp. 163–5, indicates that masculine performative models existed for (male) Attic rhetoricians in accord with which they should deliver their speeches in the assembly or in some other public context. That is, their manner of presentation was judged, in part, on the degree of manliness it conveyed.

176. Nightingale (2001), p. 148.

177. (1999), p. 45, n. 1; cf. 800b4–801a7; cf. too 812b10–813a4.

178. Cf. my chapter IV.

179. Cf. 802e8–9.

180. τὸ δὲ πρὸς κόσμιον καὶ σῶφρον—802e9–10

181. cf. 814d9–816d2 for the types of dances that will and will not be permitted; also, see below.

182. Chodorow (1999), p. 130.

183. 796b3–c2.

184. The Kuretes were mountain spirits who protected the infant Zeus. They were represented in art as youths dancing the πυρρίχη. On the armed drama of the Dioskuri, cf. Athenaios iv, 184f. The Augustan scholar Dionysius of Halikarnassos (VII.72) says that Athena invented the ἐνόπλιος ὄρχησις to celebrate the triumph of the gods over the giants. Cf. Jeanmaire (1939), pp. 421 sq. who refers to Kretan dances and other such institutions as a kind of 'club masculin'. Cf. Aghion, Barbillon and Lissarrague (1996), pp. 192–4.

185. *Le Balet Comique de la Reine* (2002), *artsci.washington.edu/drama-phd/bcpllaws.html.* Cf. Aristotle, *Politics* II.6.1265a30–35 where he is critical of Plato's insistence on moderation in the *Laws* saying that it would be better to live 'with moderation and liberally'.

186. *Laws* 814–16e.
187. 398c sq. Different types of music were regarded (not just by Plato but the ancient Greeks in general) to promote certain character types and feelings. Some varieties of the Lydian style were seen as mournful, the Ionian relaxing and, more importantly here, the Dorian and Phrygian are considered to promote self-control and courage. Cf. Lee (1974), p. 258.
188. 802a–d. This committee on musical/literary standards may well be the *nukterinos* council itself. We are not told. But there is every indication that they would be made up from the ranks of the highest ranking Guardians of the Laws.
189. 801c10–d6 . . . νομοθέτας περὶ τὰ μουσικὰ καὶ τὸν τῆς παιδείας ἐπιμελητήν.
190. 799a1–2; cp. 656d sq. He also says that the Spartans and Kretans did similarly in their refusal to allow innovation to dance and song (660b). This, as with Egypt, may represent Plato's idealised view. Note that his policy on games staying the same, mentioned above, also alluded to a similar practice amongst the Egyptians. Recourse to ancient Egyptian customs may have appealed to Plato because as Nightingale (1999), p. 119, says, 'it involves establishing fixed laws governing the creation of and participation in all areas of artistic endeavour . . . [and] these laws are inscribed and placed in temples, and have such force that they positively preclude any alteration and innovation'.
191. 799a4–b10—δίκας ἀσεβείας διὰ βίου παντὸς τῷ ἐθελήσαντι παρέχειν. The penalties for those found guilty of this charge include exile and potential execution.
192. Lest they be ἀχόρευτος ('uneducated' or 'unmusical, also wretched—654a); on this cf. Thomas (1995), p. 123.
193. 811e1–812a3. Perhaps Plato did not anticipate that this method of teaching through reading dialogues might pose an ultimate threat to undermine the authority of teachers. 'If dialogues taught a way to teach oneself', as Brant (1998), p. 76, says 'ironically, Plato could make all other teachers redundant'. He indicates that this problem was resolved in favour of pedagogical authority by 18th century scholars on the grounds that an outside opinion might be more informative than one's own alone.
194. 811a1–b5. This attitude reflects the contempt shown at *Phaedrus* 275a for versatile dilettantes. Cf. Herakleitos (fr. 16): πολυμαθίη νόον οὐ διδάσκει; cf. 819a for the Egyptian approach to teaching a variety of subjects.
195. (2002).
196. (1992), p. 44.
197. Cf. *Rep.* 398a–b
198. 275a–b; cf. Nightingale (1999), p. 103, Hesk (2000), pp. 151 sq., pp. 159–63, and Derrida (1981) s.v. 'Plato's Pharmacy'.
199. (1999), p. 103.
200. 816d3–13. Nightingale (1997), p. 175 n. 10, suggests that 'Plato did not think when he wrote the *Republic* that watching comedies could help to learn the nature of base and ridiculous characters'. But cf. *Rep.* 396a, where Sokrates indicates that it is necessary for the citizens of the *Kallipolis* to know of 'base' and 'mad' people so as to avoid imitation of them.
201. (1992), p. 44.
202. (1997), p. 185. Cf. my chapter VI for more on this in relation to *andreia*.
203. Cf. Halliwell (1998), pp. 64 sq. for comparisons with Aristotle's *Poetics*.
204. 935e5–6; cp. Ar. *Eth. Nik.* 1128a20 sq. and *Pol.* 1336b2 sq.

205. As Halliwell (1998) p. 63 indicates, the 'correct and laudable species of pleasure will be the result simply of the artistic presentation or moral truth—the dramatic portrayal, for example, of virtuous men'.
206. Cf. my chapter IV for more on this.
207. (1996), p. 5. Cf. *Rep.* 398a.
208. 817b1–d4; Cf *Rep.* 394d, 606c; *Phil.* 48a.
209. Cf. Hesk (2000), pp. 136, 157–62, for the Athenian Stranger's employment of 'noble lies' as characteristically reflective of Spartan propagandistic policies more than Athenian.
210. (1997), p. 88.
211. (1992), p. 61. Cf. Saïd (1978) p. 510, who recognises this particular tack of Platonic *mimēsis* in her discussion of his use of *hamartia,* saying, 'Ainsi, la faute tragique, avec ses ambiguïtés et ses contradictions, n'a plus de réalité aux yeux du philosophie. Elle n'est jamais qu'une illusion, un fantôme funeste qui ne peut qu'abuser les insensés. Il faut donc la banner de la cite avec son créateur.'
212. Thuc. II.35 sq. Cf. Ober (1998), pp. 45, 143. Cf. Toynbee (1972), pp. 90–92, for the view that Plato is reacting against Periklean views. It should be noted, however, that Plato has probably not written this or any part of the *Laws* in direct response to a speech given fifty years prior. It was possibly the case that he was responding to the publication of this same speech in Thucydides and the views contained therein. As Stadter (1959), p. 108, says, a 'comparison of the points made by the Athenian Stranger with passages from the "Old Oligarch" makes it clear enough that Plato is merely airing longstanding conservative prejudices against the contemporary interpretation of a view of Athenian democracy and the source of its strength—naval power—which can be traced back well into the fifth century which Plato found intolerable'.
213. In the same speech to potential performers, the Athenian Stranger says, 'so now, oh children and offspring of the mild Muses, first display your works beside those of ours before our rulers; and if your speeches seem the same as ours or better than ours, then we shall grant you a chorus, but if not, dear friends, then we can never do so' (817d4–9).
214. (1994), p. 38.
215. ... λογισμοὶ μὲν καὶ περὶ ἀριθμοὺς ἕν μάθημα, μετρητικὴ δὲ μήκους καὶ ἐπιπέδου καὶ βάθους ὡς ἐν αὐ δεύτερον, τρίτον δὲ τῆς τῶν ἄστρων περιόδου πρὸς ἄλληλα ὡς πέφυκε πορεύεσθαι. Cf. *Rep.* 526c, 527d–530c and *Epin.* 990b.
216. This is derived from mostly aristocratic customs and, as Murray says (1990), pp. 149–50, 'the fundamental potential for opposition between drinking-group and democracy is clear. However much the fifth-century democracy might try to provide public dining rooms and public occasions for feasting, the *symposion* remained largely a private and aristocratic preserve'.
217. Cf. *Theognis* 509–510, 837–840 for a similar statement of moderation in drinking. *Laws* 666a–d entails these legal regulations of age and also details the choruses composed of Magnesians over the age of forty who, as Lissarrague (1990), p. 10, says 'may "invite Dionysus" to "relieve the desiccation of old age" ... wine warms the soul and removes its stiffness, just as it removed its worries ... making the old man happy in his life and newly sociable' and 'his soul, once again pliant as that of a child, can

be reshaped, and its malleability has a direct effect during religious observances: it allows the old man to sing and to dance, which are important social activities'. This is a reward for following Magnesia's rule of moderation in drinking earlier in life. Cf. Belfiore (1986), p. 429, where he indicates that the drunkenness of Magnesia's elderly parallels the medical operation of purgation of the body.

218. Cf. Golden (1992), pp. 12–13 and Belfiore (1986), pp. 421–37, for a discussion of the use of wine in the *Laws* as a means to train emotions through a kind of forced cathartic activity.

219. The subjects should become 'fearless' (ἄφοβος) in the face of pleasure (648b9–c3). Cf. *Lak. Pol.* III.5, for a similar goal set by the Spartans.

220. 'Calculation', (λογισμός), also renderable as 'reckoning', is identified with Reason's 'golden chord' that guides the souls of mortals along the right path in the 'puppets of the gods' myth that fits into this broader discussion on the educational benefits of drinking parties (644c12–645c8). 'When λογισμός has become the δόγμα of the *polis*', says the Athenian Stranger making a musical pun, 'it is named "law"' (644d1–3). Νόμος can, of course, also mean song.

221. If a reveller is not willing 'to obey those [in charge] and the officials of Dionysus, who are aged upwards of sixty years, then he must bear shame (αἰσχύνη) equal to and greater than those who are disobedient to the commanders who are the officials of Ares, the god of war' (671d9–e3).

222. *Laws* 647a.

223. Richer (1999), p. 97. Cf. Plut. *Mor.* 7e and *Iliad* VI.441–2

224. *Lak. Pol.* II.2. *Phobos* had his own temple in Sparta and was probably attended by an all-male priesthood; relatively little is known about the religious features of *Aidōs*, but Richer (1999), p. 93, is 'tempted *a priori* to see in *Aidōs* a form of *Phobos* for the use of women'.

225. (1999), p. 99; Xenophon also stresses that the Spartan education aimed at 'inspiring great reserve (τό αἰδεῖσθαι ἰσχυρῶς ἐμφῦσαι) in its subject youth (*Lak. Pol.* III.4).

226. (1993), p. 280.

227. (1993), pp. 374–5.

228. 647a, 649c–d.

229. Cf. my chapters IV, VI.

230. This topic is discussed in greater detail in my chapter VII.

231. 'Is there a drug (φάρμακον) of fear that some god has given to humankind', the Athenian Stranger asks, that 'ultimately brings the bravest of mortals into absolute terror?' (647e1–648a1). Kleinias decides that there is no such drug in existence but he readily agrees to the proposition that a good legislator 'would be glad to be able to get hold of an "acid test"' (βάσανος) of the courage and cowardice of his citizens (648b1–2). Cf. Cairns (1993), p. 374 sq. on the *symposiarch*. One suspects that Magnesia, not unlike some modern governments, would similarly employ hallucinogens and barbiturates as available.

232. (1990), p. 9.

233. This bears similarity to Freud's account of the male *psyche* which, as Chodorow (1994), p. 25, says 'represents women, and especially the mother, not only explicitly but implicitly, or latently, as object'.

234. 841a sq.

235. The Athenian Stranger is critical of Spartan, Kretan and other traditions involving drink but he specifically indicates that the Spartans err in insisting upon enforced sobriety and thus not learning control over their pleasures as well as pains (639e). Megillus points out that, since his family were (conveniently) *proxenoi* to Athens (642b), he has seen much drunkenness—at the Great Dionysia as well as in the Spartan colony of Tarentum—but 'with us', he says, 'no such thing is possible'(637b1–6). Hodkinson (2000), p. 196, admits that we do not know whether they partook of alcohol excessively or moderately. There is evidence for either possibility, but most sources about ancient Sparta indicate, in his words, 'a degree of individual discretion' that seems to have operated 'within a setting that imposed strict social sanctions against excessive drinking'. Also cf. Michell (1964), pp. 289–90, for a survey of the sources.

236. Cf. Hodkinson (2000), p. 216, who indicates that 'As the prime locus for the practice of voluntaristic, reciprocal commensality among private groups of peers, the *symposion* was associated above all with the wealthy elite'.

237. (1990), p. 150.

238. 'When a man drinks it [wine], does it first make him immediately cheerful more so than before, and, the more he partakes of it, by as much is he filled full of good hopes and of capability in his opinion? And finally indeed is such a one, reckoning himself to be clever, filled with complete license of the tongue and a lack of inhibition (ἐλευθερίος), completely fearless, so that he will both speak anything without hesitation and also in the same way behave? Everyone, I believe, would agree with us that this is so' (*Laws* 649a9–b6). Cf. Boyancé (1951), pp. 3–19, for Plato's accurate description of the effects of alcohol.

239. (1990), p. 9.

240. 650a2–5; he says that it would be better to know this about a person before placing him in charge of one's sons or daughters.

241. 'If some state pursues the practice, which was just now discussed, with law and order as an example worthy to follow, that they exercise it with care for the sake of moderation (τοῦ σωφρονεῖν), and if that state permits other pleasures in like manner according to the same argument, as a device for the mastery of them, then in every case this same example must be followed' (673e3–e8).

242. Richer (1999), p. 100, indicates that 'Aidōs had a wide sphere of influence at Sparta, then, in connection with both men and women, and the importance of the concept in Spartan customs (supervised by the ephors) appears clearly established'.

243. (1993), p. 376.

244. I borrow the phrase 'more equal' from Orwell's *Animal Farm* and *1984*. On the Athenian Stranger's formulation of relativistic equality cf. *Laws* 744b sq., 757; cf. too *Rep.* 557a, 561b–563.

245. ἀρχὰς ὡς . . . τῷ ἀνίσῳ ξυμμέτρῳ

246. E.g. funerary honours and state positions, cf. 744c4 and below.

247. He says that 'the law has already granted him permission, and still gives permission, to choose whomever he wishes of the men and women of the state for that public commission' (813c6–9).

248. 951d8–e4. On the selection and training of this committee, cf. 951d–e, 952a, 961–69.

249. Powell (1994), p. 280.

250. Cf. Xenophon (*Lak.* Pol. XIII.10–11), for similar travel restriction in his Lykourgian Sparta.
251. 963a7–11, c11–d2, 965b5–9, 965c9–e4, 966a5–10; cp. 631c sq. As opposed to five cardinal virtues in the *Protagoras* (cf. *Protag.* 349b, 359a).
252. Cf. *Rep.* 484, 537b sq., where dialectics are described, as Bury says (1999, p. 555, n. 3), 'as a kind of induction (συναγωγή) whereby the mind ascends from "the many" particulars to "the one" universal concept or "idea": a comprehensive view of the whole that marks the dialectician (ὁ συνοπτικὸς διαλεκτικός)'.
253. . . . περὶ καλοῦ τε καὶ ἀγαθοῦ—966a5–10.
254. 966c5–7.
255. This includes the text of the *Laws* itself and potentially the *Republic*, the *Timaeus* and others—966c1–9.
256. ἀέναον οὐσίαν ἐπόρισεν—966d12–e3
257. 967d4–8; cf. 903d.
258. 966e3–967e1; cf. 818a sq. and *Rep.* 607b–c.
259. 967e2–5; cf. 710a and *Rep.* 399.
260. Cf. Goldhill (2002), p. 217 sq. for a (post)modern rebuttal to the traditional Platonic pedagogical system and its place in an industrialised world.

NOTES TO CHAPTER IV

1. *Protagoras* 351a4–b2.
2. (2000), pp. 336–7.
3. There is something vaguely like this in contemporary English usage. The words 'virtue' and 'virtuous' contain within them the Latin base 'vir', meaning 'man', and are more directly derived from the Latin 'virtus', which means, not unlike its ancient Greek equivalent, both 'manhood' and 'courage'. Other examples of this include such sexually implicit terms as *virility* and *virile*. The Stoics later appear to have connected courage and virtue along similarly sexual lines. Edwards (2002) suggests that 'Virtus', amongst the Romans of the 1st century C.E., was a 'manly' quality that women could sometimes possess (mainly Seneca's relatives it would seem) but not un-problematically. It was more readily associated with the ideal role for men.
4. (701d10–11) ὅπως ἡ νομοθετουμένη πόλις ἐλευτηέρα τε ἔσται καὶ φίλη ἑαυτῇ καὶ νοῦν ἕξει.
5. Yunis (1996), p. 215. Platonic freedom must also be construed, paradoxically, as the rational submission to proper authority (762e).
6. *GPM*, p. 161.
7. These fears are expressed by the women of Troy at *Iliad* VI.238. Such a doom was inflicted upon Skione by the Athenians in 422 and on Melos in 416; on Hysiai by the Spartans in 417, on Plataiai by the Thebans in 373 and upon Thebes, in turn, by Alexander the Great. See also Polybios II.58, 9–12 sq. for the similar fate that befell Mytilene.
8. Mossman (1995), pp. 23 sq. Cf. Eur. *Hekuba* 60–1, 98–103, 156–61, 234–5, 332–3, 444 sq., 459–6, 550–2, 741, 798, 809 sq., 821–3, 881, 905 sq., 1289, 1293–5.
9. Anderson (1997), p. 141. Cf. *Andromache* 147–53, 155, 555–6, 577–8, 583.
10. 515–16.
11. (1997), p. 139.

12. Cartledge (2001), p. 82.
13. These traits are praised both by Herodotos (III.4.1) and Xenophon (*Ages.* X.1) where the 'good man' is described in terms of 'endurance, valour and judgement when discussion is necessary'. Cf. too Demosthenes XXIV.103, 119 sq. (along with Aiskhines III.175 seq.), where defectors from a military expedition are listed alongside parricides and hoodlums.
14. Xen. *Hell.* V.1.15.
15. Eur. *Her. Fur.* 1354 sq; Soph. *Trach.* 1071–5, 1199–1201.
16. Cf. Demokritos B182; Eur. frags. 233, 236, 237, 238, 239, 240; Soph. *El.* 945; Xen. *Mem.* ii 1.28, *Kyneg.* 12.9; Ar. *Clouds* 965, 987, 1044–105; and esp. Plato, *Laws* 694c sq, 695b sq. where the 'manly' education of Kyros is contrasted with that of his sons who were raised in luxury by 'women and eunuchs' and thus grew 'soft' and decadent. Cf. *Republic* 407b sq. on how *aretē* is not promoted by excessive attention to the body.
17. Cartledge (2001), p. 84–5, discusses the ancient concept of the *koinōnia* (community/commonweal) of citizens vs. the modern post-Hobbesian State.
18. Cf. my chapter III.
19. The Hellenistic kingdoms, in many respects the heirs of Athens' legacy, often consisted of a minority of Greeks ruling over a mostly alien populace. Amongst them there was, as Browning (2002), p. 261, says, 'an almost exaggerated emphasis on Greekness'.
20. VIII.144; But which was their common language? Different forms of local dialects were labelled 'Greek' selectively, cf. Davies (2002) p. 166 sq.; on the structure of Hellenic collective orientation in the 5th century, cf. Davies (1978), pp. 21–48 and Dover (1974), pp. 3 sq.
21. *Pol.* I.1252b7–9. His Macedonian allegiances may be showing here.
22. (1989), p. 1.
23. *GPM*, p. 6.
24. Cf. Hall (1989) and Harrison (2002) p. 7, 166, 261, 291; and see below.
25. (2002), p. 291.
26. Cf. Hall (1989), pp. 16–17 on this view in other *poleis*.
27. (2002), p. 4.
28. Cf. my chapters II and VII.
29. Cf. Hall (1993), p. 110 and Halperin (1990a), p. 266. As Harrison (2002), p. 4, indicates, 'Aeschylus' celebration of Athenian and Greek victory in his *Persians* (472) contains many of the contrasts between Asia and Greece that were to be developed by later authors: between the unaccountable monarchy of the Persians and the effective, accountable democracy of Athens, between the slavish masses of the king's vast flotilla and the small band of Greeks, each 'the lord of his oar', between the empty pomp of the Persian court (with its deference to god-like kings and the excessive authority of royal women) and the masculine simplicity of the Athenians.' See below.
30. Cf. Ktesias *Persika* (*FGrH* 688 f 1–44); Xen., *Kyropaideia* III.1.13 on the Persian's effeminate garb and VIII.8.16 for the soft luxury associated with Persian furniture; Aeschylus' *Persai* (in particular 816–17, 179, 719, and 755 where Xerxes is said to have a lack of manhood—*anandreia*); Cf. also Herodotos IV.172.1 and Xenophon's *Anabasis* I.7.4 and III.2.16.
31. (2002), p. 210.

32. As Miller (2000), p. 413, says, 'while an important role in the articulation of Greek ethnic identity was played by the successful repulsion of the Persians in 490 and 480/79, Greek sense of ethnicity was not event-driven so much as a function of large-scale socio-economic developments'. The Roman historian Livy (1st B.C.E./C.E.) explains '*cum alienigenis, cum barbaris aeternum omnibus Graecis bellum est eritque*', (XXXI.29.15); cf. Eur. *Hekuba.* 1199–1201.

33. Miller (1997), figs. 1 and 2. It is probably a patriotic allusion to battle of the river Eurymedon in the early 460s; cf. *ibid.* pp. 11–12. Cf. Bovon (1963), pp. 580 sq. on Greek representations of Persian attire and its reception. This may represent a case of penetration used as violence in a kind of zero-sum way as described by Dover (cf. chapter I); however, the special circumstances here seem to preclude drawing too broad a generalization.

34. *GH,* p. 105. But cf. Davidson (2001), pp. 3–51 for an alternative view.

35. Eur. *Helen* 276; the single 'free' man was, of course, the Great King himself. Interestingly, the importation of democratic institutions into the heroic cities of drama (e.g. the Argive assembly voting in Aeschylus' *Supp.*, Theseus' disquisition on democratic theory in Euripides' *Supp.*, an evidently kingless Athens in *Eumenides,* and the procedures of debate and voting in Euripides' *Orestes*) provide a very telling anachronism. Euripides is considered to subvert the Barbarian-Greek polarity, cf. Said (1978).

36. E.g. Euripides' *Hekuba* 328 sq., 1199–20; *Helen* 276.

37. Cf. *Iphigenia in Aulis* 1400, *Telephus,* fr. 719 TGF; Thrasymachos, fr. 2 DK.

38. Cf. Nippel (2002), p. 291.

39. Cf. *Dissoi Logoi* II.9 sq. and Thomas (2002), p. 128. She indicates (p. 130) that this attitude of cultural relativism is implicitly shared by Herodotos—but he is more subdued in his approach. On this, cf. too Harrison (2002), pp. 5–23,

40. XV.15

41. Hall (1989), p. 193.

42. Cf. Dover (1974), p. 2 and Graziosi (2002), pp. 150 sq. on Homer's divine associations.

43. *Odyssey* XVII.300–320.

44. Interestingly, this association then would seem to suggest that the Athenian Stranger in the *Laws* is (atypical amongst Plato's protagonists) upholding a basically democratic Athenian value in embracing a policy of manliness that is starkly opposed to effeminacy—itself connected with a type of slavery

45. As Cohen (2000), p. 11, says 'the latest clarion call urges a move beyond binary thought and consideration of the opposition of the Greek self and Other . . . nonetheless, such opposition was an especial characteristic of the Classical Greek world'.

46. (2000), p. 48.

47. Jones (2002). Cf. Osborne (2000), p. 23 sq. and Cohen (2000), p. 11, on the dangers of over-speculation about the Greeks and the *other.*

48. Harrison (2000), pp. 56–57. This scene, as he indicates, 'reflects and develops the shared prejudices and assumptions of author and audience'.

49. Cf. Herodotos V.78.

50. Herodotos (VII.8) says that Xerxes summons his elders to council 'so as to learn their opinions and inform them all of his wishes'. Cf. Harrison (2000), p. 86.

51. *Ibid.,* p. 77. Cf. Aristophanes, *Lys.* 614–35 and Hdt. III.80.6.

52. E.g. the Persian woman in Atossa's dream is proud to serve under the yoke of slavery (192–7) and, in ref. to the Greeks, she says ' . . . who is set over them as shepherd and master of their host? Of no man are they called the slaves or vassals' (241–2). Contrast with Herodotos *Histories,* when Artabanus alone dares to speak against Xerxes' proposed expedition, the king un-democratically ignores his advice with a *thymos*-laden rebuttal (VII.10–11).

53. As Miller (1997), p. 38, points out, by the middle of the 5th century 'a large amount of Persian jewelry and clothing now in the Greek world had glutted the market'. Some of this would have been in the form of 'spoils of war'. But a great many of the Persian commodities available for Greek consumption were supplied by trade according to demand.

54. Geddes (1987), p. 319.

55. As with the Amazons, contempt was sometimes mingled with admiration. Cf. my chapter VI.

56. *Life of Perikles XIII;* 'he tunes the shell he trembled at before'.

57. Thuc. I.95.1–2. Median attire apparently also incorporated eyeliner and rouge, cf. Xen. *Kyr.* I.3.2.

58. Geddes (1987), p. 330; Cf. Herodotos III.80.1–6 for a statement of this Athenian value of 'equality' as a rebuttal to the Persian Otanes.

59. Jones (2002). Cf. Whitley (2001), p. 366, where, in funerary arrangements, 'plainness is the keynote of the early fifth century'. A similar state of democratic burial shall exist in Magnesia (*Laws* 958 sq.); cf. chapters V and VI.

60. Geddes (1987), pp. 325–6.

61. Cf. my chapter III on music in Magnesia's educational system; Plato's Sokrates had forbidden Asian musical styles to young people in the *Kallipolis* (*Rep.* 398d–399a). Aristotle, perhaps in keeping with his native Macedonian as well as his adopted Athenian values, also upholds this at *Pol.* 1340a–b, 1342a–b.

62. *Laws* 802e8–9.

63. τὸ δὲ πρὸς κόσμιον καὶ σῶφρον—802e9–10.

64. 629b. Cf. 653c–660c and see Barker (1984) pp. 141–56 on Magnesian music.

65. (1982), p. 21.

66. *Lyk.* 22.

67. *Laws* 697c; 698a.

68. *Kyr.*VIII.1–27. Cf. Isokrates IV.152 for his condemnation of corrupt Persian educational practices.

69. 695a5–b; but cf. Briant (2002), pp. 208–10 for the view that is a highly prejudicial representation.

70. Cf. my chapter III.

71. Cf. my chapter VI; see *Laws* 694d1–695b1, 728e5 sq., 744d3 sq. for examples of the Athenian Stranger's 'even-handed' approach to the Persians (cf. Hdt. III.68–88) along with my chapter II on Plato's family's Persian connections.

72. 791d5–8.

73. *Metaphysics* A.V.986a22sq. It is possible that this 'Table of Opposites' may have been an invention of the fourth century although it appears to be intrinsically Pythagorean in character. Cf. Burkert (1972), pp. 51 sq. who maintains that it was authentic and an influence on Plato, saying that 'the "table of opposites" is quite closely connected

with Academic doctrines: we have here a continuous transition between Pythagorean and Platonic'.

74. It is worth mentioning that Aristotle described Plato, in terms of his philosophy, as 'in most respects a follower of the Pythagoreans' (*Met.* A. V.987a30). We cannot fully assess the validity of this statement but see Kingsley (1995) and below.

75. Cf. Burkert (1972), pp. 125, 133 and 369 sq. on these mathematical qualities and their relationship with Platonic metempsychosis, music and other related subjects.

76. VIII.388a–e. Epsilon = 5. There he says that ' . . . no even number united with even gives an odd number, nor does it ever show any departure from its own distinctive nature, being impotent through its weakness to produce the other number, and having no power of accomplishment; but odd numbers combined with odd produce a progeny of even numbers because of their ever-present generative function'.

77. This sort of rationale connects with the medically erroneous opinion that the father was the *true* parent of the child and that the mother merely provided a receptacle in which the foetus is nourished. Cf. Aeschylus, *Eumenides* 658–61 and Aristotle, *De Generatione Animalium* 715a20 sq. Cf. my chapters III and V for some of Plato's potential views on the matter.

78. Lovibond (1994), p. 92.

79. *Laws* 781b1–4.

80. λαθραιότερον μᾶλλον καὶ ἐπικλοπώτερον ἔφυ—781a2–4. For a discussion of this passage cf. Annas (1976), pp. 307–21, and esp. pp. 316–17.

81. (1994), p. 94.

82. For a broader discussion of passages in Plato that exhibit characteristics of the Pythagorean 'Table of Opposites', cf. Irigaray (1985), pp. 188–99.

83. On tragedies cf. 658d3, and 817c4–5 sq. These passages, along with *Gorgias* 502d, have been cited as evidence that Athenian women were admitted into the theatre in Plato's time. Cf. my chapter III.

84. φρόνιμος—816d–817a.

85. Lovibond (1994), p. 96.

86. The Athenian Stranger says that 'if a native should stray to some other craft rather than the cultivation of *aretē* then the city wardens will engage in chastising him with reproaches and dishonours until they restore him to his proper course' (847a5–b2).

87. (1994), p. 97.

88. Cf. *Republic* 352e sq, 401a, 444e; *Protagoras* 349b, 359a.

89. *LSJ* s.v. ἀνανδρία.

90. Cf. Saunders (1990), pp. 65 sq.

91. England (1994), pp. 109–111.

92. Sokrates' suicide was, of course, dictated by judicial necessity and Plato has made this distinction. He is said to have faced his demise with courage declaring that 'those who practice philosophy in the right way are in training for dying and they fear death least of all' (*Phaedo* 67e).

93. We are told in the *Phaedo* that most people, being subjects of the gods, have insufficient right to take their own lives (62b–62c). Similarly, Kebes indicates that no reasonable man would willingly seek to the leave the wise mastery of the gods (62d–62e).

94. See my chapter I, and throughout, for other comparisons between the *Laws* and the *Republic*.

95. While this rather Spartan approach may be a good argument for same-sex relationships in the military, it need not be taken as Plato's own view nor, indeed, does it reveal much about what ἀνανδρία may actually mean in context. As Cairns (1993), p. 378, says of this passage, 'an entire city or army of lovers would be a powerful force, such would be its determination to avoid disgrace and pursue honour'.

96. The only other instance of ἀνανδρία in *Phaedrus* occurs at 254c8, where the 'dark' horse of Strife is said to seem to pull away from its position in a manner that is 'cowardly' or 'unmanly'.

97. Hobbs (2000), p. 228.

98. Fisher (1992), p. 486; cf. Foucault (1984), p. 220 and Davidson (1997), p. 169.

99. 836d7, d9–e1, cf. 636c6–7.

100. (2000), p. 152.

101. *Ibid.* p. 140; *Rep.* 491a7–b4; cf. pseud. Plat. *Alkibiades* I.124e, where the young Alkibiades wishes to excel in the 'manly' affairs perceived as appropriate to a gentleman.

102. σωφροσύνην δὲ ἀνανδρίαν καλοῦντές—560d4

103. I have actually left out a few passages because they bear only minor relevance here. However, I include the references in the event that the reader is interested. Cf. *Menexenus* 246e & 247b–c; *Letters* VII, 330d & 331a seq. This last one expresses disapproval of a crooked politician, who gives bad constitutional advice, as being unmanly (ἀνανδρος). It is very similar to the Athenian Stranger's condemnation of judges who have rendered false judgements mentioned above.

104. Cf. esp. *Phaedrus* 237 sq.; *Phil.* 65c sq.; *Prot.* 353c sq; *Rep.* 505b sq., 561a, 580d sq.

105. δεινὰς θωπείας κολακικάς—633d1–2.

106. μίμησιν τοῦ θήλεος ἰόντος τὴν τῆς εἰκόνος ὁμοιότητα ἆρ οὐ μέμψεται—836d5–e1-3

107. Cf. Hdt VII.101–4, where Demaratus tells Xerxes that the Greeks 'are free—yes—but not entirely free, for they have a master and that master is Law (*nomos*), which they fear much more than your subjects fear you'. Cf. my chapter II.

108. Cf. my chapters I and VI on the 'softness' of Timarkhos for submitting to excessive pleasure.

109. Cf. my chapter III.

110. 633e1–2. His use of terminology here reflects that of Eur. (*Her. Fur.* 494–6) where Herakles is told that 'to appear to your enemies even in a dream', would be sufficient to defeat them, 'for . . . they are *kakos*'. Cf. too Soph. *Phil.* 1306 sq. where cowardliness in facing a spear is described as *kakoi*.

111. μεγίστων ἡδονῶν καὶ παιδιῶν—635b5–6.

112. ἀνδρεῖοι καὶ ἐλεύθεροι—635d4–6.

113. Cf. Cairns (1993), p. 377, who discusses this issue of 'seeming' vs. 'being' good in the *Laws*.

114. On Apollo and education, cf. Aghion, Barbillon and Lissarrague (1996), pp. 45–46; on Dionysos, pp. 62–4.

115. Mactoux (1993), p. 280 and Richer (1999), p. 96. Both describe a similar practice in Sparta with the deified principle of *Phobos* and its connection to the authority of the *ephors*. Cf. *Laws* 653d and 665a for Apollo's connection to drinking parties and education and cf. my chapter III.

116. Cf. Plato's *Parmenides* 139 sq., 146d and 148a sq.; *Sophist* 254e sq., *Theaetetus* 186a; *Timaeus* 35a.

117. This can also be seen in Hektor's mode of behaviour as informed by his 'Heroic Code' of values that is opposed to Alexandros and Helen's so-called 'Pleasure Principle'.
118. Cf. my chapter I.
119. (1981), p. 12. The *oikos* became the sexually specific sphere of women; cf. my chapters V and VI.
120. *Ibid.* p. 11.
121. *Republic* 544c, 555b, 557b, 557e, 561; *Statesman* 292a, 302d sq.; *Laws* 710e etc. Unlike his father Ariston and stepfather Pyrilampes, Plato chose to avoid democratic politics as much as possible, cf. Davies (1971), pp. 332–5. Pyrilampes was a prominent supporter of Perikles and Plato was probably brought up largely in his stepfather's household. Kritias and Charmides, leaders among the extremists of the oligarchic insurgence of 404, were, respectively, cousin and brother of Periktione; both were friends of Sokrates, and through them Plato may have known him from boyhood.
122. Cf. my chapter II.
123. Loraux (1995), p. 10. Cf. Chodorow (1978), p. 182, who indicates that a key aspect of sex-role stereotyping for males is 'that certain social activities are defined as masculine and superior'.
124. (1995), p. 10.
125. Homer, *Iliad* V.875–880; Homeric Hymn 28.1.4–5, and Aghion, Barbillon and Lissarrague (1996), pp. 171–3 and 192–4.
126. Cf. the Homeric *Hymn to Dionysus,* esp. 15–21, and Aghion, Barbillon and Lissarrague (1996), pp. 62–4.
127. Hesiod, *Theogony* 453–491, and Aghion, Barbillon and Lissarrague (1996), pp. 260–2.
128. Loraux (1995), p. 12; cf. her chapters 1 and 2.
129. Cf. in particular *Phaedrus* 251d–c and my chapter III on preformationism and Plato.
130. *LSJ* s.v. ὠδίς.
131. Cf. Loraux (1995), p. 15; cf. *Republic* 490b.
132. Cf. my chapters I and II.
133. See above.
134. Cf. Soph. *Ajax* 148–161, where the chorus discusses the verbal prowess of Odysseus, or 1250–63 when Agamemnon verbally attacks Teuker's pedigree, and 1290–1307 for Teuker's rebuttal; cf. Demonsthenes LIV, *contra Konon*, 18–19, where he cites an example of verbal 'flyting;' cf. too Aristophanes, *Frogs* 756 sq., 849 sq. and *Knights* 1399–1400.
135. (2001), p. 181.
136. (1980), pp. 132–3.
137. Hesk (2002). Cf. Herzfeld (1985) p. 233, who, in ref. to modern Kretan practices derived from ancient ones, indicates that 'men (and to some extent women as well) constantly challenge social tolerance because challenge itself is a social norm'.
138. *Laws* 934d–936b.
139. On the selection and education of these Guardians of the Laws, cf. *Laws* 968c.
140. *Laws* 908a, 909a, 951d sq., 961a sq. and 968a
141. For the 'Parable of the Cave', see *Rep.* 514 sq., 532b sq (and cf. 539e).
142. Cf. my chapter VII.

143. Self-mastery, defined along similar lines, dominates Aristotle's *Nikomachaean Ethics* as well as many later Stoic doctrines.

NOTES TO CHAPTER V

1. (1977), p. 25.
2. Plato, *Laws* 627e4–628a4.
3. (1997), p. 20. Cf. *LSJ* s.v. οἶκος.
4. Cf. my chapter I.
5. *Republic* 416d sq., 420a, 422d, 464b sq., 543b.
6. The rules for a 'best' state would, quite naturally, differ. 'For that state and constitution come first', he asserts, 'and the laws are the best, where there is observed as much as possible throughout the whole of the city an old saying; as it is said: "friends have all things truly in common."' ὡς ὄντως ἐστὶ κοινὰ τά φίλων—*Laws* 739b7–c2; a Pythagorean maxim often cited by Plato; cf. *Rep.* 424a and cp. Eurip. *Orest.* 725.
7. μίαν ὅτι μάλιστα πόλιν—739d3 sq.
8. 739e3–7.
9. Cf. Pomeroy (1997), p. 62. Plato's narrator agrees with this view, see below.
10. 368e sq. This is the same reason given for composing the *Republic* as a quest to define Justice.
11. πατρίοις νόμοις—680a8–9; see below on ancient 'matriarchy'.
12. Engels (1977), p. 25, concurs.
13. 680b sq. He quotes Homer (*Odyssey* IX. 112 sq.), in reference to this type of 'constitution' being in use amongst the Kyklopes.
14. Δοκοῦσί μοι πάντες τὴν ἐν τούτῳ τῷ χρόνῳ πολιτείαν δυναστείαν καλεῖν—680b sq. Cp. Aristotle, *Pol.* 1252b 17 sq.
15. The *Kallipolis* in the *Republic* would seem to transcend this mundane limitation.
16. 917a1–7. Cp. 690a sq and see my chapter VI.
17. 690a4–6; καὶ ὅλως γονέας ἐκγόνων ἄρχειν ἀξίωμα ὀρθὸν πανταχοῦ ἂν εἴη;
18. E.g. Dem. XXIII.11; Ps. Dem. II.21–22; Isok. IV.63; Isai. IV.4.
19. (1993), p. 60.
20. The Athenian Stranger, as we saw previously, says that 'if a native should stray to some other craft rather than the cultivation of virtue then the city wardens will engage in chastising him with reproaches and dishonours until they restore him to his proper course' (847a5–b2); Cf. Xen. *Lak. Pol.* VII.1–3 sq. for a comparable Spartan practice.
21. Cf. my chapters III and IV for more on the uses of shame in the *Laws*.
22. Cf. Aghion, Barbillon and Lissarrague (1996), pp. 299–300.
23. (1983), p. 15.
24. The Athenian Stranger mentions 'private shrines of ancestral gods' (ἱδρύματα ἴδια πατρῴων θεῶν) at which it is pious to worship 'according to law' (*kata nomon*) at 717b5. The proscription against private shrines at 909d6–7 is stated as ἱερὰ μηδὲ εἰς ἐν ἰδίαις οἰκίαις ἐκτήσθω. In the first instance, in Book IV, the Athenian Stranger may be referring to privately constructed shrines in public places. This, admittedly, seems incompatible with a state in which 'private' is meant to be expunged as much as possible—but it is certainly not out of the question. It could also be that

Plato had changed his mind by the time he wrote the proscription in Book IX. However, whether Magnesian citizens are allowed to construct 'private' shrines in public or not, it seems quite clear that neither ἱδρύματα ἴδια πατρῴων θεῶν nor ἱερὰ are to be permitted within the private sphere.

25. Cf. Burkert (1987), p. 11.
26. (1968), p. 178.
27. It also seems unlikely that he is borrowing this idea from Sparta since, as Patterson (1998), p. 250, n. 12, says 'Plato's silence on any such Spartan system of indivisibility and inalienability of *klēros* while setting up just such a system in the *Laws* (in the presence of a Spartan) is strong evidence that there was none'.
28. ἐπίσκοποι δ' ἔστωσαν τούτων ἃς εἱλόμεθα γυναῖκες; these are discussed in greater detail later in the next chapter.
29. There is some evidence of a similar practice in ancient Krete (*Code of Gortyn* IV.32sq.); cf. too Aristotle, *Pol.* II.2, 5, (1263a) and Plut. *Moralia* 238e–f.
30. In Xenophon's *Oikonomikos* (VII.24), Ischomachos expresses the notion that women 'naturally' have more affection for newborn and young children than do men.
31. Plato experienced at least two households in his youth between the time that his father, Ariston, died and his mother remarried her uncle, Pyrilampes. The main one would have been Pyrilampes', the other Ariston's and/or possibly Periktione's father's (or her own, which had been Ariston's?). Cf. Davies (1971), pp. 332–5.
32. (1990), p. 127.
33. This is discussed in chapter III and elsewhere.
34. Cf. Loraux (1984) p. 23 and Blundell (1995), p. 135, for Athena's robes and Sealey (1990), p. 37, for those of Artemis.
35. (1998), pp. 36–7; cf. *Ath. Pol.* LIV.7, for the *polis'* organisation and supervision of these affairs.
36. Cf. Slabs V and VIII in particular. Whilst the male figures in the procession are represented as manly warriors, the women are characteristically associated with symbols of domesticity. Hephaistos sits on Athena's left hand side and highlights the association between technology and the crafts along with these two deities' pseudo-sexual relationship. Hephaistos had once tried to rape her and, as she rejected him, he ejaculated onto her leg. She wiped it off (symbolically) with a piece of wool and cast it to the ground from which sprang Erichthonios. Cf. Blundell (1998), p. 65 for a discussion of this myth and Kearns (1998) pp. 100–101 for the association between the ritual of the Panathenaia and the legendary daughters of Kekrops who, as the originators of the craft, first presented the *peplos* to Athena.
37. (1998), pp. 63–4.
38. Cf. Aristophanes, *Lys.* 575sq for her analogy between statecraft and women's customary labour of carding and weaving wool; cf. 712 sq.
39. Unlike Athens and elsewhere, we are told that domestic pursuits such as weaving and carding were not considered appropriate occupations for citizens (Xen. *Lak. Pol.* I.3–4). But this seems an odd proposition and may refer to idealised or imagined customs rather than actual law. Cf. *Laws* 806a5–c1, for the Athenian Stranger's view that they did engage in spinning and weaving.
40. 805e–806c.
41. *Oikonomikos* VII.10 sq. Clearly, Ischomachus 'model' wife represents an idealised (and particularly masculine) view of how women citizens of a certain class ought to

behave once married. But this view may have been quite popular amongst upper-class males.

42. *Lysistrata*, 492–7. Aristophanes' attitudes toward women, like Xenophon's, should be read in terms of the context of his class and sex.

43. XXXII.10, 12–18

44. Demosthenes XLI.17–19

45. I.170

46. (1999), p. 372. Cf. Xen. *Lak. Pol.* I.5; Plut. *Lyk.* XV.7–10.

47. Cf. Millender (1999), pp. 370–3 and below.

48. 918d–919b, perhaps recollecting Plato's experiences in Sicily.

49. 'Yet if someone—which should never happen nor ever will—were to compel (it is laughable to say but nonetheless it will be said) the best men everywhere to be inn-keepers for a period of time, or to engage in retail trade or to practice one of such like things, or likewise if one were to compel [the best] women, out of some necessity of fate, to partake of such a way of life, we would know how friendly and dear each of these things is, and if it should happen according to an uncorrupted principle, all such innkeepers would be honoured as in the guise of a mother or a nurse' (918d8–e7). Is this 'morally responsible capitalism'?

50. The Athenian Stranger says that none of the citizens who hold a share of land amongst the 5040 hearths 'is to be a retail trader, either voluntarily or involuntarily, or a merchant or a waiting-servant or to render services whatsoever to private individuals who do not return to him equal services—except for a father and mother and to those household members of a younger generation and to all those elder than himself [or herself], as many as are free and freely served' (919d3–e2).

51. LVII.31

52. (1998), pp. 6–13.

53. (1981), p. 168.

54. (1988), p. 170. She and Derrida are specifically discussing the *Phaedrus* but these arguments apply to Plato's works in general. Cf. my chapters III and IV. For other objections to Derrida here, cf. Ferrari (1987).

55. But cf. my chapters IV and VII for 'birth in beauty' and the myth of 'the two horses'.

56. Pomeroy (1997), p. 33. New Comedy (Men. *Pk.*1012–15) offers a brief formula for marriage that probably applied in the Hellenic age as well as the Hellenistic: FATHER: I give you my daughter to sow for the purpose of producing legitimate children. GROOM: I take her. FATHER: I also give you a dowry of three talents. GROOM: I take it, too, gladly. Cf. also *Sam.* 897–900, *Dysk.* 842–5.

57. Chodorow (1978), p. 194, points out that, in a patriarchal society, a girl is often encouraged to identify with her mother's role from an early age so, when married, 'she *becomes* the mother (phylogenetically the all-embracing sea, ontogenetically the womb)'.

58. (1997), p. 20. Plato's mother, Periktione, remarried her paternal uncle, Pyrilampes, after the death of Ariston; on this cf. Davies (1971), pp. 332–5 and above.

59. Pseud. Dem. XLIV.18, indicates that 'whatever woman is pledged on just terms to be a wife by her father, or by her brother who has the same father, or by her paternal grandfather, the children born of her shall be legitimate'.

60. (1995), p. 126. This is in contrast to funerary representations where 'the handshake is a symbol not only of unity and of farewell or greeting but also . . . of the equality of those involved'.

61. Hdt. VI.122.

62. Plut. *Kimon* IV.7; also cf. *ibid* 9 for Kimon himself, and Dem. XL. 27 for an account of a man said to be in love with his wife; for Peisistratos' daughter see Plut. *Moralia* 189c.

63. Cf. *Lak. Pol.* IX.5 on the alleged degrees of freedom allowed Spartan women and I.5–10 on wife-sharing. But, as Cartledge (2001), p. 121, says, 'we cannot automatically infer that ownership of property conferred on Spartan women personal independence, let alone political power'. A Spartan *kurios* may have acted in the same or similar capacity in making betrothals as his Athenian counterpart. Cf. Millender (1999), p. 360 sq. on Spartan women's perceived 'liberation'.

64. (1990), p. 155 sq. Cf. Lefkowitz and Fant (1982), pp. 33–4 on these Kretan laws.

65. Cf. Dem. LIX.122 where it is said that 'marriage consists in this, that one has children and one introduces sons to one's *phrateres* and to one's fellow demesmen. But one gives daughters as one's own in marriage to men'. The supposed Spartan custom of youths 'capturing' their brides is not based upon any Classical evidence although, as Hodkinson (2000), p. 98, says 'matrimonial rites may have included a symbolic marriage by capture (Plut. *Lyk.* XV.3)'; cf. Hdt. VI.65 on King Demaratos who carried off the woman betrothed to his kinsman Leotychidas. Herodotos and Aristotle regard this anecdote as indicative that, as Hodkinson (*ibid.*) says, 'it was Leotychidas' method of acquiring a wife which was the norm and that marriages were typically preceded by a betrothal arranged by the brides parents or next-of-kin'.

66. Rankin (1964), p. 85. Contrast Hdt. I.196–99 for the alleged Babylonian 'wife market' and women's participation in temple-bound concubinage as examples of Platonic-style theorizing on curious ways of organising society and marriage projected onto an ethnographic example (see also IV.19 on the Issedonian women). But, as Pembroke (1967), pp. 4–5, says 'marriage in Babylon, as Herodotos describes it, does seem to require the market-place . . . even so, he cannot bring himself to set the scene in one; he has the girls rather vaguely "collected together in one place" instead'. Babylonian temple prostitution, as Harrison (2000), p. 217, says 'is described by Herodotus as "the most shameful of customs" (ὁ δὲ δὴ αἴσχιστος τῶν νόμων, I.199)'. Cf. Burkert (1990), p. 24 on some of the distinctions between ethnography and moral relativism in Hdt.

67. (772e7–e4). If the wealthy only marry the wealthy and the poor marry only the poor, in time the division between the classes will be so great as to cause tensions and possibly class conflicts that Plato's narrator seeks to avoid (cf. 744a8–745b1).

68. *Rep.* 459d–460b. Cf. *Republic* 546a1–547a6 for the infamous 'Nuptial Number;' there are numerous works dealing with this complex passage among which include, but are not limited to, Aristotle, *Pol.* E 12. 1316a4 sq.; Macrobius *Somn. Scip.* II 11. 10 on the so called 'Great Year' or 'Cycle'; Proclus *In. Remp.* II p. 38; cf. Adam (1891), p. 79. Cf. Hesk (2000), pp. 152–4, 159–62 on the Platonic 'Myth of Metals' as propagandistic deception and persuasive rhetoric.

69. Cf. *Laws* 684d for the difficulty of land distribution; there are 5040 (a number divisible by 1, 2, 3, 4, 5, 6, 7, 8, 9, 10, 12 etc. without remainder) administrative units

for land-holdings by the citizens of the city (737e); each lot supports one family, the number of families is meant to remain at more or less a constant of 5040 (740b–c): one of the male children will inherit the holding and the females are given in marriage where appropriate; excess offspring will be obliged to emigrate (740d–e, 741). As Purcell (1990), p. 45, points out, 'instances of "overpopulation" [in the ancient world] causing emigration are more plausibly to be attributed to resource fluctuations or to increase in community size through immigration than to demographic increase (and that is all the famous passage of advice about *apoikiai* in Plato's *Laws* 4.707d–708d means)'. As we saw in my chapters II and III, the Athenian Stranger has provided safeguards against immigration being a problem.

70. This appears to correspond, at least in some respects, with Xenophon's account of Spartan principles on land distribution, cf. Xen. *Lak. Pol.* I.9 and VII.3–6. Polybios (c.205–c.120 B.C.E.) also indicates that Spartan land laws were such that 'no citizen may own more than another, but all possess an equal share' (*Hist.* VI.45, 3–5). However, such equality was not always the case; cf. Cartledge (2001), pp. 121 sq. Polybios drew upon Xenophon's account of the Spartan laws for his histories and so, like much of Xenophon's ethnographic data on Sparta, one must take it with a grain of salt.

71. (1964), p. 90.

72. 771e5–772a3; cp. 672e5, 656c2, and for the role assigned to pleasure and festivals in the theory of education see 653c sq.

73. Cf. *GH* pp 171 sq., for a discussion of (sic) 'heterosexual' *erōs* and marriage, cf. pp. 163, 167, on this in regard to Plato's philosophy.

74. See below on seduction and incitement to passion. Cf. too *GH* pp. 171 sq. for more on this.

75. Isaios I.39 concerning the obligation to arrange marriages for orphaned cousins; cf. Lysias (born c. 445B.C.E.) XIII.45 and XII.21 for views on the wrongful deprivation of marriage.

76. Cf. 707d–708d and 740c4 and e6.

77. 923e4–6. This compares well with ancient Hebrew law where, 'If a man die, and have no sons, then ye shall cause his inheritance to pass unto his daughter' (*Numbers* 27.8), she then passes the inheritance on to her offspring via her husband (whether of the same clan or not—*ibid.* 36.3, 36.8).

78. Stears (1998), p. 116, the *anchisteia* is a bilateral kinship grouping centred on an individual and extending to the children of cousins. Cf. my chapter VI for more on this.

79. 'The fact that, even in Classical times when succession was through males, the claim of a woman, who had no brothers, to the family land remains paramount points directly to a time when all property descended through women', writes Willetts (1967), p. 24. See below and elsewhere on the *mutterrecht*.

80. Such as the Lykians of Asia Minor who allegedly named themselves after their mothers, I.173sq. On the Amazons, cf. my chapter VI.

81. Channel 4 (2002a). Varying theories suggest that they were women's teaching tools for sex-education, that they were a type of pornography for men or, possibly, cultic artefacts. As with the so-called *mutterrecht*, one should be careful about 'xeroxing' modern views onto the past. According to this programme on Channel 4, prehistoric societies were probably more sexually 'equal' than one-sided. The subjugation

of women's labour of childbirth seems to have begun with the formation of cities and the advent of the large-scale ownership of private property (e.g. the house).

82. (1967), p. 1.

83. (1993), p. 240. Cf. *Menex.* 237e4 and 239a1–2. Attic soil is 'both their earth and their mother', so Athenian *andres* are all 'brothers, children of the same mother'. As Loraux (1993), p. 121, indicates 'the Attic earth is never only "mother" in the funeral orations, but, through a return in full force of the paternal signifier, it is always both "mother and father" (*mētēr kai patris:* mother and earth of fathers)'.

84. 680a8–9. He says that some of the 'patriarchal constitutions' would occasionally have mothers in charge but he does not seem to regard this as having been the norm.

85. Cf. von Bachofen (1897) for more on this theory of matrilineal descent.

86. The list of heirs and their order of succession is as follows: 1.) A brother of the deceased by the same father (but not necessarily by the same mother); 2.) A brother of the deceased by the same mother (but not necessarily by the same father); 3.) A son of the deceased's brother (providing that he and the heiress are of the appropriate ages); 4.) A son of the deceased's sister (same guidelines as #3 above); 5.) A brother of the deceased's father; 6.) A son of #5 above; 6.) A son of the sister of the deceased's father; Pomeroy (1975), pp. 168–9, says that 'such endogamous arrangements were common among propertied Athenians'. The inclusion of the maternal brother is contrary to Attic law. The *Code of Gortyn* offers a very similar line of succession excluding the maternal relatives (Col. VII, 15–27). On the marriage of ancient heiresses to cousins cf. Davies (1971), p. 3716b. Also see Thompson (1967), pp. 273–82.

87. Sealey (1990), p. 29. Cf. Lefkowitz and Fant (1982), p. 34.

88. Cf. *Laws* 924e2–925a1, where 'the males come before the females in any single generation'.

89. 925a2–5. Herm. (*Juris Dom.* 27), reckoning this situation to be the same as is that referred to at Aristophanes' *Vesp.* 578, deems Plato's legislation to be in keeping with Attic precedent.

90. (1921), p. 527.

91. I.e. not part of her *anchisteia.*

92. Cf. my chapters I and esp. VI.

93. (1977), p. 323.

94. 16–19. Some, like the character of Theagenes wife (64), might consult Hekate before leaving the house.

95. (1978), p. 254.

96. (2001), p. 116; see below on the Spartans.

97. Cf. *Laws* 772a7–774a1, 783b2–c4

98. Cf. Chodorow (1978), p. 79 sq., for her discussion of some of the self-replicating features, specifically in terms of sex-roles, of the patriarchal family.

99. Cf. McKinnon (1982), p. 543 and my chapter I.

100. 774a3–c2. Cf. Clem. Alex. *Strom.* ii. 423a, concerning this law, who calls the monetary penalty τροφὴν γυναικός, and suggests that there would be magistrates' fees to be paid in addition; Strabo (c.67 B.C.E.–19 C.E.) 10.482, citing Ephorus of Kyme (early 4th century B.C.E.), says that Kretan youths were customarily obliged to marry at the same time upon graduation from the *agela* of childhood. Persistent bachelorhood could conceivably incur psychological penalties from one's age-mates or society

in general. The *Code of Gortyn* (VII 29–47) decrees that a judge must compel a male heir, who is of age and unwilling to marry, to wed his legally betrothed πατροίοκος within a two month time span. Nonetheless, since it is left to the family of the heiress to pursue the matter in the courts, presumably, under some circumstances, a would-be bachelor might escape any restrictions.

101. The subject of when to marry can be observed as part of a broader cultural discourse represented in surviving texts. In the *Republic*, Sokrates had favoured twenty-five and older for males and Aristotle seems to have supported thirty-seven or a little bit younger for males and eighteen for females; Aristotle, *Pol.* VII.14, 6 (1335a). Cf. also 721b, 785b; *Republic* 460e. Hesiod (c. 700 B.C.E.—*Works and Days* 695 sq.) recommended that women marry about the age of eighteen or nineteen.

102. At age fifty-nine, an Athenian's military service ended and he was therefore considered an 'old man' indicates Lacey (1968), p. 107. Retirees were considered ἔξω τοῦ καταλόγου and they became arbitrators for a year (*Ath. Pol.* LIII. 4), but did not simply vanish thereafter—e.g. Sokrates served as president of the Assembly in 405 at the age of about sixty-four (Xen. *Mem.* I.1, 18 and Plato *Apology* 32b–c).

103. Cf. my chapter VI and below.

104. But cf. Dem. XXVIII.15–16 and XXIX.43 for some exceptions.

105. (1993), p. 182. Cf. Isaios VIII.18–20, on the character of private marriage celebrations.

106. The importance of such a civic kinship-group which is not necessarily indicative of actual kinship, whether in Magnesia or Athens, connects well with Engels (1977), p. 176, who indicates that the evolving social institutions within the city-state had 'created a public force which was now no longer simply identical with the whole body of armed people . . . it divided the people for public purposes, not by groups of kinship, but by *common place of residence*'.

107. The Apatouria was associated with the boy's sacrifice on the same day when they cut their hair signifying the end of childhood (cp. Isac. VI. 64, VIII. 19); some later sources suggest that boys and girls may have been introduced into the *phratries* during the Hellenistic period or in cities other than Athens in the Classical (Julius Polydeuces of Naucratis [lat. Pollux, end of the 2nd century C.E.] VIII, 107, and the *Suda* [10th century Byzantine Greek historical encyclopedia of the ancient Mediterranean world, derived from the scholia to critical editions of canonical works and from compilations by yet earlier authors] pp. 265–6). For more on *phratries*, cf. Lambert (1993), 143–61; Wade-Gery (1931), pp. 129–143; also, Sadao Ito (1981), pp, 35–60, rejects Pollux's statement that the the *gamelia* was sacrificed by members of *phratries* when girls reached puberty. Plato (*Laws* 785a) mentions that Magnesian women will be inducted into *phratries*. The Byzantine scholars may have misinterpreted Isaios III. 73, where there is some indication that, under certain circumstances, women could be 'introduced' to a *phratry*. This discussion is taken up and expanded upon in my next chapter.

108. Cf. Aristotle, *Ath. Pol.* 26.4 for Perikles' famous marriage law that insisted upon a form of pedigree for Athenian citizenship.

109. VIII.39 and XII.17–19.

110. Cf. Cartledge (2001), pp. 119, 120. Spartan marriages, as will be discussed later in this chapter in the context of adultery, by their very nature do not form typical family structures as one would expect to find in ancient Athens or Gortyn.

111. ἐν ἀκμαῖς σωμάτων . . . *Lak. Pol.* I.6–8; cf. Plut. *Lys.* XXX.7.
112. Xenophon's reports on the Spartans may or may not represent the customs and practices established by the reformer Lykourgos. However, by the time that Xenophon wrote his account (and certainly by the time Plato was writing the *Laws*) many things had changed. 'If anyone should ask me', writes Xenophon (*Lak. Pol.* XIV.1–2), 'whether now the laws of Lykourgos seem to me still to remain unchanged, by Zeus, I could not say that with confidence'. Many of the Athenian Stranger's borrowings may actually be from a Sparta that no longer existed except in memory or possibly in imagination only.
113. *Lyk.* XV.3, *Kleom.* I
114. (2001), p. 116.
115. *Ibid.*
116. 1265a13. At 1276a29, Babylon 'it is said, had been captured for two whole days before some of the inhabitants knew of the fact'.
117. (1990), p. 163.
118. Hodkinson (1994), p. 204; Plutarch's account being largely influenced by Xenophon's idealised Spartan texts and probably Plato's dramatic dialogues as well. Cf. Hodkinson (2000), pp. 44–5 on this and for Plato's alleged influence on third-century Spartan revolutionaries.
119. *Laws* 929e9–930a5. They are to be matched with mates who have more complementary temperaments.
120. England (1921), p. 547, note on 930a6; cp. also *Laws* 773c5.
121. MacDowell (1978), p. 88.
122. (1990), p. 36. For divorces initiated by women cf. e.g. Dem. XXX.15,17, 26, 31; Isaios III.8.7.
123. The elder Demosthenes, displaying a marked difference between his city and the Athenian Stranger's, had betrothed both his wife to his sister's son and his 5-year-old daughter to his brother's son *while he still* lived, Dem. XXVII.5, XXVIII.15, XXIX.43. It was not uncommon for an Athenian husband to make arrangements for his wife's subsequent remarriage in their wills. On this cf. Dem. XXX.7, LVII.41 and Isae. II.7–9. For other examples of the remarriage of widows cf. Thompson (1972), pp. 211–25.
124. Dem. XXXVI.8.
125. *Code of Gortyn*, II.45–53.
126. Sealey (1990), pp. 64–65.
127. μὴ μητρυὰν ἐπαψόμενον—930b3–6; England (1921), p. 548, says of this passage that 'the participial clause here contains the more important verb; "spare the children a stepmother!"'
128. Golden (1990), p. 143; cf. Hesiod, *Works and Days* 825 and, Menander, *Monos.* 127, for the proverb that good days are 'mothers' and bad days 'stepmothers', and the negative qualities associated with a 'stepmother of ships'.
129. XII.5.
130. XXXII.17.
131. 302–309. It is probably this passage from Euripides to which the Athenian Stranger is making reference at 930b3–6.
132. Hdt. IV.154.2; cf. Eur. *Alk.* 313–319.
133. *De Gen. Anim.* III.759a36.

134. τῷ τε οἴκῳ καὶ τῇ πόλει—930b6–c1.
135. γυναῖκες ἐπιμελουμένες τῶν γάμων—930c1.
136. *Code of Gortyn* VIII.42–IX.17.
137. (1997), p. 169.
138. Cf. Ogden (1996) and *Laws* 930d1–e2 for an account, albeit brief, of how rulings on the status of children are to be decided 'when there is no dispute about the parentage of offspring'. The Athenian Stranger appears to be not particularly fearful, as one might expect from a typical Athenian of his day, about an infestation of illegitimate offspring. Of course, the author of the *Laws* was not typical in many respects and he either did not anticipate this to be a problem in his hypothetical state or he thought that existing institutions (like the Marriage Guardians) could easily cope with it.
139. Pomeroy (1997), p. 178.
140. Strauss (1993), p. 65.
141. Cf. *Rep.* 547b–548b on the perceived overthrow of these values that characterised Spartan decline. Burnett (1976), p. 3 and plate 1.1, discusses the use of weighted metal ingots as a means of exchange amongst cultures of the ancient near East and Early Roman transactions that were conducted through the use of un-cast bronze lumps (the so-called *aes rude*) or bronze bars with a large component of iron (the *aes signatum*).
142. *Lak. Pol.* VI. 5–6; Polybios, *Hist.* IV, 45, 4–6, also says that money was esteemed of no value among the Spartans. Yet this apparently diminished significance of wealth probably represents an *ethos* from an idealised past that either never happened or was no longer in practice by the time of Plato's *Laws*. As even Xenophon (*Lak. Pol.* XIV.3–4) reports, 'in former days they were afraid to be discovered possessing gold; but nowadays there are some who boastfully display their property'.
143. (2000), p. 167. Sparta minted no coinage of her own until the 260s or 250s. As he says, 'several sources from the fourth century onwards claim that gold and silver coinage issued by other states was excluded by Lykourgos and that this prohibition remained in force until 404 when the booty sent to Sparta by Lysander was admitted for public use'.
144. Svoronos (1906), pp. 192–202 suggests that they might have taken the form of a roasting spit, or *obelos*—hence the subsequent use of the related term *obolos* in Southern Greek coinage systems. Cf. Hodkinson (2000), pp. 162–4.
145. Hodkinson (2000), p. 98; cf. Patterson (1998), p. 250.
146. *Mor.* 227 sq., Hermippos fr. 87 *apud* Athenaios 555c. According to Plut. *Mor.* 242b, 'a poor [Spartan] girl, being asked what dowry she brought to the man who married her, replied, "the family *sōphrosynē*"'.
147. Hodkinson (2000), p. 44–5, 72 and 93–4 for third-century Spartan revolutionary connections with Plato (and esp. the *Laws*). Cf. Cartledge (2001), pp. 119–120 on Aristotle's criticism of Kretan and Spartan dowries and inheritance laws
148. Hodkinson (2000), p. 99. The *Code of Gortyn* (VI.9–12) also refers to the transfer of property to a bride by her father and indicates that, as in Sparta, it remained under her control.
149. Cartledge (1981), p. 98, argues that 'what Aristotle calls "large dowries" were really . . . marriage-settlements consisting of landed property together with any movables that a rich father (or mother) saw fit to bestow on a daughter'. Cf. Pomeroy (1997), p.

55; for Hellenistic and Roman sources on Spartan 'dowries' cf. Plut. *Mor.* 227f–228a, *Lys.* XXX.5–6; Ael. VH VI.6; Ath. XIII.555c and Justin III.3.8.

150. ὕβρις δὲ ἧττον γυναιξὶ; Justinian (iii.3) seems to have adopted Plato's attitude and speaks of dowries as 'frena'.

151. Saunders (1970), p. 254, n. 14.

152. (1992), p. 480; cf. too *ibid.* n. 119.

153. (1987), p. 14.

154. XI.40; III.49.

155. XXVII, 42–5; cf. Archippe's huge dowry, Dem. XLV. 28. It consisted of 'a talent from Peparethos, a talent from here, a lodging house worth 100 *minai*, female slaves, the gold jewellery and other things of hers'.

156. Letter XIII, 361d–e.

157. *Code of Gortyn* Col. X. 14–20

158. *ibid.* Col. III, 40–44; also for Athenian regulations on women, regardless of their social class, who reclaimed their dowries cf. Isae. III.8 and III.78. For examples of widows' dowries, cf. Dem. XXVII. 5, 13–14, 13 with *id.* XLV, 28; Isae. VIII.8; Lysias XXXII.6; and see Hypereides (390–322B.C.E.), *Lykophron*, I.5 where a widow's *kurios* (her brother) arranged her marriage, but her child's guardian, who was administrating her first dowry, provided her with the dowry.

159. (1990), p. 29.

160. (1968), p. 109.

161. According to Plutarch (*Moralia* 227 sq), the Spartan lawgiver had forbidden dowries by legislation believing, much as the Athenian Stranger, that character rather than wealth should determine the choice of a bride.

162. Cf. Pomeroy (1997), p. 43. Hodkinson (2000), pp. 98–103, on this complex passage from the *Politics* of Aristotle. He indicates, p. 103, that 'Even if one rejects my hypothesis of universal female inheritance and prefers to view landed dowries as voluntary gifts, it is apparent that by the fourth century marriage-settlements were often quite large'. See next note.

163. *Politics* II.9.1269b12–1270a6. Aristotle, in his statement about 'heiresses' and 'dowries', could have been referring, says Blundell, 'somewhat inaccurately, to two types of female inheritance, one where the daughter inherited the entire estate, and one where she received a share of it on marriage' (1995), p. 156.

164. As mentioned, 5040 is the smallest number that may be divided by the numbers 1, 2, 3, 4, 5, 6, 7, 8, 9, 10 and 12 without a remainder. This arithmetical peculiarity makes an easy division for administrative purposes. But the number of citizens is huge for an ancient *polis*; as Nixon and Price (1990), pp. 162–3 say, 'Plato in certain parts of the *Laws* takes over current practices from Athens or other states; with the number of citizens he is led by theoretical principles to offer a number much larger than that possible for the majority of tribute payers'. This was a concern for Aristotle in the *Politics* (see above), but Magnesia's monetary policies are other than traditional and may function without the need for so many tribute payers. 'Tribute', as such, comes in the form of food for common meals and labour for service, building and maintenance. These will be provided by agrarian and municipal slaves owned by the *polis*.

165. *Laws* 740d; the 'highest and most distinguished' official is to be appointed to oversee population control. Cf. also 818d8, *Protagoras* 345d, and Simonides Fr. 5. Cf.

Hippokrates (4th B.C.E.) *Nature of Women* 98, for herbal methods of contraception available and, also, Lefkowitz and Fant (1982), pp. 88–9.

166. 740c4–e6.

167. ... παίδων καταλείποντα ἀεὶ τῷ θεῷ ὑπηρέτας ἀνθ᾽ αὑτοῦ παραδιδόναι.— 773e5–774a1.

168. Cf. my chapters IV and VII.

169. ' ... when they arrive at the appropriate age, a husband is wedded to a wife, as a matter of personal preference (κατὰ χάριν), and a wife to a husband, and for their remaining time they live piously and justly, being staunchly true to their first love-contracts' (840d6–e1). Cf. Eur. *Hel.* 190.

170. Cp. Hdt. II.64 and IV.180 for a contrasting animalistic analogy. At II.64, he indicates that 'only the Egyptians and the Greeks' do not behave like animals since they forbade sexual intercourse in temples (e.g. unlike the Babylonians and other barbarians). At IV.180, he discusses the savage Machyles and Auses (tribes near Libya) who share their women in common 'like animals'. Cf. Rosellini and Saïd (1978), p. 965 on Herodotos' slanted ethnography of 'savage' promiscuity amongst foreign peoples and cf. my chapter VII for more on this analogy in Plato. Some have interpreted Egyptian archaeology to suggest that they placed less emphasis on virginity and same-sex intercourse than the Athenians of Plato's era (Channel 4, 2002b).

171. Cf. Hesk (2000), pp. 153–6, 159–62 on Platonic *pharmaka*. In contrast to Plato, Diogenes the Cynic, in his hypothetical constitution, considered promiscuity with mutual consent to be the most satisfactory sexual arrangement and he regarded the sexual act (as with eating, masturbation and excretion) as not especially private (Diogenes Laertes VI.72, 97). On comparable modes of sexual propaganda cf. Xen. *Lak. Pol.* I.7–9 for alleged Spartan wife swapping and, again, on Herodotos who portrayed barbarian cultures as being sexually promiscuous, cf. I.203, III.101, IV.180 and also Rosellini and Saïd (1978), pp. 955–66.

172. Cf. my chapter VII on the issue of same-sex liaisons.

173. Rhodes (1981), p. 331, MacDowell (1978), p. 89–90 and Harrison (1971), pp. 13–17; cf. Dem. XXIII, Aristotle, *Ath. Pol.* LIII, Gell. XV.30.vi and Ath. XIII. Before Perikles' law, the male offspring of such unions could become citizens; afterwards, with emphasis squarely focused on the mother's legitimacy. Such offspring were then regarded as bastards (*nothoi*). Cf. Harrison (1971), pp. 24–8, 61–8 for an assemblage of the evidence on mixed marriages and bastards. The law on citizenship was relaxed, whether officially or otherwise, in the closing years of the Peloponnesian wars (see below).

174. 841d6–e4 ... ὡς ὄντως ὄντα ξενικόν. Some question remains as to whether or not this law has actually been (or will be) passed. The laws on sexual conduct present considerable difficulties in interpretation. For more on this subject, cf. my chapters VI and VII. The prescribed remedy is to make the crime known to the public and thereby, one may interpret, discourage them from further wrongdoing through shame and public censure.

175. 874c2–5.

176. (1992), p. 482; cf. Dem. XXIII.53; and cf. too Morrow (1960), p. 465 sq. and MacDowell (1978), pp. 89, 124 for Athenian parallels.

177. Cf. my chapter VII and below.

178. Cf. Omitowoju (2002), pp. 113–114.

179. Cf. Dover (1974), p. 147 and Pomeroy (1975), p. 87. Cohen (1990), p. 148, indicates, 'whereas modern law focuses on coercive, non-consensual sexual transactions, making rape the pre-eminent sexual delict, Athenian law accords this place of honour to adultery, which is clearly the paradigmatic sexual offence'. But see below.

180. (1997), p. 191. Cf. Harris (1990) for this view of Lysias I.

181. Hdt. II.115.4–5.

182. (1997), p. 191. These sentiments are echoed in Lysias I (32 sq.) where the object of violent assault is said to hate her attacker, but the *psyche* of a woman seduced was regarded as damaged.

183. Sealey (1990), p. 29.

184. *Ibid.* p. 194. As Omitowoju (2002), p. 114 indicates, 'in this punishment we have the social aspect of the offence spelled out to us because the punishment is designed to demonstrate before the whole city, defined in its religious configuration . . . who possesses respectability and who does not'.

185. (1993), p. 279.

186. Cf. my chapters I and VII.

187. Note the use of active and passive language construction—whether in Greek or English: ὁ μὲν οὖν πείσας ὡς ἀναγκάσας ἀδικεῖ, ἡ δὲ πεισθεῖσα ὡς ἀναγκασθεῖσα τῷ λόγῳ μάτην ἀκούει κακῶς (12–13).

188. Croally (1994), p. 155, indicates that Helen 'uses the first, second and last of Gorgias' arguments (as well as some of her own). It was Aphrodite who offered her to Paris (929–31), thus making her abduction a decision of the gods (Gorg. *Hel.* 6.); Paris married her by force (962/*Hel.* 7); and Aphrodite, the goddess of love, is a powerful divinity who cannot be resisted (940, 945–50/*Hel.* 19)'. But Menelaos condemns her claiming (1037) that she went willingly.

189. (1994), p. 157. and even Helen, as Croally pp. 156–7 says, 'explicitly admits that she is talking about the irrational'; Euripides' Hekuba 'ridicules Helen's story of Aphrodite's presence' and 'from the substance of the arguments themselves, it would have been difficult for the audience to decide whom to favour as a winner of the debate (something they may have been able to do with Medea, or Andromache, or Hecuba)'.

190. Dem. LIX.86–7.

191. Hypereides, *Lykophron* I.12–13

192. Aiskhines (I.182–3) indicates that, for an Athenian woman, not being able to dress up for the festivals would have 'made life not worth living'. Cf. Sealey (1990), pp. 28–9.

193. (1997), p. 29; cf. Aiskhines' I.183 again for the observation that Solon wanted to make the life of an adulterous woman 'unliveable'. Cf. Plut. *Sol.* 23, where Solon stops a man from having the right to sell his daughter or sister into slavery 'unless he should find her in [unsanctioned] intercourse with a man'.

194. I.183 sq.

195. Lysias I.33. Plutarch (*Solon* XXIII.2) says that Solon's law decreed that an Athenian girl *seduced* into adultery be sold into slavery as she would no longer be psychologically fit to become a bride.

196. Sealey (1990), p. 29.

197. Cf. Dem. XXIII.53–6; cf. Aristotle, *Ath. Pol.* LVII.3, for lawful killings associated with adultery.

198. Lysias I.49, Ar. *Clouds* 1083, *Wealth* 168.
199. (1997), p. 28.
200. Cf. my chapter III on Aspasia.
201. (1994), p. 1579. Nussbaum cites Dover who 'suggests that loss of semen plays such a large role in folklore and psychopathology that one may wonder whether Plato thought that semen was a nonrenewable resource'. She attests that she received a letter from Prof. Sir Kenneth Dover highlighting this phenomenon but does not include it in her article.
202. Dem. XLVII.53. Diogenes Laertius (II.26) alleged that the Athenians temporarily loosened some of their stringent policies on legitimacy and marital sanctity after the Sicilian disaster and plague of 413, when they were faced with an immediate need to repopulate their state (he says that Sokrates had two wives). Rhodes (1981), p. 331, says that 'the law was still in force in 414 (Ar. Av. 1649–52), but in the last years of the Peloponnesian War it was either annulled or ignored'. The Athenian concern had been and, later, continued to be over legitimacy lest an adulterer impregnate a man's wife and the issuing offspring being reared as if it were a 'proper' heir; cf. Lysias I.33. Cf. MacDowell (1978), p. 91, where he indicates that 'the decree making a concubine's children legitimate, if it did exist, must have been annulled by the end of the fifth century; in the fourth-century, it is clear that only the children of a duly married wife were legitimate'.
203. (1969), p. 123. On the subject of matrimony in Plato's *Laws*, Field says that 'his attitude is in many respects the same as that expressed in the words of our English Prayer Book, so distressingly unromantic to modern taste. The institution of marriage, we read there, is ordained first for the procreation of children, and secondly, as 'a remedy against sin' (p.124). Extra-marital liaisons are not forbidden in Magnesia, although, as we have seen, they are strongly discouraged.
204. Cf. my chapters III and IV.
205. *Lyk.* 49c sq. and Xen. *Lak. Pol.* I.6–10.
206. (2001), p. 125.
207. The only adultery that we know of in ancient Sparta, aside from the literary case of Helen and Alexandros, was the reported instance of Queen Timaea who bore a son fathered by Alkibiades (Plut. *Alk.* XXIII.7–8; *Ages.* III.1–2). Anaxandridas allegedly resorted to bigamy rather than adultery because he had no children by his first wife (Hdt. V.39–41). We do not know to what extent these practices were undertaken by the average Spartiate since it is precisely because they were about nobles that these stories were seen to bear significance enough to be recorded.
208. Pomeroy (1997), p. 56.
209. Polyb. XII.6b5; Strabo VI.3.3 (279–80); but as Pomeroy (1997), p. 56, indicates, this may be an aetiological myth to account for the pre-existing phenomenon of sexual license.
210. *Code of Gortyn*, II.10–27.
211. *Ibid.* II, 10–15;Lacey (1968) p. 113.
212. (1968), p. 114.
213. 917a4–6, cf. my chapter VI.
214. (1978), p. 178.
215. This is a fundamental feature of sex-role stereotyping according to Chodorow (1978), p. 181.

216. *Laws* 928e3–4; ἐν παγκάκων ἤθεσιν ἀνθρώπων γίγνεσθαι.
217. We are not told whether a mother can do this as well.
218. *LSJ* s.v. υἱός and ἄνθρωπος.
219. 929b2–3, her *anchisteia*.
220. Demosthenes XXXIX.39.
221. (1978), p. 91. The *Code of Gortyn* (XI.10–15) reveals that a Kretan procedure existed for disinheriting an *adopted* son but says nothing about disinheriting a natural one. If a Kretan father should wish to disinherit an adopted son, then he must bring his case before an assembly of the people and would be liable to pay ten staters to the disowned in the event that he is successful in his case. The general assembly in Krete would have consisted of many adopted 'relatives' of the would-be orphan whose testimony might be taken as primary evidence. There is no indication in the *Code of Gortyn* that a disowned son would be required to emigrate—but this might have been necessary without a citizen-father as his protector.
222. Golden (1990), p. 110.
223. *Ibid*. Cf. also Aristotle, *Ath. Pol.* 56.6, Ar. *Nub.* 844–846, Xen. *Mem.* I.2.49, Aiskhines III.251. Aristotle recognised the dangers posed by senile *kurioi* and so he recommended retirement around the age of seventy 'when a man begins to lose his vigour' (*Pol.* VII.1335a36). Note that Magnesia's version of this legality requires an official consultation with the Guardians of the Laws before the case can be brought to a magistrate.
224. Apul. *Apol.* XXXVII.1.2, Luc. *Macr.* 24, Plut. *Mor.* 785a, Cic. *Sen.* VII.22.
225. 717b sq., 917a, 927b1 sq.; cp. 680e sq, 690a and 714e.
226. (1993), p. 65.
227. Golden (1990), p. 101.
228. *Contra Leokrates*, 94. Cf. Aiskhines III.252.
229. E.g. Aeschylus. *Supp.* 707–709; Xen. *Mem.* IV.4.20; Dem. XXIV.60; XXV.66; Aeschylus. I.28; Antiphanes fr. 262E; Men. Fr. 715E; Aristotle, *Nic. Eth.* IX.1164b5, 1165a24. This subject of the importance of parental respect is also a primary theme of Aristophanes' *Clouds* and *Wasps*.
230. Powell (1994), p. 276. Cf. II.39 for customs of similar respect ethnographically projected onto Egyptians, Skythians and Hdt. I.131 for the Persians to a lesser extent.
231. Cf. 755a, 951d–e, 952a and 961a on the requisite ages of these. Magnesia's gerontocratic leanings may have something to do with Plato's own advanced age at the time he composed the *Law.*
232. *Mem.* III.5.15. Cf. Hdt. I.30 sq. on Solon's myths of Tellus and his children, along with Kleobis and Biton, as exemplars of ideal parent-child behaviour; cp. II.35–6 for a contrast with alleged Egyptian disrespect for parents.
233. Hesk (2000), p. 145 sees this tactic in Plato's writing as representative of 4th century 'political and legal debate as a discourse transformed by a new technology of rhetoric into an "efficacious discourse" of persuasion—a discourse that always threatened to persuade through deceptive communication rather than truth'. Cf. my chapter II.
234. 'Let it thus be established: everyone shall revere his elder both by deed and word; whosoever, man or woman, exceeds him in age by twenty years he shall regard as a father or a mother, and he shall keep his hands off that person, and he shall ever refrain himself, for the sake of the gods of birth, from all reproductive acts with those

who might be his own bearers and begetters' 879c5–d2; cf. *Rep.* 461d–e for a similar law in the *Kallipolis*. Cf. Diogens Laertius, VII.129 sq. for a similar formulation in Zeno's *Republic*.

235. Cf. 917a1–7 for this hierarchy and above.

236. 880e9–881d7. The Athenian Stranger states at 880e8–9 that ideally this situation should never arise in Magnesia. Fear of the penalties that such offenders earn in Hades should keep them in line (881a3–5)—but the length and elaborateness of his legal formula for dealing with potential parent-beaters suggests a fear that it might nonetheless happen even in the second-best *polis*.

237. Temple robbers and parricides are to be denied interment within tombs in Magnesia (960b). A similar statute existed in ancient Athens whereby temple robbers were said to have been denied burial in all of Attica (Xen. *Hellenika* I.7.22).

238. Not unlike the case of the noble Hippolytos in Euripides' play by the same name (1401–1446)—except that the roles of parent and child are reversed in comparison to the Athenian Stranger's law.

239. E.g., if they were suffering from senility or other mental debilities, as discussed above—928d sq.

240. ... ἡ δὲ ἄδεια ἀναισχυντίαν ἐνέτεκε—701a9. Cf. my chapter III.

241. 701b7–8; cf. *Rep.* 424e.

242. 701b11–14; he indicates that something similar happened to the Titans.

243. 717d8–718a3. Cf. my chapter VI.

244. Cf. Polyb. VI.53.6 on the Roman *imagines* and their propagandistic use in funerals; cf. my chapters III and IV for more on the uses of *aidōs* in Magnesia.

245. (1996), p. 14.

246. 717a4–a7.

247. (1995), p. 128.

248. Thuc. II.34–47.

249. Cf. my chapter II on persuasive rhetoric and *paramyth* in the *Laws*.

250. Thuc. II.43

251. Thuc. II.39–40

252. Although not always. Plato's Sokrates, at *Menex.* 236b, is perhaps as Stadter (1978a), p. 119 says, being 'especially ironic' in suggesting that Aspasia composed the 'Funeral Oration'.

253. Plato took exception, as Stadter (1978a), p. 120, indicates, 'to the contemporary interpretation of a view of empire and democracy'. Cf. my chapters IV and II. On Toynbee's assertion (1972), pp. 90–2, that *Laws* 704a–707c (where he indicates that Magnesia will not organise its economy on naval strength or empire) is a direct criticism of the 'Funeral Oration'; cf. too Macdonald (1959), p. 108, who indicates that a 'comparison of the points made by the Athenian Stranger with passages from the "Old Oligarch" makes it clear enough that Plato is merely airing longstanding conservative prejudices'. There is merit in both arguments.

254. Cf. Pomeroy (1995), p. 111.

255. That is, if men and women sing separate religious songs, then this seems logical; cf. my chapters III and IV on Magnesian music.

256. The Priests and Priestesses of Apollo and the Sun are an exception to this rule cf. my chapter VI for more on these.

257. 958e8–959a1. The upright stone slab or *stele* and its variations was also in use in Classical Athens but comprised only one of many possible styles available, cf. Stears (1995), p. 113.
258. ... ὡς εἰς ἄψυχον χθονίων βωμόν—959d1.
259. 959d3–6. These restrictions of expenditure follow-up the comments which the Athenian Stranger made at 719d–e where he indicated that a poet might praise a costly funeral for a wealthy woman as well as a skimpy funeral for a poor man as both being well-measured 'but one must tell what and how much is a "measured" amount' before it can become law. It is perhaps worth noting that Plato (Letter XIII, 361e) reported a planned expenditure of ten minae for the tomb of his mother, Periktione.
260. On representations of families (and especially of women) in ancient Athenian funerary practices, cf. Osborne (1997), 3–33 and Stears (1995), pp. 113 sq. Cf. Rubinstein (1989), pp. 411–20, for a survey of Athenian funerary monuments in relation to economic class.
261. Cf. Dem. XLIII.62 and Plut. *Solon* 21. Pomeroy (1995), p. 112, discusses these Solonian funerary laws, which bear a striking resemblance to Magnesia's, in greater detail. Cf. my chapter VI for more on this and below.
262. 959e3–5.
263. 'In life itself, what constitutes each of us is nothing other than the soul, but the body following each of us is a semblance; and it is noble to say that the bodies of the deceased are images of the dead, while the being that is really each of us, named the immortal soul, goes off to other gods to give an account, just as the ancestral law says' (959a6–b5). The word he uses here for 'image' (εἴδωλον) was frequently applied by Homer to the souls of the deceased. The underworld deities are sometimes referred to as the 'other' gods such as at *Phaedo* 63b and in Aeschylus, *Supplices* 230–31.

NOTES TO CHAPTER VI

1. Homer, *Iliad* VI.490–493. Cf. Aristophanes, *Lys.* 714, where, like Andromache, when she tried to broach public policy with her husband and he similarly declared, 'war will be the concern of men'.
2. *Laws* 806c4–7
3. Aristophanes, *Lys.* 536–8.
4. *Principia Discordia*, qtd. in Formosa (2002) http://jubal.westnet.com/hyperdiscordia/psycho_metaphysics.html
5. As Cartledge (1981), p. 86, indicates, there was a sort of '"Lakonomania" which infected certain upper-class circles in democratic Athens', and Plato was as much affected by this as Xenophon (but not Aristotle).
6. Cf. chapter III on education.
7. Plutarch, following Xenophon, reports that Spartan women also took up the arts of running, wrestling and throwing the discus (*Lyk.* XIV.2). Cf. Aristophanes, *Lys.* 81 sq. on the Spartan Lampito's comedic characterisation as a 'manly' woman.
8. Much as with Magnesia, slaves and servants relieved Spartan citizen women of many household duties. Unlike Athens and elsewhere, we are told that domestic pursuits such as weaving and carding were not considered appropriate occupations for citizens

(Xen. *Lak. Pol.* I.3–4). Whether this is true or not is debatable. Xenophon may be referring to men only, cf. chapter V.

9. Aristotle, *Pol.* 1270 sq. Indicates that the Spartan women's 'license' was due, in part, to the male army being away for so long at a time and that Lykourgos 'gave up' trying to bring them under control when they resisted his reforms. Whether Aristotle realised it or not, this would also seem to point to their role in homeland defence out of necessity in the absence of the men.

10. 806a5–c1. As Cartledge (2001), p. 113, says, a 'Spartan girl—like her counterparts in other Greek states (cf. Hesiod, *Op.* 520)—resided with her parents until marriage. Specifically, she continued to reside with her mother, for the matricentral character of a Spartan girls' home-life was heavily accentuated by the fact that her father was expected to spend most of his time living communally and in public with his male peers'. See below on the Sauromatians and Amazons.

11. Herodotos' *Histories,* as Harrison (1997), p. 191, indicates, 'suggest the belief in women as "legal minors"' permanently in need of restraint. But, compare this with their capacity for responsibility enshrined in Athenian law as described by Gould (1980), pp. 44–5. Harrison goes on to say that 'when Athenian women (in the dim, distant past) stab to death with their brooches the bearer of the news of the deaths of their husbands . . . the Athenian response is only to change their style of dress from Dorian to Ionian, so that they would no longer wear brooches (V.87.2–3); they could not be trusted to hold back from similar hysterical outbursts (equally perhaps any punishment would have been pointless?)'.

12. 804e. Cf. Hartog (1988), pp. 31–2 and 39.

13. The Skythians reportedly called the Amazons *oiorpata* which means 'killers of men' (Hdt. IV.27). This perhaps recalls Homer's term for them at *Iliad* III.171 sq. and VI.186, which is *antianeirai* and, as Hartog *ibid.* p. 240, indicates, is 'playing on the prefix *anti,* both the "equals" and the "enemies" of males'. Cf. *ibid.* pp. 3 sq. on the 'imaginary Skythians'.

14. Cf. chapter IV for more on Graeco-Asian relations.

15. (1989), p. 132. Cf. Thomas (2000), pp. 61–2 on Herodotos' ethnography of the Skythians and Amazons in terms of ancient medical beliefs about the effects of herbs and types of edible game in relation to the 'humours' and 'bile'. Such regional influences are considered to have affected the particular development of the Amazons. The grass in Skythia was thought to produce more 'bile' than all other 'grasses that we know' (Hdt. IV.58).

16. Cf. Harrison (1997), p. 187.

17. Hippokrates, *Airs, Waters, Places* XVII. Cf. Thomas (2000), p. 88.

18. (1998), p. 171. Cf. Bovon (1963), pp. 580 sq. on modes of 'barbarian' attire and, p. 598 sq. on its reception in Greece as 'decadent' and 'soft'.

19. Except, perhaps to some degree the Spartans. Cf. Hardwick (1996), pp. 173–4 who also discusses the Amazonian/Lakonian female Guardians of *Republic* V.

20. (1988), p. 222.

21. The earliest known Athenian literary reference is probably that at Euripides' *Herakles* 408–419. They also appear on vase paintings from 575 onwards and frequently portray the Amazons in Herakles' 9th labour and Theseus' famous rape of *Hippolyte.* Cf. Tyrrell (1984), pp. 2–3.

22. Aristotle (*Pol.* 1327b18–34) condemns Asiatics as inferior, as does Herodotos (IX.122.3), largely by virtue of their local climate and where they live (e.g. not Greece). Ephorus (Steph. Byz., s.v. *Amazones*) applied similar 'geographical predestination' to the Amazons. Cf. my chapter IV for more on Greeks and barbarians. Cf. Thomas (2000), p. 56. Hardwick (1996), pp. 158, 161 discusses this along with some of the modern associations between Amazons, lesbians and feminists as altogether 'manly' women.

23. (1998), p. 55.

24. Tyrrell (1984), p. 66, says that Amazons 'are beautiful women who arouse men sexually, but their erotic appeal cannot be civilised in marriage, its proper sphere, and so is loose, socially unproductive, and dangerous'. But they are 'civilised' through conquest and marriage in popular art and myth, see below.

25. Perhaps, as Harrison (1997), pp. 186–7, says, 'we identify a handful of heroines [in Herodotos], Medea, Artemisia, Antigone, and see them as evidence that Greek women envisaged the possibility of their own emancipation; male stereotypes of women show their fear of the opposite sex, their (unconscious) acknowledgement that the oppression of women was wrong, that it could not ultimately be sustained'.

26. Cf. Homer, *Iliad* VI.490–493 (quoted at the beginning of this chapter) and cf. my chapters I and V.

27. In the *Laws*, female Magnesians must adopt a 'masculine' attitude toward sex in terms of self-control and mastery of their desires. This sort of reversal is not considered 'unnatural' but more like an upgrade from emotional femininity to rational masculinity, see below. The author of the Hippokratic text on *Diseases of Women* indicates (I.6) that the healthiest type of woman is 'masculine', but such a one is less inclined toward maternity and conception.

28. (1988), p. 216.

29. Strabo XI.5.1; female children were kept and reared as Amazons, male children were returned to their fathers. But some accounts show a nefarious intent against the male sex. Amongst the Hippokratic *corpus*, the author of *On Joints* (53.iv.232, 7–13) discusses the dislocation of joints and adds the anecdotal detail that the Amazons dislocated the joints of their male children who, thus hobbled, would be less capable of causing difficulties for the women. He admits that he does not know if this report is truthful, cf. Thomas (2000), pp. 61, 245.

30. III.35. Cf, *GH,* pp. 100–101, on male expectations of sexual passivity for Athenian women.

31. Cp. Hdt. IV.110 sq.

32. Hartog (1988), p. 217. Cf. my chapter III for more on the *ephēbeia.*

33. Cf. *GPM,* pp. 101 sq. on ancient Greeks views of androgyny and women.

34. (2001), p. 114. Cf. Ibykos (fr. 58) on these figurines and Cartledge *ibid.* n. 47. Cf. Plut. *Lyk.* XIV.4–7 on the public nudity of prepubescent Spartan girls and cf. my chapter V for this practice in the *Laws.* Cf. also *GH,* pp. 193 sq.

35. Cf. Cartledge *ibid.* who says, 'It is not, I think, fanciful to associate this feature with the strongly homosexual [sic] orientation of the average Spartan male'.

36. Homer, *Iliad* III.239, VI.186–223; Arktinos of Miletos (fl. 776 B.C.E.) wrote the *Aithiopis* as a direct sequel to the *Iliad.* It is best known for its opening scene in which Penthesilea and her Amazons come to the aid of the Trojans after the death of Hektor.

Achilles kills the queen, then mourns for her. When Thersites makes fun of him for this, Achilles slays him too. Cf. Aghion, Barbillon and Lissarrague (1996) s.v. Achilles and Penthesilea. Hardwick (1996), figs. 1–4 graphically depict many of these scenes of Amazon defeat.

Only fragments remain of *Aithiopus,* but Quintus of Smyrna is thought to have re-written Arktinos' poems. Cf. Quintus Smyrnaeus (mid 4th c.e.), *The Fall of Troy* I.61–66, I.621, I.843–88.

37. Plutarch, *The Life of Theseus;* cf. Isokrates, *Panathenaicus* 192, 194 who says they lost and were all killed or expelled; Lysias' *Funeral Oration* VI says they lost; Aristides' *Panathenic Oration* 83–84 says 'now from this point, as if a rope had broken, all snapped back, and the Amazons' march of empire was undone. And here too the city aided the whole race, and now it is doubtful if Amazons ever existed'. Cf. Aghion, Barbillon and Lissarrague (1996) s.v. Amazons.

38. Apollod. *Bibl.* II.3; Hom. *Iliad* 6.219; Pind. *Ol.* XIII.91 and 130; Plut. *Mor.* XVII.248. They battle Herakles/Theseus over Hippolyte's girdle. Antiope (or Hippolyte, depending on the story) is abducted, and married King Theseus in Greece (cf. Euripides *Phaedra* and Plutarch's *Life of Theseus).*

39. Cf. Romm (1988), p. 200 sq. for these. Interestingly, they are also credited with having been the first to mount horses and use iron, cf. Lysias, *Funeral Oration* IV.

40. II.6; cf. Blundell (1998), p. 55–6.

41. Cf. Harrison (2000), p. 37, for the common association between Amazons and Persians in Herodotos and amongst Athenian speechwriters.

42. Cf. Pindar *Ol.* XIII.87–90, for Bellerophon's defeat of the *gunaikeion straton* of Amazons.

43. (1996), p. 166.

44. Hall (1989), pp. 62–8. She argues that they, as with other barbarians, acted as a foil for Athenian self-definition; cf. my chapter IV.

45. Cf. *ibid.* pp. 175–6 and Just (1989) chapters 9 and 10, who regards them as 'the savages without' as opposed to 'the enemies within'. He indicates that the Amazons belonged to a category of women defined by their alien quality, like Medea, in whom this trait is associated with emotional forces perceived as a threat to civilised society. Thus they were outsiders in need of 'proper' acculturation.

46. Strabo (c. 63 b.c.e.–21 c.e. or later), Diodorus Siculus (1st c.e.), Plutarch (c. 46–c. 126 c.e.) and others cannot count as cultural context for Plato. They are representing the views of different eras altogether. But many of them will have approached their subjects having read ancient writers like Herodotos, Lysias and others that we do not today posses who had more direct insight into Plato and his era.

47. Hdt. IV.180 describes a similar practice amongst the barbarous Machyles and Auses, near Libya, whose maidens dress in armour and practice war games in honour of Athena.

48. Cf. my chapter III on education and sex role stereotyping.

49. Cf. my chapter III for a discussion of the educational uses of Magnesian *syssitia* and some comparisons with similar Spartan practices.

50. Like the *Kallipolis* of the *Republic,* the sorts of healthy foods served at these, according to Wilkins, Harvey and Dobson (1995), p. 8, will consist of 'the staples wheat, barley and wine, to which strong flavours are added by vegetables and nuts . . . meat and the works of pastry cooks'. Cf. my chapter V on the Spartan diet.

51. *FGrH* 3B:458, F2; 4.143a–d, quoting Dosiadas of Krete (end of the 3rd century B.C.E.).

52. *Politics* 1271b20–1272b23. At 1272a21 he confirms that 'women children and men' ate at these communal meals. Sealey (1990), p.54, says that the Kretan communal dining houses (*hetaireiai*) were probably a near-approximation of the Athenian *phratries* in that they were both similar types of hereditary, civic organisations but 'to say that is to explain the unknown by the little known'. Presently, this chapter will consider some of the 'little known' about Athenian *phratries*.

53. As Xenophon, *Lak. Pol.* IV, 2–5, indicates, the result being 'that as long as they are together, their table is never without food'; cf. Pomeroy (1997), p. 212, on the notion that the Spartan *andreia* were 'hotbeds' of institutionalised same-sex activity.

54. Wilkins, Harvey and Dobson (1995), p. 8.

55. *Ibid.*, p. 30; 'Solon ruled that those who dined at state expense at the town hall—the most signal honour Athens could provide—should receive *maza* [barley-cakes] on ordinary days, and wheaten bread only during festivals'. Sokrates had, with irony, suggested this honour as his penalty in Plato's *Apology* 17a–42a. Cf. MacDowell (1978), pp. 253–7.

56. Cf. Aristotle, *Politics* II.6.1265a5–10.

57. εἰς τὸ φῶς ἦκται

58. λαθραιότερον μᾶλλον καὶ ἐπικλοπώτερον ἔφυ

59. This suggest that a charge of undue license may be levelled against Spartan and Kretan women if we are to believe Euripides (*Andromeda* 595 sq.); On the phrase εἰς τὸ φῶς as a poetical expression cf. *Prot.* 320d, *Theaet.* 157d, *Tim.* 91d, *Laws* 869c, and *Rep.* 461c.

60. Philo of Alexandria, fond of merging Platonic philosophy with Jewish ideas, considered the female sex to be more inclined toward sensuality and thus *naturally* impeded with regard to virtue (*Allegorical Interpretations* III.56). He identified Eve with sensory perception and associated her with the Pleasure principle. The Judeo-Christian Fall, as Philo and others have interpreted it, brought consequences for women such that they must to bear children through painful labour and then rear their offspring whilst the men-folk toiled and developed technical skills (associated with the Mind). Additionally, Philo believed that a direct consequence of the Fall was that women should lose their freedom and accept the mastery of their husbands (*On Creation* 167). Plato's narrator, as we have seen, has Magnesian women bound by marriage and engaged in childbearing but he has also provided slaves and servants to educate and rear the offspring. It is difficult to determine how subservient a Magnesian wife would have to be to her husband in consequence of her questionable *nature*.

61. Their 'disorderly' characterisation here recollects similar observations made in my chapter IV on Platonic *andreia*; cf. too chapter V.

62. The use of such language in describing women, as Scott (1986), p. 10, argues, may be regarded as casting them in an implicitly negative light or 'verbally projecting' such characteristics upon them.

63. Eupheletos (Lysias I.6) indicates that, after marrying, he kept a close eye on his wife's activities and that her indiscretion with Eratosthenes was in part the result of his later laxity in exercising this supervision.

64. *Oik.* VII.30.

65. Isai. III.13–14.

66. Lyk., *contra Leokrates* 40.
67. Cf. Lysias III.6–7; Demosthenes XLVII.35–38; and see too Euripides, *Electra* 343–4, where Electra's husband warns her that 'it is shameful for a woman to be standing with young men'. See too Lysias I.4 where one of the charges against Eratosthenes was that he entered Euphiletos' house and saw his wife privately.
68. Schaps (1977), p. 330. Cf. Dem. XXXIX.9 where Mantitheos, suing to prevent his half-brother from also calling himself Mantitheos son of Mantias, reveals the name his half-brother's mother, Plangon, in the speech but not his own mother's.
69. Cf. my chapters III, IV and V for this *leitmotif*. This appears to be a common, male conceptualisation of women.
70. 781b8–c2. This may be 'tongue-in-cheek' since Plato would have been aware that many individuals who might take issue with these ideas would be reading the *Laws*. In addition to acknowledging the opposition's views, it may also serve to stress the fictional or 'mythic' quality of this dramatic dialogue. Cf. my chapter II.
71. *Laws* 745a sq. and cf. 457a sq. on how 12 tribes is a convenient division of the 5040 households.
72. Engels (1977), p. 176, suggests, such evolving social institutions within the *polis* had 'created a public force which was now no longer simply identical with the whole body of armed people . . . it divided the people for public purposes, not by groups of kinship, but *by common place of residence*'. Cf. Hall (1997) on the perceived kinship relations in *phratries*.
73. Cf. my chapter V for the *phratry's* relationship with the *oikos* in terms of inheritance.
74. Nestor, trying to calm dissent amongst the Achaian camp, says, 'The man who loves the horror of war amongst his own people is an outlaw, without *phratēres* and without a home'. (*Il.* IX.63–4).
75. It was a two-stage process. Males were first introduced in infancy at a ceremony called the *meion*, they were later admitted, during adolescence, at a ceremony called the *koureion* prior to being inducted into their fathers' *demes* at the age of eighteen. Cf. Lambert (1993), p. 36, pp. 172–4. The speaker in Isaios, *On the Estate of Apollodoros*, VII.16, says that the *genos* and *phratry* have the same admission policies, he says 'they have the same law, whether one introduces one's born son or an adoptive son. With one's hand upon the sacrificial victims one must swear that the son whom one is introducing, whether one's by birth or by adoption, is the child of a female citizen and has been rightly born'. "Rightly born," as Sealey (1990), p. 34, indicates 'was a circumlocution for "born to a woman united by *engyesis* to the father."'
76. (1993), p. 31.
77. *Ibid.*, p. 32, pp. 43–9, 53–4.
78. 764–5. 'What is normally shameful', boast the birds, 'is creditable with us . . . Anyone who is a slave and a Karian like Exekestides, let him grow wings with us, and he'll become a *phratēr*'. Cf. Cawkwell (1997), pp. 103–4.
79. On Perikles' citizenship law, cf. Lambert (1993), pp. 43 sq., Rhodes (1981), pp. 331 sq. and MacDowell (1978) pp. 89–90. Also, cf. Plut. *Per.* XXXVII.5, for Perikles allegedly being allowed to introduce his son by the foreign woman Aspasia into his *phratry*.
80. Isaios III.73. But this translation may be misleading, see below.

81. (1993), p. 181; cf. Isaios III.73, 76.
82. (1995), p. 117.
83. Pollux VIII.107 and Σ Ar. *Ach* 146. It is notable that the *gamelia* was not mentioned by Theomnestos and Apollodoros in their prosecution of Stephanos for his marriage to the non-Athenian Neaira in Dem. LIX. He may have introduced her and the prosecution intentionally neglected to mention it—but this is not certain.
84. At VIII.107, he describes the *gamelia* as the female equivalent of the *koureion*.
85. (1855), 346; lines 5–7.
86. Cf. von Silke (2002); cf. Pomeroy (1995), p. 117 and esp. n. 23 and n. 24.
87. Isaios III.76, 79; Pollux VIII.107. A fragment from Didymos describes 'the introduction of women to the *phrateres*', *FGrH* 325 F 17; but cf. Harpokration (s.v. γαμηλία) who declares that Didymos reported that Phanodemos' definition was in error. Although Didymos' report states that Phanodemos had said that wives were introduced into the *phratry* at the *gamelia,* it is contested whether he (Phanodemos) actually ever said such a thing (cf. Pomeroy 1995, p. 117).
88. III.79.8.
89. LVII.43.
90. Lambert (1993), p. 183 and n. 220. 'In other words', as Pomeroy (1995), pp. 117–118, says 'the *gamelia* served as an occasion at which a marriage was made public and created witnesses to the legitimacy of the children born as a result of it'.
91. *Ibid.*, p. 184. Each *phratry's* laws (*nomoi*) for the *gamelia* would have been different as well.
92. 785a3–b2.
93. The 'women in charge of marriages' . . . γυναῖκες ἐπιμελουμένες τῶν γάμων—783b–784b, and cf. 930c1–7 where they are consecrated to Eileithuia (Artemis of Childbirth) and meet each day in her temple; see below.
94. At 731d, the unjust soul may be tempered toward justice by ceasing from 'womanly' (γυναικείως) raging. This is another example of excessive emotionality being associated with femininity. Cf. the Pythagorean Table of Opposites in my chapter IV.
95. . . . μήτε οἴκτοις γυναικείοις—949b1–3. This recollects Sokrates' comments at *Apology* 34c sq. where he makes much of refusing to bring in his relatives to beg melodramatically for his acquittal as was apparently not an uncommon occurrence in such cases.
96. Cf. e.g. Thuc. II.24.2, Dem. XXVIII.3, LIX, LVII.37, pseud. Dem. XL, Isai. V.5, VI.12, X.4 and below.
97. Agariste was the daughter of Kleisthenes, ruler of Sikyon, and the mother of Kleisthenes the famous reformer. Cf. MacDowell (1978), pp. 67, 87.
98. Andokides I.16; Cf. Rhodes (1981), p. 465, on the rules governing the celebration of the mysteries and cf. MacDowell (1978), pp. 198–9.
99. As MacDowell (1978), p. 84, indicates, 'a metic woman might have no male relatives in Athens and so be '*kyrios* of herself' (Demosthenes LIX.46), though, as a metic she would have a sponsor (prostates) who might speak for her in legal affairs'. Cf. *ibid.* pp. 85–103.
100. (1977), p. 330. Cf. Dem. XXXIX.9 and above.
101. At 715c9–10, the Athenian Stranger says 'and those who were called "rulers" (ἄρχοντας) I have now called "ministers of the laws" (ὑπηρέτας τοῖς νόμοις),

not for the sake of coining a new phrase, but in the belief that the salvation or ruin of a *polis* hangs upon nothing so much as this'. These elected "ministers of the laws" have more limited authority than the appointees on the *nukterinos* council—to whom the Guardians of the Laws ultimately answer.

102.   753b–c. Curiously, at 715b–c2, the Athenian Stranger stated that 'we will not apportion offices in your city on the grounds of someone's wealth or any such possessions, whether physical strength, size or descent'. He seems to have backtracked somewhat on the issue of wealth and possessions in terms of selecting magistrates. Indeed, amongst the four necessarily unequal property classes of Magnesia (outlined at 744a–745b), when it comes to 'offices, revenues and distributions, the honour due to each individual person will depend not only upon the virtue of his ancestors and himself, and the strength and handsomeness of bodies, but also according to the way one uses wealth or poverty' (744b5–c2). There is a clear sense that the wealthy may have greater inclination for *aretē*.

103.   Cf. my chapter III.

104.   (2002), p. 448.

105.   756c9–10; this process is quite elaborate and involves a random lottery at the final stage, after all the rounds of voting, to decide the candidates who then must be scrutinised, see below; cf. Plut. *Solon* XVIII.4–5 and sq., for this common democratic formula of 'anyone who wishes' in Solon's reforms.

106.   755b sq.

107.   They are officially identified as functioning in a 'watchdog' capacity, making recommendations and keeping the ship of state 'on course' (960–65), but their actual power is nearly absolute—just below that of the laws. Cf. my chapter III on their special education and II on their authority. In many ways, they are reminiscent of the Spartan *Gerousia*, cf. Cartledge (2001) pp. 34–5, 60, 84 on their powers.

108.   951d8–e4; cf. 813c6–8.

109.   Cf. my chapter II for more on such legal preambles.

110.   773e5–774a1. This would appear to be an example of the sort of 'mystification' (or idealisation) that certain modern feminists accuse some men of associating with the act of reproduction; cf. O'Brien (1981), pp. 8–15, 46.

111.   Cf. my chapter V.

112.   Cf. McKinnon (1982), p. 518, for the characterisation of this sort of thing as a principal means of male domination of women through the deployment of the socio-economic forces at their disposal.

113.   Cf. my chapter V.

114.   Eileithuia figured prominently into Athenian women's religious lives. We are told that the robes of women who had died while giving birth were dedicated to Artemis at Brauron who was patroness of the life cycle of women (Eur. *Iph. Taur.* 1404–9). Cf. also Sealey (1990), p. 37 and Cole (1998), pp. 36 sq. on woven items offered along with gold and silver representations of breasts, vulvae and and wombs. Artemis, along with Apollo and the Dioskuri, was a principal deity of Sparta, cf. Parker (1989), p. 145 sq.

115.   784a–b. Cf. Lambert (1993), p. 182, for similar 'sacred rites' in Athenian marriages.

116.   784d1–5. Cf. chapter V on the relative harshness of this penalty.

117.   Cf. my chapter III for the Spartan connotations of 'herds' (ἀγέλαι) of children.

118. 'Ideally no man', says he, 'would dare to have sexual relations with a respectable free-woman other than his wedded wife, nor would he dare to sow unhallowed and bastard seed among concubines, nor sterile seed in males contrary to nature' (841d1–5). Cf. chapters V and VII.

119. 841d6–e4.

120. Cf. chapter VII.

121. 743d2–6. Running a bordello would be considered, at most, a banausic trade and, at least, contrary to the pursuit of virtue.

122. Cf. Dem. LIX.87, Aiskhines. I.14, 183–184 and Plu. *Solon* 23.I for Athenian penalties for citizens who undertook prostitution or ran a procurement service.

123. . . . πλὴν τοῦ σωφρονεῖν—850b3. On *metic* taxation in Athens, cf. MacDowell (1978), pp. 76 sq.

124. The distinctions between prostitutes, concubines and sexual companions (*pornai, pallakai, hetairai*), exclusive to non-citizen women, are complex, cf. my chapter II and below. Of course, 'the rest' could also include males as well as females, cf. my chapter VII.

125. Davidson (1997), p. 77. Cf. my chapter II for more on prostitutes in ancient Athens.

126. I.29–32. Cf. *GPM* 41, 289 sq., 302. As Dover (*GH* p. 20), indicates, the 'sale of one's own body' is rendered from the verb '*peporneumenos*' which 'is the perfect participle of the verb *porneusthai*, "behave as a *pornē* or *pornos*"'.

127. *GH* p. 32. Cf. Aiskh. I.192 sq., 123 sq.

128. Cf. my chapter VII on the questionable prohibition of same-sex intercourse.

129. Cf. Lysias I.8 sq. where Euphiletos indicates that it was at his mother's funeral that his wife met Eratosthenes. The only relatives of the deceased permitted were of the family's *anchisteia*; see below and my Chapter V.

130. 909e3–8; this would seem to be addressing another aspect of their perceived 'secretiveness'.

131. Cf. my chapter VI on the characterisation of these types of music according to sex.

132. In chapter V, we saw that private religious ceremonies are forbidden in Magnesia.

133. Cf. my chapters III and IV.

134. (1995), p. 114.

135. *Ibid.* In Stears (1998), p. 116, she describes the *anchisteia* as 'a bilateral kinship grouping centred on an *ego* and extending to the children of cousins'.

136. Stears (1995), p. 114.; cf. Sealey (1990), p. 15 on the *anchisteia* and inheritance. In Aristophanes' *Birds* (1650–52), Pisthetairos startles Herakles by accusing him of being a *nothos* (more or less translatable as 'illigtimate') since his mother was an alien women. He cites legal code to prove this (1660–66) saying that the *nothos* has no *anchisteia* if there are legitimate (*gnēsioi*) children present.

137. Lysias I; Isaios VI.64; Aiskh. *Fals. Leg.* XXXIII.1. This will not be a problem in Magnesia as the public rolls and the registries of *phratries* will be comprehensive and accurate.

138. Temple robbers and parricides are to be denied interment within tombs (960b). A similar statute existed in ancient Athens whereby temple robbers were denied burial in Attica (Xen. *Hellenika* I.7.22). See below for other exceptions due to class and status and cf. my chapter V.

139. (1997), p. 11.
140. Cf. Ibid. pp. 11–12 and Stears (1995), p. 113 sq. The Athenians stopped erecting these c.500 possibly due to democratic reforms being legislated, but this remains uncertain (cf. Cic. *de leg.* II.26.64–5).
141. (1995), p. 114; 88 extant monuments record a male and female couple, yet amongst the single inscriptions there are 234 male examples as opposed to 102 female ones.
142. Cf. my chapter V and below.
143. Plut. *Lyk.* XXVII; Herod. VI.58. Cf. also Plato *Minos* 315d, Michell (1964), pp. 62–3 and Cartledge (2001), p. 200, n. 71. Michell suggests that this was to prevent the angry spirits of bad kings from entering the city.
144. (1964), p. 62.
145. (1964), p. 63.
146. Morrow (1960), p. 203, has observed that 'even in rare cases in which a guardian acts alone—as in making arrangements for a funeral—the penalty for disobedience is determined by the board' of Guardians acting together.
147. As we saw in chapter V, 'Let it be a noble thing to his credit', says the Athenian Stranger, 'when the matters regarding the dead transpire well and in due measure, but a shameful thing if they transpire ignobly' (959e3–5).
148. 959e7–960a2. This compares well with Solon's funeral legislation, see below.
149. Stears (1998), p. 114. The mouth would be closed and the body, as she says, would be 'washed and then wrapped in a number of layers of fabric, including a shroud and a top cover. On the bier it was laid out with the feet toward the door and a pillow under the head. It was then decked with herbs and sometimes with garlands and occasionally jewellery . . . '
150. Cf. *Ibid.* p. 18, and above, for the prominence of women in these ceremonies in Athens.
151. 960a3–5. Solon's reforms also required the *ekphora* to be completed before dawn as well as limiting public expression of grief; cf. (Dem.) XLIII.62, Plut. *Solon* XXI, Cic. *de leg.* II.64, and see below.
152. 717e. Cf. my chapter V on this yearly ceremony and its relation to the family.
153. Cf. Hdt. IX.85 and Plut. *Lyk* XXVII,3 and Parker (1989), pp. 144–5, esp. n. 4 for some deeper explication of these passages.
154. As Parker (1989), p. 146, writes 'The Spartiate who looked up at the colossal archaic statue of Apollo at Amyclae, 45 feet high and doubtless the most sacred object in all Laconia, saw there an image of a supernatural warrior, with bow in one hand, spear truculently raised in the other'. Cf. Aghion, Barbillon and Lissarrague (1996), pp. 45–6.
155. . . . ἄνδρας αὐτῶν τρεῖς—945e6–946a1.
156. 947d1–3. As apparently was also the case amongst the Spartans where comparable religious ceremonies involved children of both sexes together; cf. Plut. *Mor.* 239c as well as Hodkinson and Powell (1999), p. 110, n.107. Cf. Parker (1989), pp. 143–4 and 146. See below on the exclusion of women of childbearing age not in the deceased's *anchisteia*.
157. There is evidence for a similar practice of annual ceremonies for certain 'honoured' dead in the 4th century. But, unlike the Magnesians, these wealthy individuals set up foundations to secure their tombs' continued attentions and observances of ceremony; cf. Pomeroy (1997), p. 108.

158. Pseud. Dem. XLIII.62; Plut., *Solon* 4, 21. These reforms, if they actually occurred, were probably not always practised; cf. Michell (1964), pp. 62–3.
159. (1975), p. 80.
160. (1978), p 109.
161. (1998), p. 117. Even so, she indicates that women have been particularly identified as the 'central producers of noisy lamentations at the funerals'. Cf. Plato *Laws* 800e and Hdt. II.61.
162. (1998), p. 119. The baby, as we have seen, would go through a series of public presentations (especially if it was male) overseen by the bride's father and husband.
163. Cf. Parker (1983) for a broader discussion of this issue.
164. Ibid., p. 122. Cf. (Dem) XLIII.63 where the absence of an opponent's wife and mother at a familial *prothesis* and *ekphora* was used as evidence in the rival claim of an estate.
165. (1983), p. 15.
166. See chapter III on education for a more detailed analysis.
167. E.g. in court or at a funeral. See chapter V for more on funerary practices and the restrictions of emotionality directed specifically toward women.

NOTES TO CHAPTER VII

1. From the *Ballad of Reading Gaol,* ed. Ross (1991), p. 47.
2. It is absolutely essential to bear in mind that Plato had no concept of 'homosexuality' or 'heterosexuality' in the modern sense *per se* because this dualism is actually a cultural construction of the last century and a half by the industrialised West. When I employ the term 'same-sex', I mean it in reference to sexual acts involving members of the same sex (men with men and women with women—as opposed to men with women, or 'mixed-sex' relationships). Cf. my chapter I.
3. Cf. Cairns (1993) pp. 27–47 on 'shame-culture' in the ancient world in general and pp. 142–3 for instances in Homer and cf. my chapter VI.
4. *Laws* 626d sq., 839e sq. Cf. *Republic* 430e sq., 443d sq.
5. Cf. *Iliad* XX.231 sq. on the Kretan reputation for boy-love (which rivalled if not exceeded that of the Spartans), see too Athenaios XIII.602 and cf. Aristotle, *Politics* III.1.1272a24–26; Sextus Empiricus *Pyrrhonism* III.199; and Maxwell-Stuart (1975), pp. 13–15. Interestingly, when Aristotle indicates (*Politics* II.9.1269b25–7) that states which honour wealth and luxury tend to be both warlike and dominated by women, he excludes the Celts and others 'in which open sexual relations between men' are favoured but he omits Sparta as one of these. This makes one wonder if sexual relations between Spartan men were any more or less "open" than in Athens. One must take care in differentiating pederasty from the state of being sexually interested in members of the same sex. One must also take care not to impose modern ethics and morals upon the ancients who lacked our current insights. As will be shortly seen, what the Athenian Stranger is criticising here and in Book VIII is largely sexual relations between consenting individuals of the same sex and not simply pederasty or boy-love.
6. England (1921), p.230, accepts Boeckh's πάλαι ὄν νόμιμον in his edition but indicates that Burnet's reading of manuscripts A and O was παλαιὸν νόμον, corrected by the writer to παλαιῶν νόμων. England says that he examined the passage in A and 'thought it was by a later hand'. He believes that a later editor altered the ω's back

to o and wrote νόμιμον as a variant for νόμον in the margin. Likewise, England says that it is a mistake to take νόμον as being in apposition to τὰς περὶ τὰ ἀφροδίσια ἡδονάς as he reckons this to be the erroneous view of some scribe who took κατὰ φύσιν, along with παλαιὸν, to qualify νόμον. He states that 'the ἡδοναί are φύσει as opposed to νόμῳ, and the force of the passage seems weakened if they are spoken of as νόμος' (*ibid.*). Whilst I am frequently inclined to agree with England's views, I believe that he has missed the mark on this one. I prefer to follow Schöpsdau's commentary (1994), p. 203, n. on *Laws* 636b4–6, which indicates that the texts of A and O (παλαιὸν νόμον) are rightly supported by Burnet and, he writes that 'καὶ κατὰ φύσιν ist parallel zu παλαιόν als Attribut auf νόμον zu beziehen' and 'τὰς περὶ τὰ ἀφροδίσια ἡδονὰς . . . θηρίων ist Apposition zu παλαιὸν νόμον, das seinerseits Objekt zu διεφθαρκέναι ist'.

7. Cf. Pangle (1980), p. 515–16 n. 35 and my chapter I.
8. 636b1–c1. Cf. *Theaet.* 162b, 169a–b. According to Cartledge (2002), p. 102, the fact that they performed athletics in the nude indicates that the 'Spartans put a premium on gymnastic exercise' and that 'the cult of the nude male body is likely to have been pushed to extremes, as it is known to have been in other Greek cities'. Thuc. I.6.5, suggests that the Spartans were the ones who first established the custom of exercising naked.
9. 780–781. He is aware that there will be opposition to women attending. Cf. Morrow (1960), p. 393 sq.
10. Plut. *Lys.* VIII. Cf. also Freeman (1950), pp.165–66.
11. Cloché (1950), pp. 95–112.
12. Aristotle, *Politics* V.7.1307a27, 1307b6.
13. The Athenian Stranger seems to be implying that the youths in these cities named were literally "spoiling" for a fight because they were so well trained. Aristotle (*Politics* V. 7) in discussing the factionalism at Thurii says γενόμενοί τινες πολεμικοὶ τῶν νεωτέρων. Cp. Alkidamas (4th century B.C.E.), *Odysseus* 1.19 who states that: οὐδ' ἐν παλαίστρια οὐδ' ἐν συμποσίῳ, ἔνθα φιλεῖ ἔριδας πλείστας καὶ λοιδορίας γενέσθαι.
14. Book V of the *Politics* lists many revolutions that occurred through public festivals, but no one ever says that festivals should be banned as a result.
15. Theirs is to be a highly supervised form of physical fitness. Cf. my chapter III.
16. On their associations with same-sex intercourse, cf. Ephorus of Kyme, *FrGH* 70, 2a; F149.14 and F97.3.
17. *Deipnosophistae* XIII.602a. Aristotle (*Politics* V.10.1311a16–18) has also indicated that some tyrants fell due to a lack of control over their desires as evidenced in their pursuit of same-sex pleasures.
18. *Deipn.* XIII.602a7–b1. Cf. Plutarch (*Pelopidas* 18) who attributes the founding of this order to Gorgidas.
19. *Pol.* 1311a38.
20. Cf. also Aiskhines I.132–140.
21. Euripides' *Ion* treats similar criticisms of myth.
22. The views expressed at *Republic* 468b and Aristophanes' and Pausanias' speech in the *Symposium* could be taken for evidence that this passage in the *Laws* might represent a change in Plato's attitudes towards same sex relations. But we cannot know this for certain given the dialogue form, cf. my chapter II.

23. This is the only passage in the *Laws* that refers directly to same-sex intercourse between women. There is an implied reference to the erotic activities of female youths at 836a6–b2. Its sparseness in Plato's works is fairly typical amongst ancient Greek writers and may reflect an unspoken cultural taboo on the subject.

24. παρὰ φύσιν, in its six occurrences in the *Laws*, has the sense of 'contrary to nature' or 'unnatural' as opposed to κατὰ φύσιν, 'according to nature', and these phrases occasionally occur together in pairs to denote opposed states such as in the above passage and at 655e1–3, and 733a7–8.

25. The Athenian Stranger later explicitly prohibits sexual intercourse between any free person and slaves of either gender (777e6–778a4). Gould's (1963), p. 144, avowal that 'Plato draws a, for him unprecedented, distinction between heterosexual [sic] pleasure, which he calls natural, and homosexual [sic] pleasure, which he calls contrary to nature', while pertinent, reminds us to have a care in distinguishing between Plato and his narrator, the Athenian Stranger.

26. Dover, Letter III, qtd. in Nussbaum (1994), p. 1630, n. 423; he cites *Symposium* 197e7 and the *Gorgias* as examples.

27. Paul Friedländer (1958), p. 288, asserted that 'Although, if men would listen to him [Plato], his goals were possible of achievement, he understood fully that his proposal was visionary (632e, 712b), an old man's game of jurisprudence (685a), and he had no expectation that his ideal would be realised in practice. He was merely insisting upon the necessity of abstraction or hypothesis as controls in societal inquiry (739e)'.

28. (1994), pp. 1579, 1581, 1581, 1648.

29. Rist (1997), p. 78. He also argues that Dover and Nussbaum are contradicted by *Laws* 636b–c.

30. (1997), p. 78. Cf. *Laws* 839e5–840b1 for Ikkos of Tarentum who was said to have avoided sexual activity during training before athletic events.

31. This corresponds to Nussbaum's (1994) reading at 1637–1638.

32. England (1921), p. 231, indicates that it is difficult to understand why εἶναι is in the present after ἀποδεδόσθαι. He also says that δι' ἀκράτειαν ἡδονῆς makes an awkward predicate for εἶναι—although both he and Burnet keep εἶναι in their editions of the text.

33. (1921), p. 231.

34. *GH*, pp. 186 and 165. It seems a curious thing that many of the philological issues of textual validity in the *Laws*, but not all, seem to occur around the subject of same-sex relations; see below.

35. (1994), p. 1626, italics in original

36. Cf. Aiskhines, *Against Timarkhos*, I. 134, where same-sex, male attraction is also not considered abnormal.

37. She cites *Laws* 839d–842a (considered below), in support of this.

38. Cf. *LSJ*, p. 1627.

39. Qtd. in Hamilton and Cairns (1989), p. 1237.

40. *LSJ* s.v. τόλμημα.

41. (1994), p. 1627; cf. *Phaedrus* 247c on daring to speak the truth; *Symposium* 177c, on the daring required to give worthy praise to Erōs, 179d, for the daring of one who gives his life for a loved one, 179e, on Achilles daring to risk his life to avenge the death of Patroklos; *Republic* 474b and 503b4, on the daring proposition that

philosophers ought to rule a city. At *Laws* 661a, the Athenian Stranger uses τολμάω in reference to the daring involved in military courage.

42. Nussbaum (1994), p. 1628, n. 416.

43. 835e2–836a6. Cf. my chapter III on education.

44. Cf. my chapter I.

45. See below.

46. Manuscripts A and O omitted the πρὸ before the τοῦ, L preserved it; all the early editors before Stalb omitted the τοῦ. On the myth of Laios and some alternatives (which I shall later examine) cf. Athenaios XIII.602f sq.

47. ὀρθῶς εἶχεν is here what England (1921), p/343, calls the 'philosophic' imperfect and indicates something like 'it was right, as you see', or 'it was always right'. This is comparable to (but not the same as) the imperfect of customary action, cf. Smyth (1984 ed.) p. 424, par. 1893.

48. τάχ᾽ ἂν χρῷτο πιθανῷ λόγῳ, καὶ ταῖς ὑμετέραις πόλεσιν οὐδαμος συμφωνοῖ is indicated in the MSS; however England, Dies and Badham all concur in reading ἀπιθανῷ and England proposes, with confidence, to read συμφώνῳ for συμφωνοῖ. Yet Hermann's suggestion is to keep πιθανῷ and read εἰ καί for καί thus rendering the passage ' . . . his argument would probably be persuasive, even if not at all in harmony with your cities'. I am inclined to agree, in part, with England (1921), pp. 342–343, where he says that the subject of the whole passage (835d–842a) 'is *the regulation of sexual passions in general*. The Cretan vice of paederasty is an *extreme* instance of unregulated "sexual" passion'. England also states that this passage deals with 'unnatural lust', and he groups paedophilia together with same-sex relationships in general.

49. Cf. Hdt. II.64 and IV.180 where animalistic sexual behaviour amongst 'savage' barbarians is identified as excessively promiscuous and impious. Cf. Rosellini and Saïd (1978), pp. 955–66 for more on this theme in Herodotos and also my chapter V.

50. In the *Philebus* passage above quoted, Sokrates is discussing pleasure and argues that one ought not derive one's way of thinking on the matter from the beasts and birds. Of course, I suppose that this does not exclude the possibility that one might draw logical conclusions about pleasure from animals should their actions happen to be in accord with philosophy—but this is not what is said in the text.

51. (1994), p. 1631.

52. *GH*, p. 167. Rist (1997), p. 71, believes that Plato has outlined (in the *Phaedrus*) a hierarchical ranking of the types of erotic relationship wherein the best condition is that in which any same-sex desires may be sublimated into genuine friendship but the lovers 'refrain from [sexual] intercourse'. The second-best tier is much like the first except they do engage in occasional sexual intercourse and this 'partial enslavement' results in the eventual abandonment of the life of philosophy. This position is not necessarily in conflict with the view expressed in the *Laws*.

53. By 'psychic solvency' I refer to the ideally Platonic state of the soul wherein Reason (implicitly with the aid of moderation) has command over the appetites. Cf. my chapter III for the supervised drinking parties.

54. XIII.602f8–603a3 . . . τοιούτων ἐρώτων κατάρξασθαι Λάιον ξενωθέντα.

55. Praxilla of Sicyon (5th century B.C.E.), according to Athenaios (*ibid*), said that prince Chrysippos was actually carried off by Zeus. However it is also a possibility that it was by both Laios and Oidipūs that the handsome youth was loved and this has been

considered by some as the source of conflict between the two. This is supported by Schol. Eur. *Phoen.* 60, who declares that 'τινὲς δέ φασιν ὅτι Λάιος ἀνηρέθη ὑπὸ Οἰδίποδος ὅτι ἀμφότεροι ἥρων Χρυσίππου'. Cf. also Devereaux (1953), pp. 32–141. As with the myth of Ganymede and Zeus, Plato deals with the Homeric tale of Achilles and Patrokles by positing, through his narrators that the former was erroneously called the lover of the latter (*Symposium* 180a). Cf. Aiskhines I.133–144 sq. on a varying interpretation of Achilles' and Patrokles' relationship. In Euripides (fr. 840), Laios declares helplessly, in reference to his actions with Chrysippos, that 'I have understanding, but nature forces me'. Cf. too Aeschylus' *Myrmidons.*

56. *FHG*, i. 201. This may have some kernel of truth to it if we accept the historical version of events to the effect that the Minoans first settled mainland Greece.

57. *PLG*, iii. 247.

58. I am aware that the use of the term 'sublimation' carries with it a Freudian connotation. I am not employing this term in the strictest Freudian sense (although there are similarities) but 'sublimation' seems to be the best term to describe this process that the Athenian Stranger recommends. Vlastos' 'transmutation' might suffice as well.

59. (1969), p. 123.

60. See *Lysis* 218a, 221; *Phaedrus* 237d sq., 253d sq.; *Philebus* 35b sq., 41c sq., 34c sq.; *Republic* 430b sq., 437d sq., 558d sq., 559a sq., 571c sq.; *Symposium* 191 sq., 200 sq. (cp. *Phaedrus* 237d sq., 251); *Theaetetus* 156b; *Timaeus* 69d sq.—although these provide a good example of the sheer amount of passages concerned with love and desire, some of which will figure heavily into this chapter, it is by no means a complete list of all the love-references in Plato. For a good, broad spectrum of the subject of love in the works of Plato, see Gould (1963).

61. I suggest that his particular definition of φιλία in the *Laws* ultimately signifies an extension of earlier Pythagorean thought transmitted and developed throughout the whole of the Platonic *corpus*. The subject of Pythagorean influences in Plato is too vast and complex to be here adequately discussed. Cf. Burkert (1972), pp 8, 27, 57–71, 79–83, 85, 92, 201, 371 sq., Kingsley (1995), pp. 88–115, 131–132, and Burnett (1920), pp. 221–299, for more on Pythagorean connections in Plato. Leonid Zhmud (2001) has recently pointed out that Kingsley's criticism of Diels' doxographic placement of Empedokles, along with his particular reformulation of Pythagorean history and philosophy, are not without their faults. He likewise has questioned Burnett's approach to Diels' *Doxographici Graeci*. Nonetheless, Zhmud freely acknowledges the profound Pythagorean influence upon Plato.

62. (1997), p. 73.

63. Cf. *GH*, pp. 49–50.

64. Cf. *Symposium* 200a sq., where ἐρᾶν is associated with ἐπιθυμειν.

65. *GH* p. 50, n.20.

66. Prodikos, in the late 5th century B.C.E., defined *erōs* as 'desire doubled' (ἐπιθυμία) and added that '*erōs* doubled is insanity' (*DK*, B7). Likewise, Xenophon (*Mem.* III.9.7) said 'that those whose aberrations are slight are not considered by most people as insane, but just as one calls strong desires "*erōs*," so one calls substantial distortion of a person's thinking "insanity."'

67. 837b2–3. So too in the quasi-scientific speech of Eryximachos in the *Symposium* do we hear of the stormy affections between opposites (τὸ δὲ ἀνόμοιον ἀνομοίων ἐπιθυμεῖ τε καὶ ἐρᾳ–186b).

68. Cf. *Phaedrus* 253d sq., and *Republic* 571c where fleshly desires are said to be in conflict with Reason; also cp. *Laws* 686e sq. where similar sentiments are expressed.

69. φίλον . . . ὅμοιον ὁμοίῳ—837a6; he quotes *Odyssey* XVII.218 here.

70. There it is rendered in a similar manner, as ὁ ὅμοιον τῷ ὁμοίῳ ἀνάγκη ἀεὶ φίλον εἶναι. Cp. *Gorgias* 510b2, where ἴσον is employed as a synonym with the qualifying κατ' ἀρετήν (see *Lysis* 214d), which is to be taken both with ὅμοιον and ἴσον. Plato's Sokrates (*Lysis* 214a6–b1) quotes *Odyssey* XVII.218, saying, 'αἰεί τοι τὸν ὁμοῖον ἄγει θεὸς ὡς τὸν ὁμοῖον καὶ ποιεῖ γνώριμον'. Homer's view stands opposed to Hesiod's (*Works and Days* 25) which maintained that the closer two things are to being like one another, the more they are repelled. Amongst other things, the subject of whether or not 'like' is actually attracted to 'like' is taken up to no small degree in the *Lysis*. Although no real conclusion to the matter is there attained, Sokrates delineates three kinds of friendship (212b–d) suggesting that someone is 'neither the friend of the other unless both love each other', and he allows 'like' to be attracted to 'like' at 219b–c. Similarly at 214d–e, it seems to be the case that 'like' is attracted to 'like' in some ways since only 'the good man is a friend to the good man alone, but the evil man never engages in friendship' with anyone.

71. *Lak. Pol.* II.13. But this was probably not the case in the terms that Xenophon describes, cf. Cartledge (2001), pp. 91, 189–90.

72. (1973) p. 23; Plato was, nonetheless, clearly aware of the extreme degree of susceptibility to physical beauty as indicated at *Phaedrus* 250c–e and *Symposium* 219c4.

73. 'To use St. John's phraseology', as England (1921), p. 346, says 'ἡ ἐπιθυμία τοῦ σαρκός is replaced by ἡ ἐπιθυμία τῶν ὀφθαλμῶν. The eye may be the instrument or handmaid of the "higher" nature, as well as of the "lower."—Plato was doubtless attracted by the assonance'. That is of ὁρῶν δὲ μᾶλλον ἢ ἐρῶν.

74. According to Vlastos (1973), pp.22–23, the sort of same-sex love that is fully sensual but denies consummation, 'transmuting physical excitement into imaginative and intellectual energy' was suggested in the *Symposium* as a 'rebuff' to Alkibiades' attempt at seduction in 219b–d. It is, however, clearly indicated as a superior form of love at *Phaedrus* 250e and 255e–256e and at *Republic* 403b–c.

75. The Athenian Stranger has also made a similar association between courage, wisdom, moderation and justice (being the four cardinal virtues) at 630b.

76. This is one of the rare occasions where Megillus, the normally laconic Spartan, engages the conversation—albeit to a limited degree since the Athenian Stranger does most of the talking. But typically his rather one-sided dialogue is with Kleinias.

77. *LSJ*, s.v. ὕβρις.

78. England (1921), p. 346, says that 'the introduction of μεγαλοπρεπές takes from the passage the air of a stock philosophical quote'.

79. Cf. Cartledge (2001), p.p. 83–5, on comparable terminology amongst the Spartans, and cf. my chapter III.

80. Pangle (1980), p. 486, translates *hubris* here as 'wantonness' as does Taylor (1934). Fisher (1992), p. 482, says that 'the traditional associations of *hybris* with youth, energy and leisure naturally are equally appropriate to this use of it as the dominance of excessive sexual desires'.

81. Cf. my chapters III and IV on the uses of shame/modesty in Magnesia.

82. (1992), p. 480.

83. 874c2–5. Fisher (1992), p. 482, indicates that this law is very similar to that at Athens in terms of crime and punishment (Demosthenes XXIII.53). Cf. also Morrow (1960), p. 465 sq. and MacDowell (1978), pp. 89, 124 for Athenian parallels. Cf. my chapter V.

84. Cf. *Republic* 349 sq. for the notion that those who seek to 'outdo' or 'get the better of' (*pleonezein*) one another lack the control of Reason and thus suffer from a disorderly psychic state; cf. too *Laws* 757 sq. for the idea that, amongst 'equals', there must be no seeking advantage over one another even in the pursuit of Reason.

85. 'When Sokrates makes a speech in the *Phaedrus* on the same subject as the speech which Phaedrus has recited, he treats *erōs* as desire which induces *hubris* and is in conflict with Reason (*Phdr.* 237cd, 238bc)' (*GH* p. 43, n.11).

86. (1990), p. 30; cf. Foucault (1984), p.215.

87. Aiskhines (II.150–1) on the case against Demosthenes.

88. Cf. Davidson (2001), esp. 13 and 17; and my chapter I.

89. (1993), p. 378, n. 103.

90. Fisher (1992), p. 486; cf. Foucault (1984), p. 220 and Davidson (1997), p. 169.

91. (1992), p. 487; cf. Price (1989), p. 123 sq. and *GH*, p. 167; cf. too Cairns (1993), p. 377.

92. (2000), p. 152, cf. my chapter IV.

93. This position was later taken up by other authors but never to such an extent as in Plato. Cf. Theopompos of Chios (b.376B.C.E.) *FGrH* 11f F213; Aristotle *Nicomachean Ethics* 1149b20 sq, 1149b30–6.

94. Cf. Davidson below for this line of reasoning.

95. Davidson (1997), p. 176.

96. Aeschylus fr. 243 in *TGF*; Sophocles fr. 932; Aristophanes' *Thesm.* 504sq., *Ecc.* 468–70, 616–20, *Clouds* 553sq. Alkiphron (I.6.2) depicts female sexual voracity as a 'Charybdis', and warns another man that his *hetaera* will devour him whole (3.33).

97. λύττης ἐρωτικῆς καὶ μανίας–839a9–b1.

98. See below on the Athenian Stranger's final summation of the law on sex where I have treated this matter in greater detail.

99. Saunders (1972), p 76, points out that 'one cannot be quite sure, but ἐλευθέρον, which all translators understand in the general sense of "free", is probably to be taken in the more restricted sense of "citizen" women. The complementary adjective γεννᾱίων surely excludes foreign women, as with rare exceptions aliens in Magnesia are anything but γενναῖα' (cf. 841e, 850a sq., 919c sq., 952d sq.). Cf. my chapter V.

100. Fisher (1992), p. 483. For a (perhaps somewhat idealised) view of the Spartan emphasis on consensus and social ostracism in the control of their citizenry, cf. e.g. Xenophon *Lak. Pol.* 2.10, 5.5–7, 6.2, 8 and Aristotle, *Politics* II.9.1270b28–31, 1275b9–13. Also cf. Pierart (1973), p. 416 sq.

101. Cf. my chapter V.

102. Cf. 250e3–251a; cf. 254.

103. On this see Rist (1997), p. 66, n. 4 and Nussbaum (1994), p. 1578.

104. It is altogether possible that Plato did not actually share the same attitudes that he would impose upon his subjects—not that it is necessary for him to share them. Rist (1997), p. 78, says 'the fact remains that he [Plato] separated reproductive love from spiritual love, which at its highest is celibate, involving male or "really male" (i.e.

female) souls alone. In addition to condemning same-sex intercourse, Plato did not marry. In this he differed from the inhabitants of the second-best city of his *Laws*, where, as Price says, 'no-one is expected to be wholly abstinent'. Cf. Price (1989), p. 232. It is necessary to bear in mind that Rist cannot know for certain whether or not Plato actually married but there is precious little evidence to suggest that he did as opposed to others (like Sokrates) on whose family life more has been recorded.

105. Cf. Hesk (2001), p. 153–6, 159–62 on Plato's use of 'pharmacological' lying and pp. 177–8 on ethical falsehood. Cf. my chapter II.

106. Inasmuch as we can regard such evidence as valid, a recent Channel 4 (2002) documentary indicated that not only do animals engage in same-sex intercourse, but many people have been selectively denying this fact for some time—especially in terms of arguing for the 'unnaturalness' of it in humans. Animals that have been scientifically proven to partake sexually of the same-sex acts include, but are not limited to, swans, chimpanzees, dogs, sheep, seagulls, African buffalo and dolphins. A longer list includes many other types of birds, reptiles and mammals.

107. *GH*, p. 166.

108. This view is subject to much debate and I deal with it more in chapter V. What appears to be indicated here is the notion that each sperm, or 'seed', was thought to contain a whole and immature human being which would then germinate in a woman's womb to develop into a baby. Therefore same-sex intercourse between males, as well as masturbation, could be seen to amount to a kind of murder–'killing the species of humankind'.

109. *GH*, p. 168.

110. Cf. also *Republic* 474d; and cf. too Aiskhines I.135–137, for an indication that same-sex attraction was regarded as quite normal in fifth–fourth century Athens. A hypothetical 'Athenian father', as Dover, *GH*, pp. 88–9, says, 'who sternly told his fourteen-year-old son never to speak to strange men on the way home from the gymnasium, yet betrayed by a glint in the eye and a curl of the lip that he was not wholly displeased by a rumour that his twenty-year-old son had "caught" the fourteen-year-old boy next door, was acting as humans act'.

111. As Winkler (1990), p. 172, says 'Athens was a society in which philosophers were often ignored and, when noticed, were easily represented not as authority figures but as cranks and buffoons'. Ameipsias had a chorus of 'thinkers' or 'worriers' (*phrontistai*); Eupolis' *Flatterers* portrayed the wealthy Kallias with his household of dodgy philosophers; and, of course, there is the comical representation of Sokrates in Aristophanes' *Clouds*.

112. *GH, p. 168.*

113. Cf. my chapter II on 'unwritten law'.

114. ἀναίδεια–841a8–9. Pangle (1980) p. 233, renders ἀναίδεια hereas 'awe'.

115. The 'mistress' in question, δέσποινα, represents excessive desires which master Reason. Taylor (1934), p. 1406, translates it as 'the tyranny of the appetite'. Cairns (1993), p. 144, highlights the importance of early socialisation for this use of shame as a means of behavioural control in ancient societies.

116. (1921), p. 12, italics in original.

117. … ἀλλ' οὐ τὸ μὴ πάντως δρᾶν—841b2–5.

118. (1993), pp. 376, but, as he rightly indicates (p. 377), 'it is important that, if possible, the [Magnesian] citizens should *be* rather than merely seem good' (emphasis mine). For

similar uses of shame cf. *Laws* 631e–632c, 634a, 663c, 671e, 711c, 721d, 730b–731a, 742b, 755a, 762a, 762c, 773e, 774c, 784d, 808e, 841e, 879e, 881b–c, 921d–922a, 926d, 944d–e (the coward to be treated as a woman). Cf. my chapter IV.

119.   England (1921), p. 356, says that, in the Athenian Stranger's use of τάχα δ' ἄν, 'he passes, I think, from the region of aspiration to that of what he may hope for as possible in the actual present "with God's help"; even though the love of spiritual beauty should not generally develop'.

120.   MSS. A and O omit the words τε καὶ οὐκ ὀρθῶς which are added in the margin of A.

121.   (1921), p. 357, italics in original.

122.   England (1921), p. 356, reckons that both of the alternatives represent 'a state of society in which the fear of God and the fear of man either (1) kept men altogether straight in sexual matters, or (2) both (a) confined their unlawful connexions to those with women, and (b) made them hide even these from the rest of the world'.

123.   (1989), p. 234.

124.   Cf. *Phaedrus* 239–241c on the harm done to the beloved by an intemperate lover. As Price (1989), p. 232, says, 'it is evident that Plato is far from the more recent attitude which finds same sex activity "unnatural" to the extent that it manifests a disposition of same sex desire; he lacks the conception to make that objection'.

125.   On the Athenian Stranger's use of so-called 'noble lies' in the *Laws* reflecting Spartan (more so than Athenian) policies of statecraft, cf. Hesk (2000), pp. 157–62.

126.   The Athenian Stranger says that γένεσις is the principal process whereby humankind may render service to 'the Good', the supreme object of religious worship (τὸ πάντων ἄριστον—728d1). He indicates that those who render service to the Highest have contact with τῆς ἀειγενοῦς φύσεως, which corresponds to true, indestructible Being. At 903c, he says that every γένεσις fashions an instrument for helping to secure the happiness of the universe as a whole. This would seem consistent with Diotima's thesis at *Symposium* 206e2–5 where *erōs* is described as both a longing for offspring 'in accordance with the Good' and, at 207a3–4, as 'the longing for the Immortal'. Cf. my chapters IV and V.

127.   Cp. 721c6; also cf. Aristotle, *De An.* 415a29, … ἵνα τοῦ ἀεὶ καὶ τοῦ θείου μετέχωσιν, ᾗ δύνανται.

128.   Cf. my chapters V and VI.

129.   (1989), p. 233. A similar stance was taken by the commission whose majority report recommended to Pope Paul VI that certain acts of contraception should be permitted within a marriage so long as its general purpose should remain reproductive. For an account of this cf. Napier (1969).

130.   *Laws* 740d; the 'highest and most distinguished' official is to be appointed to oversee population control. Cp. also 818d8, *Protagoras* 345d, and Simonides of Ceos (556–448 B.C.E.) Fr. 5. Cf. my chapter V.

131.   See my chapter II for Classical instances where the 'active' penetrator may also be accused of failing to master himself by submitting to a 'feminine' desire for overindulgence in sex.

132.   Cf. Davidson (2001), 20–23.

133.   Aristotle, *Rhetoric* 2.6.1384a15–20; cf. *GPM*, p. 215 and Foucault (1978), p.243.

134.   As in Aiskhines I.185; cf. *GH*, pp. 67–8. However, nowhere does Aiskhines clearly indicate that Timarkhos was the 'receptive' partner; rather, the issue is that he has

allegedly given sexual favours in exchange for money and that he partakes of excessive pleasure.

135. Cf. *Laws* 626e7; *Republic* 430c7; *Phaedrus* 232a4–5.
136. Cf. *Republic* 431a3–b2.
137. *Laws* 839a7; cf. *Phaedrus* 241a4 and *Republic* 403a10.
138. *Laws* 838d5; cf. *Republic* 577d2, 579d10 and *Phaedrus* 238e3; *GPM*, p. 208.
139. Konstan (1997), pp. 71–2.
140. (1994), p. 94. Cf. my chapter IV.
141. Cf. my chapter III on education.
142. Cf. my chapter I.
143. Of course, madness has also been associated with the pursuit of philosophy in the *Phaedrus*, but evidently that sort of 'madness' is not of the harmful variety. Cf. *Phaedrus* 244–245c and 249d–e on the 'good' type of madness send by the gods.
144. (1920), p. 345.
145. (1963), p. 144.
146. That is, if we are to take her words seriously (although it would be imprudent to regard Diotima, or any other Platonic character, as an *exclusive* 'mouthpiece' for Plato's innermost thoughts).
147. 203a6–8. Perhaps a better rendering would be something like 'a superior variety [implicit in μέγας] of spiritual entity'; see the following note.
148. Whether or not love (*Erōs*) is a god is a subject of much discussion in Plato's works. For example, in the *Phaedrus*, *Erōs* is characterised as a great god (242d sq) and therefore incapable of evil (242e). *Erōs*' divinity is further supported by the Platonic Sokrates praying to it at *Phaedrus* 257a. Nevertheless, we should not disregard Diotima's suggestion that it is some other type of spiritual being on account of these things as Plato is perfectly entitled to change his mind. *Erōs* is clearly considered in Plato's dialogues to be a divine entity of a powerful nature. 'Typically', as Gould (1991), p. 179, indicates, 'Δαίμονες and τὸ δαιμόνιον represent the mysterious agencies by which the gods communicate with mortals'. It can also be used to refer to any god, the souls of the heroes of the golden age and, later, any souls of the deceased; cf. *LSJ* s.v. δαίμων.
149. XXIV.525–6.
150. fr. 7.2–6 (DK).
151. A 32.24–25 (DK).
152. Cp. *Republic*, 437d sq., on mundane vs. 'higher' desires.
153. As Gould (1963), p. 139, says, 'we have little evidence that Plato actually ceased to believe in the description he gave of love in the *Symposium* and the *Phaedrus*. Indeed, the *Phaedrus* may well have been written fairly late in Plato's life'.
154. For immortality of the soul in Plato see also *Letter* VII.334e; *Meno*, 81b, 85c; *Phaedo*, 72e–76, 85e–91 sq. 105 sq., 107c; *Republic*, 498c, 608c sq., *Timaeus*, 41c sq., 69c; *Symposium*, 208c, amongst others.
155. (1997), p. 69.
156. (1989), p. 60. Cf. my chapter IV on doxastic self-mastery.
157. *Ibid.* p. 61.
158. These 'rival impulses' may also result from confusion on the part of the lover between the active and passive senses of φίλος, as discussed at *Lysis* 212a sq.

159. ὥρας καθάπερ ὀπώρας πεινῶν–note the pun.
160. *Phaedrus* 239b.
161. *mania–Phaedrus* 265a–266a sq.
162. This issue was likewise glossed in the *Symposium* (218b) in that Phaedrus, Agathon, Eryximachus, Pausanias, Aristodemus, Aristophanes and Sokrates have all had a taste of this 'philosophic and Bacchic madness' (τῆς φιλοσόφου μανίας τε καὶ βακχείας).
163. (1973), p. 27. n.80.
164. (1964), p. 49 sq. But it is reasonable to question this presumption given the unknowability of Plato's thoughts.
165. Indeed, the Athenian Stranger recommends a sort of 'Dionysiac treatment' for mothers to use in putting babies to sleep at *Laws* 790e and, at *Republic* 479d–e, the narrator Sokrates informs Glaucon that the revellers at the Dionysiac festivals bear a certain likeness to philosophers.
166. It is possible that we should not read the *Laws* with recourse to Plato's earlier works and that it should stand alone. However, there is evidence for no small doxographic compatibility and some indication that the Magnesians (at least the *nukertinos*) will have access to the Platonic canon, cf. my chapter II.
167. Cf. Thuc. II.43.1 for Perikles' erotic imagery and Aristophanes, *Knights* 732 and 1340–44 for a mocking of Kleon's overuse of this type of language.
168. (2000), p. 64.
169. Halperin (1990), p. 25, maintains that 'sexuality' in general is a modern construct that is defined as a 'separate, sexual domain within the larger field of man's psychophysical nature'. While I do not disagree with this in principle, I believe that one can speak of ancient concepts of 'sexuality'. One does so even if they are defined in terms of 'active' subjects and 'passive' objects–although any such conceptualisation of ancient thought is at least reductive and, at best, inaccurate.
170. Cf. my chapters I and II, and cf. Davidson (2001), p. 27.
171. Cf. my chapter V.
172. Halperin (1990), p. 41.
173. The Hippokratic text *On Diseases of Women* indicates (I.6) that the healthiest type of woman is 'masculine', but less inclined toward maternity and conception.
174. Cf. Davidson (2001), p. 28 sq.
175. *De morbis chronicis*, IV.9.132–3.
176. Cf. 847a5–b2; . . . τὴν τῆς ἀρετῆς ἐπιμέλειαν.
177. Aiskhines condemns Timarkhos as a man 'who has outraged (*hubrizein*) himself contrary to nature' (qtd. in *GH*, p. 60). Dover says that 'if Aeschines really means that same sex relations in general are unnatural, he is adopting a standpoint otherwise expounded only in one strand of the Socratic-Platonic philosophical tradition' (*ibid.*).
178. cf. my chapter IV.
179. (1994), p. 95.
180. (1997), p. 179. The notion that habitual practice can cause something to become 'second nature' can be found at *Republic* 359d, 'when men persist in imitations long after youth is past, that imitative behaviour becomes their established habit and nature'. Aristotle likewise maintained that habit becomes 'second nature' (*Rhet.* I.11.1370a6–9).

181. Davidson (1997), p. 174. He is talking specifically here about Sokrates' characterisation of the *kinaidos* in his argument with Kallikles over the nature of desire at *Gorgias* 493a–494e. Cf. Davidson (2001), pp. 23–25.

182. Cf. my chapters II, III and IV.

NOTES TO CHAPTER VIII

1. *Laws* 969b5–9, cp. 964d sq.
2. From the *Excursion* in Morley ed. (1888), p. 417.
3. 701d, cf. 693 b–c.
4. 969c8–10. By the phrase 'in the task of settling the *polis*' (. . . ἐπὶ τὴν τῆς πόλεως κατοίκισιν), he means 'to settle' it in the sense of colonisation, but the double meaning appears applicable both in the Greek and in English.

Bibliography

Adam, James ed. Plato. *Respublica*. Clay & Sons: London, 1891.

———. Plato. *The Republic*. vols. I–II. Cambridge University Press: Cambridge, 1902.

Adkins, A. W. *From the Many to the One: A Study of Personality and Views of Human Nature in the Context of Ancient Greek Society, Values and Beliefs*. Clarendon Press: Oxford, 1960.

Aghion, Iréne, Claire Barbillon and François Lissarrague eds. *Gods and Heroes of Classical Antiquity*, trans. by Leonardo N. Amico. Flammarion: Paris and New York, 1996.

Anderson, Michael J. *The Fall of Troy in Early Greek Poetry and Art*. Clarendon Press: Oxford, 1997.

Annas, J. 'Plato's *Republic* and Feminism', *Philosophy* 51, (1976), pp. 307–21.

Archer, L., S. Fischler and M. Wyke. *Women in Ancient Societies: An Illusion of the Night*. Macmillan: London, 1994.

Arjava, Anitti. *Women and Law in Late Antiquity*. Clarendon Press: Oxford, 1996.

Asimov, Isaac. *Foundation and Earth*. Nightfall Inc.: Glasgow, 1996

Auden, W. H. *Forewords and Afterwords*, ed. E. Mendelsohn. Faber: London, 1973.

Austin, M. M. and P. Vidal-Naquet. *Economic & Social History of Ancient Greece: An Introduction*. B. T. Batsford Ltd.: London, 1977.

Badawi, A., ed. *Theology of Aristotle* (Cairo, 1955), trans. by G. L. Lewis in *Plotini opera*, ed. P. Henry and and H. R. Schwyzer, ii. Paris and Brussels, 1959.

Bain, David. 'Six Greek Verbs of Sexual Congress', *Classical Quarterly*, new series, xli (1991), pp. 51–77.

Banks, Iain M. *Use of Weapons*. Orbit: London, 2000.

———. *State of the Art*. Orbit: London, 2001.

Barclay, William. *Educational Ideals in the Ancient World*. Collins: London, 1959.

Barker, Andrew. *Greek Musical Writings: Vol 1, The Musician and His Art*. Cambridge University Press: London 1984.

Beck, Frederick A. G. *Greek Education*. Methuen & Co. LTD: London, 1964.

Belfiore, E. 'Wine and Catharsis of the Emotions in Plato's *Laws*', *Classical Quarterly, xxxvi* (1986), pp. 421–37.

Benhabib, Seyla, Judith Butler, Drucilla Cornell, Nancy Fraser and Linda Nicholson. *Feminist Contentions: A Philosophical Exchange*. Routledge: New York, 1995.

Berger, Maurice, Brian Wallis and Simon Watson eds. *Constructing Masculinity*. Routledge: New York, 1995.

Bergk, Theodor ed. *Poetae Lyrici Graeci*. 4th edition. Teubner: Leipzig, 1878–82. (*PLG*)

Bignone, E. *Empedocle: studio critico*. Bocca: Turin, 1916.

Blondell, Ruby. *The Play of Character.* Cambridge University Press: Cambridge, 2002.

Bluck, R. S. *Plato's Seventh and Eighth Letters.* Cambridge University Press: Cambridge, 1947.

Blundell, Sue. 'Marriage and the Maiden: narratives on the Parthenon', in Blundell and Williamson (1998), pp. 47–70.

———. *Women in Ancient Greece.* British Museum Press: London, 1995.

Blundell, Sue and Margaret Williamson eds. *The Sacred and the Feminine in Ancient Greece.* Routledge: London, 1998.

Bobonich, Christopher. *Plato's Utopia Recast: His Later Ethics and Politics.* Clarendon Press: Oxford, 2002.

———. 'Persuasion, Compulsion and Freedom in Plato's *Laws*', in *Classical Quarterly* xli.ii (1991), pp. 365–388.

Bonner, Robert J. *Aspects of Athenian Democracy.* University of California Press: Berkeley, 1933.

Bowman, Alan K. and Greg Woolf eds. *Literacy and Power in the Ancient World.* Cambridge University Press: Cambridge, 1994.

Bovon, Anne. 'La Représentation des Guerriers Perses et la Notion de Barbare dans la Ire Moitié du Ve Siécle', in *BCH* 87 (1963), pp. 579–602.

Boyancé, P. 'Platon et le vin', in *BAGB, Lettres d'humanité* (1951), pp. 3–19.

Brant, Clare. 'The Politics of Teaching and Political Education in Late Eighteenth Century Dialogues', in Too and Livingstone (1998), pp. 67–82.

Bray, Alan. *Homosexuality in Renaissance England.* Gay Men's Press: London, 1992.

Bremmer, Jan ed. *Interpretations of Greek Mythology.* Croom Helm: London, 1987.

———. 'Adolescents, *Symposion,* and Pederasty', in Murray (1990), pp. 135–148.

Briant, Pierre. 'History and Ideology: The Greeks and "Persian Decadence,"' trans. by Antonia Nevill, in Harrison (2002), pp. 193–210.

Brisson, Luc. 'The Vigilance Committee', presented at the I International Congress on Ancient Thought: *The Laws of Plato and their Historical Significance.* Hosted by the University of Salamanca, Spain: 25 November 1998.

———. 'Proclus et l'Orphisme', in J. Pepin and H. D. Saffrey eds. (1997), pp. 43–104.

———. *Plato the Mythmaker.* Gerard Naddaf, trans. and ed. The University of Chicago Press: Chicago, 1994.

———. *Platon, les mots et les myths.* Paris: 1982.

British Library (2002) http://pages.britishlibrary.net/mikepymm/utilitar.html

Browning, Robert. 'Greeks and Others: From Antiquity to the Renaissance,' in Harrison (2002), pp. 257–277.

Burkert, Walter. *The Orientalizing Revolution: Near Eastern Influences on Greek Culture in the Early Archaic Age.* Harvard University Press: Cambridge, Mass., 1992.

———. 'Herodot als Historiker fremder Religionen', in Burkert et al., *Hérodote et les peuples non-grecs,* Fondation Hardt Entretiens 35 (1990), pp. 1–39.

———. *Ancient Mystery Cults.* Harvard University Press: Cambridge, Mass., 1987.

———. *Lore and Science in Ancient Pythagoreanism,* trans. Edwin L. Minar Jr. Harvard University Press: Cambridge, MS, 1972.

Burnet, John ed. Plato. *The Laws.* Clarendon Press: Oxford, 1913.

———. *Early Greek Philosophy,* Third ed. A&C Black Ltd.: London, 1920.

———. *Greek Philosophy: Thales to Plato.* Macmillan: London, 1930.

Burnett, Andrew. *Coinage in the Roman World.* Seaby: London, 1976.

Burnett, C. ed. Hermann of Carinthia. *De essentiis.* Brill: Leiden, 1982.

Bury, R. G. ed., trans. Plato. *The Laws.* vols. I–II. St. Edmundsbury Press Ltd.: Bury St. Edmunds, Suffolk, 1999.

Butler, Judith. 'Contingent Foundations', in Benhabib, Butler, Cornell, Fraser and Nicholson (1995), pp. 35–58.

Buxton, Richard. *From Myth to Reason? Studies in the Development of Greek Thought.* Oxford University Press: Oxford, 1999.

———. *Imaginary Greece: The Contexts of Mythology.* Cambridge University Press: Cambridge, 1995.

Cairns, Douglas L. *Aidōs: The Psychology and Ethics of Honour and Shame in Ancient Greek Literature.* Clarendon Press: Oxford, 1993.

Cameron, Averil and Amélie Kuhrt eds. *Images of Women in Antiquity.* Croom Helm: London and Canberra, 1983.

Cantarella, Eva. *Bisexuality in the Ancient World.* Yale University Press: New Haven, 1992.

Carradice, Ian. *Greek Coins.* The Bath Press (for the British Museum): Suffolk, 1995.

Cartledge, Paul. 'Spartan Wives: Liberation or License?' in *Classical Quarterly* XXXI.i, (1981), pp. 84–105.

———. *The Greeks: A Portrait of Self and Others.* Oxford University Press: Oxford, 1993.

———. 'Classics: from discipline in crisis to (multi-)cultural capital', in Too and Livingstone (1998), pp. 16–28.

———. *Spartan Reflections.* Duckworth: London, 2001.

Cartledge, Paul, Paul Millett and Stephen Todd eds. *Nomos: Essays in Athenian Law, Politics and Society.* Cambridge University Press: Cambridge, 1990.

Castle, E. B. *Ancient Education and Today.* Penguin: Hammondsworth, Middlesex, 1962.

Cawkwell, George. *Thucydides and the Peloponesian War.* Routledge: London, 1997.

Cawkwell, George Law. 'The peace between Athens and Persia,' in *Phoenix, The Journal of the Classical Association of Canada.* (Toronto). Vol. 51 (1997a), pp. 115–130.

Chambers, M. ed. Aristotle. *The Athenian Constitution.* B. G. Teubner: Leipzig, 1994.

Channel 4. *The Truth About Gay Animals.* Aired 22 April 2002, 10:35 P.M.

———. *Sex B.C.* Aired 29 July 2002(a), 5 August 2002 (b) and 12 August 2002 (c) at 9:00 P.M.

Chase, A. H. 'The Influence of Athenian Institutions upon the *Laws* of Plato', *Harvard Studies in Classical Philology,* XLIV (1933) pp. 131–192.

Ch'êng-ên, Wu. *Monkey.* Nihon Television: Japan, 1979.

Chodorow, Nancy. *The Power of Feelings: Personal Meaning in Psychoanalysis, Gender and Culture.* Yale University Press: New Haven, 1999.

———*Femininities Masculinities Sexualities: Freud and Beyond.* Free Association Books: London, 1994.

———*The Reproduction of Mothering: Psychoanalysis and the Sociology of Gender.* The University of California Press: Berkeley, 1978.

———'Family Structure and Feminine Personality', in Rosaldo, Michell Z. and Louise Lamphere (1974), pp. 43–66.

Chomsky, Noam. Interview in *The Whole Shebang.* BBC2, aired 1 April 2002.

Chroust, A. H. 'A Second (and Closer) Look at Plato's Philosophy', *Archiv für Staatswissenschaften und Geschichte,* 48 (1962), pp 575–597.

Clairmont, C. *Classical Attic Tombstones,* vols. i–vii with plates. Arkanthus: Kilchberg, 1993.

Cloché, Paul. *Thebes de Béotie.* Descleé de Brouwer: Paris, 1950.

Cohen, Beth ed. *Not the Classical Ideal: Athens and the Construction of the Other in Greek Art.* Koninklijke Brill NV: Leiden, 2000.

Cohen, D. 'The social context of adultery at Athens', in Cartledge, Millet and Todd (1990), pp. 147–65.

Cole, Susan G. 'Domesticating Artemis', in Blundell and Williamson (1998), pp. 27–44.

Croally, N. T. *Euripidean Polemic: The* Trojan Women *and the function of tragedy.* Cambridge University Press: Cambridge, 1994.

Crombie, I. M. *An Examination of Plato's Doctrines,* vol. I. Routledge: London, 1962.

Davidson, James. *Courtesans and Fishcakes: The Consuming Passions of Classical Athens.* Fontana Press: London, 1997.

———. 'Dover, Foucault and Greek Homosexuality: Penetration and the Truth of Sex', *Past and Present,* 170 (February 2001), pp. 3–51.

Davies, Anna Morpurgo. 'The Greek Notion of Dialect,' in Harrison (2002), pp. 153–171.

Davies, J. K. *Athenian Propertied Families.* Clarendon Press: Oxford, 1971.

———. *Democracy and Classical Greece.* Fontana: London, 1978.

De Marcellus, Henri Venable. *The Origins and Nature of the Attic Ephēbeia to 200 B.C.* Oxford University D. Phil. Thesis, 1994.

Deacy, S. and K. Pierce, eds. *Rape in Antiquity.* Duckworth: London, 1997.

Deacy, Susan. 'The vulnerability of Athena: *parthenoi* and rape in Greek myth', in Deacy and Pierce, (1997), pp. 43–64.

de Beauvoir, Simone. *The Second Sex,* trans. and ed. by H. M. Parshley. Johnathan Cape: London, 1953.

de Vogel, C. J. *Pythagoras and Early Pythagoreanism: An Interpretation of Neglected Evidence on the Philosopher Pythagoras.* Royal VanGorcum Ltd., Assen: Netherlands, 1966.

Derrida, Jacques. *Of Grammatology,* trans. by Gayatri Chakravorty Spivak. Johns Hopkins University Press: Baltimore, MD, 1998.

———. *Dissemination,* trans by Barbara Johnson. University of Chicago Press: Chicago, 1981.

Devereaux, G. 'Why Oedipus Killed Laius', *International Journal of Psychoanalysis,* xxxiv (1953), pp. 32–141.

Diehl, Ernst ed. *Anthologia Lyrica Graeca,* vol. II, 3rd ed. Teubner: Liepzig, 1950.

Diels, Hermann. *Doxographici Graeci.* Weidmann: Berlin, 1879.

———. *Poetarum philusuphurum fragmenta.* Weidmann: Berlin, 1901.

———. *Die Fragmente der Vorsokratiker,* Tenth ed., ed. by W. Kranz. Weidmann: Berlin, 1951–2. (DK)

Diels, Hermann and Wilhelm Schubart eds. *Anonymer Kommentar zu Platons Theaetet (Papyrus 9782), nebst drei Bruchstücken philosophischen Inhalts (Pap. N.8; P. 9766, 9569) unter Mitwirkung von J. L. Heiberg bearbeitet von H. Diels und W. Schubart.* Weidmann: Berlin, 1904. (Diels-Schubart)

Dindorf, G. *Scholia graeca in Homeri Odysseam: ex codicibus aucta et emendata; edidit Gulielmus Dindorfius.* Oxonii: E Typographeo Academico, 1855.

Dover, Sir Kenneth J. *Aristophanes: Clouds.* Oxford University Press: Oxford, 1968.

——— *The Greeks.* British Broadcasting Corporation: London, 1980.

——— *Greek Homosexuality.* Duckworth: London, 1978. (*GH*)

——— *Greek Homosexuality,* 2nd ed. MJF Books: New York, 1989.

——— *Greek Popular Morality in the Time of Plato and Aristotle.* Oxford University Press: Oxford, 1974 (*GPM*).

DuBois, Page. *Sowing the Body: Psychoanalysis and Ancient Representations of Women.* The University of Chicago Press: Chicago, 1988.

Edwards, Catharine. 'Seneca and Stoic virility', presented at the University of St. Andrews, School of Greek, Latin and Ancient History Class Seminar, 22 February 2002.

Elshtain, Jean Bethke. *Public Man, Private Woman: Women in Social and Political Thought.* Martin Robertson: Oxford, 1981.

Engels, Frederick. *The Origin of the Family, Private Property and the State.* Lawrence & Wishart: London, 1977.

England, E. B., ed. Plato. *The Laws.* vols. I–II. Manchester University Press: Manchester, 1921.

Ferrari, G.R.F. *Listening to the Cicadas : A Study of Plato's Phaedrus.* Cambridge University Press, Cambridge: 1987.

Field, G. C. *The Philosophy of Plato,* 2nd ed. Oxford University Press: Oxford, 1969.

Finley, Sir M. I. *The Use and Abuse of History.* The Logarth Press: London, 1986.

Fisher, N. R. E. *Hybris.* Aris and Phillips Ltd.: Wiltshire, 1992.

Flower, Harriet I. *Ancester Masks and Aristocratic Power in Roman Culture.* Clarendon Press: Oxford, 1996.

Foley, Helene P. *Reflections of Women in Antiquity.* Gordon and Breach Science Publishers: London, 1985.

Formosa, Joe. *Hyperdiscordia* (2002), http://jubal.westnet.com/hyperdiscordia/

Foucault, M. *L'Usage des plaisirs.* Rilem: Paris, 1984

———. *The History of Sexuality, vol. I: an Introduction,* trans. by Robert Hurley. Vintage Books: New York, 1978.

Foxhall, Lin and John Salmon eds. *Thinking Men: Masculinity and its Self-Representation in the Classical Tradition.* Routledge: London and New York, 1998.

Freeman, Kathleen. *God, Man and State: Greek Concepts.* MacDonald: London, 1952.

———. *Greek City States.* MacDonald: London, 1950.

Friedländer, Paul. *Plato: An Introduction,* trans. by Hans Meyerhoff. Pantheon Books: New York, 1958.

Garner, Richard. *Law and Society in Classical Athens.* Croom Helm Ltd.: London, 1987.

Geddes, A. G. 'Rags and Riches: the Costume of Athenian Men in the Fifth Century', *Classical Quarterly,* ii (1987), pp. 307–331.

Gerson, L. P. *God and Greek Philosophy.* Routledge: London, 1990.

Gill, Christopher. *Personality in Greek Epic, Tragedy and Philosophy: The Self in Dialogue.* Clarendon Press: Oxford, 1996.

Gilpatrick, Leslie. *Reading With Children: Helping Children Learn Skills for Reading Success.* McCloud Publishing: Santa Cruz, CA, 2000.

Gleason, Maud W. *Making Men: Sophists and Self-Presentation in Ancient Rome.* Princeton University Press: Princeton, NJ, 1995.

Golden, Leon. 'Aristotle on Tragic and Comic *Mimesis,*' *American Philological Association: American Classical Studies* (29), Scholars Press: Atlanta, 1992.

Golden, Mark. *Children and Childhood in Classical Athens.* Johns Hopkins University Press: Baltimore, 1990.

Golden, Mark and P. Toohey, eds. *Inventing Ancient Culture: Historicism, Periodization, and the Ancient World.* Routledge: London, 1997.

Goldhill, Simon. *Who Needs Greek? Contests in the Cultural History of Hellenism.* Cambridge University Press: Cambridge, 2002.

———. 'Representing Democracy: Women at the Great Dionysia', in Osborne and Hornblower (1994), pp. 347–369.

Goold, G. P. ed. *Plato: Lysis, Symposium, Gorgias,* trans. by W. R. M. Lamb. Loeb Classical Library. St. Edmundsbury Press Ltd.: Bury St. Edmunds, Suffolk, 1991.

Gould, John. *Herodotus.* Weidenfeld and Nicolson: London, 1989.

———. 'Law, custom and myth: aspects of the social position of women in Classical Athens', *JHS* 100 (1980), pp. 38–59.

Gould, Thomas. *Platonic Love.* Routledge & Kegan Paul: London, 1963.

Graves, Frank P. *A History of Education Before the Middle Ages.* Macmillan: New York, 1910.

Graves, Robert. *The Greek Myths.* Penguin Books: London, 1960.

Graziosi, Barbara. *Inventing Homer.* Cambridge University Press: Cambridge, 2002.

Green, Peter. *Alexander of Macedon, 356–323 B.C : A Historical Biography.* Harmondsworth: Penguin, 1974.

Griffith, Mark. 'Public and Private in Early Greek Institutions of Education', in Too (2001), pp. 23–84.

Grosz, Elizabeth. *Jaques Lacan: A Feminist Introduction.* Routledge: London, 1990.

Gunderson, Erik. *Staging Masculinity: The Rhetoric of Performance in the Roman World.* The University of Michigan Press: Ann Arbor, 2000.

Guthrie, W. K. C. *A history of Greek philosophy/Vol.5, The later Plato and the Academy.* Cambridge University Press: Cambridge, 1978.

Halsall, Paul. 'The Law Code of Gortyn', in *Ancient History Sourcebook,* 1998, http://www.fordham.edu/halsall/ancient/450-gortyn.html, pp. 1–3.

Hall, Catherine. *White, Male and Middle Class: Explorations in Feminism and History.* Polity Press: Cambridge, 1992.

Hall, Edith. *Inventing the Barbarian: Greek Self-Definition through Tragedy.* Clarendon Press: Oxford, 1989.

———. 'Asia Unmanned', in Rich and Shipley (1993), pp. 108–133.

Hall, Jonathan M. *Ethnic Identity in Greek Antiquity.* Cambridge University Press: Cambridge, 1997.

Hall, Robert William. *Plato and the Individual.* Martinus Nijhoff: The Hague, 1963.

Halliwell, Stephen. *Aristotle's Poetics.* Duckworth: London 1998.

Halperin, David M., John J. Winkler and Froma I. Zeitlin eds. *Before Sexuality: The Construction of Erotic Experience in the Ancient Greek World.* Princeton University Press: Princeton, NJ, 1990.

Halperin, David M. *One Hundred Years of Homosexuality and Other Essays on Greek Love.* Routledge: New York and London, 1990.

Hamilton, Edith and Huntington Cairns. *The Collected Dialogues of Plato, Including the Letters.* Princeton University Press: Princeton, NJ, 1989.

Hardwick, Lorna. 'Amazons: Heroes, Outsiders, or Women?' in McAuslan and Walcot (1996), pp. 158–176.

Harris, William V. *Ancient Literacy.* Harvard University Press: Cambridge, Mass., 1989.

Harrison, A. R. W. *The Law of Athens: Procedure.* The Clarendon Press: Oxford, 1971.

———. 'Law-making at Athens at the End of the Fifth Century B.C.', *Journal of Hellenic Studies,* 75 (1955) pp. 33–5.

Harrison, Thomas ed. *Greeks and Barbarians.* Edinburgh University Press: Edinburgh, 2002.

Harrison, Thomas. *The Emptiness of Asia: Aeschylus' Persians and the History of the Fifth Century.* Duckworth & Co. Ltd.: London, 2000.

———. 'Herodotus and the ancient Greek idea of rape', in Deacy and Pierce (1997), pp. 185–208.

Hartog, Francois. *The Mirror of Herodotus: The Representation of the Other in the Writing of History*, trans. by Janet Lloyd. University of California Press: Berkeley, 1988.

Hawley, Richard and Barbara Levick eds. *Women in Antiquity: New Assessments*. Routledge: London and New York, 1995.

Hermann, Karl Friedrich. *Appendix Platonica*. Heidelberg University Press: Heidelberg, 1852–64.

Herzfeld, Michael. *The Poetics of Manhood: Contest and Identity in a Cretan Mountain Village*. Princeton University Press: Princeton, 1985.

Hesk, J. 'Flyte Club: an Idiom of Contest in Athenian Drama and Culture', presented at the University of St. Andrews' School of Greek, Latin and Ancient History's Class. Seminar, 22 March 2002.

———. *Deception and Democracy in Classical Athens*. Cambridge University Press: Cambridge, 2000.

Hignett, C. *A History of the Athenian Constitution to the End of the Fifth Century B.C.* Oxford University Press: Oxford, 1952.

Hobbs, Angela. *Plato and the Hero: Courage, Manliness and the Impersonal Good*. Cambridge University Press: Cambridge, 2000.

Hodkinson, Stephen and Anton Powell, eds. *Sparta: New Perspectives*. Duckworth & Co. Ltd: London, 1999.

Hodkinson Stephen '"Blind *Ploutos*"? Contemporary Images of the Role of Wealth in Classical Sparta', in Powell and Hodkinson (1994), pp. 183–222.

———*Property and Wealth in Classical Sparta*. Duckworth and the Classical Press of Wales: London, 2000.

Hornblower, Simon. 'The Old Oligarch (Pseudo-Xenophon's *Athenian Politeia*) and Thucydides: A Fourth Century Date for the *Old Oligarch*?' in Pernille, Nielsen and Rubinstein eds. (2000), pp. 363–384.

Humphreys, S. C. 'Law, Custom and Culture in Herodotus,' in *Arethusa* (1987), I.2, pp. 211–220.

———. *The Family, Women and Death: Comparative Studies*. Routledge & Kegan Paul: London, 1983.

Immerwahr, Henry R. 'Pathology of Power in the Speeches in Thucydides', in Stadter ed. (1973), pp. 16–31.

Irigaray, L. *Speculum of the Other Woman*, trans. by C. Gill. Cornell University Press: Ithaca, New York, 1985.

Ito, Sadao. 'The Enrolment of Athenian Phratries', *Legal History Review*, 31 (1981), pp. 35–60.

Jackson, H. 'On *Laws* 896d'. *Cambridge Philosphical Society*, Lent Term 1912.

Jacoby, F ed. *Die Fragmente der griechischen Historiker* Brill: Leiden, 1926–1958. (*FGrH*)

Jaeger, Werner. *Aristoteles: Grundlegung einer Geschichte seiner Entwicklung*. Weidmann: Berlin, 1923.

———*Paideia: the Ideals of Greek Culture*, trans. by Gilbert Highet. Basil Blackwell: Oxford, 1939.

Jeanmaire, H. *Couroi et Courêtes: Essai sur l'éducation spartiate et sur les rites d'adolescence dans l'antiquité hellénique*. Bibliothéque Universitaire Lille: 1939.

Jocelyn, H. D. 'A Greek Indecency and its Students: ΛΑΙΚΑΖΕΙΝ', *Proceedings of the Cambridge Philological Society*, xxvi (1980), pp. 12–66.

Jones, Ian. 'Aeschylus, the Persians and Tyrant Mania', presented at the University of St. Andrews postgraduate seminar, 6th March 2002.

Jones, J. W. *Law and Legal Theory of the Greeks: an Introduction.* The Clarendon Press: Oxford, 1956.

Jost, K. 'Das Beispiel und Vorbild der Vorfaren bei den anrischen Redern und Geschichtssch-reiben bis Demosthenes', *Rhetorische Studien* 19, Paderborn (1936), pp. 140–45.

Joyal, Mark ed. *Studies in Plato and the Platonic Tradition.* Ashgate Publishing Ltd.: Aldershot, 1997.

Just, Roger. *Women in Athenian Law and Life.* Routledge: London and New York, 1989.

Kahn, Charles H. *Plato and the Socratic Dialogue: The Philosophical Use of the Literary Form.* Cambridge University Press: Cambridge, 1996.

Kahrstedt, U. 'Untersuchungen zu athenischen Behörden', *Klio* 31 (1938), pp. 1–25.

Kassel, R and C. Austin eds. *Poetae comici Graecae.* de Gruyter: Berlin, 1968. (*PCG*)

Kearns, Emily. 'The nature of heroines', in Blundell and Williamson (1998), pp. 96–110.

Kennell, Nigel M. *The Gymnasium of Virtue: Education and Culture in Ancient Sparta.* University of North Carolina Press: Chapel Hill, 1995.

Kern, Otto. *Inscriptiones Graecae.* Walter de Gruyter & Co.: Berlin, 1913. (*IG*)

———. *Inschriften von Magnesia am Maeander.* Walter de Gruyter & Co.: Berlin, 1900.

Kingsley, Peter. *Ancient Philosophy, Mystery, and Magic: Empedocles and the Pythagorean Tradition.* Clarendon Press: Oxford, 1995.

Kinkel G. ed. *Epicorum Graecorum Fragmenta.* Vandenhoek & Ruprecht: Gottingen, 1988. (*Frag. ep.*)

Konstan, David. *Friendship in the Classical World: Key Themes in Ancient History.* Cambridge University Press: Cambridge, 1997.

Kranz, W. *Empedokles: Antike Gestalt und romantische Neuschoepfung.* Weidmann: Zurich, 1949.

Kurke, Leslie. *Coins, Bodies, Games and Gold: the Politics of Meaning in Archaic Greece.* Princeton University Press: Princeton, 1999.

Lacey, W. K. *The Family in Classical Greece.* Cornel University Press: New York, NY, 1968.

Lambert, S. D. *The Phratries of Attica.* The University of Michigan Press: Anne Arbor, 1993.

Laqueur, Thomas. *Making Sex: Body and Gender from the Greeks to Freud.* Harvard University Press: Cambridge Massachusetts & London, 1990.

Le Balet Comique de la Reine. University of Washington. *artsci.washington.edu/drama-phd/bctextp1.html* (2002)

Lee, Desmond, ed. and trans. *Plato: The Republic* (2nd ed.). Penguin Books: Middlesex, 1974.

Lefkowitz, M. R. and M. B. Fant, eds. *Women's Life in Greece and Rome.* Duckworth: London, 1982.

Lesky, Erna. 'Die Zeugungs-und Vererbungslehren der Antike und ihr Nachwirkin', Abhandl. Der Geistes- und Sozialwissenshaftlichen Klasse. *Mainz* 19 (1950), p. 20.

Liddell, Henry George and Robert Scott revised and ed. by Sir Henry Stuart Jones. *A Greek-English Lexicon,* 9th edition. The Clarendon Press, Oxford, 1994. (*LSJ*)

Linforth, I. M. 'The Corybantic Rites in Plato', *University of California Publications in Classical Philology,* XIII (1946), pp. 21–62

Lissarrague, François. *The Aesthetics of the Greek Banquet: Images of Wine and Ritual (Un Flot d'Images),* trans. by Andrew Szegedy-Maszak. Princeton University Press: Princeton, 1990.

Loraux, Nicole. *The Children of Athena: Athenian Ideas About Citizenship and the Division Between the Sexes,* trans. by Caroline Levine. Princeton University Press: Princeton, NJ, 1993.

————. *The Experiences of Tiresias: The Feminine and the Greek Man,* trans. by Paula Wissing. Princeton University Press: Princeton, 1995.

Lovibond, Sabina. 'An Ancient Theory of Gender', in Archer, Fischler and Wyke, (1994), pp. 89–101.

Lyons, Deborah. *Gender and Immortality: Heroines in Ancient Greek Myth and Cult.* Princeton University Press, Princeton, NJ, 1997.

McAuslan, Ian and Peter Walcot eds. *Women in Antiquity.* Oxford University Press: Oxford, 1996.

McKinnon, Catherine. 'Feminism, Marxism, Method and the State: An Agenda for Theory', *Signs,* (vol 7, no. 3) Spring 1982, pp. 515–544.

MacDonald, C. 'Plato, Laws 704a–707c and Thucydides II.35–46', *Classical Review* IX.1959, pp. 108–109.

MacDowell, Douglas M. *The Law in Classical Athens: Aspects of Greek and Roman Life.* ed. H. Scullard. Cornell University Press: Ithaca, New York, 1978.

————, ed. Gorgias. *The Encomium of Helen.* Duckworth & Co. Ltd.: London, 1982.

Macherey, Pierre. *A Theory of Literary Production,* trans. by Geoffrey Wall. Routledge: London, 1978.

Mactoux, M. 'Phobos à Sparte', *RHR* 210.3 (1993), pp. 279–90.

Marrou, H. I. *A History of Education in Antiquity,* trans. by George Lamb. The University of Wisconsin Press: Madison, Wisconsin, 1982.

Marx, Karl. *Capital : a Critique of Political Economy.* Frederick Engels, ed; translated from the first German edition by Ernest Untermann. Chicago: Kerr, 1909.

Maxwell-Stuart, P. G. 'Antipater's Eupalamus', *American Journal of Philology* 96 (1975), pp 13–15.

Michell, H. *Sparta.* Cambridge University Press: Cambridge, 1964.

Millender, Ellen G. 'Athenian ideology and the empowered Spartan woman', in Hodkinson and Powell (1999), pp. 355–392.

Miller, Margaret C. 'The Myth of Bousiris: Ethnicity and Art,' in Cohen (2000), pp. 413–442.

————. *Athens and Persia in the Fifth Century BC: a Study in Cultural Receptivity.* Cambridge University Press: London, 1997.

Monoson, S. Sara. *Plato's Democratic Entanglements: Athenian Politics and the Practice of Philosophy.* Princeton University Press: Princeton, NJ, 2000.

More, St Thomas. *Utopia.* J. Churton Collins, ed. The Clarendon Press: Oxford, 1930.

Morgan, Kathryn A. *Myth and Philosophy from the Presocratics to Plato.* Cambridge University Press: Cambridge, 2000.

Morley, John ed. *The Complete Poetical Works of William Wordsworth.* Macmillan & Co.: London, 1888.

Morrow, Glenn A. *Plato's Cretan City: A Historical Interpretation of* the Laws. Princeton University Press: Princeton, NJ, 1960.

————*Plato's Epistles.* The Bobbs-Merrill Co. Inc.: New York, 1962.

Mortely, Raoule. *Womanhood: the Feminine in Ancient Hellenism, Gnosticism, Christianity and Islam.* Delacroix Press: Sydney, 1981

Mossman, Judith. *Wild Justice: A Study of Euripides'* Hecuba. Clarendon Press: Oxford, 1995.

Motluk, Alison. 'Read My Mind'. *New Scientist,* No.2275 (27 January 2001), pp. 23–26.

Müller, C. ed. *Fragmenta Historicorum Graecorum.* Firmin Didot: Paris, 1841–72. (*FHG*)

Murray, Oswyn ed. *Sympotica: a Symposium on the Symposion.* Clarendon Press: Oxford, 1990.

Murray, Oswyn and Simon Price eds. *The Greek City: From Homer to Alexander.* Clarendon
    Press: Oxford, 1990.
Murray, Oswyn. 'The Affair of the Mysteries: Democracy and the Drinking Group', in Murray
    (1990), pp.149–161.
Murray, Penelope. 'What is *Muthos* for Plato?' in Buxton ed. 1999.
———. *Plato on Poetry.* Cambridge University Press: Cambridge, 1996.
Napier, Charles. *The Design of the Creator: A Guide to Humanae Vitae.* Methuen: London,
    1969.
Nauck A. ed. *Tragicorum Graecorum Fragmenta.* 2nd edition. Hildersheim: Olms, 1962.
    (*TGF*)
Needham, J. *Science and Civilisation in China.* London University Press: Cambridge,
    1954–84.
Nightingale, Andrea Wilson. 'Liberal Education in Plato's *Republic* and Aristotle's *Politics*', in
    Too (2001), pp. 133–174.
———. 'Plato's Lawcode in Context: Rule by Written Law in Athens and Magnesia', in *Clas-
    sical Quarterly,* xlix.1 (1999), pp. 100–122
———. *Genres in Dialogue: Plato and the Construct of Philosophy.* Cambridge University Press:
    Cambridge, 1997.
Nippel, Wilfred. 'The Construction of the "Other"', trans. by Antonia Nevill. In Harrison
    (2002), pp. 278–310.
Nixon, Lucia and Simon Price. 'The Size and Resources of Greek Cities', in Murray and Price
    (1990), pp. 137–70.
Novotny, Frantisek. *The Posthumous Life of Plato.* Martinus Nijhoff: The Hague, 1977.
Nussbaum, Martha C. 'Platonic love and Colorado Law', *Virginia Law Review,* 80.7 (October
    1994), pp. 1515–1651.
Nuttal, A. D. *Why Does Tragedy Give Pleasure?* Clarendon Press: Oxford, 1996.
Ober, Josiah. 'The Debate Over Civic Education in Classical Athens', in Too (2001), pp.
    175–208.
———. *Political Dissent in Democratic Athens: Intellectual Critics of Popular Rule.* Princeton
    University Press: Princeton, 1998.
———. 'Fortress Attica', in *Mnemosyne: Bibliotheca Classica Batava, supplementum octogesi-
    mum quartum* (84). E.J. Brill: Leiden, 1985.
O'Brien, Mary. *The Politics of Reproduction.* Routledge and Kagen Paul: London, 1981.
Ogden Daniel. 'Rape, adultery and protection of bloodlines in classical Athens', in Deacy and
    Pierce (1997), pp. 25–41.
———. *Greek Bastardy in the Classical and Hellenistic Periods.* Oxford University Press: Ox-
    ford, 1996.
Omitowoju, Rosanna. *Rape and the Politics of Consent in Classical Athens.* Cambridge Univer-
    sity Press: Cambridge, 2002.
———. 'Regulating Rape: Soap Operas and Self-Interest in the Athenian Courts', in Deacy
    and Pierce (1997), pp. 1–24.
Osborne, Robin. 'An Other View: An Essay in Political History', in Cohen (2000), pp.
    21–42.
———. 'Law, the Democratic Citizen and the Representation of Women in Classical Athens',
    Past and Present, 155 (May 1997), pp. 3–34.
Osborne, Robin and Simon Hornblower eds. *Ritual, Financem Politics: Athenian Democratic
    Accounts Presented to David Lewis.* Clarendon Press: Oxford, 1994.

Ostwald, Martin. *Nomos and the Beginnings of the Athenian Democracy.* Clarendon Press: Oxford, 1969.

———. *From Popular Sovereignty to the Sovereignty of Law: Law, Society, and Politics in Fifth Century Athens.* University of California Press: Berkeley, 1986.

Pangle, Thomas L. *The Laws of Plato Translated with Notes and an Interpretive Essay.* The University of Chicago Press: Chicago and London, 1980.

Parker, Robert. 'Spartan Religion', in Powell (1989), pp. 142–172.

———. *Miasma: Pollution and Purification in Early Greek Religion.* The Clarendon Press: Oxford, 1983.

Patterson, C. J. *The Family in Greek History.* Harvard University Press: Cambridge, MA and London, 1998.

Pembroke, Simon. 'Women in Charge: The Function of Alternatives in Early Greek Tradition and the Ancient Idea of Matriarchy', in the *Journal of the Warburg and Courtauld Institutes,* XXX (1967), pp. 1–35.

Pepin, J. and H. D. Saffrey eds. *Proclus: Lecteur et interprete des anciens.* Actes du colloque international du CNRS: Paris, 1997.

Peradotto, John and J. P. Sullivan eds. *Women in the Ancient World: The Arethusa Papers.* State University of New York Press: Albany, 1984.

Pernille Flensted-Jensen, Thomas Heine Nielsen and Lene Rubinstein eds. *Polis and Politics: Studies in Ancient Greek History.* Museum Tusculanum Press: Copenhagen, 2000.

Pieper, J. *Enthusiasm and Divine Madness,* trans. by Richard and Clara Winston. New York, 1964

Pierart, Marcel. *Platon et la Cité Grecque.* Brussels, 1973.

Plessner, M. 'The Place of the *Turba Philosophorum* in the Development of Alchemy', *Isis* (45) 1954, pp. 331–8.

Pomeroy, Sarah B. *Families in Classical and Hellenistic Greece: Representation and Realities.* Clarendon Press: Oxford, 1997.

———. 'Women's Identity and the Family in the Classical *polis*', in Hawley and Levick (1995), pp. 111–121.

———. '*Technikai kai Mousikai:* The Education of Women in the Fourth Century and in the Hellenistic Period', *American Journal of Ancient History,* 2 (1977), pp. 51–68.

———. *Goddesses, Whores, Wives and Slaves: Women in Classical Antiquity.* Pimilco: London, 1975.

Powell, Anton and Stephen Hodkinson eds. *The Shadow of Sparta.* Routledge: London, 1994.

Powell, Anton. 'Plato and Sparta: modes of rule and non-rational persuasion in the *Laws*', in Powell and Hodkinson, (1994), pp. 273–322.

———. ed. *Classical Sparta: Techniques Behind Her Success.* Routledge: London, 1989.

Praechter, K. 'Platon Praformist?' *Philologus,* Bd. 83 (1928), pp. 18–30.

Price, A. W. *Love and Friendship in Plato and Aristotle.* Clarendon Press: Oxford, 1989.

Purcell, Nicholas. 'Mobility and the Polis', Murray and Price (1990), pp. 29–58.

Rankin, H. D. *Plato and the Individual.* Methuen & Co. Ltd.: London, 1964.

Rawson, Elizabeth. *The Spartan Tradition in European Thought.* Clarendon Press: Oxford, 1969.

Redfield, James. 'The Women of Sparta', in *Classical Journal,* (73) 1977–8, pp. 146–61.

Reinmuth, O. W. 'The Ephebic Inscriptions of the Fourth Century B.C'. *Mnemosyne: Bibliotheca Classica Batava.* E.J. Brill: Leiden (1971), pp. 123–138.

Rhodes, P. J. 'The Athenian code of laws, 410–499 B.C'., in *JHS* 111 (1991), pp. 87–100.

———. *A Commentary on the Aristotelian Athenaion Politeia.* Clarendon Press: Oxford 198.

Rich, John and Graham Shipley eds. *War and Society in the Greek World.* Routledge: London, 1993.

Richer, Nicolas. '*Aidōs* at Sparta', in Hodkinson and Powell (1999), pp. 91–116.

Rist, John M. 'Plato and Professor Nussbaum on Acts "Contrary to Nature,"' in Joyal (1997).

Ritter, H. and L. Preller. *Historia Philosophiae Graecae,* (VIII ed.) Edward Wellmann: Gotha, 1898. (*RP*)

Robinson, Dave and Judy Groves. *Introducing Plato.* Icon Books Ltd.: Cambridge, 2000.

Romm, James. *Herodotus.* Yale University Press: New Haven, 1998.

Rosaldo, Michell Z. and Louise Lamphere, eds. *Woman, Culture and Society.* Stanford University Press: Stanford, CA, 1974.

Rosaldo, Michell Z. 'Woman, Culture, and Society: A Theoretical Overview', in Rosaldo and Lamphere (1974), pp. 17–42.

Rosellini, M. and S. Saïd. 'Usages de Femmes et Autres *NOMOI* Chez les 'sauvages' d'Hérodote: Essai de Lecture Structurale', in *Annali della Scuola Normale Superiore di Pisa,* classe di lettere e filosofia (series III), vol. VIII.3, 1978.

Ross, Robert ed. *Selected Poems of Oscar Wilde.* Methuen & Co. Ltd.: London, 1911.

Ross, W. D. ed. Aristotle. *The Politics.* Oxford University Press: Oxford, 1957.

Rowe, C. J. *Philosophers in Context: Plato.* ed. Stephen Körner. The Harvester Press: Sussex, 1984.

Rubenstein, L. 'Athenian grave monuments and social class', *GRBS,* 30 (1989), 411–420.

Rutherford, R.B. *The Art of Plato.* Gerald Duckworth & Co., Ltd.: London, 1995.

Saïd, E. W. *Orientalism.* Pantheon: New York, 1978.

Saïd, Suzanne. *La faute tragique.* F. Maspero: Paris, 1978.

Saunders, Trevor J. *Plato's Penal Code: Tradition, Controversy and Reform in Greek Penology.* Clarendon Press: Oxford, 1991.

———. 'Plato and the Athenian law of theft', in Millet and Todd (1990), pp. 63–82.

———. trans. *Plato: The Laws.* Penguin Books Ltd.: Harmondsworth, Middlesex, 1970.

———. 'Notes on the *Laws* of Plato'. *Bulletin of the Institute of Classical Studies.* Supplement No. 28: 1972.

Schaps, David. 'The Woman Least Mentioned: Etiquette and Women's Names', in *Classical Quarterly,* (1977) new series xxvii, pp. 323–330.

Schöpsdau, Klaus. *Platon: Nomoi, Buch I–III Übersetzung und Kommentar von Klaus Schöpsdau.* Vandenhoek & Ruprecht: Gottingen, 1994.

Scott, Joan W. 'Women's History: The Modern Period', *Past and Present,* (1983), pp. 141–57.

———. 'Gender: A Useful Category of Historical Analysis', *American Historical Review* (91) 1986, pp. 1053–1075.

Sealey, Raphael. *Women and Law in Classical Greece.* The University of North Carolina Press: Chapel Hill, 1990.

Sinfield, Alan. *Cultural Politics—Queer Reading.* Routledge: London, 1994.

Singor, H. W. 'Admission to the *syssitia* in fifth-century Sparta', in Hodkinson and Powell (1999), pp. 67–90.

Smyth, Herbert Weir. *Greek Grammar.* Harvard University Press: Harvard, 1984.

Snodgrass, Anthony. 'Survey Archaeology and Rural Landscape', in Murray and Price (1990), pp. 113–136.

Spencer, Nigel ed. *Time, Tradition and Society in Greek Archaeology: Bridging the Great Divide.* Routledge: London, 1995.

Stadter, Philip A. ed. with intro. *The Speeches in Thucydides: A Collection of Original Studies With a Bibliography.* The University of North Carolina Press: Chapel Hill, 1973.

Stadter, Philip A. 'Thucydidean Orators in Plutarch', in Stadter ed. (1973a), pp. 109–123.

Stalley, R. F. *An Introduction to Plato's Laws.* Basil Blackwell: Oxford, 1983.

Stears, Karen. 'Death becomes her: gender and Athenian death ritual', in Blundale and Williamson (1998), pp. 113–127.

———'Dead women's society: constructing female gender in Classical Athenian funerary sculpture', in Spencer (1995), pp. 109–131.

Strauss, Barry S. *Fathers and Sons in Athens: Ideology and Society in the Era of the Peloponnesian War.* Routledge: London, 1993.

Svoronos, I. N. 'ΜΑΘΗΜΑΤΑ ΝΟΜΙΣΜΑΤΙΚΗΣ', in *Journal International d'Archéologio Numismatique* IX, 1906, pp. 147–236 (in Greek); English trans. in *American Journal of Numismatics* 43–44 (1908–10).

Swerdlow, Joel L. 'Quiet Miracles of the Brain', *National Geographic*, 187.6 (1995), pp. 2–26.

Taran, Leonardo. *Academica: Plato, Phillip of Opus and the Pseudo-Platonic Epinomis.* American Philosophical Society: Philadelphia, 1975.

Taylor, A. E. The Laws *of Plato Translated into English.* J. M. Dent & Sons Ltd.: London, 1934.

———. *Philosophers Ancient and Modern: Plato.* Archibald Constable & Co. Ltd.: London, 1908.

Tertullian. *De Anima.* ed. J. H. Waszink. B. R. Grüner: Amsterdam, 1947.

Theon of Smyrna. *On Mathematical Topics which are useful for the Study of Plato.* J. Dupuis ed. Paris: 1892.

Thomas, Rosalind. *Herodotus in Context.* Cambridge University Press: Cambridge, 2000.

———. *Literacy and Orality in Ancient Greece.* Cambridge University Press: Cambridge, 1995.

———. 'Literacy and the city-state in archaic and classical Greece', in Bowman and Woolf (1994), pp. 33–50.

Thompson, Wesley. 'The Marriage of First Cousins in Athenian Society', *Phoenix*, 21 (1967), pp. 273–82.

———. 'Athenian Marriage Patterns: Remarriage', *California Studies in Classical Antiquity*, 5 (1972), pp. 211–25.

Todd, Stephen. *The Shape of Athenian Law.* Oxford University Press: Oxford, 1993.

Todd, Stephen and Paul Millett, 'Law, Society and Athens', in Cartledge, Millett and Todd (1990), pp. 1–18.

Too, Yun Lee. *The Rhetoric of Identity in Isocrates.* Cambridge University Press: Cambridge, 1995.

Too, Yun Lee, ed. *Education in Greek and Roman Antiquity.* Brill: Leiden, 2001.

Too, Yun Lee and Niall Livingstone eds. *Pedagogy and Power: Rhetorics of Classical Learning.* Cambridge University Press: Cambridge, 1998.

Toynbee, A. J. *Study of History*, vol. III. Oxford University Press: Thames and Hudges, 1972.

Turkle, Sherry. 'Jacques Lacan and Co.: A History of Psychoanalysis in France, 1925–1985', *London Review of Books*, 6 December 1990, pp. 3–9.

Tyrrell, William Blake. *Amazons: A Study in Athenian Mythmaking.* The Johns Hopkins University Press: Baltimore, MD, 1984.

van der Ben, N. *The Proems of Empedokles' Peri Physios*. B. R. Grüner: Amsterdam, 1975.

van Groningen, B. A. *In the Grip of the Past: Essay on an Aspect of Greek Thought*. E. J. Brill: Leiden, 1953.

Vance, Carol. 'Social Construction Theory and Sexuality', in Berger, Wallis and Watson (1995), pp. 37–48.

Vatai, Frank Leslie. *Intellectuals in Politics in the Greek World: From Early Times to the Hellenistic Age*. Croom Helm: London, 1984.

Vidal-Naquet, Pierre. *The Black Hunter: Forms of Thought and Forms of Society in the Greek World*, trans. by Andrew Szegedy-Maszak. The Johns Hopkins University Press: Baltimore, Maryland, 1986.

———. 'The Black Hunter Revisited', in *PCPS* 32, (1986b), pp. 126–44.

Vlastos, Gregory. *Platonic Studies*. Princeton University Press: Princeton, 1973.

von Bachofen, J. J. *Das Mutterrecht : Eine Untersuchung über die Gynaikokratie der alten Welt nach ihrer religiösen und rechtlichen Natur*. B. Schwabe: Basel, 1897.

von Fritz, Kurt. *Platon in Sizilien und das Problem der Philosophenherrschaft*. Walter de Gruyter & Co.: Berlin, 1968.

von Silke, Trojahn. *Die auf Papyri erhaltenen Kommentare zur Alten Komödie : ein Beitrag zur Geschichte der antiken Philologie*. K.G. Saur: München, 2002.

von Wilamowitz-Moellendorff, Ulrich. 'Die Herkuft der Magneten am Menander', *Hermes* XXX (1895), pp. 177–198.

———. 'Die *Katharmoi* des Empedokles'. *SPAW* 94 (1929): 626–61. (Reprinted in his *Kleine Schriften*. Weidmann: Berlin, 1935).

Wade-Gery, Henry. 'Studies in the Structure of Attic Society', *Classical Quarterly*, XXV, 1–2 (1931), pp. 129–143.

Walbank, F. W. 'The Problem of Greek Nationality,' in Harrison (2002), pp. 234–256.

Walters, Nick. *Dr. Who? Superior Beings*. BBC Worldwide Ltd.: London, 2001.

Wheeler, B. I. *Dionysos and Immortality*. G. P. Putnam's Sons: London, 1899.

Whitby, Michael, ed. *Sparta*. Edinburgh University Press: Edinburgh, 2001.

Wilkins, John, David Harvey and Mike Dobson, eds. *Food in Antiquity*. University of Exeter Press: Exeter, 1995.

Willetts, Ronald F., ed. *The Law Code of Gortyn*. Walter de Gruyter & Co.: Berlin, 1967.

Winkler, John. 'Laying Down the Law', in Halperin, Winkler and Zeitlin, (1990), pp. 171–209.

———. 'The Ephebe's Song: Tragoidia and Polis', in Winkler and Zeitlin (1990), pp. 20–62. [Winkler (1990b)].

Winkler, John and Froma Zeitlin eds. *Nothing to do with Dionysos?* Princeton University Press: Princeton, 1990.

Wright, M. R. Ed. *Empedocles: the Extant Fragments*. Yale University Press: New Haven, Ct. 1981.

Yunis, Harvey. *Taming Democracy: Models of Political Rhetoric in Classical Athens*. Cornell University Press: Ithaca, NY, 1996.

Zhmud, Leonid. 'From the ancient to the new doxography: Aristotle, Theophrastus and Diels (and beyond)', presented at the University of St. Andrews' School of Greek, Latin and Ancient History's Class Seminar, 13 April 2001.

Zuntz, G. *Persephone, Book II: Empedokles' Katharmoi*. Clarendon Press: Oxford, 1971.

Index